THE B
COMPLETE
DISCOGRAPHY

THE BEATLES COMPLETE DISCOGRAPHY

JEFF RUSSELL

UNIVERSE

First published in the United States of America in 2006 by
Universe Publishing
a division of Rizzoli International Publications, Inc.
300 Park Avenue South
New York, NY 10010
www.rizzoliusa.com

First published in Great Britain in 1982 by Cassell

Originally published in Great Britain in 2005 as
The Beatles Album File and Complete Discography by
Cassell Illustrated
a division of Octopus Publishing Group Limited
2-4 Heron Quays, London E14 4JP

ISBN 0-7893-1373-1
Library of Congress Control Number 2005907163

2006 2007 2008 2009 / 10 9 8 7 6 5 4 3 2 1

Design: Design 23
Editor: John Bailey
Additional text: Mike Evans

Printed in China

CONTENTS

The Beatles on Record   7

The British Albums   11

The American Albums   215

Further British Albums   249

The Christmas Albums   361

Appendices   373

Discography   417

Index   454

The Beatles on Record

The Beatles were the biggest phenomenon the world of music has ever known. Their music brings joy and excitement to millions of people worldwide, and never before or since has so much been said or written about any recording artists. They captured the hearts and affection of the world's youth and created a mystique that fascinates fans even now, nearly 35 years after they split up and went their different ways. In those thirty-five years many books have been published giving various accounts of their success. Their history has been well documented in a number of those books, particularly in Hunter Davies's excellently researched *The Beatles: The Authorised Biography*, and Mark Lewisohn's two books, *The Beatles Live!* and *The Beatles' Recording Sessions*. They are all excellent books within the realms of their content but, unfortunately for Beatles' fans worldwide those books, despite their excellence, can never be added to. The Beatles, as a group, no longer exist and with the deaths of John Lennon in 1980 and George Harrison in 2001, can never exist as a group again. There is therefore very little that can be added to their history that hasn't already been written; they will never perform live again and there will never be another Beatles recording session. So what's left? What's left is what The Beatles were all about - their music and, in particular, their records.

The Beatles had numerous recording sessions to produce those records; they performed the songs hundreds of times worldwide and if they hadn't made those records their history would have been extremely limited.

This book deals solely with those records. Not the records that were made individually by John, Paul, George or Ringo after they split up, but the records that The Beatles recorded as a group. During the sessions that produced those records The Beatles also recorded a wealth of material that, for various reasons, remains unreleased. However, the release of further Beatles records will always remain a possibility.

Within the pages of this book you will find information relating to every song The Beatles officially issued on record, the titles of albums and individual tracks, release dates, composer credits, timings and comments on each track with details of who plays and sings what, together with odd bits and pieces of information included here and there.

Some previous discussions of The Beatles' songs have fallen into the trap of losing sight of the original music while attempting highly technical explanations and over-analysis of the lyrics. In this book, there is a return to that original music - it's there and it always will be there, to *listen* to and enjoy, not to analyse.

Throughout the book, attempts have been made to identify the actual known writer of a song - John Lennon or Paul McCartney – even when the official and registered composing credit is Lennon and McCartney.

The first part of the book has been set out chronologically, with the albums in their basic order of release in Britain and internationally. The inevitable exceptions to this are *The Beatles First*, *The Decca Sessions 1.1.62* and *The Beatles' Historic Sessions*.

Although not issued until 1964, 1987 and 1981 respectively, these albums were recorded prior to The Beatles' EMI/Parlophone signing, and therefore have been included before the *Please Please Me* album. Also, the *Magical Mystery Tour* and *Hey Jude* albums, although not issued in Britain until 1976 and 1979 respectively, have been placed in their international order of release, i.e. as the follow-up albums to *Sgt. Pepper's Lonely Hearts Club Band* and *Abbey Road*. Also included is *The Beatles Box*, that although not generally available in the stores, is obtainable through World Records, EMI's mail order division. Also covered for interest and completeness is *The Songs Lennon and McCartney Gave Away*, an album including songs, written by Lennon and McCartney and recorded by other artists, but never issued by The Beatles.

Following the chapters on British albums are chapters on the records released in the USA by Capitol Records. The albums discussed are those from *Meet The Beatles* to *Revolver* plus the *American Rarities* and *20 Greatest Hits* – 14 albums altogether. These also are in chronological order and each track is usefully cross-referenced to a British album. These fourteen albums are the only American albums listed separately, as all albums from *Sgt. Pepper's Lonely Hearts Club Band* onwards were issued in basically the same order worldwide.

After the album reviews, Chapter 50 The Alternative Versions, discusses the alternative versions of recordings issued by The Beatles around the world. These have been a favourite topic among Beatles fans for years. In Chapter 51 The Unreleased Tracks, there are listed some 200 songs recorded by The Beatles in one form or another, but never released. The Non-Album Tracks, covers recordings issued that are not available on album.

Lastly comes the Discography, giving a complete listing of all The Beatles' records released in the UK, USA and Australia up to December 2004.

Also included, both in the main text and the Discography, are the compact discs released internationally by EMI during 1987/8. The contents of these, that are based on the British albums, are the same worldwide. So whether you are in London, New York, Sydney or indeed wherever you are, you can play your compact discs with the knowledge that everyone, for the first time ever, is able to listen to exactly the same compact disc.

Since the first edition of this book in which was predicted the release of 'How Do You Do It?' and 'Leave My Kitten Alone' as a single, EMI have tried on at least one other occasion (January 1985) to release both these and a further 11 unreleased tracks as an album entitled *Sessions*. This, together with a single featuring 'Leave My Kitten Alone' and an alternative unreleased version of 'Ob La Di, Ob La Da', didn't make it to the stores either.

Like Beatles fans everywhere my hopes of seeing The Beatles re-form were destroyed by the radio announcement I heard at 7.00am GMT on Tuesday 9 December 1980. With the murder of John Lennon in New York, shortly after his return to the music scene after five years of self-imposed exile, a little bit died in all of us.

Ironically, his death led to Paul, George and Ringo getting together to record a George Harrison song, *All Those Years Ago*, as a tribute to John.

My tribute to John Lennon, to George Harrison and to the memory of The Beatles, is this book – written by a fan for other fans everywhere as a guide to Beatles records and, for a new generation, as an introduction to the fabulous sound of The Beatles.

Jeff Russell, Liverpool.

THE
BRITISH
ALBUMS

THE EARLY TAPES OF

THE BEATLES
THE BEATLES with TONY SHERIDAN
TONY SHERIDAN and the BEAT BROTHERS

Polydor
823 701-2

THE EARLY TAPES OF THE BEATLES

UK Release: 10 December 1984
US Release: 10 December 1984
Intl CD No: 823 701-2
Running Time: 40:17

Polydor 823 701-2
Polydor 823 70 1-2
Producer: Bert Kaempfert

Ain't She Sweet; Cry For A Shadow; When The Saints Go Marching In; Why;
If You Love Me, Baby; (What'd I Say); Sweet Georgia Brown; (Let's Dance); (Ruby Baby);
My Bonnie; Nobody's Child; (Ready Teddy); (Ya Ya Parts 1+2); (Kansas City).

The Beatles' first album, recorded in Hamburg in 1961, features eight recordings made in their pre-Parlophone days. Of those eight, there are only two that could be called Beatles recordings. The remaining six feature The Beatles backing Tony Sheridan. To make the album worthwhile Polydor included a further four Tony Sheridan recordings backed by another group called The Beat Brothers, who were not, as many thought, The Beatles recording under a pseudonym.

The history behind this album is similar to the story of the meeting between The Beatles and Brian Epstein, only in this case it was Bert Kaempfert. He had heard reports of a group playing around the clubs in Hamburg's red light district that was attracting a great deal of interest and went to investigate. Arriving at the Top Ten Club in the notorious Reeperbahn, he witnessed an impressively enthusiastic group, Tony Sheridan and The Beatles. Kaempfert was aware of the effect they had on the audience. What he was not aware of at the time was that Tony Sheridan and The Beatles were not all members of the same group. He approached them and finally persuaded them to sign a three-year recording contract with him.

The first recordings The Beatles made with Bert Kaempfert were 'My Bonnie', 'When The Saints Go Marching In', 'Why (Can't You Love Me Again)' – all featuring Tony Sheridan on lead vocal – and 'Cry For A Shadow' (a Harrison-Lennon instrumental). The line-up for these recordings was John Lennon, Paul McCartney, George Harrison and Pete Best (Stuart Sutcliffe having left the group to study art), together with Tony Sheridan. The first release from this session was a single. 'My Bonnie'/'The Saints' was released in Germany on Polydor 24 673 in June 1961. The record sold extremely well and The Beatles were soon in the German Top Ten.

A week after their first session The Beatles returned for a further recording session with Polydor at which they recorded 'Ain't She Sweet' (featuring a lead vocal from John Lennon), 'If You Love Me, Baby', 'Nobody's Child' and 'Sweet Georgia Brown', all of which have a lead vocal from Tony Sheridan. With the exception of 'Sweet Georgia Brown', that was included on the *Ya Ya* EP (Polydor H 21485) issued in Germany in October 1962, these new titles remained unissued until 1964. Then, after the success of The Beatles' first five singles and first two LPs on Parlophone, Polydor resurrected all eight tracks. Initially they issued 'Ain't She Sweet'/'Take Out Some Insurance On Me Baby' (Polydor NH 52317) on 29 May1964, but amidst a host of Parlophone number ones, this reached only No. 29 in the British charts. The remaining six Polydor tracks also were issued as singles but none reached the top fifty in Britain. Polydor, determined to have some success with their Beatles recordings, took all eight tracks plus four recorded by Tony Sheridan and The Beat Brothers and subsequently compiled the album *The Beatles First* (Polydor 236 201) (US release: *The Beatles - Circa 1960 - In The Beginning* Polydor 24-4504) again without much luck. The album has been reissued a number of times, with an equal number of titles, the most recent being on compact disc as both *The Beatles First* and *The Early Tapes Of The Beatles* (Polydor 823 701-2) that also includes a further two Sheridan/Beat Brothers tracks, 'Ready Teddy' and 'Kansas City' and is the version of the album used here. Although The Beatles' recordings featured here hint at what was to come on future recordings, they are really only of interest to Beatles collectors, mainly for their historical rather than their musical value.

In addition to these eight recordings a further tape reputed to be from these sessions came to light in 1985. The contents have yet to be revealed and at present are open to speculation, but the tape is thought to contain at least two tracks that feature John Lennon on lead vocal: 'Some Other Guy' and 'Rock and Roll Music'.

Ain't She Sweet (Yellen-Ager)   2:12
Recorded: 22/23 June 1961, Hamburg-Harburg-Friedrich-Ebert-Halle, Hamburg, West Germany
The Beatles

John Lennon: Rhythm Guitar and Solo Vocal   **Paul McCartney:** Bass Guitar
George Harrison: Lead Guitar   **Pete Best:** Drums

This opening track features John Lennon's first officially recorded vocal performance. This is the only recording on the album to feature any of The Beatles on lead vocal. John gives the song the distinctive Lennon treatment; his raw nasal vocal almost jumps out of the speakers. The instrumental backing accentuates John's vocal without imposing on it. Overall the recording comes across well, although in places it sounds rather shallow. This was no doubt due to Bert Kaempfert's production techniques that, although flawless with his own orchestra, just do not seem to work with a beat group. Eighteen months later they were to meet George Martin, who was to bring out that distinctive Beatles sound.

Cry For A Shadow (Harrison-Lennon)   2:23
Recorded: 22/23 June 1961, Hamburg-Harburg-Friedrich-Ebert-Halle, Hamburg, West Germany
The Beatles

John Lennon: Rhythm Guitar   **Paul McCartney:** Bass Guitar
George Harrison: Lead Guitar   **Pete Best:** Drums

Co-written by George and John, this instrumental is the only published or unpublished Harrison-Lennon collaboration. The opening and main theme was thought up by George Harrison; John Lennon later added the rhythm sections. It is an interesting, although simple, piece of music consisting of opening and main theme, that is played through three times, with a few other bars added for the ending. George Harrison's lead guitar playing here is by far the best on the album - he is not given the opportunity on other tracks. The music is given more excitement by various screams and shouts from the four Beatles. The title was not chosen until after the recordings were finished. The toss of a coin decided that 'Cry For A Shadow' and not 'Beatle Bop' should be used. The Beatles had, in any case, felt that the latter title was rather coy so it was dismissed and 'Cry For A Shadow' was agreed.

When The Saints Go Marching In (Trad. Arr. Sheridan)   3:18
Recorded: 22/23 June 1961, Hamburg-Harburg-Friedrich-Ebert-Halle, Hamburg, West Germany
The Beatles with Tony Sheridan

John Lennon: Rhythm Guitar   **Paul McCartney:** Bass Guitar
George Harrison: Lead Guitar   **Pete Best:** Drums
Tony Sheridan: Solo Vocal

The B side of the now famous 'My Bonnie' single features a solo vocal from Tony Sheridan
together with some very enthusiastic and exciting backing music from The Beatles.

Why (Can't You Love Me Again) (Crompton-Sheridan)   2:58
Recorded: 22/23 June 1961, Hamburg-Harburg-Friedrich-Ebert-Halle, Hamburg, West Germany
The Beatles with Tony Sheridan

John Lennon: Rhythm Guitar and Backing Vocal
Paul McCartney: Bass Guitar and Backing Vocal
George Harrison: Lead Guitar and Backing Vocal
Pete Best: Drums   **Tony Sheridan:** Lead Vocal

Partly written by Tony Sheridan, this pleading song seems to suit his voice perfectly. The Beatles
provide an adequate musical backing, together with harmony vocals and hand-clapping.

If You Love Me, Baby (aka: Take Out Some Insurance On Me Baby) (Singleton-Hall)   2:53
Recorded: 24 June 1961, Studio Rahlstedt, Hamburg, West Germany
The Beatles with Tony Sheridan

John Lennon: Rhythm Guitar   **Paul McCartney:** Bass Guitar
George Harrison: Lead Guitar   **Pete Best:** Drums
Tony Sheridan: Solo Vocal

One of Tony Sheridan's favourite songs. Here The Beatles provide Sheridan with an excellent
backing for his solo vocal.

What'd I Say (Charles) 2:39
Recorded: 31 January 1963, Studio Rahlstedt, Hamburg, West Germany
Tony Sheridan and The Beat Brothers

Sweet Georgia Brown (Bernie-Pinkard-Casey) 2:05
Recorded: 21 December 1961, Musikhalle, Hamburg, West Germany
The Beatles with Tony Sheridan
John Lennon: Rhythm Guitar and Backing Vocal
Paul McCartney: Bass Guitar, Piano and Backing Vocal
George Harrison: Lead Guitar and Backing Vocal
Pete Best: Drums   **Tony Sheridan:** Lead Vocal
Once again, The Beatles provide a very enthusiastic backing to Tony Sheridan's vocal talents.
Incidentally, in 1963 Sheridan re-recorded the vocals with specially adapted lyrics that refer to
the length of The Beatles' hair and the recently formed Beatles' Fan Club. This is that version.
The original appears on the 1962 German EP *Ya Ya* (Polydor H 21485).

Let's Dance (Lee) 2:33
Recorded: 18 October 1962, Studio Rahlstedt, Hamburg, West Germany
Tony Sheridan and The Beat Brothers

Ruby Baby (Leiber-Stoller) 2:52
Recorded: 31 January 1963, Studio Rahlstedt, Hamburg, West Germany
Tony Sheridan and The Beat Brothers

My Bonnie (Pratt) 2:42
Recorded: 22/23 June1961, Hamburg-Harburg-Friedrich-Ebert-Halle, Hamburg, West Germany
The Beatles with Tony Sheridan
John Lennon: Rhythm Guitar and Backing Vocal
Paul McCartney: Bass Guitar and Backing Vocal
George Harrison: Lead Guitar and Backing Vocal
Pete Best: Drums   **Tony Sheridan:** Lead Vocal

This must be the most famous track on the album, the A-side of the single issued in Germany in 1961, and the reason for the meeting between Brian Epstein and The Beatles. Tony Sheridan's lead vocal is given a rousing musical and vocal backing by The Beatles, who also supply some enthusiastic handclapping.

When this track was originally issued as a single in Germany (Polydor 24 673) it featured a slow introduction in German. When it was later issued in Britain (Polydor NH 66-833) the introduction was in English, and it is that version that is included here.

Nobody's Child (Foree-Coben) 3:55
Recorded: 22/23 June 1961, Hamburg-Harburg-Friedrich-Ebert-Halle, Hamburg, West Germany
The Beatles with Tony Sheridan
John Lennon: Rhythm Guitar   **Paul McCartney:** Bass Guitar
George Harrison: Lead Guitar   **Pete Best:** Drums
Tony Sheridan: Solo Vocal
This old country-and-western song is brought up to date here by Tony Sheridan, who is given an excellent backing by The Beatles.

Ready Teddy (Blackwell-Marascalco) 2:01
Recorded: 21 December 1961, Musikhalle, Hamburg, West Germany
Tony Sheridan and The Beat Brothers

Ya Ya (Parts 1 + 2) (Robinson-Dorsey-Lewis) 5:08
Recorded: 28 August 1962, Studio Rahlstedt, Hamburg, West Germany
Tony Sheridan and The Beat Brothers

Kansas City (Leiber-Stoller)   2:38
Recorded: Unknown
Tony Sheridan and The Beat Brothers

When The Beatles returned to Liverpool in October 1961, they brought a few copies of 'My Bonnie' with them for their friends. One person to receive a copy was Bob Wooller, the DJ at the Cavern Club, who gave the record a considerable amount of play. Soon, several members of the club were asking for the record at NEMS (North End Music Stores) the nearby music shop.

The manager, Brian Epstein, knew that the record was not in stock but wanted to know who the artists were so that he could obtain it. Brian was told that the record was by a German group called The Beatles. He made enquiries around Liverpool and found out that The Beatles were not German but English and, above all, a local group who were currently playing at the Cavern Club just around the corner from his music shop. Intrigued, he went along to the CavernClub to find out more about them and their record. He watched their performance and recognised the four scruffy lads who came into his shop on Saturday afternoons to listen to records, but who never bought anything. He also could not fail to notice the enormous amount of excitement they generated within the audience. It seemed as though the moment they appeared on stage the atmosphere became electrically charged. Brian was fascinated. How could these four scruffs have so much effect on an audience? No wonder he was having so many requests for their record.

After their performance, Brian met The Beatles and found out that the record was on the Polydor label. He then began extensive enquiries among record importers, but drew a blank. Being the businessman he was, he contacted Polydor Records in Germany and imported 200 copies himself. Brian also made enquiries about how to manage a group. Receiving what he considered to be sufficient information, he invited The Beatles along to his office to discuss becoming their manager.

The Beatles told Brian that they were under a management contract to Allan Williams. Brian also learned that their recording contract with Polydor Records still had two years to run. He went along to see Allan Williams, who was glad to get rid of The Beatles. He readily agreed that Brian could have them, adding that The Beatles had caused him nothing but trouble. It was a decision that he was soon to regret.

Brian then contacted Polydor Records who told him they were interested in The Beatles only as a backing group for Tony Sheridan, and that they had no plans whatsoever to record The

Beatles on their own. After some discussion Polydor Records released The Beatles totally and unconditionally from their contract. Both situations now resolved, The Beatles signed a contract, witnessed by Alistair Taylor, Brian's personal assistant, that made Brian Epstein their new manager. Brian never signed that contract and never revealed why.

The first thing Brian did was to take over the responsibility of making bookings for the group from Pete Best. Next, he talked them into wearing suits on stage and told them to work out a regular stage performance during which they were to play only their best numbers. He also banned them from smoking, eating, drinking alcohol or chewing gum during their performances. Before every booking he would issue each of them with typewritten instructions about where they would be playing and the time they were to be there - at least half an hour before the start of the performance.

Having organised The Beatles and given them a new appearance Brian decided the next task was to get his newly signed group a recording contract.

THE DECCA SESSIONS 1.1.62

UK Release: 19 October 1987
US Release: Various
Producer: Mike Smith

Topline Top 181
Intl CD No: Various
Running Time: 32:02

SIDE ONE: Three Cool Cats; Memphis, Tennessee; Besame Mucho; The Sheik Of Araby; Till There Was You; Searchin'.

SIDE TWO: Sure To Fall (In Love With You); Take Good Care Of My Baby; Money; To Know Her Is To Love Her; September In The Rain; Crying, Waiting, Hoping.

Brian Epstein, determined to get The Beatles a recording contract, managed through his various contacts in the music business, to convince Mike Smith, an A & R manager at Decca Records, to come to the Cavern Club in Liverpool during December 1961 to see the group performing live. What he saw, unlike Bert Kaempfert's first impression, was a clean-cut, smartly dressed quartet who, no matter what they played, managed to drive the regulars at the Cavern wild. After seeing their performance, that impressed him immensely, Smith agreed to give The Beatles an audition on 1 January 1962, at Decca's West Hampstead studios. Both Brian Epstein and The Beatles were delighted. Brian told The Beatles to rehearse their best numbers for the audition and not to use any of their own compositions: a decision that although open to a great deal of speculation possibly cost them a contract with Decca.

On New Year's Eve 1961, The Beatles together with Neil Aspinall loaded their equipment into a van and drove down to London. Brian Epstein travelled by train. Arriving at about 10pm they booked into The Royal Hotel in Russell Square, and then went out on the town to join the New Year revellers in Trafalgar Square.

The following morning The Beatles and Neil Aspinall arrived at Decca's studios to find that Brian Epstein was already there. Brian was annoyed, it was approaching 11am, the time of the audition, and no one from Decca had yet arrived. Mike Smith eventually arrived at 11.30 and The Beatles began to unload their equipment only to be told that it wasn't required and that they were to use the guitars and equipment provided.

The Beatles, now in the relatively calm and controlled environment of the recording studio, ran through the songs they had selected from their repertoire, eventually recording at least 15 songs, including three of their own that they had included despite Brian's instructions. The session finished at about 2pm and Mike Smith, impressed with their recordings, told them there would not be an immediate decision, as that would come from higher above.

About 20 years after that audition, AFE Records became the first of many record companies to officially issue 12 of the 15 recordings that, over the years, have become known as *The Decca Tapes*. AFE's release, *The Complete Silver Beatles* (UK: AFE AFELP 1047; US: AFE AR 2452) contained all but the three Lennon-McCartney originals: 'Like Dreamers Do', 'Love Of The Loved' and 'Hello Little Girl'. What were included, though, were early versions of both 'Money' and 'Till There Was You', that The Beatles eventually re-recorded and included on the 1963 album *With The Beatles*. The remaining ten tracks include Beatles versions of the Coasters' hits 'Three Cool Cats' and 'Searchin'', together with Chuck Berry's 'Memphis, Tennessee', along with seven other tracks that The Beatles were including in their stage act during 1960-61.

Over the years since *The Decca Tapes* made their first official appearance, the recordings seem to have been issued by as many different record companies as there are tracks and in as many different running orders. The first company to issue these recordings on compact disc was Topline Records who issued them as *The Decca Sessions 1.1.62* (Topline TOP CD 523). As the recordings will no doubt be issued by other record companies at some point, I have used that album as a sample release. Unfortunately, it doesn't contain 'Like Dreamers Do', 'Love Of The Loved' or 'Hello Little Girl' apparently because of copyright legalities. To offer a complete commentary on the entire 15, although other sources claim there were more original recordings, these three tracks have been included after the album.

SIDE ONE
Three Cool Cats (Leiber-Stoller) 2:41
Recorded: 1 January 1962, Decca Studios, West Hampstead, London
John Lennon: Rhythm Guitar and Backing Vocal
Paul McCartney: Bass Guitar and Backing Vocal   **George Harrison:** Lead Guitar and Lead Vocal
Pete Best: Drums
George is in excellent form on lead vocal in this complete send-up of the 1959 Coasters hit. John and Paul aid and abet with various humorous interjections of 'I want that little chick' and 'Hey man, save one chick for me'. This comes across as a less-than-serious attempt to record the song.

Memphis, Tennessee (Berry) 2:40
Recorded: 1 January 1962, Decca Studios, West Hampstead, London
John Lennon: Rhythm Guitar and Solo Vocal   **Paul McCartney:** Bass Guitar
George Harrison: Lead Guitar   **Pete Best:** Drums
John's lead vocal on this late 50s Chuck Berry standard is by far one of his best performances on the album. It puts Chuck Berry's original version to shame although The Beatles do not stray far from his original arrangement. During their numerous BBC radio appearances in the early 1960s The Beatles featured this song on a number of occasions.

Besame Mucho (Velazquez-Skylar) 2:33
Recorded: 1 January 1962, Decca Studios, West Hampstead, London
John Lennon: Rhythm Guitar and Backing Vocal   **Paul McCartney:** Bass Guitar and Lead Vocal
George Harrison: Lead Guitar and Backing Vocal   **Pete Best:** Drums
This must be one of The Beatles' all-time favourite songs. Although not officially released previously, various versions by The Beatles had cropped up on bootleg records. During the early 60s The Beatles recorded this song for a number of radio broadcasts. It also cropped up a few years later during the sessions for *Let It Be* as a much better version, although it was never released. Paul always sings the lead vocal, with backing from John and George. They do an excellent job on this old 1930s song that was revived in 1959 by The Coasters.

The Sheik of Araby (Snyder-Wheeler-Smith) 1:37
Recorded: 1 January 1962, Decca Studios, West Hampstead, London

John Lennon: Rhythm Guitar   **Paul McCartney:** Bass Guitar
George Harrison: Lead Guitar and Solo Vocal   **Pete Best:** Drums

Although one of the best, this is unfortunately one of the shortest tracks on the album. George gives a rousing rendition of this ancient song and is given an equally rousing backing. John inserts some ad lib comments that give the song a lighter feel than other recordings on the album and turn it into a send-up. This is a good recording, although the ending is sloppy.

Till There Was You (Willson) 2:55
Recorded: 1 January 1962, Decca Studios, West Hampstead, London

John Lennon: Rhythm Guitar   **Paul McCartney:** Bass Guitar and Solo Vocal
George Harrison: Lead Guitar   **Pete Best:** Drums

This is the first of two tracks on the album that were later re-recorded and released by The Beatles on the *With The Beatles* album. Paul's lead vocal is backed by his own bass guitar, George's lead guitar and Pete Best's drumming. The song is given a similar treatment to that of the later version, although the lead guitar and drums don't seem at ease.

Searchin' (Leiber-Stoller) 3:44
Recorded: 1 January 1962, Decca Studios, West Hampstead, London

John Lennon: Rhythm Guitar and Backing Vocal   **Paul McCartney:** Bass Guitar and Lead Vocal
George Harrison: Lead Guitar and Backing Vocal   **Pete Best:** Drums

The sixth track of the album is another song originally recorded by The Coasters; this one dates back to 1957. The Beatles featured it now and again in their stage act. Paul sings lead vocal with John and George adding harmonies for the chorus. The two sections of falsetto come from John Lennon who nervously tries to inject some humour into the situation.

SIDE TWO
Sure To Fall (In Love With You) Perkins-Cantrell-Claunch) 2:48
Recorded: 1 January 1962, Decca Studios, West Hampstead, London
John Lennon: Rhythm Guitar and Harmony Vocal   **Paul McCartney:** Bass Guitar and Lead Vocal
George Harrison: Lead Guitar and Harmony Vocal   **Pete Best:** Drums
The old Carl Perkins number is given The Beatles treatment, with lead vocal from Paul and harmonies from John and George here and there. This is either a very straight-faced send-up or Paul has stage fright. Nevertheless it is still an enjoyable track.

Take Good Care Of My Baby (Goffin-King) 2:51
Recorded: 1 January 1962, Decca Studios, West Hampstead, London
John Lennon: Rhythm Guitar and Harmony Vocal
Paul McCartney: Bass Guitar and Harmony Vocal
George Harrison: Lead Guitar and Lead Vocal   **Pete Best:** Drums
Lead vocals are from George with harmonies in places from John and Paul. The Beatles stick closely to the original Bobby Vee recording.

Money (Bradford-Gordy) 2:57
Recorded: 1 January 1962, Decca Studios, West Hampstead, London
John Lennon: Rhythm Guitar and Lead Vocal
Paul McCartney: Bass Guitar and Backing Vocal
George Harrison: Lead Guitar and Backing Vocal   **Pete Best:** Drums
This track was also re-recorded and later issued by The Beatles on the album *With The Beatles*. This is much faster than the later version, and instead of piano it starts with John Lennon's rhythm guitar. The lead vocal also comes from John. He sounds like he would during a live performance, and the echo given to his voice emphasises this effect. The backing vocals from Paul and George are sung in a similar way to the later released version, but musically it doesn't compare – the song as recorded on *With The Beatles* is far superior.

To Know Her Is To Love Her (Spector) 2:27
Recorded: 1 January 1962, Decca Studios, West Hampstead, London
John Lennon: Rhythm Guitar and Lead Vocal
Paul McCartney: Bass Guitar and Backing Vocal
George Harrison: Lead Guitar and Backing Vocal   **Pete Best:** Drums
This was originally recorded by the Teddy Bears in 1958 and produced by the now legendary Phil
Spector. The Beatles stick closely to Phil Spector's original arrangement but change the title and
lyrics from a female to a male point of view. Again John sings lead vocal with Paul and George
supplying the da, da, da, backing. The Beatles used to feature this during their early stage act, and a
live version can be heard on *The Star Club Tapes.*

September In The Rain (Dubin-Warren) 2:17
Recorded: 1 January 1962, Decca Studios, West Hampstead, London
John Lennon: Rhythm Guitar   **Paul McCartney:** Bass Guitar and Solo Vocal
George Harrison: Lead Guitar   **Pete Best:** Drums
Originally a hit for Dinah Washington in 1961, this must be one of the strongest tracks on the album.
Paul gives the song a true Beatles feel in the mould of 'I Saw Her Standing There'. This is the only track
that sounds as though The Beatles are thoroughly enjoying themselves.

Crying, Waiting, Hoping (Holly) 1:58
Recorded: 1 January 1962, Decca Studios, West Hampstead, London
John Lennon: Rhythm Guitar and Backing Vocal
Paul McCartney: Bass Guitar and Backing Vocal
George Harrison: Lead Guitar and Lead Vocal   **Pete Best:** Drums
The Beatles recorded quite a few Buddy Holly songs. Prior to the release of *The Decca Tapes* the only
Holly song that had been issued was 'Words of Love' on *The Beatles For Sale* album. The lead vocal
on this song comes from George, with backing vocals from John and Paul.

 Although the following three tracks do not appear on this album, they are included here for the
sake of completeness. In 1982 'Like Dreamers Do' and 'Love Of The Loved' appeared on an American
album of dubious legality but, along with 'Hello Little Girl', they have yet to appear on a British album.

Love Of The Loved (Lennon-McCartney)   1:48
Recorded: 1 January 1962, Decca Studios, West Hampstead, London
John Lennon: Rhythm Guitar   **Paul McCartney:** Bass Guitar and Solo Vocal
George Harrison: Lead Guitar   **Pete Best:** Drums
This McCartney-written song was eventually given away to Cilla Black who recorded it in 1963 (Parlophone R 5065). Here Paul sings lead vocal backed by John and George playing an incessant riff that appears throughout the recording.

Like Dreamers Do (Lennon-McCartney)   2:30
Recorded: 1 January 1962, Decca Studios, West Hampstead, London
John Lennon: Rhythm Guitar   **Paul McCartney:** Bass Guitar and Solo Vocal
George Harrison: Lead Guitar   **Pete Best:** Drums
This song was eventually recorded in 1964 by The Applejacks (Decca F11916) and produced by Mike Smith who also produced this version. Paul sings lead vocal in a slightly toned-down Little Richard voice. The recording generates as much excitement as many later releases, although because this was an audition, a certain amount of fear can be heard in Paul's voice. The backing sounds more enthusiastic than on the Polydor sessions, and Pete Best's performance is a great improvement over the monotonous drumming on those recordings.

Hello Little Girl (Lennon-McCartney)   1:36
Recorded: 1 January 1962, Decca Studios, West Hampstead, London
John Lennon: Rhythm Guitar and Lead Vocal   **Paul McCartney:** Bass Guitar and Lead Vocal
George Harrison: Lead Guitar and Harmony Vocal   **Pete Best:** Drums
This track was written by John, who once said of the song, 'This was one of the first songs I ever finished. I was then about 18 and we gave it to The Fourmost. I think it was the first song of my own that I ever attempted to do with the group.'

   The Fourmost did record this song in 1963 with The Beatles' future producer, George Martin. In comparison to The Fourmost's recording (Parlophone R 5056), this leaves much to be desired. The lead vocal is a duet between John and Paul, with John singing solo in places. For the chorus they are joined by George.

Having completed their recording session The Beatles returned to Liverpool and awaited Decca's decision. Three months later, in March 1962, Brian Epstein received a reply from Decca - they had turned down The Beatles. Disappointed, but still hopeful, Brian took the audition tapes to every record label he could find, and in quick succession was turned down by Pye, Philips, Columbia and just about every other record label in London. A rather despondent Brian, determined that somebody was going to like The Beatles, decided to have one final try.

Deciding that the best way to present The Beatles was by having records made from the tapes, he ended up in the HMV shop in London's Oxford Street. Here, for approximately £1.50, an album could be made from tapes and Brian did just that. The cutting engineer, impressed with what he was hearing, recommended that Brian take his records upstairs to the offices of Ardmore and Beechwood. There Brian met Syd Coleman who, after hearing the records, recommended that he went to see a friend of his, George Martin at Parlophone. The following day Brian went along to see George Martin and played him the tapes. George was not very impressed after hearing them, but decided to take a chance and agreed to give The Beatles a recording test on Wednesday 6 June 1962.

On that day, The Beatles gave their first performance for their future producer. Although again not too impressed George Martin had a feeling that there was a certain something that needed to be brought out. After the audition, George told Brian and The Beatles that he would give them a decision within a month. Having been disappointed by Decca's decision, The Beatles didn't pay much attention to George Martin's comment and, rather dejected, returned to Liverpool and subsequently to Hamburg to play an engagement at the Star Club. Meanwhile, George Martin was listening to the audition tapes over and over again. He could hear The Beatles' potential, but there was something not quite right with the drumming. It was not regular enough and, in his opinion, did not give the right sort of sound. George informed Brian Epstein that he was prepared to sign The Beatles to a recording contract, but they would have to find a new drummer – he was not prepared to sign Pete Best.

The Beatles, still in Hamburg, received the following telegram from Brian: CONGRATULATIONS BOYS, EMI REQUEST RECORDING SESSION, PLEASE REHEARSE NEW MATERIAL. This was what they had been waiting for. On their return from Hamburg, Brian was told that John, Paul and George had decided independently that they wanted Pete Best out and Ringo Starr in. He was now faced with the unenviable task of sacking Pete Best.

With Ringo Starr as their new drummer, George Martin offered The Beatles a recording contract in which he agreed to record two singles in the first year. The date set for the first recording session was Tuesday 4 September 1962, when they were to record two tracks for release as a single. The two tracks selected for that first single were 'Love Me Do'/'P. S. I Love You' and the single was issued on 5 October 1962. Within a few weeks it had reached No. 17 in the charts, the lowest position any Beatles record issued on Parlophone was to reach during their entire recording career.

The Beatles were delighted, and so was George Martin who set up a second session for the follow-up. This was set for Monday 26 November 1962. The result was 'Please Please Me'/'Ask Me Why',although George Martin wanted The Beatles to record 'How Do You Do?' that later was a hit for Gerry and The Pacemakers, another Liverpool group. The Beatles, although not enthusiastic about 'How Do You Do It?', made a recording of it to please George Martin. After the second session The Beatles set off for Hamburg again to fulfil a Christmas residency at the Star Club that was to last from 18 to 31 December 1962. During that two-week period, Adrian Barber, formerly with The Big Three, made some recordings on a domestic tape recorder with a single microphone, that included recordings of The Beatles.

THE BEATLES HISTORIC SESSIONS

UK Release: 25 September 1981
US Release: Various
Producer: None

AFE AFELD 1018
Intl CD No: Various
Running Time: 73:50

SIDE ONE: I'm Gonna Sit Right Down And Cry (Over You); I Saw Her Standing There; Roll Over Beethoven; Hippy Hippy Shake; Sweet Little Sixteen; Lend Me Your Comb; Your Feets Too Big.

SIDE TWO: Twist And Shout; Mr. Moonlight; A Taste Of Honey; Besame Mucho; Reminiscing; Kansas City/Hey Hey Hey Hey; Where Have You Been All My Life.

SIDE THREE: Till There Was You; Nothin Shakin' (But The Leaves On The Trees); To Know Her Is To Love Her; Little Queenie; Falling In Love Again; Ask Me Why; Be Bop A Lula; Hallelujah, I Love Her So.

SIDE FOUR: Sheila; Red Sails In The Sunset; Everybody's Trying To Be My Baby; Matchbox; (I'm) Talking About You; Shimmy Shake; Long Tall Sally; I Remember You.

The recordings as available on this album originally were made in the Star Club in Hamburg, Germany, sometime between 18 and 31 December 1962. Adrian Barber, formerly of The Big Three, set up a domestic tape recorder and over that two-week period, recorded about 20 hours of various Liverpool groups including The Beatles. The recordings were then given to Ted Taylor of Kingsize Taylor and The Dominoes who offered them to The Beatles' manager Brian Epstein in 1964, after The Beatles had become famous. After listening to them, Epstein turned Taylor down, but nevertheless offered him £20 for the recordings. Taylor refused. During the 1960s Taylor gave the tapes to a recording engineer in Liverpool with the hope of eventually getting them released, but to no avail. The tapes were then put aside until the early 1970s when Allan Williams, The Beatles' first manager, discovered that the tapes were still around. Williams attempted to sell them to various record companies, hopefully to have them released. Eventually, after threatening to destroy them, he found a buyer.

It was reported at the time that $50,000 was spent transferring the original $3^3/_4$-inches-per-second mono recordings on to professional 16-track tape. With the aid of various filters, equalisers and compressors the recordings were cleaned up. Although they cannot be regarded as high quality,

The Beatles Historic Sessions

STAR CLUB HAMBURG, WEST GERMANY, DECEMBER 31st 1962

JOHN LENNON
PAUL McCARTNEY
GEORGE HARRISON
RINGO STARR

BEATLES

"We reached our stage peak in Hamburg . . . .
We got very tight as a band because we had to
play for eight hours a night . . . That was well
before we became famous so the people who
came along to see us were drawn by our music
or whatever atmosphere we created".

George Harrison, Sept. 1969

the original mono recording was scarcely that anyway, the overall sound is quite acceptable considering the way they were recorded.

From the recordings by The Beatles, 30 tracks were selected for release. Among those tracks that apparently remain unreleased, are reported to be mostly alternative versions of those issued, and reputedly a Beatles rendition of 'My Girl Is Red Hot' featuring a lead vocal from John Lennon.

Of those 30 that are available, 26 were issued as a double album by Bellaphon Records in West Germany on 8 April 1977 as *The Beatles Live! At the Star Club in Hamburg; Germany, 1962* (Bellaphon 5560). Then Lingasong Records, using the same title, issued the album in Britain (LNL 1) on which four of the tracks differed, on 25 May 1977 and in America (LS-2-7001) on 13 June 1977.

In 1981, AFE Records using all 30 tracks, issued this double album. As the recordings featured here have been, are or will be available from various record companies, this album has been used as a sample release.

On the whole, the album makes for interesting listening and contains some pre-Parlophone recordings of 'I Saw Her Standing There'; 'Ask Me Why' and 'Twist and Shout' that were included on the first Parlophone album *Please Please Me* some three months after these recordings were made. Another eight songs also can be compared with the later studio versions that were issued on *With The Beatles* and *Beatles For Sale* albums and *Long Tall Sally* EP.

Finally, two of the recordings included here, 'Hallelujah, I Love Her So' and 'Be Bop A Lula', feature vocals by Horst Obber, a waiter at the Star Club, who had joined The Beatles on stage.

SIDE ONE 17:41

I'm Gonna Sit Right Down and Cry (Over You) (Thomas-Biggs) 2:30
Recorded: 18-31 December 1962, The Star Club, Grosse Freiheit 39, Hamburg, West Germany
John Lennon: Rhythm Guitar and Lead Vocal   **Paul McCartney:** Bass Guitar and Backing Vocal
George Harrison: Lead Guitar and Backing Vocal   **Ringo Starr:** Drums

I Saw Her Standing There (Lennon-McCartney) 2:25
Recorded: 18-31 December 1962, The Star Club, Grosse Freiheit 39, Hamburg, West Germany
John Lennon: Rhythm Guitar and Harmony Vocal   **Paul McCartney:** Bass Guitar and Lead Vocal
George Harrison: Lead Guitar   **Ringo Starr:** Drums

Roll Over Beethoven (Berry) 2:17
Recorded: 18-31 December 1962, The Star Club, Grosse Freiheit 39, Hamburg, West Germany
John Lennon: Rhythm Guitar   **Paul McCartney:** Bass Guitar
George Harrison: Lead Guitar and Solo Vocal   **Ringo Starr:** Drums

Hippy Hippy Shake (Romero) 1:42
Recorded: 18-31 December 1962, The Star Club, Grosse Freiheit 39, Hamburg, West Germany
John Lennon: Rhythm Guitar   **Paul McCartney:** Bass Guitar and Solo Vocal
George Harrison: Lead Guitar   **Ringo Starr:** Drums

Sweet Little Sixteen (Berry) 2:50
Recorded: 18-31 December 1962, The Star Club, Grosse Freiheit 39, Hamburg, West Germany
John Lennon: Rhythm Guitar and Solo Vocal   **Paul McCartney:** Bass Guitar
George Harrison: Lead Guitar   **Ringo Starr:** Drums

Lend Me Your Comb (Wise-Weisman-Twomey) 1:45
Recorded: 18-31 December 1962, The Star Club, Grosse Freiheit 39, Hamburg, West Germany
John Lennon: Rhythm Guitar and Lead Vocal   **Paul McCartney:** Bass Guitar and Lead Vocal
George Harrison: Lead Guitar   **Ringo Starr:** Drums

Your Feets Too Big (Benson-Fisher) 2:21
Recorded: 18-31 December 1962, The Star Club, Grosse Freiheit 39, Hamburg, West Germany
John Lennon: Rhythm Guitar and Harmony Vocal   **Paul McCartney:** Bass Guitar and Lead Vocal
George Harrison: Lead Guitar   **Ringo Starr:** Drums

SIDE TWO 16:57
Twist and Shout (Medley-Russell) 2:12
Recorded: 18-31 December 1962, The Star Club, Grosse Freiheit 39, Hamburg, West Germany
John Lennon: Rhythm Guitar and Lead Vocal
Paul McCartney: Bass Guitar and Backing Vocal
George Harrison: Lead Guitar and Backing Vocal   **Ringo Star:** Drums

Mr. Moonlight (Johnson) 2:10
Recorded: 18-31 December 1962, The Star Club, Grosse Freiheit 39, Hamburg, West Germany
John Lennon: Rhythm Guitar and Lead Vocal
Paul McCartney: Bass Guitar and Harmony Vocal
George Harrison: Lead Guitar   **Ringo Starr:** Drums

A Taste Of Honey (Marlow-Scott) 1:55
Recorded: 18-31 December 1962, The Star Club, Grosse Freiheit 39, Hamburg, West Germany
John Lennon: Rhythm Guitar and Backing Vocal   **Paul McCartney:** Bass Guitar and Lead Vocal
George Harrison: Lead Guitar and Backing Vocal   **Ringo Starr:** Drums

Besame Mucho (Velazquez-Skylar) 2:40
Recorded: 18-31 December 1962, The Star Club, Grosse Freiheit 39, Hamburg, West Germany
John Lennon: Rhythm Guitar and Backing Vocal   **Paul McCartney:** Bass Guitar and Lead Vocal
George Harrison: Lead Guitar and Backing Vocal   **Ringo Starr:** Drums

Reminiscing (Curtis) 1:41
Recorded: 18-31 December 1962, The Star Club, Grosse Freiheit 39, Hamburg, West Germany
John Lennon: Rhythm Guitar   **Paul McCartney:** Bass Guitar
George Harrison: Lead Guitar and Solo Vocal   **Ringo Starr:** Drums

Kansas City (Leiber-Stoller)**/Hey Hey Hey Hey** (Penniman) 2:10
Recorded: 18-31 December 1962, The Star Club, Grosse Freiheit 39, Hamburg, West Germany
John Lennon: Rhythm Guitar and Backing Vocal   **Paul McCartney:** Bass Guitar and Lead Vocal
George Harrison: Lead Guitar and Backing Vocal   **Ringo Starr:** Drums

Where Have You Been All My Life (Mann-Weill) 1:45
Recorded: 18-31 December 1962, The Star Club, Grosse Freiheit 39, Hamburg, West Germany
John Lennon: Rhythm Guitar and Lead Vocal   **Paul McCartney:** Bass Guitar and Backing Vocal
George Harrison: Lead Guitar and Backing Vocal   **Ringo Starr:** Drums

SIDE THREE 20:43
Till There Was You (Wilison) 1:55
Recorded: 18-31 December 1962, The Star Club, Grosse Freiheit 39, Hamburg, West Germany
John Lennon: Rhythm Guitar   **Paul McCartney:** Bass Guitar and Solo Vocal
George Harrison: Lead Guitar   **Ringo Starr:** Drums

Nothin' Shakin' (But The Leaves On The Trees) (Colacrai-Fontaine-Lampert-Cleveland) 1:15
Recorded: 18-31 December 1962, The Star Club, Grosse Freiheit 39, Hamburg, West Germany
John Lennon: Rhythm Guitar   **Paul McCartney:** Bass Guitar
George Harrison: Lead Guitar and Solo Vocal   **Ringo Starr:** Drums

To Know Her Is To Love Her (Spector) 3:05
Recorded: 18-31 December 1962, The Star Club, Grosse Freiheit 39, Hamburg, West Germany
John Lennon: Rhythm Guitar and Harmony Vocal
Paul McCartney: Bass Guitar and Harmony Vocal
George Harrison: Lead Guitar and Lead Vocal   **Ringo Starr:** Drums

Little Queenie (Berry)   3:57
Recorded: 18-31 December 1962, The Star Club, Grosse Freiheit 39, Hamburg, West Germany
John Lennon: Rhythm Guitar   **Paul McCartney:** Bass Guitar and Solo Vocal
George Harrison: Lead Guitar   **Ringo Starr:** Drums

Falling In Love Again (Hollander-Lerner)   1:58
Recorded: 18-31 December 1962, The Star Club, Grosse Freiheit 39, Hamburg, West Germany
John Lennon: Rhythm Guitar   **Paul McCartney:** Bass Guitar and Solo Vocal
George Harrison: Lead Guitar   **Ringo Starr:** Drums

Ask Me Why (Lennon-McCartney)   2:30
Recorded: 18-31 December 1962, The Star Club, Grosse Freiheit 39, Hamburg, West Germany
John Lennon: Rhythm Guitar and Lead Vocal   **Paul McCartney:** Bass Guitar and Backing Vocal
George Harrison: Lead Guitar and Backing Vocal   **Ringo Starr:** Drums

Be Bop A Lula (Vincent-Davis)   2:28
Recorded: 18-31 December 1962, The Star Club, Grosse Freiheit 39, Hamburg, West Germany
John Lennon: Rhythm Guitar   **Paul McCartney:** Bass Guitar
George Harrison: Lead Guitar   **Ringo Starr:** Drums
Horst Obber: Solo Vocal

Hallelujah, I Love Her So (Charles)   2:07
Recorded: 18-31 December 1962, The Star Club, Grosse Freiheit 39, Hamburg, West Germany
John Lennon: Rhythm Guitar   **Paul McCartney:** Bass Guitar
George Harrison: Lead Guitar   **Ringo Starr:** Drums
Horst Obber: Solo Vocal

SIDE FOUR 18:29
Sheila (Roe) 1:55
Recorded: 18-31 December 1962, The Star Club, Grosse Freiheit 39, Hamburg, West Germany
John Lennon: Rhythm Guitar
Paul McCartney: Bass Guitar
George Harrison: Lead Guitar and Solo Vocal
Ringo Starr: Drums

Red Sails In The Sunset (Kennedy-Williams) 2:00
Recorded: 18-31 December 1962, The Star Club, Grosse Freiheit 39, Hamburg, West Germany
John Lennon: Rhythm Guitar
Paul McCartney: Bass Guitar and Solo Vocal
George Harrison: Lead Guitar
Ringo Starr: Drums

Everybody's Trying To Be My Baby (Perkins) 2:25
Recorded: 18-31 December 1962, The Star Club, Grosse Freiheit 39, Hamburg, West Germany
John Lennon: Rhythm Guitar
Paul McCartney: Bass Guitar
George Harrison: Lead Guitar and Solo Vocal
Ringo Starr: Drums

Matchbox (Perkins) 2:35
Recorded: 18-31 December 1962, The Star Club, Grosse Freiheit 39, Hamburg, West Germany
John Lennon: Rhythm Guitar and Solo Vocal
Paul McCartney: Bass Guitar
George Harrison: Lead Guitar
Ringo Starr: Drums

(I'm) Talking About You (Berry) 1:50
Recorded: 18-31 December 1962, The Star Club, Grosse Freiheit 39, Hamburg, West Germany
John Lennon: Rhythm Guitar and Solo Vocal
Paul McCartney: Bass Guitar
George Harrison: Lead Guitar
Ringo Starr: Drums

Shimmy Shake (South-Land) 2:18
Recorded: 18-31 December 1962, The Star Club, Grosse Freiheit 39, Hamburg, West Germany
John Lennon: Rhythm Guitar and Lead Vocal
Paul McCartney: Bass Guitar and Lead Vocal
George Harrison: Lead Guitar
Ringo Starr: Drums

Long Tall Sally (Johnson-Penniman-Blackwell)   1:50
Recorded: 18-31 December 1962, The Star Club, Grosse Freiheit 39, Hamburg, West Germany
John Lennon: Rhythm Guitar   **Paul McCartney**: Bass Guitar and Solo Vocal
George Harrison: Lead Guitar   **Ringo Starr**: Drums

I Remember You (Mercer-Schertzinger)   1:51
Recorded: 18-31 December 1962, The Star Club, Grosse Freiheit 39, Hamburg, West Germany
John Lennon: Rhythm Guitar and Harmonica   **Paul McCartney**: Bass Guitar and Solo Vocal
George Harrison: Lead Guitar   **Ringo Starr**: Drums

PLEASE PLEASE ME

UK Release: 22 March 1963
US Release: February 1987
Intl CD No: CDP 7 46435 2
Running Time: 31:48

**Parlophone PMC 1202: PCS 3042
Capitol CLJ 46435
Producer:** George Martin

SIDE ONE: I Saw Her Standing There; Misery; Anna (Go To Him); Chains; Boys; Ask Me Why; Please Please Me.

SIDE TWO: Love Me Do; P.S. I Love You; Baby It's You; Do You Want To Know A Secret; A Taste Of Honey; There's A Place; Twist And Shout.

The Beatles' first album for Parlophone combines their two previously issued singles 'Love Me Do'/'P.S. I Love You' and 'Please Please Me'/'Ask Me Why' with ten newly recorded songs. Four of the new songs are Lennon-McCartney originals, while the remaining six are Beatles versions of some of their favourite songs they had included in their live performances at the Cavern Club in Liverpool and the Star Club in Hamburg for some time before getting a recording contract with EMI.

Despite the success of the two singles – 'Please Please Me' had just reached No. 1 – EMI were still not convinced that The Beatles were going to last. But, wanting to meet the overwhelming demand for their records, EMI asked The Beatles to make an album as soon as possible, and preferably call it *Please Please Me* so that it would be instantly recognisable to the buyers of the single.

George Martin initially planned to record a live album capturing all the excitement of a Beatles performance at the Cavern Club in Liverpool, but the idea proved to be impractical and was quickly dropped in favour of a studio recording of songs they would have performed on a live album.

On 11 February 1963 The Beatles, and George Martin, went to EMI's Abbey Road studios to record the remaining tracks on this album in one long exhaustive recording session that lasted from 10am to 11pm. As he had not decided on the content of this album, George Martin asked The Beatles to run through some of their favourite songs. From these he selected nine of the final ten album titles. The tenth was 'Twist and Shout'. With the contents now decided, and with the knowledge that The Beatles had been playing these songs for years, Martin started the recording session.

Thirteen hours, ten songs and £400 later the album was finished. To record an album, mix it and

have it ready to go into production in one day was no mean feat but they managed it. It is interesting to note that at the time of this recording Lennon and McCartney had written nearly 100 songs and were heavily criticised for not including more of their own songs on this album. Nevertheless EMI were delighted with the recordings when the album was released and decided that two tracks from the album should be issued as a single.

To avoid that plan, and with the knowledge that four of the album tracks had already been issued as singles, a further recording session on 5 March 1963 produced 'From Me To You' and 'Thank You Girl'. These were released as a single, on 12 April 1963, two weeks after the release of the album. Like 'Please Please Me', its predecessor, this single went to No. 1

The release of the album changed the British music scene. Previously the British album chart had been filled with film sound-track albums, recordings of London and Broadway musicals and, with the exception of Elvis Presley and two or three other American artists, very little else. The only British pop music artists who had had any sort of success in the British album charts before The Beatles were Cliff Richard and The Shadows.

SIDE ONE
I Saw Her Standing There (Lennon-McCartney) 2:50
John Lennon: Rhythm Guitar and Harmony Vocal   **Paul McCartney:** Bass Guitar and Lead Vocal
George Harrison: Lead Guitar   **Ringo Starr:** Drums

A great opener to the album, this was initial proof that Lennon and McCartney could and would write good old rock'n'roll. It is hard to imagine a better start to The Beatles' first album than Paul counting in 'one-two-three-four'. Paul's lead vocal with harmonies from John is backed by some excellent Shadows-style lead guitar from George. The recording features some of The Beatles' early trademarks, including handclapping, used to add more excitement to an already exciting recording, and 'oooo' that was to be put to good use on future recordings. Overall, this is a good chunk of pounding rock'n'roll that featured in Beatles live performances and was a huge favourite among members at both the Cavern and Star clubs.

On 28 November 1974 John Lennon recorded this song with Elton John. After a concert given by Elton John at Madison Square Garden, Lennon joined him on stage and announced 'we thought we'd do a number of an old estranged fiancé of mine, called Paul'.

Misery (Lennon-McCartney) 1:43
John Lennon: Rhythm Guitar and Lead Vocal   **Paul McCartney**: Bass Guitar and Lead Vocal
George Harrison: Lead Guitar   **Ringo Starr**: Drums
The lead vocal on this up-tempo ballad sounds double-tracked; it is, in fact, a close-harmony duet between John and Paul, and is a fine example of how they blended their voices to sound like one. It is also proof that Lennon and McCartney could sing as well as write songs.

Anna (Go To Him) (Alexander) 2:56
John Lennon: Rhythm Guitar and Lead Vocal
Paul McCartney: Bass Guitar and Backing Vocal
George Harrison: Lead Guitar and Backing Vocal   **Ringo Starr**: Drums
John's powerful pleading lead vocals do justice to this Arthur Alexander song that Arthur had recorded a year earlier for the Dot label. As John Lennon later revealed, Arthur Alexander was a big influence on his early writing. This song and the equally mournful 'You Better Move On', recorded by the Rolling Stones, are two of Arthur's internationally famous songs.

Chains (Goffin-King) 2:21
John Lennon: Rhythm Guitar, Harmonica and Harmony Vocal
Paul McCartney: Bass Guitar and Harmony Vocal
George Harrison: Lead Guitar and Lead Vocal   **Ringo Starr**: Drums
The musical introduction to this Goffin-King song, originally recorded by American girl group The Cookies, heralds the first appearance on the album of John's harmonica. The vocals are a three-part harmony between John, Paul and George, with George singing solo between the chanting chorus line that dominates the song.

Boys (Dixon-Farrell) 2:24
John Lennon: Rhythm Guitar and Backing Vocal
Paul McCartney: Bass Guitar and Backing Vocal
George Harrison: Lead Guitar and Backing Vocal   **Ringo Starr:** Drums and Lead Vocal
This song, originally recorded by the Shirelles, gives Ringo his first appearance on the album as vocalist. He belts out the lyrics in fine form, sounding like any good rock'n'roller should sound. John, Paul and George supply the 'bop-shoo-wop' backing as Ringo hurtles his way through his beloved Shirelles song. Luther Dixon and Wes Farrell surely thought this was a good rendition of their song.

Ask Me Why (Lennon-McCartney) 2:24
John Lennon: Rhythm Guitar and Lead Vocal
Paul McCartney: Bass Guitar and Harmony Vocal
George Harrison: Lead Guitar and Harmony Vocal   **Ringo Starr:** Drums
Released as the B side to 'Please Please Me', The Beatles' second single for Parlophone, this is the first song on the album not to have been recorded at the 11 February session. One of John's early attempts at ballad writing, it features him on lead vocal with some very pleasant harmonies from Paul and George. Falsetto, another of The Beatles' early trademarks, can be heard on this song.

Please Please Me (Lennon-McCartney) 2:00
John Lennon: Rhythm Guitar, Harmonica and Lead Vocal
Paul McCartney: Bass Guitar and Harmony Vocal
George Harrison: Lead Guitar and Harmony Vocal   **Ringo Starr:** Drums
Two minutes of sheer excellence. This highly commercial recording was the title track of the album and also the title of The Beatles' second single for Parlophone that shot up to the top of the charts within weeks of being released. John's lead vocal is given some fine close harmony backing from Paul and George. The track is interspersed with some interesting harmonica from John. This recording is quite amazing because it manages to condense so much into such a short space of time. Paul has since given George Martin credit for improving the tempo of this track that was the main reason for its success.

SIDE TWO

Love Me Do (Lennon-McCartney) 2:19
John Lennon: Harmonica and Lead Vocal
Paul McCartney: Bass Guitar and Lead Vocal
George Harrison: Acoustic Guitar and Harmony Vocal
Ringo Starr: Tambourine   **Andy White:** Drums

This recording was the A side of The Beatles' first single for Parlophone. The next track, 'P. S. I Love You' was the B side. Released on 5 October 1962, it hovered around the lower half of the Top 20 at No. 17. It was on the chart for six weeks that was short by later standards. The recording is dominated by John's harmonica. The main lead vocals are a duet from John and Paul, with John singing solo at various times. The lyrics are sparse but with the dominant harmonica and John's asthmatic Liverpudlian scouse vocals it was definitely an ear catcher in 1962.

There are two recordings of 'Love Me Do'; one features Ringo on drums and the other features Andy White a session musician. This version is the Andy White version with Ringo on tambourine. The single featured Ringo on drums.

The reason for the two recordings was that after Ringo replaced Pete Best, George Martin who had not heard him play, brought in Andy White in case Ringo's drumming didn't match up to expectations. Martin insisted that The Beatles used Andy White as the drummer but The Beatles wanted Ringo. As a compromise, two recordings were made. None of The Beatles was particularly pleased about a session musician being used on their records, or about the fact that Ringo had been given a tambourine, and they insisted that the version featuring Ringo on drums be released as the single. The version featuring Ringo is included on Record 1 of *The Beatles Box*.

P.S. I Love You (Lennon-McCartney) 2:02
John Lennon: Acoustic Guitar and Lead Vocal   **Paul McCartney:** Bass Guitar and Lead Vocal
George Harrison: Lead Guitar   **Ringo Starr:** Maracas
Andy White: Drums

Previously released as the B side to 'Love Me Do', this sounds rather like a Paul McCartney re-write of John Lennon's 'Ask Me Why', although it is still a very pleasant song.

Baby It's You (David-Williams-Bacharach) 2:36
John Lennon: Rhythm Guitar and Lead Vocal
Paul McCartney: Bass Guitar and Backing Vocal
George Harrison: Lead Guitar and Backing Vocal
Ringo Starr: Drums   **George Martin:** Piano
This easy-going ballad was previously recorded by The Shirelles, one of The Beatles' favourite groups. John's lead vocals are backed by Paul and George who supply the sha, la, la, la, la backing. John Lennon's ability to change the tone, pitch and feeling in his voice is finely displayed on this recording.

Do You Want To Know A Secret (Lennon-McCartney) 1:55
John Lennon: Rhythm Guitar and Backing Vocal
Paul McCartney: Bass Guitar and Backing Vocal
George Harrison: Lead Guitar and Lead Vocal   **Ringo Starr:** Drums
George Harrison's first appearance on the album as a vocalist is on this song, of which John Lennon was once quoted as saying 'I wrote this one for George'. Unfortunately for George the whole recording is badly mixed, with George's lead guitar mixed into oblivion somewhere down the right channel, and John and Paul's backing vocals given far too much echo, producing an out-of-keeping, almost ethereal atmosphere. The song was later recorded by Billy J. Kramer and The Dakotas and reached No. 1 in the British charts.

A Taste Of Honey (Marlow-Scott) 2:02
John Lennon: Rhythm Guitar and Harmony Vocal   **Paul McCartney:** Bass Guitar and Lead Vocal
George Harrison: Lead Guitar and Harmony Vocal   **Ringo Starr:** Drums
Taken from the theme music of the film of the same name, 'A Taste Of Honey' has been recorded by many musicians, from blues singers to classical orchestras. This song featured in The Beatles' early stage performances, was very popular in the early 60s, and was a good vehicle for Paul McCartney's voice. John and George supply harmonies.

There's A Place (Lennon-McCartney)   1:44
John Lennon: Rhythm Guitar, Harmonica and Lead Vocal
Paul McCartney: Bass Guitar and Harmony Vocal
George Harrison: Lead Guitar   **Ringo Starr:** Drums

The tight harmony of John and Paul, with John singing solo at times, combine perfectly with the wailing soulful harmonica on this fine example of John's early ballad writing. This is an extremely pleasant, well-recorded song.

Twist And Shout (Medley-Russell)   2:32
John Lennon: Rhythm Guitar and Lead Vocal
Paul McCartney: Bass Guitar and Backing Vocal
George Harrison: Lead Guitar and Backing Vocal   **Ringo Starr:** Drums.

This is the strongest track on the album and one of the few songs that Lennon and McCartney must have wished they had written themselves. Originally recorded by the Isley Brothers in 1962, this Phil Medley and Bert Russell song was a Beatles show-stopper at early concerts, the song that most people would remember after the show was over. John's rasping, leathery vocals turn the invitation to twist and shout into a demand. The chunky combination of the lead and rhythm guitars, coupled with Paul's chugging bass guitar and Ringo's tight drum beat makes this a truly magnificent recording. According to legend, when The Beatles had finished the recordings for the *Please Please Me* album they still had some studio time left, so, in one take, they recorded 'Twist and Shout'. Every time I listen to the track I wonder how long it took John Lennon to recover from the sore throat he must have suffered after recording this track.

WITH THE BEATLES

UK Release: 22 November 1963
US Release: February 1987
Intl CD No: CDP 7 46436 2
Running Time: 32:44

Parlophone PMC 1206: PCS 3045
Capitol CLJ 46436
Producer: George Martin

SIDE ONE: It Won't Be Long; All I've Got To Do; All My Loving; Don't Bother Me; little Child; Till There Was You; Please Mister Postman.

SIDE TWO: Roll Over Beethoven; Hold Me Tight; You Really Got A Hold On Me; I Wanna Be Your Man; Devil In Her Heart; Not A Second Time; Money.

The Beatles' second album for Parlophone features 14 newly recorded songs. Seven were written by Lennon-McCartney, one by George Harrison and the remaining six are a further selection of The Beatles' personal favourites.

After the huge success of the *Please Please Me* album it was important to follow it with another equally good, or a better, album and The Beatles came up with the goods. On three of the tracks The Beatles are joined by producer George Martin on piano. They are 'You Really Got a Hold On Me' the old Miracles number, Lennon and McCartney's 'Not A Second Time' and finally John's powerful rendition of the Janie Bradford/Berry Gordy song, 'Money'.

Unlike *Please Please Me*, this album is not dependent on earlier single releases. To ensure that none of the tracks was extracted for release as a single, The Beatles recorded 'I Want To Hold Your Hand' and 'This Boy' on 19 october 1963. These were issued as a single on 29 November 1963, exactly one week after the release of the album.

with
the
beatles

stereo

SIDE ONE

It Won't Be Long (Lennon-McCartney)   2:11
John Lennon: Rhythm Guitar and Lead Vocal
Paul McCartney: Bass Guitar and Backing Vocal
George Harrison: Lead Guitar and Backing Vocal   **Ringo Starr:** Drums
John's double-tracked lead vocal on this song is given some neat close-harmony backing by Paul and George. The song is structured in a similar way to 'Money', the album's closing track; John sings the statement-style lyrics and Paul and George reply with yeah-yeah. The recording also makes use of a repetitive, although not over-obvious or annoying, riff.

All I've Got To Do (Lennon-McCartney)   2:05
John Lennon: Rhythm Guitar and Lead Vocal
Paul McCartney: Bass Guitar and Harmony Vocal
George Harrison: Lead Guitar   **Ringo Starr:** Drums
This recording starts with an unusual semi-blues/country beat. It then moves at a much faster pace before reverting to the earlier beat. John handles the lyrics perfectly, with Paul supplying harmonies. The combination works extremely well.

All My Loving (Lennon-McCartney)   2:04
John Lennon: Rhythm Guitar and Harmony Vocal   **Paul McCartney:** Bass Guitar and Lead Vocal
George Harrison: Lead Guitar and Harmony Vocal   **Ringo Starr:** Drums
Paul's first lead-vocal performance on the album in 'All My Loving' has become one of The Beatles' standards and has been recorded by many artists in many styles. Paul's voice is double-tracked on this powerful song that tears along at a furious pace. The song starts and stops unobtrusively and makes effective use of a second or so of silence – an effect that was used often on future recordings. Listen to George's country-and-western guitar playing during the instrumental break; it fits in with the rest of the track perfectly to make this one of Paul McCartney's most likeable songs.

Don't Bother Me (Harrison) 2:28
John Lennon: Rhythm Guitar and Tambourine   **Paul McCartney:** Bass Guitar and Claves
George Harrison: Lead Guitar and Solo Vocal
Ringo Starr: Drums, Bongos and Loose-Skinned Arabian Bongo

This was the first George Harrison song to appear on a Beatles album, although it was not his first composition. He had written the instrumental 'Cry For A Shadow' with John that was included on the Polydor album *The Beatles First*.

This song probably would never have been written had it not been for Bill Harry, editor/owner in the early 60s of the Merseyside newspaper *Merseybeat*. He repeatedly teased George, asking him when he was going to start writing songs like John and Paul. Finally, George came up with 'Don't Bother Me'. It was a good first song from George. It is structured like 'All My Loving', starting and stopping in a similar manner. In addition to the normal instrumentation, George's double-tracked lead vocals are backed by Paul beating out the rhythm on claves, John joining in on tambourine, and Ringo on a loose-skinned Arabian bongo.

Little Child (Lennon-McCartney) 1:46
John Lennon: Rhythm Guitar, Harmonica and Lead Vocal
Paul McCartney: Bass Guitar, Piano and Lead Vocal
George Harrison: Lead Guitar   **Ringo Starr:** Drums

John's harmonica leads into this rhythm-and-blues song, one of very few recorded by The Beatles. The lead vocal is a duet between John and Paul, although John predominates. His superb blues harmonica contribution is very derivative of Cyril Davies, the exponent of some fine harmonica playing on many British rhythm-and-blues records during the late 50s and early 60s when he worked with Alexis Korner's Blues Incorporated.

The influence of Cyril Davies on John, and of Nicky Hopkins another early British exponent of rhythm and blues on Paul who plays piano on the track, was evident on the call and answer of the vocals versus the harmonica and piano and give the song a strong Rolling Stones feel.

Till There Was You (Willson) 2:12
John Lennon: Acoustic Guitar
George Harrison: Acoustic Guitar

Paul McCartney: Bass Guitar and Solo Vocal
Ringo Starr: Bongos

Taken from the stage show/film *The Music Man*, this song had been used for a long time by The Beatles in their stage performances. It always went down extremely well at the Cavern and Star clubs and was used as a slow melodic breather between up-tempo dance beat songs. With almost magical control The Beatles would bring an audience to near silence whenever they performed this number. For proof of this listen to *The Beatles' Historic Sessions* album. The lead vocal is a solo from Paul with John and George playing acoustic guitars and Ringo tapping out a gentle beat on a set of bongos. The only electrically powered instrument on this track is Paul's bass guitar.

Please Mister Postman (Holland) 2:34
John Lennon: Rhythm Guitar and Lead Vocal
Paul McCartney: Bass Guitar and Harmony Vocal
George Harrison: Lead Guitar and Harmony Vocal   **Ringo Starr**: Drums

Another early Beatles favourite, this one-time American chart-topper for American girl group The Marvelettes features John Lennon on lead vocal with Paul and George adding harmonies and some interesting backing vocals. What sounds like a duet between John and Paul is actually John's voice double-tracked. This is another song that The Beatles probably wished they had written themselves.

SIDE TWO
Roll Over Beethoven (Berry) 2:44
John Lennon: Rhythm Guitar
George Harrison: Lead Guitar and Solo Vocal

Paul McCartney: Bass Guitar
Ringo Starr: Drums

With John's rhythm guitar chugging away, George double-tracks the lead vocals for this rendition of the Chuck Berry classic. The Beatles performed this song quite often during their early days at the Cavern and Star clubs and it was a popular request number. An early live recording of the song can be heard on *The Star Club Tapes*.

Hold Me Tight (Lennon-McCartney)   2:30
John Lennon: Rhythm Guitar and Backing Vocal   **Paul McCartney:** Bass Guitar and Lead Vocal
George Harrison: Lead Guitar and Backing Vocal   **Ringo Starr:** Drums.
Paul is on lead vocal for this one with John and George adding energetic backing vocals and joining on chorus. Paul sings with a slightly Little Richard sound similar to 'I Saw Her Standing There' on the first album. Both songs show Paul's increasing interest in writing his own rock'n'roll songs.

You Really Got A Hold On Me (Robinson)   2:58
John Lennon: Rhythm Guitar and Lead Vocal
Paul McCartney: Bass Guitar and Backing Vocal
George Harrison: Lead Guitar and Lead Vocal
Ringo Starr: Drums   **George Martin:** Piano
The lead vocal for this song, originally recorded by American group The Miracles, is brilliantly handled by John. It is not the easiest of songs to sing, but he does it well. George duets with John and alternates with him on the main line of the song. Paul joins them both for the chorus, while George Martin adds a dramatic piano.

In the late 50s and early 60s, American soul was virtually unknown in Britain, and almost nobody had heard of The Miracles or Smokey Robinson. It was not until The Beatles and other Liverpudlian groups started to put out their versions of American records such as 'You Really Got a Hold On Me' that interest in the originals began to grow. Smokey Robinson later went on to write such classics as 'The Tracks Of My Tears' and 'The Tears Of A Clown'.

I Wanna Be Your Man (Lennon-McCartney)   1:59
John Lennon: Rhythm Guitar, Hammond Organ and Harmony Vocal
Paul McCartney: Bass Guitar and Harmony Vocal   **George Harrison:** Lead Guitar
Ringo Starr: Drums, Maracas and Lead Vocal
After the public response to Ringo's performance of the Shirelles' number 'Boys' on *Please Please Me*, John and Paul came up with 'I Wanna Be Your Man' for him. Ringo handles the lyrics professionally, with a helping hand from John and Paul on chorus. The instrumentation for this track is supplemented by a Hammond organ played by John and maracas added by Ringo.

After failing to reach the Top 20 with their first single 'Come On', the Rolling Stones recorded 'I Wanna Be Your Man' as their follow-up and the song took them to No. 12 in the British charts.

Devil In Her Heart (Drapkin)   2:23
John Lennon: Rhythm Guitar and Harmony Vocal
Paul McCartney: Bass Guitar and Harmony Vocal
George Harrison: Lead Guitar and Lead Vocal   **Ringo Starr:** Drums and Maracas
When The Beatles got hold of this song that was originally recorded by American girl group the Donays, they changed the lyrics slightly for George to sing. He handles the song skilfully and John and Paul add harmonies and backing vocals. During their career The Beatles were to record in many styles; on this track they play a samba beat, and the final chord almost could have been replaced with a vocal cha, cha, cha.

Not A Second Time (Lennon-McCartney)   2:03
John Lennon: Acoustic Guitar and Solo Vocal   **Paul McCartney:** Not Present
George Harrison: Not Present   **Ringo Starr:** Drums
George Martin: Piano
The last Lennon and McCartney song on the album features a double-tracked vocal from John with George Martin on piano. This is one of their few early songs without backing vocals. The track is backed by Martin, John on acoustic guitar and Ringo on drums.

This is the song that William Mann of *The Times* described so graphically in 1963. After writing about Lennon and McCartney at great length as 'the outstanding English composers of 1963', Mann then gave a review of 'This Boy' and continued with 'but harmonic interest is typical of their quicker songs too, and one gets the impression that they think simultaneously of harmony and melody, so firmly are the major tonic sevenths and ninths built into their tunes, and the flat submediant key switches, so natural in the Aeolian cadence at the end of 'Not A Second Time' (the chord progression that ends Mahler's Song of the Earth)' to which John Lennon replied, 'Really it was chords just like any other chords'.

Money (Bradford-Gordy)   2:47
John Lennon: Rhythm Guitar and Lead Vocal
Paul McCartney: Bass Guitar and Backing Vocal
George Harrison: Lead Guitar and Backing Vocal   **Ringo Starr:** Drums
George Martin: Piano

John shouts out his demands for money with the full force of his raw leathery voice. Paul and George add the backing answers to his demands, and Ringo adds an almost hypnotic jungle beat on drums. George Martin is again featured on piano, one of the predominant instruments on this powerful rendition. The song was partly written by Berry Gordy, the boss of Motown Records and originally recorded by American artist Barratt Strong for the American Anna record label in 1959. It was subsequently re-issued on the Motown label in 1960.

A HARD DAY'S NIGHT

UK Release: 10 July 1964
US Release: February 1987
Intl CD No: CDP 7 46437 2
Running Time: 29:53

Parlophone PMC 1230: PCS 3058
Capitol CLJ 46437
Producer: George Martin

SIDE ONE: A Hard Day's Night; I Should Have Known Better; If I Fell; I'm Happy Just To Dance With You; And I Love Her; Tell Me Why; Can't Buy Me Love.

SIDE TWO: Any Time At All; I'll Cry Instead; Things We Said Today; When I Get Home; You Can't Do That; I'll Be Back.

The soundtrack album from The Beatles' first film features 13 new Lennon and McCartney songs and was to be the only Beatles album to consist entirely of Lennon and McCartney compositions. Future albums always contained at least one track written by George Harrison and in two cases tracks written by Ringo Starr.

The first side features seven new songs used in the film, from the powerful opening title track to the slow melodic 'And I Love Her'. The soundtrack also used some of The Beatles' older songs such as 'I Wanna Be Your Man', 'Don't Bother Me', 'All My Loving' and 'She Loves You' but these are not included on the album. The second side has a further selection of Lennon and McCartney originals including 'I'll Cry Instead', that was written for the film, but was not considered strong enough for inclusion by the film's director, Dick Lester. Among the remaining five tracks is 'You Can't Do That', issued with 'Can't Buy Me Love' as a single about three months before the release of this album. The album title track along with 'Things We Said Today' was issued as a single.

The film, that also stars Wilfred Brambell as Paul's grandfather, depicts two days in the lives of The Beatles. It begins with them boarding a train in Liverpool (shot at Marylebone Station, London) on their way to give a concert that is shown at the end of the film. It has some hilarious moments and is very enjoyable.

THE BEATLES

A HARD DAY'S NIGHT

SIDE ONE
A Hard Day's Night (Lennon-McCartney) 2:32
John Lennon: Rhythm Guitar and Lead Vocal
Paul McCartney: Bass Guitar and Harmony Vocal
George Harrison: Lead Guitar
Ringo Starr: Drums   **George Martin:** Piano

The opening chord of this strong opening track shows typical Beatles originality and sounds more like
the end of a record than the beginning. As the chord fades, John double-tracks the lead vocals with
Paul harmonising in part and sometimes also singing lead vocals. In the excellent instrumental break
in the middle George's guitar sounds like a harpsichord and Ringo's backing beat rounds the whole
thing off. A good strong solid opening track that is played over the film's opening titles.

I Should Have Known Better (Lennon-McCartney) 2:42
John Lennon: Acoustic Guitar, Harmonica and Solo Vocal
Paul McCartney: Bass Guitar   **George Harrison:** Lead Guitar
Ringo Starr: Drums

John's wailing harmonica introduces this song that also features him on lead vocals in a double-
tracked solo with an extremely energetic backing. The song's early appearance in the film
accompanies a scene where The Beatles are playing cards in a train.

If I Fell (Lennon-McCartney) 2:16
John Lennon: Acoustic Guitar and Lead Vocal   **Paul McCartney:** Bass Guitar and Lead Vocal
George Harrison: Lead Guitar   **Ringo Starr:** Drums

This pleasant up-tempo ballad opens with a solo vocal from John on the first verse before he is joined
by Paul in a duet for the rest of the song. In the film The Beatles are seen performing this during
rehearsals for a television show.

I'm Happy Just To Dance With You (Lennon-McCartney) 1:59
John Lennon: Rhythm Guitar and Backing Vocal
Paul McCartney: Bass Guitar and Backing Vocal   **George Harrison:** Lead Guitar and Lead Vocal
Ringo Starr: Drums and Loose-Skinned Arabian Bongo

George is on lead vocals for this song, written for him by John. The Oh-oh backing comes from John and Paul, and Ringo's loose-skinned Arabian bongo that produces a hollow thumping sound, makes its second appearance on a Beatles record. It was first used in 'Don't Bother Me' on *With The Beatles*.

And I Love Her (Lennon-McCartney) 2:27
John Lennon: Acoustic Guitar
Paul McCartney: Acoustic Guitar and Solo Vocal
George Harrison: Claves and Acoustic Guitar Solo   **Ringo Starr:** Bongos
Paul McCartney's earliest ballad has become an international standard recorded by scores of artists, each with a different treatment. George Martin's orchestral version is included on the American album; here, the song features Paul on lead vocals, first double-tracked then triple-tracked to add his own harmonies. It also features a striking and memorable acoustic guitar riff accompanied by claves, two further acoustic guitars and bongos.

Tell Me Why (Lennon-McCartney) 2:04
John Lennon: Rhythm Guitar and Lead Vocal
Paul McCartney: Bass Guitar and Harmony Vocal   **George Harrison:** Lead Guitar
Ringo Starr: Drums
The vocals on this track are an interesting and unusual three-part harmony between John and Paul, with John's vocals double-tracked and Paul harmonising. The recording also features an effective use of falsetto by John and Paul, who manage to sound like a crowd of children.

Can't Buy Me Love (Lennon-McCartney) 2:15
John Lennon: Rhythm Guitar   **Paul McCartney:** Bass Guitar and Solo Vocal
George Harrison: Lead Guitar   **Ringo Starr:** Drums
Previously issued as a single, three months before this album, the song features a double-tracked vocal from Paul and sounds rather like a re-write of 'A Hard Day's Night', minus the opening chord. The recording also features an interesting double-tracked guitar during the instrumental break. The Beatles first recorded 'Can't Buy Me Love' in a theatre dressing room. The recording started with the verses instead of the chorus as it does here. Only three of The Beatles were on that recording, John and Paul singing and playing guitar and Ringo adding the backing beat, courtesy of a suitcase. George had gone to the toilet, and at the end of the song there is the sound of a toilet being flushed. The Beatles wanted to issue that version as a single but George Martin was not amused so this recording was made instead.

SIDE TWO
Any Time At All (Lennon-McCartney) 2:10
John Lennon: Acoustic Guitar and Solo Vocal   **Paul McCartney:** Bass Guitar and Piano
George Harrison: Lead Guitar   **Ringo Starr:** Drums
A lively song featuring a solo vocal from John and enthusiastic backing that includes a guitar/piano duet between George and Paul during the instrumental break. Neither this nor the remaining five tracks on this side of the album are featured in the film.

I'll Cry Instead (Lennon-McCartney) 1:44
John Lennon: Acoustic Guitar, Tambourine and Lead Vocal
Paul McCartney: Bass Guitar and Lead Vocal   **George Harrison:** Lead Guitar
Ringo Starr: Drums
This country-and-western influenced song written by John for inclusion in the film features a lead vocal duet between John and Paul with George playing some neat country-and-western/rockabilly guitar.

Things We Said Today (Lennon-McCartney) 2:35
John Lennon: Acoustic Guitar, Tambourine and Harmony Vocal
Paul McCartney: Bass Guitar and Lead Vocal   **George Harrison:** Lead Guitar
Ringo Starr: Drums
The opening riff is reminiscent of the Shadows' 'Guitar Tango', although it was uncharacteristic for The Beatles to borrow from other artists' material. Paul double-tracks the lead vocal with John harmonising in places. The song is a pleasant up-beat ballad written by Paul.

When I Get Home (Lennon-McCartney) 2:14
John Lennon: Rhythm Guitar and Lead Vocal
Paul McCartney: Bass Guitar and Harmony Vocal
George Harrison: Lead Guitar   **Ringo Starr:** Drums
Lead vocals are from John on this one with Paul harmonising in parts. Unfortunately the over-emphatic use of the line whoa-ho-I overshadows the rest of the song.

You Can't Do That (Lennon-McCartney)   2:33
John Lennon: Rhythm Guitar and Lead Vocal
Paul McCartney: Bass Guitar and Harmony Vocal
George Harrison: Twelve String Lead Guitar and Harmony Vocal
Ringo Starr: Drums, Cowbell and Bongos
This was previously issued as the B side to 'Can't Buy Me Love'. John's gravelly lead vocal shouts out the lyrics in an attempt at being Wilson Pickett, as he later admitted, and Paul and George harmonise on the chorus. Ringo bangs out a metallic beat on a cowbell and for good measure bongos are added.

I'll Be Back (Lennon-McCartney)   2:22
John Lennon: Acoustic Guitar and Lead Vocal
Paul McCartney: Bass Guitar, Acoustic Guitar and Harmony Vocal
George Harrison: Acoustic Guitar   **Ringo Starr:** Drums
The closing track is a pleasant up-tempo ballad featuring a double-tracked lead vocal from John, with Paul harmonising in places. The sentiment expressed in the title was a nice way to finish the album.

BEATLES FOR SALE

UK Release: 4 December 1964
US Release : February 1987
Intl CD No: CDP 7 46438 2
Running Time: 36:58

**Parlophone PMC 1240: PCS 3062
Capitol CLJ 46438
Producer:** George Martin

SIDE ONE: No Reply; I'm A Loser; Baby's In Black; Rock And Roll Music; I'll Follow The Sun; Mr. Moonlight; Kansas City/Hey Hey Hey Hey.

SIDE TWO: Eight Days A Week; Words Of Love; Honey Don't; Every Little Thing; I Don't Want To Spoil The Party; What You're Doing; Everybody's Trying To Be My Baby.

For this album Lennon and McCartney wrote eight new songs, and added a further six from the vast repertoire of material that they had been performing for some time. Three of the new songs, 'Eight Days A Week', 'No Reply' and 'I'm A Loser', were all considered as possible singles but once again The Beatles did not want to issue a single from the album. Instead John came up with 'I Feel Fine' and Paul with 'She's A Woman', that were issued as a single on 27 November 1964, one week prior to the release of this album. The Beatles had just completed their second major tour of the USA when they began work on this album during mid to late August 1964 and their obvious exhaustion can be heard in some of the tracks. On 'Every Little Thing' and 'I Don't Want To Spoil The Party' for example, the vocals sound rather weary and slightly strained. They had issued an album in time for the Christmas market of 1963 and planned to do the same for Christmas 1964 so recording continued. They were to repeat this each year, issuing Christmas singles until 1969.

In spite of the strain that shows through on a couple of tracks, this album contains some of The Beatles' classic early recordings such as John's powerful rendition of the old Chuck Berry standard 'Rock and Roll Music', Roy Lee Johnson's classic 'Mr. Moonlight and Paul's new song 'I'll Follow The Sun'. As with the previous three albums, both George and Ringo feature on one track each. Ringo sings the old Carl Perkins standard 'Honey Don't' and George takes lead vocal on another Carl Perkins track, 'Everybody's Trying To Be My Baby'.

The sleeve photographs for this album also reveal the strain in the form of four unsmiling Beatles. The inner photograph shows The Beatles standing against a background of photographs of various

music-hall and film stars, pieced together to form a collage. This is an obvious presage to the sleeve for the 1967 Sgt. Pepper album.

SIDE ONE

No Reply (Lennon-McCartney)   2:15
John Lennon: Acoustic Guitar and Lead Vocal
Paul McCartney: Bass Guitar and Harmony Vocal
George Harrison: Lead Guitar and Harmony Vocal   **Ringo Starr:** Drums
George Martin: Piano
This strong opening track features a double-tracked lead vocal from John, with Paul helping here and there and George joining them for the chorus. They go straight into the lyrics without musical introduction or opening chorus. This was a style of writing used by John and Paul for quite some time. It was often George Martin who would add a chorus as an introduction before the main lyrics.

I'm A Loser (Lennon-McCartney)   2:31
John Lennon: Acoustic Guitar, Harmonica and Lead Vocal
Paul McCartney: Bass Guitar and Harmony Vocal
George Harrison: Lead Guitar   **Ringo Starr:** Drums and Tambourine
Lead vocals again are from John with Paul harmonising in parts and joining John for the chorus. At the time of writing this song, John had become influenced by Bob Dylan. Here he uses many of Dylan's expressions and nuances.

Baby's In Black (Lennon-McCartney)   2:02
John Lennon: Acoustic Guitar and Lead Vocal   **Paul McCartney:** Bass Guitar and Lead Vocal
George Harrison: Lead Guitar   **Ringo Starr:** Drums and Tambourine
Lead vocals on this track are a duet between John and Paul. Some 18 months after this recording was released, the Rolling Stones and a group called Los Bravos had hit records with 'Paint It Black' and 'Black Is Black', respectively, both might well have been inspired by this song. All three tracks convey the black feeling of lost love.

Rock And Roll Music (Berry) 2:02
John Lennon: Rhythm Guitar, Piano and Solo Vocal   **Paul McCartney:** Bass Guitar and Piano
George Harrison: Acoustic Guitar   **Ringo Starr:** Drums
George Martin: Piano (with John and Paul)

John's leathery vocals make a far better job of this Chuck Berry classic than Berry ever did, and do the song justice. It tears along at breakneck speed. As well as singing, John joins George Martin *and* Paul McCartney to add the piano backing. Yes, they are all on the same piano, and all at the same time.

I'll Follow The Sun (Lennon-McCartney) 1:46
John Lennon: Acoustic Guitar and Harmony Vocal
Paul McCartney: Acoustic Guitar and Lead Vocal   **George Harrison:** Lead Guitar
Ringo Starr: Bongos

Paul's lead vocal on this song is mostly double-tracked with John harmonising in places. Ringo adds some gentle taps on a set of bongos and George's lead guitar puts in a brief appearance during the instrumental break of this very pleasant, relaxing song.

Mr. Moonlight (Johnson) 2:35
John Lennon: Acoustic Guitar and Lead Vocal
Paul McCartney: Bass Guitar, Hammond Organ and Harmony Vocal
George Harrison: Lead Guitar and African Drum   **Ringo Starr:** Bongos

John screams out the opening of Mr. Moonlight with all the power and expression the Lennon larynx can supply. As may be guessed, he is the lead vocalist on this track with Paul harmonising in parts. Paul also plays a dramatic Hammond organ, sounding at times like something from the Phantom of the Opera. Ringo adds the backing beat on a set of bongos, while George supplies that hollow thump on an ancient African drum.

Kansas City (Leiber-Stoller)**/Hey Hey Hey Hey** (Penniman) 2:30

John Lennon: Rhythm Guitar and Backing Vocal **Paul McCartney:** Bass Guitar and Lead Vocal
George Harrison: Lead Guitar and Backing Vocal **Ringo Starr:** Drums and Backing Vocal
George Martin: Piano

Originally, it was Little Richard's idea to join Kansas City together with his own Hey Hey Hey Hey in 1955. Paul, being a great fan of Little Richard, used this medley during The Beatles' early stage performances. It was recorded here exactly as they had always performed it, with Paul on lead vocal using his best Little Richard voice and John, George and Ringo supplying the 'hey hey hey hey' backing for the second song. There was an error on the album cover that listed this track as Kansas City. This was corrected on the record label by adding the Hey Hey Hey Hey credit and on later covers of albums that included the track.

SIDE TWO

Eight Days A Week (Lennon-McCartney) 2:43

John Lennon: Rhythm Guitar, Acoustic Guitar and Lead Vocal
Paul McCartney: Bass Guitar and Harmony Vocal **George Harrison:** Lead Guitar
Ringo Starr: Drums

The fade-in, build-up of guitars at the beginning of this track, thought to be innovative at the time, has since been copied many times. John's lead vocal is double-tracked, and he also supplies his own harmonies for this song. Many people considered this song to be dedicated to Brian Epstein because of his problems at that time: he was trying to manage too many groups and solo artists and so trying to live eight days a week.

The song was written by John when The Beatles were approached to make a second film, tentatively called *Eight Arms To Hold You*. John set about writing a song with the same title, but it turned out as 'Eight Days A Week'; he then came up with Help!, and the title of the film was changed.

Words Of Love (Holly) 2:10
John Lennon: Rhythm Guitar and Lead Vocal   **Paul McCartney:** Bass Guitar and Lead Vocal
George Harrison: Lead Guitar   **Ringo Starr:** Drums and Packing Case
John and Paul's close harmony on this, the only Buddy Holly song that The Beatles released on record, is the best example of how John and Paul blended their voices. Buddy Holly was one of Paul McCartney's favourite American artists and he has acquired all publishing rights to every Buddy Holly song.

The hand-clapping sound on the backing is Ringo playing a packing case!

Honey Don't (Perkins) 2:56
John Lennon: Acoustic Guitar and Tambourine   **Paul McCartney:** Bass Guitar
George Harrison: Lead Guitar   **Ringo Starr:** Drums and Solo Vocal
On Ringo's usual one-track-per-album opportunity, he eases his way through the words of this old Carl Perkins song, producing his own sing-a-long style that suited his voice so well, and that he was to use on many recordings.

Carl Perkins was present at the session when this and some of his other songs were recorded by The Beatles. He was reported to have thoroughly enjoyed watching the session, although he did not take part. In 1982, Perkins joined Paul McCartney for a song on McCartney's *Tug of War* album.

Every Little Thing (Lennon-McCartney) 2:01
John Lennon: Acoustic Guitar and Lead Vocal
Paul McCartney: Bass Guitar, Piano and Lead Vocal
George Harrison: Lead Guitar   **Ringo Starr:** Drums and Timpani
More close harmonies from John and Paul on this track that has the interesting inclusion of a timpani drum, played by Ringo, to accentuate sections of the song; George adds some very pleasant country-and-western-style guitar.

I Don't Want To Spoil The Party (Lennon-McCartney) 2:33
John Lennon: Acoustic Guitar and Lead Vocal   **Paul McCartney:** Bass Guitar and Lead Vocal
George Harrison: Lead Guitar   **Ringo Starr:** Drums and Tambourine
John and Paul again harmonise on lead vocals, sounding very much as they do on 'Words of Love'. This interesting track has a square-dance style backing, but John and Paul's vocals sound rather tired.

What You're Doing (Lennon-McCartney)   2:30
John Lennon: Acoustic Guitar and Backing Vocal   **Paul McCartney:** Bass Guitar and Lead Vocal
George Harrison: Lead Guitar   **Ringo Starr:** Drums
George Martin: Piano

On many early Beatles recordings, they paid homage to various artists. Here, they pay tribute to Phil Spector. The drum intro is a straight lift from the Spector-produced 'Be My Baby' by The Ronettes. It is even used again at the end, exactly as it is on the Ronettes' record. The vocals on this track come from Paul.

Everybody's Trying To Be My Baby (Perkins)   2:24
John Lennon: Acoustic Guitar and Tambourine   **Paul McCartney:** Bass Guitar
George Harrison: Lead Guitar and Solo Vocal   **Ringo Starr:** Drums

The second Carl Perkins song to be included on this album. This was recorded a week earlier than 'Honey Don't' and features George on lead vocals although he is somewhat swamped by echo and country-and-western guitar.

HELP!

UK Release: 6 August 1965
US Release: April 1987
Intl CD No: CDP 7 46439 2
Running Time: 33: 06

Parlophone PMC 1255: PCS 3071
Capitol CLJ 46439
Producer: George Martin

SIDE ONE: Help! The Night Before; You've Got To Hide Your Love Away; I Need You; Another Girl; You're Going To Lose That Girl; Ticket To Ride.

SIDE TWO: Act Naturally; It's Only Love; You Like Me Too Much; Tell Me What You See; I've Just Seen A Face; Yesterday; Dizzy Miss Lizzy.

The Beatles' fifth album for Parlophone was also the sound track from their second film. The first side contains seven of the eight Beatles songs featured in the film. The eighth, 'She's A Woman', is not included on this album.

Among the seven tracks, 'Another Girl' and 'Ticket To Ride' feature Paul McCartney playing lead guitar for the first time on record. The second side has four Lennon and McCartney originals; 'It's Only Love', with an unusual quavering guitar sound, 'Tell Me What You See', 'I've Just Seen A Face' and the brilliant 'Yesterday'.

Of the other three tracks featured on the second side, 'You Like Me Too Much' is written by George Harrison and 'Act Naturally' and 'Dizzy Miss Lizzy' are two of the last non-Beatle written songs that they recorded. 'Bad Boy', although recorded at the same time, was unavailable in Britain for 18 months. Eventually it was included on the compilation album *A Collection of Beatles Oldies*. Previously the track was available on the American album *Beatles VI* (Capitol ST 2358).

With *Help!* The Beatles began to progress away from the simple three guitar and drums format towards a more complex sound, particularly on tracks such as 'You've Got To Hide Your Love Away', 'It's Only Love' and 'Yesterday'. The latter features Paul and a string quartet. Progression was particularly noticeable four months later when the *Rubber Soul* album was issued.

The sleeves of the British and American albums differ greatly. Basically the American sleeve is an advertisement for the film, in the form of a gatefold with stills from the film and information about it.

Also, on the front cover of the American sleeve, someone has made the amusing mistake of

THE BEATLES stereo

rearranging the four photographs of The Beatles so that the semaphore that is supposed to spell out H-E-L-P! as on the British sleeve, in fact spells H-P-E-L!

SIDE ONE

Help! (Lennon-McCartney) 2:16
John Lennon: Acoustic Guitar and Lead Vocal
Paul McCartney: Bass Guitar and Backing Vocal
George Harrison: Lead Guitar and Backing Vocal   **Ringo Starr:** Drums and Tambourine
John's nasal lead vocals are supported by Paul and George on chorus and backing. This is one of the first Beatles lyrics not to have a boy-meets-girl/boy-loses-girl storyline. It is a real plea from John for help, comparing the situation he found himself in at the time to earlier, less complicated days. He said later 'I meant it – it's real. The lyric is as good now as it was then. It is no different, and it makes me feel secure to know that I was aware of myself then. I was just singing "help" and I meant it.'

The Night Before (Lennon-McCartney) 2:33
John Lennon: Electric Piano and Backing Vocal   **Paul McCartney:** Bass Guitar and Lead Vocal
George Harrison: Lead Guitar and Backing Vocal   **Ringo Starr:** Drums
Double-tracked lead vocals are from Paul with backing vocals from John and George effectively mixed into the song like fragments of a half-remembered dream. The electric piano is played by John.

You've Got To Hide Your Love Away (Lennon-McCartney) 2:08
John Lennon: Acoustic Guitar and Solo Vocal   **Paul McCartney:** Acoustic Guitar
George Harrison: Acoustic Guitar   **Ringo Starr:** Tambourine
Session Musicians: Flutes
John Lennon's intriguing lyrics show the influence of Dylan. The vocal is a solo from John; near the end he is joined by flutes.

I Need You (Harrison)   2:28
John Lennon: Acoustic Guitar and Backing Vocal
Paul McCartney: Bass Guitar and Backing Vocal
George Harrison: Lead Guitar and Lead Vocal   **Ringo Starr:** Drums
A double-tracked lead vocal from George on this, his own song, proves he could write songs as good as John and Paul's.

The backing vocals and pleasant harmony are added by John and Paul. The eerie guitar sound played by George is achieved with the volume/tone control pedal he was to use on a number of other tracks during 1965. At the end of the song it sounds as if he might play a guitar solo, but not having mastered the pedal he decided against it.

Another Girl (Lennon-McCartney)   2:02
John Lennon: Acoustic Guitar and Backing Vocal
Paul McCartney: Bass Guitar, Lead Guitar and Lead Vocal
George Harrison: Lead Guitar and Backing Vocal   **Ringo Starr:** Drums
Lead vocals are from Paul on this track, with John and George harmonising on the main line and chorus. The song has the same syncopated beat used in 'She's A Woman'. The lead guitar is played by Paul for the first time on a Beatles album and his solo at the end is really worth listening to.

You're Going To Lose That Girl (Lennon-McCartney)   2:18
John Lennon: Acoustic Guitar and Lead Vocal
Paul McCartney: Bass Guitar, Piano and Backing Vocal
George Harrison: Lead Guitar and Backing Vocal   **Ringo Starr:** Drums and Bongos
John's nasal lead vocal again works perfectly on this song. Paul and George add the backing vocals, plus some vocal support on chorus. Lead guitar comes from George and Ringo adds bongos.

Ticket To Ride (Lennon-McCartney)   3:03
John Lennon: Rhythm Guitar, Tambourine and Lead Vocal
Paul McCartney: Bass Guitar, Lead Guitar and Harmony Vocal
George Harrison: Lead Guitar   **Ringo Starr:** Drums
Previously issued as a single, this song features mainly John on lead vocal with Paul harmonising in parts and making his second appearance on lead guitar.

SIDE TWO

Act Naturally (Morrison-Russell) 2:27
John Lennon: Acoustic Guitar
Paul McCartney: Bass Guitar and Harmony Vocal
George Harrison: Lead Guitar   **Ringo Starr:** Drums and Lead Vocal

Lead vocals are from Ringo, his only appearance as a vocalist on this album. Paul helps out with some harmony vocals, while John and George play the country-and-western/rockabilly guitars in the backing.

It's Only Love (Lennon-McCartney) 1:53
John Lennon: Acoustic Guitar, Tambourine and Solo Vocal
Paul McCartney: Bass Guitar   **George Harrison:** Lead Guitar
Ringo Starr: Drums

This started life with the intriguing title of 'That's A Nice Hat', before John wrote the lyrics. George Martin recorded an orchestral arrangement of the original instrumental, and included it on his orchestral version of the *Help!* album. This must be John's first inoffensive wandering into expanded consciousness lyrics; the song starts with the words 'I get high'. The quavering lead guitar is further experimentation by George on the volume/tone control pedal. He did not perfect his technique until 'Yes It Is'.

You Like Me Too Much (Harrison) 2:34
John Lennon: Acoustic Guitar and Electric Piano
Paul McCartney: Steinway Piano and Harmony Vocal
George Harrison: Lead Guitar and Lead Vocal   **Ringo Starr:** Drums and Tambourine
George Martin: Steinway Piano (with Paul)

George provides lead vocals with harmonies from Paul on the chorus. The piano introduction features Paul and George Martin on the same Steinway. John plays electric piano in the backing and on the call-and-answer-style instrumental break, that also features George on lead guitar. George's talent as a song writer is evident in this song as well as in 'I Need You' featured on the first side of this album.

Tell Me What You See (Lennon-McCartney)   2:35
John Lennon: Washboard and Lead Vocal
Paul McCartney: Bass Guitar, Electric Piano and Lead Vocal
George Harrison: Lead Guitar and Tambourine   **Ringo Starr:** Drums and Claves
The vocal structure of this song is unusual, John and Paul duet on the statement-style lyrics and Paul sings solo on the answers. Paul also plays the electric piano in the backing.

I've Just Seen A Face (Lennon-McCartney)   2:04
John Lennon: Acoustic Guitar
Paul McCartney: Acoustic Guitar and Solo Vocal
George Harrison: Acoustic Guitar   **Ringo Starr:** Drums and Maracas
This track started life as an instrumental entitled 'Aunty Gin's Theme'; it was also recorded by George Martin under that title. Paul's lyrics show a slight Dylan influence although the song is more like an up-tempo 'Rocky Racoon'.

Yesterday (Lennon-McCartney)   2:04
John Lennon: Not Present
Paul McCartney: Acoustic Guitar and Solo Vocal
George Harrison: Not Present   **Ringo Starr:** Not Present
Session Musicians: String Quartet
Paul McCartney's most famous song started life as an instrumental entitled 'Scrambled Eggs' and has the same history as both 'It's Only Love' and 'I've Just Seen A Face'. For the first time none of the other Beatles appears on this recording so it can be classified as a Paul McCartney solo song. It features a solo vocal from Paul who also plays an acoustic guitar backed by a string quartet.

Dizzy Miss Lizzy (Williams)   2:51
John Lennon: Hammond Organ and Solo Vocal   **Paul McCartney:** Bass Guitar
George Harrison: Lead Guitar   **Ringo Starr:** Drums
John Lennon's leathery lead vocals are once again put to effective use on this Larry Williams song that was another of The Beatles' Cavern Club standards. They stick closely to the original arrangement of the song, but include some oooos and ows to give it more of a live sound.

RUBBER SOUL

UK Release: 3 December 1965
US Release: April 1987
Intl CD No: CDP 7 46440 2
Running Time: 34:50

Parlophone PMC 1267: PCS 3075
Capitol CLJ 46440
Producer: George Martin

SIDE ONE: Drive My Car; Norwegian Wood (This Bird Has Flown); You Won't See Me; Nowhere Man; Think For Yourself; The Word; Michelle.

SIDE TWO: What Goes On; Girl; I'm Looking Through You; In My Life; Wait; If I Needed Someone; Run For Your Life.

This sixth album from The Beatles showed a new musical direction. Here they move even further away from the instant pop product of their first five albums towards the second stage of their recording career. This album contains some of The Beatles most classic mid-60s songs, such as 'Norwegian Wood' and 'Girl', that sound as fresh now as they did in 1965. It was after the release of this album, and the realisation that its contents could not be reproduced live, that The Beatles decided to give up live performances and concentrate solely on making records.

On this album John gives a foretaste of the events of 1967 with the mysterious lyrics of 'The Word' and a glimpse into his past with 'In My Life'. Paul dabbles with the French language in the lyrics of 'Michelle'. George, as on *Help!*, has two songs included, 'Think For Yourself' and 'If I Needed Someone', and Ringo joins forces with John and Paul to come up with the country-and-western flavoured 'What Goes On'. On two of these tracks, The Beatles try out new instruments. George tries out the sitar on John's 'Norwegian Wood' and Paul tries out the newly invented fuzz bass guitar on George's 'Think For Yourself'.

Like *The Beatles For Sale* sleeve, this album sleeve shows four unsmiling faces. At the time fans complained that the photograph made The Beatles look rather anaemic. However, the music is far from being anaemic.

SIDE ONE
Drive My Car (Lennon-McCartney) 2:25
John Lennon: Tambourine and Lead Vocal
Paul McCartney: Bass Guitar, Piano and Lead Vocal
George Harrison: Lead Guitar and Backing Vocal   **Ringo Starr:** Drums
Paul uses his Little Richard voice once again for a duet with John on lead vocals, and George joins them here and there throughout the song for the chorus. George also plays some nice blues-sounding guitar on the intro and during the instrumental break. Paul plays piano during this blues/Motown-influenced song.

Norwegian Wood (This Bird Has Flown) (Lennon-McCartney) 2:00
John Lennon: Acoustic Guitar and Lead Vocal
Paul McCartney: Bass Guitar and Harmony Vocal
George Harrison: Sitar   **Ringo Starr:** Tambourine
The introduction to the first classic track on the album reveals George playing a sitar for the first time. The sitar was featured in the incidental music to *Help!* The Beatles' second film. George was fascinated by its sound and acquired one. He achieved his effect by tuning his new instrument to western notes. As usual this led the way for other artists to copy The Beatles' innovation and many records featuring the sitar, some good, some bad, were soon on the market. The song, that is really an account of a love affair set to music, has John on lead with additional vocals in places from Paul.

You Won't See Me (Lennon-McCartney) 3:19
John Lennon: Tambourine and Backing Vocal
Paul McCartney: Bass Guitar, Piano and Lead Vocal
George Harrison: Lead Guitar and Backing Vocal   **Ringo Starr:** Drums
Mal Evans: Hammond Organ
Paul is on lead vocals with John and George supplying harmony for chorus and backing. Mal Evans, one of The Beatles' roadies, is heard for the first time playing the Hammond organ. The piano is played by Paul.

Nowhere Man (Lennon-McCartney)   2:40

John Lennon: Acoustic Guitar and Lead Vocal   **Paul McCartney:** Bass Guitar and Lead Vocal
George Harrison: Lead Guitar and Lead Vocal   **Ringo Starr:** Drums

Initially, John brought this surrealistic character to life as a self-description. Later, after he admitted taking drugs, the character became one of the focal points for analysts who decided that the 'Nowhere Man' was anything from a drug pusher to the captain of the Yellow Submarine.

   John, Paul and George harmonise for the a cappella intro. John sings lead vocals with Paul and George adding backing harmonies and joining John for the chorus.

Think For Yourself (Harrison)   2:16

John Lennon: Tambourine and Backing Vocal
Paul McCartney: Fuzz Bass Guitar and Backing Vocal
George Harrison: Lead Guitar and Lead Vocal   **Ringo Starr:** Drums and Maracas

The first of two tracks on the album written by George features him on lead vocal with John and Paul harmonising in places. Paul also can be heard trying out the newly invented fuzz bass guitar. Obviously he cannot have been too impressed by it because it was four years before he was to use it again on a Beatles record.

The Word (Lennon-McCartney)   2:42

John Lennon: Rhythm Guitar and Lead Vocal
Paul McCartney: Bass Guitar, Piano and Lead Vocal
George Harrison: Lead Guitar and Lead Vocal
Ringo Starr: Drums and Maracas   **George Martin:** Harmonium

A foretaste of what was to come later with 'All You Need Is Love'. The phrase the word is love and the love one another theme were both to be adopted by the hippy movement.

   John, Paul and George harmonise with John mainly singing lead. George Martin plays harmonium and Paul joins in on piano. The recording seems to fade out rather early, giving the impression of an incomplete ending.

Michelle (Lennon-McCartney) 2:42
John Lennon: Acoustic Guitar and Backing Vocal
Paul McCartney: Bass Guitar and Lead Vocal
George Harrison: Acoustic Guitar and Backing Vocal   **Ringo Starr:** Drums
Written by Paul for the daughter of an American millionaire, Michelle features Paul on lead vocals with John and George adding the close harmony backing. This was another of The Beatles' songs that became an all-time standard. The song lapses into French now and again with phrases such as Ma belle (My beautiful) and Sont les mots qui vont très bien ensemble (These are words that go together very well). When 'Michelle' was issued in France as the title track of an EP, it shot to the No. 1 spot. The French did not release singles at that time and all 45 rpm records were EPs.

SIDE TWO
What Goes On (Lennon-McCartney-Starkey) 2:44
John Lennon: Rhythm Guitar and Backing Vocal
Paul McCartney: Bass Guitar and Backing Vocal
George Harrison: Lead Guitar   **Ringo Starr:** Drums and Lead Vocal
Co-written by John, Paul and Ringo, this song provided Ringo with another of the sing-a-long, rockabilly numbers that always seemed to suit his voice. John and Paul provide the harmony vocals for the chorus and George adds some nice country-and-western-style guitar.

Girl (Lennon-McCartney) 2:26
John Lennon: Acoustic Guitar and Lead Vocal
Paul McCartney: Bass Guitar and Backing Vocal
George Harrison: Sitar and Backing Vocal   **Ringo Starr:** Drums
Lead vocals are from John with Paul and George adding a wordless and a tit-tit backing vocal and also joining John for the chorus. There is an interesting section where the backing vocals build up and dissolve along with John's voice into the chorus.

I'm Looking Through You (Lennon-McCartney)   2:20
John Lennon: Acoustic Guitar and Harmony Vocal   **Paul McCartney:** Bass Guitar and Lead Vocal
George Harrison: Lead Guitar and Tambourine   **Ringo Starr:** Drums and Hammond Organ
Paul on lead vocals on this semi-rock'n'roll song reveals the influences of both Little Richard and
Buddy Holly. It sounds rather like a re-written version of Buddy Holly's 'Everyday' sung with a Little
Richard voice but curiously enough it works. The recording also features Ringo on a Hammond organ
mixed so far into the backing it might as well not be there.

    The American stereo version of this track includes two false starts but is then identical to this
version.

In My Life (Lennon-McCartney)   2:23
John Lennon: Lead Vocal
Paul McCartney: Bass Guitar and Harmony Vocal
George Harrison: Lead Guitar   **Ringo Starr:** Drums
George Martin: Piano
Nostalgically John recalls people and places who played an important part in his younger days. The
song is beautifully set to unobtrusive music, and is reminiscent of 'Penny Lane' or 'Strawberry Fields
Forever'.

Wait (Lennon-McCartney)   2:13
John Lennon: Tambourine and Lead Vocal
Paul McCartney: Bass Guitar and Lead Vocal
George Harrison: Lead Guitar   **Ringo Starr:** Drums and Maracas
A lively track featuring a lead vocal duet between John and Paul that for some reason does not seem
to fit in with the album's previous tracks. It sounds almost as if it were left over from either *Beatles For
Sale* or *Help!*

If I Needed Someone (Harrison)   2:19
John Lennon: Tambourine and Backing Vocal
Paul McCartney: Bass Guitar and Backing Vocal
George Harrison: Lead Guitar and Lead Vocal   **Ringo Starr:** Drums
George Martin: Harmonium

A George Harrison composition that shows how much he improved with each new song he wrote. This can be compared with a few Lennon and McCartney songs of the same period.

The Beatles make use of an extremely pleasant guitar riff that crops up every now and then and accentuates both the lyrics and the style of George Harrison's singing.

Run For Your Life (Lennon-McCartney)   2:21
John Lennon: Acoustic Guitar and Lead Vocal
Paul McCartny: Bass Guitar and Backing Vocal
George Harrison: Lead Guitar and Backing Vocal   **Ringo Starr:** Drums
George Martin: Tambourine

This is not one of John and Paul's best compositions. It sounds rather like a mixture of their previous 'Little Child' from the album *With The Beatles*, and the Larry Williams song 'Bad Boy'. Even John Lennon, who wrote it, went on record as not liking it.

REVOLVER

UK Release: 5 August 1966
US Release: April 1987
Intl CD No: CDP 7 46441 2
Running Time: 35:01

Parlophone PMC 7009: PCS 7009
Capitol CLJ 46441
Producer: George Martin

SIDE ONE: Taxman; Eleanor Rigby; I'm Only Sleeping; Love You To; Here, There And Everywhere; Yellow Submarine; She Said, She Said.

SIDE TWO: Good Day Sunshine; And Your Bird Can Sing; For No One; Dr. Robert; I Want To Tell You; Got To Get You Into My Life; Tomorrow Never Knows.

The musical direction The Beatles appeared to be taking with *Rubber Soul* changed quickly with *Revolver*. Released eight months after *Rubber Soul*, this album contains brilliant, diverse music and moves further into the realms of fantasy. *Revolver* contains some rather interesting social statements from The Beatles in the form of George Harrison's sarcastic comments on 'Taxman' and Paul McCartney's sad tale of loneliness on 'Eleanor Rigby'. Various flights of fantasy and strange lyrics feature on a range of titles from the sing-along 'Yellow Submarine' to the weird and frightening 'Tomorrow Never Knows'.

The sleeve shows a collage of drawings by Klaus Voormann and photographs of The Beatles that include two of the photographs previously used on the back of Rubber Soul. A collection of faces, as on the inner photograph of *The Beatles For Sale* album, again is used just as it would be used even more effectively on the sleeve of the *Sgt. Pepper's Lonely Hearts Club Band* album.

Although fans did not realise it at the time, The Beatles were to give their last full concert three weeks after the release of this album. Their music had progressed to such a point that *Rubber Soul* and *Revolver* were almost impossible to reproduce live.

REVOLVER

SIDE ONE
Taxman (Harrison) 2:36
John Lennon: Tambourine and Backing Vocal
Paul McCartney: Bass Guitar and Backing Vocal
George Harrison: Lead Guitar and Lead Vocal   **Ringo Starr:** Drums
George's first song to make a social comment takes a swipe at the taxman. Lead vocal is from George with backing and harmony vocals from John and Paul. The musical accompaniment is as harsh as the lyrics, with a very strong attacking lead-guitar riff.

Eleanor Rigby (Lennon-McCartney) 2:11
John Lennon: Not Present   **Paul McCartney:** Solo Vocal
George Harrison: Not Present   **Ringo Starr:** Not Present
Session Musicians: Four Violins, two Violas, and two Cellos
This classic McCartney composition has become another of his standards. Here it features a lead vocal from Paul who double-tracks in part to produce his own harmonies. Like 'Yesterday' on the *Help!* album, this features only Paul McCartney. John, George and Ringo do not sing or play any instrument on this recording. All of the backing music is played by a string octet.

The lyrics make a valid social statement about the loneliness of Eleanor Rigby and Father McKenzie's empty church. It is thought that Paul wrote this song after John made his now-famous comment 'Christianity will go. It will vanish and shrink. I needn't argue about that. I'm right and I will be proved right. We're more popular than Jesus now. I don't know which will go first, rock'n'roll or Christianity'.

I'm Only Sleeping (Lennon-McCartney) 2:58
John Lennon: Acoustic Guitar and Lead Vocal
Paul McCartney: Bass Guitar and Backing Vocal
George Harrison: Lead Guitar and Backing Vocal   **Ringo Starr:** Drums
The song idles along at tick-over speed and with John's lethargic vocal interpretation creates a lazy, stay-in-bed atmosphere mirroring the lyrics about him lying in bed watching the world go by. The strange guitar sound is George's overdubbed, backwards lead guitar.

Love You To (Harrison)   3:00

John Lennon: Not Present   **Paul McCartney:** Not Present
George Harrison: Solo Vocal   **Ringo Starr:** Not Present
Anil Bhagwat: Tabla   **Session Musicians:** All Other Instruments

After George Harrison had become interested in the sitar and played it on 'Norwegian Wood' he enlisted the help of Anil Bhagwat to play the tabla on this recording, the second of three on the album written by George Harrison, and also the first full-scale use of Indian instruments by George for a Beatles recording. None of the other Beatles play on this track.

Here, There And Everywhere (Lennon-McCartney)   2:29

John Lennon: Backing Vocal
Paul McCartney: Acoustic Guitar and Lead Vocal
George Harrison: Lead Guitar and Backing Vocal   **Ringo Starr:** Drums

This is a gentle but slightly up-tempo ballad from Paul, featuring his lead vocal multi-tracked and spread across the stereo sound stage. The wordless backing vocals from John, Paul and George are mixed onto the left-hand channel and blend in with the lead vocal creating the pleasing impression of a single voice.

Yellow Submarine (Lennon-McCartney)   2:40

John Lennon: Acoustic Guitar and Backing Vocal
Paul McCartney: Acoustic Guitar and Backing Vocal
George Harrison: Tambourine and Backing Vocal   **Ringo Starr:** Drums and Lead Vocal
Chorus: Includes George Martin, Patti Harrison, Mal Evans, Neil Aspinall and Geoff Emerick
Session Musicians: Brass Band

Issued as a single with 'Eleanor Rigby', on the same day as the album, this is one of The Beatles' most famous sing-along records. It has an extremely catchy chorus. The lead vocal comes from Ringo, this is the only track to feature him as vocalist, with John, Paul and George joining in on the chorus. The many sound effects included John blowing bubbles through a straw into a bucket of water, George swirling water round in another bucket, cocktail party sounds, a brass band, various engine-room noises and shouted orders. The final chorus makes use of all the people present at the recording: The Beatles, George Martin, Patti Harrison, roadies Mal Evans and Neil Aspinall, Geoff Emerick and presumably several more. The song was to inspire the cartoon film of the same name that was released three years after this recording. (See the *Yellow Submarine* album.)

She Said She Said (Lennon-McCartney) 2:39
John Lennon: Acoustic Guitar and Solo Vocal   **Paul McCartney:** Bass Guitar
George Harrison: Lead Guitar   **Ringo Starr:** Drums
Apparently this is John Lennon's account of a conversation with Peter Fonda during an LSD trip. If the backing to this track is anything to go by, the trip must have been chaotic.

SIDE TWO
Good Day Sunshine (Lennon-McCartney) 2:08
John Lennon: Harmony Vocal   **Paul McCartney:** Lead Vocal
George Harrison: Harmony Vocal   **Ringo Starr:** Drums
George Martin: Piano
The lead vocal on this track comes from Paul with harmonies from John, reflecting influences from the 30s that include a honky-tonk New-Orleans-style piano break. This interesting and inventive recording features two separate drum beats, one on each channel. With this track The Beatles began experimenting with stereo imaging. On the fade the title/chorus line comes out of each of the speakers alternately.

And Your Bird Can Sing (Lennon-McCartney) 2:02
John Lennon: Rhythm Guitar and Lead Vocal
Paul McCartney: Bass Guitar and Harmony Vocal
George Harrison: Lead Guitar and Harmony Vocal   **Ringo Starr:** Drums and Tambourine
Lead vocal is from John with Paul harmonising here and there. The recording features a very prominent lead-guitar riff mixed so far forward it becomes part of the main recording rather than part of the backing.

For No One (Lennon-McCartney) 2:03
John Lennon: Not Present
Paul McCartney: Bass Guitar, Piano and Solo Vocal   **George Harrison:** Not Present
Ringo Starr: Drums and Tambourine   **Alan Civil:** Horn
This is a very pleasant track featuring a solo vocal from Paul who also plays a bouncy piano. An unobtrusive horn is played by Alan Civil.

Dr. Robert (Lennon-McCartney) 2:14
John Lennon: Maracas, Harmonium and Lead Vocal
Paul McCartney: Bass Guitar and Harmony Vocal
George Harrison: Lead Guitar   **Ringo Starr:** Drums
Aapparently the lyrics of this song were based on a real character in New York who supplied anyone and everyone with drugs of various kinds. The lead vocals are from John with harmonies in part from Paul.

I Want To Tell You (Harrison) 2:30
John Lennon: Tambourine and Harmony Vocal
Paul McCartney: Bass Guitar, Piano and Harmony Vocal
George Harrison: Lead Guitar and Lead Vocal   **Ringo Starr:** Drums
Lead vocals are from George with John and Paul harmonising in places. This is not one of George Harrison's better compositions, it sounds slightly off-key with a rather erratic backing beat.

Got To Get You Into My Life (Lennon-McCartney) 2:31
John Lennon: Tambourine   **Paul McCartney:** Bass Guitar and Solo Vocal
George Harrison: Lead Guitar   **Ringo Starr:** Drums
George Martin: Organ   **Eddy Thornton:** Trumpet
Ian Hamer: Trumpet   **Les Conlon:** Trumpet
Alan Branscombe: Tenor Sax   **Pete Coe:** Tenor Sax
Heavily influenced by the Motown sound, this track features a solo vocal from Paul with brass backing played by Eddy Thornton, Ian Hamer and Les Conlon on trumpets and Alan Branscombe and Peter Coe on tenor sax. A good strong solid track. Later to be recorded by Cliff Bennett and the Rebel Rousers, who had a British Top 10 hit with it.

Tomorrow Never Knows (Lennon-McCartney)   3:00

John Lennon: Tambourine and Solo Vocal   **Paul McCartney:** Bass Guitar
George Harrison: Sitar and Lead Guitar   **Ringo Starr:** Drums
George Martin: Piano

Sounds effects devised by John and Ringo and arranged by Paul. Some of the lyrics of this song, that had the working title of Mark 1, come straight from the Tibetan *Book of the Dead*. They are set to an hypnotic drum beat with a collage of sound effects made up of backward-running tapes and tape loops that sound at times like a herd of rampaging elephants. John's solo vocal, treated to various studio effects, filters through like a nightmare set to music. This was The Beatles' most experimental recording to date, and a very successful experiment at that, both musically and lyrically. Lyrics like listen to the colour of your dreams herald the appearance of psychedelia. Curiously, nowhere in the lyrics do the words tomorrow never knows appear. This was a title invented by Ringo.

A COLLECTION OF BEATLES OLDIES

UK Release: 10 December 1966
US Release: None
Producer: George Martin

Parlophone PMC 7016: PCS 7016
Intl CD No: None
Running Time: 38:06

SIDE ONE: She Loves You; From Me To You; We Can Work It Out; Help!; Michelle; Yesterday; I Feel Fine; Yellow Submarine.

SIDE TWO: Can't Buy Me Love; Bad Boy; Day Tripper; A Hard Day's Night; Ticket To Ride; Paperback Writer; Eleanor Rigby; I Want To Hold Your Hand.

Following the recording of the *Revolver* album The Beatles embarked on what proved to be their final world tour that ended with a concert on 29 August 1966 at San Francisco's Candlestick Park. Their final UK concert had been some months earlier on 1 May when they performed at The Empire Pool, Wembley, during the New Musical Express Poll Winner's Show. During 1966 they also became involved in various personal projects: John appeared in the film *How I Won The War*, shot in Germany and Spain; Paul wrote the soundtrack for the film *The Family Way*, and George became more involved with Indian music, at one point flying to India to take sitar lessons from Ravi Shankar.

During this period that extended from June to December 1966, and because of their various activities, The Beatles were not involved in any recording sessions so for their pre-Christmas release this album was compiled.

It is a rather makeshift release containing eight tracks not previously included on a British album together with a further eight tracks that had appeared previously on the *A Hard Day's Night*, *Help!*, *Rubber Soul* and *Revolver* albums. Among the new material included here is 'Bad Boy' that had previously been available only on the American album *Beatles VI* (Capitol ST 2358) released 18 months earlier. The remaining seven tracks included on a British album for the first time are 'She Loves You', 'From Me To You', 'We Can Work It Out', 'I Feel Fine', 'Day Tripper', 'Paperback Writer' and 'I Want To Hold Your Hand'. Not having a stereo master available, George Martin tried to create a stereo version of 'She Loves You' for the stereo version of the album from mono recordings. Although abandoned, the various stereo mixes are still on file at EMI.

As a greatest-hits album this seemed to fit the bill at the time, but more recently all the tracks not previously included on albums have been more sensibly repackaged on *Past Masters/Volumes One and Two*. At the time of release of *A Collection Of Beatles Oldies* there were 19 tracks available plus the German-language versions of 'She Loves You' and 'I Want To Hold Your Hand' that had not previously been included on any British album, but surprisingly The Beatles chose to use only eight.

SIDE ONE

She Loves You (Lennon-McCartney)   2:18
Recorded: 1 July 1963, EMI Studios, Abbey Road, London
John Lennon: Rhythm Guitar and Lead Vocal   **Paul McCartney:** Bass Guitar and Lead Vocal
George Harrison: Lead Guitar and Harmony Vocal   **Ringo Starr:** Drums
The A side of The Beatles' fourth single, issued on Parlophone in Britain on 23 August 1963, features the usual lead vocal duet from John and Paul. The song includes the now famous catchy chorus line of yeah, yeah, yeah and the equally famous oooo, that was previously used in 'I Saw Her Standing There' on the *Please Please Me* album. If 'Love Me Do', 'Please Please Me' and 'From Me To You' had not convinced people that The Beatles had staying power the catchy chorus line and excitement generated by 'She Loves You' surely must have done so.

From Me To You (Lennon-McCartney)   1:55
Recorded: 5 March 1963, EMI Studios, Abbey Road, London
John Lennon: Rhythm Guitar, Harmonica and Lead Vocal
Paul McCartney: Bass Guitar and Lead Vocal
George Harrison: Lead Guitar and Harmony Vocal   **Ringo Starr:** Drums
With this, the follow-up single to 'Please Please Me' and The Beatles' second No. 1, they began to prove that they had both musical and song-writing ability. According to some charts 'Please Please Me' reached only No. 2, and 'From Me to You' was their first No. 1 single. If it were, it began a string of 11 consecutive No. 1 singles – a record that has never been equalled to date. Like so many of The Beatles' early recordings the lead vocal is shared by John and Paul with George joining in here and there, and on chorus. The recording also makes very effective use of John's harmonica.

   'From Me To You' was reputed to have been written on 28 February 1963 after John and Paul had read the letters column, From You To Us, in the *New Musical Express* during a coach journey from York to Shrewsbury while they were on tour as the support act with Helen Shapiro.

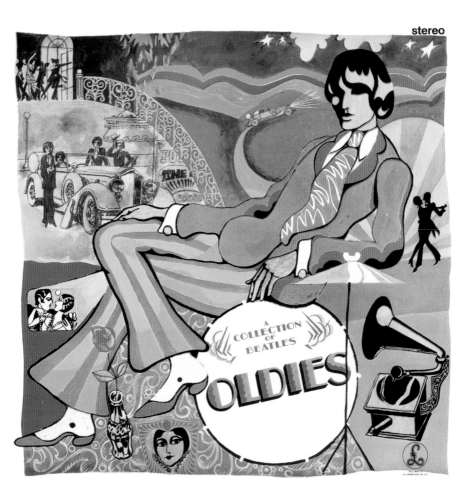

During the early 60s The Beatles had their own BBC radio show. Some episodes of the show were entitled From Us To You, and featured a reworded recording of 'From Me To You'.

We Can Work It Out (Lennon-McCartney) 2:10
Recorded: 20 and 29 October 1965, EMI Studios, Abbey Road, London
John Lennon: Harmonium and Harmony Vocal   **Paul McCartney:** Bass Guitar and Lead Vocal
George Harrison: Acoustic Guitar and Tambourine   **Ringo Starr:** Drums
This could be classified as The Beatles' first peace song. It predated 'All You Need Is Love' by two years and 'Give Peace A Chance' by four years. Released as the follow-up to 'Help!' in 1965 this is The Beatles' 11th Parlophone single and their ninth No. 1. By 1965 The Beatles had progressed from the beat group sound of some of their early 1963-4 singles to a more technically and musically proficient group of musicians. Lead vocal on this is by Paul, with John joining in for the chorus and also playing harmonium. At various times the recording lapses into a slow waltz but then picks up again for the verses. John later used the same style for the instrumental break in the middle of 'Being For The Benefit of Mr. Kite' on *Sgt. Pepper's Lonely Hearts Club Band*. Paul's optimistic main lyrics are countered by John's realism in the verse beginning Life is very short. John did a similar thing with Paul's 'Getting Better' on *Sgt. Pepper*. The main part of the track was recorded in two takes on 20 October and completed with an overdub on 29 October.

Help! (Lennon-McCartney) 2:16
John Lennon: Acoustic Guitar and Lead Vocal
Paul McCartney: Bass Guitar and Backing Vocal
George Harrison: Lead Guitar and Backing Vocal   **Ringo Starr:** Drums and Tambourine
Previously included on the album *Help!*

Michelle (Lennon-McCartney) 2:42
John Lennon: Acoustic Guitar and Backing Vocal   **Paul McCartney:** Bass Guitar and Lead Vocal
George Harrison: Acoustic Guitar and Backing Vocal
Ringo Starr: Drums
Previously included on the album *Rubber Soul*.

Yesterday (Lennon-McCartney)   2:04
John Lennon: Not Present
Paul McCartney: Acoustic Guitar and Solo Vocal
George Harrison: Not Present   **Ringo Starr:** Not Present
Session Musicians: String Quartet
Previously included on the album *Help!*

I Feel Fine (Lennon-McCartney)   2:19
Recorded: 18 October 1964, EMI Studios, Abbey Road, London
John Lennon: Rhythm Guitar, Lead Guitar and Lead Vocal
Paul McCartney: Bass Guitar and Backing Vocal
George Harrison: Lead Guitar and Backing Vocal
Ringo Starr: Drums
With advance orders of three quarters of a million copies, this was issued as a single on 27 November 1964 as the follow-up to 'A Hard Day's Night'. It was The Beatles' eighth single and sixth consecutive No. 1. The recording, that was completed in nine takes, opens with a single note of feedback that goes into the riff around which the song is constructed. This was the first time that feedback had been used on a record, and it gave ideas to many musicians like Jimi Hendrix, who later used feedback as a musical note and not just as noise. Theories at the time about the sound at the beginning of the record included the idea of an amplified humming bee. In fact The Beatles did not use pre-recorded sound effects until 1966, two years later. The lead vocal is from John with Paul and George joining him on the chorus. Paul and George also sing a wordless vocal backing.

Yellow Submarine (Lennon-McCartney)   2:40
John Lennon: Acoustic Guitar and Backing Vocal
Paul McCartney: Acoustic Guitar and Backing Vocal
George Harrison: Tambourine and Backing Vocal   **Ringo Starr:** Drums and Lead Vocal
Chorus: Includes George Martin, Patti Harrison, Mal Evans, Neil Aspinall and Geoff Emerick
Session Musicians: Brass Band
Previously included on the album *Revolver*.

SIDE TWO
Can't Buy Me Love (Lennon-McCartney) 2:15

John Lennon: Rhythm Guitar

George Harrison: Lead Guitar

Paul McCartney: Bass Guitar and Solo Vocal

Ringo Starr: Drums

Previously included on the album *A Hard Day's Night*.

Bad Boy (Williams) 2:17

Recorded: 10-11 May 1965, EMI Studios, Abbey Road, London

John Lennon: Rhythm Guitar, Hammond Organ and Solo Vocal

Paul McCartney: Bass Guitar and Electric Piano   **George Harrison:** Lead Guitar

Ringo Starr: Drums and Tambourine

This was originally issued as part of the American album *Beatles VI* on 14 June 1965 and later included on the British album *A Collection Of Beatles Oldies* released on 9 December 1966. The recording, that was completed in four takes, features a solo vocal from John and a very enthusiastic backing from the rest of The Beatles. Apart from the short rendition of 'Maggie May' on *Let it Be* and another Larry Williams song, 'Dizzy Miss Lizzy' recorded during the same session, these were the last two songs issued by The Beatles during their collective career that they did not write themselves.

Day Tripper (Lennon-McCartney) 2:37

Recorded: 16 October 1965, EMI Studios, Abbey Road, London

John Lennon: Rhythm Guitar, Tambourine and Lead Vocal

Paul McCartney: Bass Guitar and Lead Vocal

George Harrison: Lead Guitar and Harmony Vocal

Ringo Starr: Drums

This track was issued together with 'We Can Work It Out' as a double-A-sided single on 3 December 1965; the same day that the *Rubber Soul* album was released. It was written mainly by John with Paul contributing some of the lyrics. These are reminiscent of the earlier 'Ticket To Ride' and the title is similar. It was recorded in three takes on 16 October 1965 and features a lead vocal duet between John and Paul with George joining them for the harmony sections. It entered the British charts at No. 1 when it was released where it stayed for five weeks, selling over one million copies before the end of the month.

A Hard Day's Night (Lennon-McCartney) 2:32
John Lennon: Rhythm Guitar and Lead Vocal
Paul McCartney: Bass Guitar and Harmony Vocal
George Harrison: Lead Guitar　　　　　　**Ringo Starr:** Drums
George Martin: Piano
Previously included on the album *A Hard Day's Night*.

Ticket To Ride (Lennon-McCartney) 3:03
John Lennon: Rhythm Guitar, Tambourine and Lead Vocal
Paul McCartney: Bass Guitar and Harmony Vocal　　**George Harrison:** Lead Guitar
Ringo Starr: Drums
Previously included on the album *Help!*

Paperback Writer (Lennon-McCartney) 2:25
John Lennon: Rhythm Guitar and Backing Vocal　　**Paul McCartney:** Bass Guitar and Lead Vocal
George Harrison: Lead Guitar and Backing Vocal　　**Ringo Starr:** Drums
As this is also included on the *Hey Jude* album, along with 'Rain' its B side, it is discussed with that album.

Eleanor Rigby (Lennon-McCartney) 2:11
John Lennon: Not Present　　　　　　**Paul McCartney:** Solo Vocal
George Harrison: Not Present　　　　　**Ringo Starr:** Not Present
Session Musicians: Four Violins, two Violas and two Cellos.
Previously included on the album *Revolver*.

I Want To Hold Your Hand (Lennon-McCartney) 2:24
Recorded: 17 October 1963, EMI Studios, Abbey Road, London
John Lennon: Rhythm Guitar and Lead Vocal
Paul McCartney: Bass Guitar and Lead Vocal
George Harrison: Lead Guitar and Harmony Vocal　　**Ringo Starr:** Drums
As a single, this record sold over 15 million copies worldwide. In fact, prior to its release in Britain on 19 November 1963, there were advance orders approaching one million copies. Needless to say, it

entered the charts at No. 1 in Britain, where it remained for six weeks. This was the record that in 1964 gave birth to Beatlemania in America, where it sold nearly five million copies and opened up the American market for other British artists.

The recording opens with John's rhythm guitar, a sound that builds up to an intense pitch and then virtually explodes as John and Paul begin their lead vocal duet. For the chorus line John and Paul are joined by George and all three add excited hand-clapping to make this one of their most powerful early recordings.

Recorded in 17 takes on 17 October 1963, this was The Beatles' first four-track recording. This enabled George Martin to produce a better stereo image and make other improvements over the two-track recordings of earlier sessions.

SGT. PEPPER'S LONELY HEARTS CLUB BAND

UK Release: 1 June 1967
US Release: 2 June 1967
Intl CD No: CDP 7 46442 2
Running Time: 39:02

Parlophone PMC 7027: PCS 7027
Capitol MAS 2653: SMAS 2653
Producer: George Martin

SIDE ONE: Sgt. Peppers Lonely Hearts Club Band; With A Little Help From My Friends; Lucy In The Sky With Diamonds; Getting Better; Fixing A Hole; She's Leaving Home; Being For the Benefit of Mr. Kite.

SIDE TWO: Within You, Without You; When I'm Sixty-Four; Lovely Rita; Good Morning, Good Morning; Sgt. Pepper's Lonely Hearts Club Band (Reprise); A Day In The Life.

Regarded by many as The Beatles' finest album, Sgt. Pepper has been copied, emulated and drawn from, but never equalled. The title has slipped into everyday language in the music world to describe any artist's new album as being their finest achievement, their Sgt. Pepper.

The album took four months and £50,000 to make, staggering figures when compared with The Beatles' first Parlophone album, *Please Please Me*, that was recorded in one 13-hour session and cost £400.

This album's concept began to take shape during the late summer/early autumn of 1966 when Paul came up with the title song. Ideas were then exchanged and it was decided that Sgt. Pepper should be the theme for the album with the track opening the album and appearing again near the end. So the title was recorded twice and the second recording slotted in just before 'A Day In The Life', the album's final track. After this, the album, in the words of The Beatles 'generated its own togetherness' and as each new recording was made it seemed to fall into place.

Recording began in November 1966 with 'Strawberry Fields Forever', 'When I'm Sixty-Four' and 'Penny Lane', but it was decided to issue 'Penny Lane/Strawberry Fields Forever' as a single, and these tracks were extracted from the recordings already made. After a Christmas break, recording recommenced on 19 January 1967 when The Beatles began work on the album's closing track 'A Day

In The Life'. Recording continued through to 3 April 1967 when, with the exception of a few final overdubs of strings, the album was completed.

The first rock music album to be issued with a continual theme running through it, Sgt. Pepper was dubbed the first concept album. As a result concept albums by other artists of varying degrees of quality soon began to appear.

Like its contents, the sleeve of this album is highly original. Designed by Peter Blake from ideas by The Beatles, it shows a collection of faces of people they admired or who had influenced them in various ways. Among the 50-odd faces are W. C. Fields, Aldous Huxley, Fred Astaire, Bob Dylan, Tony Curtis, Laurel and Hardy, Max Miller and a host of others. The only person missing from the collage of faces was Adolf Hitler who was reputed to have been picked by John. His photograph had been selected and blown up to fit in with the rest, but at the last minute it was decided that the inclusion of Adolf Hitler would be in bad taste. The collage also includes wax models of The Beatles, Sonny Liston and Diana Dors, all of which were loaned from Madame Tussauds in Marylebone Road, London. Other features of the cover photograph include The Beatles dressed in bright satin uniforms as Sgt. Pepper's band, with their name painted on a bass drum. The foreground is set out as a garden with the word 'Beatles' spelt out in flowers and also a guitar shaped out of flowers. Across the top of the garden and foreground right are marijuana plants, included as a protest about the non-legalisation of the drug. Statues and ornaments included in the foreground were from various Beatles' homes. The Beatles are holding instruments they did not normally play, John has a French horn, Ringo a trumpet, Paul a cor anglais and George a flute. A line printed on the back of the sleeve sums up the intention of the album: 'a splendid time is guaranteed for all'.

SIDE ONE
Sgt. Pepper's Lonely Hearts Club Band (Lennon-McCartney) 1:59
John Lennon: Lead Guitar and Backing Vocal

Paul McCartney: Bass Guitar and Lead Vocal

George Harrison: Lead Guitar and Backing Vocal

Ringo Starr: Drums

George Martin: Organ

Session Musicians: Four Horns

The album opens with the sound of an orchestra tuning up and an expectant audience. The Sgt. Pepper band then strikes up the first few chords on guitars, and the album begins. The Beatles had introduced heavy guitar sounds on 'Rain' issued as the B side to 'Paperback Writer' about 12 months earlier, but here is their first full use of guitars as a sound, as opposed to just backing instruments. The Beatles' instrumentation on this track is supplemented by George Martin on organ near the end of the track and a group of four studio musicians who add the horns to make the Sgt. Pepper band a semi-rock/brass outfit. Lead vocals are from Paul, who also joins John and George for the backing and the chorus.

With this album The Beatles started experimenting with stereo and discovered that sound could actually appear to move between left and right speakers. On this track the chorus starts on the left-hand channel then begins to drift across to the centre of the sound stage. When Paul sings again he starts on the right-hand channel.

With A Little Help From My Friends (Lennon-McCartney) 2:46
John Lennon: Backing Vocal

Paul McCartney: Bass Guitar, Piano and Backing Vocal

George Harrison: Tambourine

Ringo Starr: Drums and Lead Vocal

Ringo is in the vocal spotlight with vocal support from John and Paul on both the backing and the chorus. His vocal performance on this song is rated by many to be one of his best. This is another Lennon and McCartney song that had a working title bearing no relation to the finished song. It started out as 'Bad Finger Boogie', and is said to have influenced one of the groups signed to the Apple label in their choice of name. They started out as The Ivies before becoming Badfinger.

Lucy In The Sky With Diamonds (Lennon-McCartney) 3:25
John Lennon: Lead Guitar and Lead Vocal
Paul McCartney: Bass Guitar, Hammond Organ and Harmony Vocal
George Harrison: Sitar and Harmony Vocal   **Ringo Starr:** Drums

John Lennon went on record as saying that his most surrealistic lyrics were inspired not by an LSD trip as many thought and some still maintain, but by a painting that his son Julian had brought home from school. When John asked what it was, Julian replied 'It's Lucy in the sky with diamonds'. Lucy, Julian's best friend at school, had inspired Julian to paint a girl on a black background surrounded by stars, that he insisted were not stars but diamonds.

   Lead vocals are by John with Paul and George joining in on chorus and also supplying backing vocals. The track opens with what sounds like a string instrument, but is in fact a Hammond organ. Its in-built special effects were used to produce a harpsichord/celeste sound.

Getting Better (Lennon-McCartney) 2:47
John Lennon: Lead Guitar and Backing Vocal
Paul McCartney: Bass Guitar and Lead/Backing Vocal
George Harrison: Lead Guitar, Tamboura and Backing Vocal
Ringo Starr: Drums and Bongos   **George Martin:** Piano
It certainly is. Paul's lyrics are set to the same syncopated beat that he had used a few years earlier on tracks such as 'She's A Woman'. Lead vocals are from Paul who also joins John for the backing. George had experimented with the sitar on earlier Beatles albums and here he tries a new Indian instrument, the tamboura. This looks like an oversized sitar, but doesn't produce musical notes in terms of western music. Instead it produces a droning resonant tone that in Indian music is used as it is here more as a backing tone than as part of the instrumentation. Near the end of the track George Martin joins in with a piano. Interestingly he doesn't play the keyboard but strikes the strings instead.

Fixing A Hole (Lennon-McCartney)   2:33
John Lennon: Maracas and Backing Vocal
Paul McCartney: Harpsichord, Bass Guitar, Lead Guitar and Lead Vocal
George Harrison: Lead Guitar and Backing Vocal   **Ringo Starr:** Drums
Lead vocal on this one again comes from Paul, who also plays the harpschord. The guitar solo in the
middle is played by George. This is a good up-tempo song from Paul but its lyrics, like 'Lucy In The Sky
With Diamonds' have been misconstrued. Paul McCartney commented 'This song is just about the hole in
the road where the rain gets in; a good old analogy; the hole in your make-up which lets the rain in and
stops your mind from going where it will. It's you interfering with things. If you're a junkie sitting in a room
fixing a hole then that's what it will mean to you, but when I wrote it I meant if there's a crack or the
room is uncolourful, then I'll paint it.'

She's Leaving Home (Lennon-McCartney)   3:24
John Lennon: Lead/Backing Vocal   **Paul McCartney:** Lead/Backing Vocal
George Harrison: Not Present   **Ringo Starr:** Not Present
Session Musicians: Harp and Strings
This is another classic McCartney ballad, and a sad social statement about a girl running away
from home and 'everything that money could buy' because love and attention were missing
from her life. Paul had said he was inspired to write the song by a newspaper article that
reminded him of the same loneliness he had conveyed in 'Eleanor Rigby'. The vocals are
interestingly interwoven. Paul sings a double-tracked lead vocal with John singing here and there.
This is the only track on the album where The Beatles do not play any of the backing; they are
accompanied by a harp and some sweet-sounding violins that were scored by Mike Leander.

Being For The Benefit of Mr. Kite (Lennon-McCartney)   2:36
John Lennon: Hammond Organ and Solo Vocal
Paul McCartney: Bass Guitar and Lead Guitar
George Harrison: Harmonica
George Martin: Wurlitzer Organ and Piano   **Ringo Starr:** Harmonica
Neil Aspinall: Harmonica   **Mal Evans:** Harmonica
John was inspired to write this song by a Victorian poster for a circus for the benefit of Mr. Kite –
a grand circus, The Hendersons and Pablo Fanques Fair'. Among the acts appearing in the circus

was Henry The Horse. John's vivid imagination helped him to collect these characters together and create the lyrics for the track. After reading them and those for 'Lucy In The Sky With Diamonds', George Martin described John as 'an oral Salvador Dali'. John sings the solo lead vocal on the track and plays Hammond organ. Paul plays a guitar solo and Ringo, George and Beatles roadies Neil Aspinall and Mal Evans each play a different type of harmonica. George Martin adds a few touches with a Wurlitzer organ, and the whole thing is rounded off with recorded snippets of a Victorian steam organ. To achieve the required random effect with the recording of the fairground organ, it was cut into 12-inch long strips, hurled into the air, then edited back together again, parts being played backwards and parts forward.

SIDE TWO
Within You, Without You (Harrison)   5:03

John Lennon: Not Present

George Harrison: Tamboura and Solo Vocal

Neil Aspinall: Tamboura

Paul McCartney: Not Present

Ringo Starr: Not Present

Session Musicians: Dilruba, Tamboura, Tabla and Swordmandel

Session Musicians: Eight Violins and three Cellos

Having previously tried his hand at recording Indian music with 'Love You To' on *Revolver*, George Harrison's dabblings go one step further on this track. He merges an assortment of Indian instruments including a dilruba, tabla, a swordmandel and three tambouras, two played by George and Neil Aspinall, with eight violins and three cellos. This is more of an event than a recording and at five minutes and three seconds it either sends you into a trance or to sleep, you either love it or hate it. George is the only member of The Beatles featured and in addition to playing one of the three tambouras he has a solo vocal. The sound of raucous laughter breaks the atmosphere and closes the track.

When I'm Sixty-Four (Lennon-McCartney)   2:38
John Lennon: Lead Guitar and Backing Vocal
Paul McCartney: Bass Guitar, Piano and Lead/Backing Vocal
George Harrison: Backing Vocal   **Ringo Starr:** Drums
Session Musicians: Two Clarinets and one Bass Clarinet
The track opens with the sound of two clarinets plus a bass clarinet played by session musicians.
Paul wrote the song for his father who had just turned 64. Its inoffensive lyrics and its equally
inoffensive accompaniment jog along at a pleasant pace and divert us from the Indian temple and
the raga-rock of George's extravaganza on the previous track. Lead vocal is from Paul with a
three-part harmony backing from John, Paul and George. The piano is played by Paul.

Lovely Rita (Lennon-McCartney)   2:43
John Lennon: Acoustic Guitar, Comb and Paper and Backing Vocal
Paul McCartney: Bass Guitar, Piano, Comb and Paper and Lead/BackingVocal
George Harrison: Acoustic Guitar, Comb and Paper and Backing Vocal
Ringo Starr: Drums   **George Martin:** Piano
Lead vocal comes from Paul who also plays piano, although the honky-tonk piano in the middle is
George Martin. John, Paul and George sing backing vocals and also use comb and paper to
produce the sha, sha, sha sound. The last 60 seconds include a fine blues/jazz piano from Paul
and various grunting and groaning noises. The Beatles were to use a similar ending on the *Magical
Mystery Tour* title track later in 1967.

Good Morning, Good Morning (Lennon-McCartney)   2:35
John Lennon: Lead/Backing Vocal
Paul McCartney: Bass Guitar, Lead Guitar and Backing Vocal
George Harrison: Lead Guitar   **Ringo Starr:** Drums
Sounds Incorporated: Three Saxophones, two Trombones and one French Horn
This lively track opens with the sound of a cock crowing and then some very solid brass from
three saxophones, two trumpets and a French horn played by Sounds Incorporated, a Liverpool
group who were great friends of The Beatles. The lead vocal is by John, joined by Paul for the
chorus. The guitar solo is by Paul. The ending can be described only as recorded chaos. Among

the sound effects used are a fox-hunt that gallops away across the stereo, bleating sheep, a mooing cow and a clucking chicken that George Martin had noticed sounded like the opening guitar note of the next track. He carefully edited this so that the clucking sound blended into the guitar note and so we are transported from the farmyard back into the theatre.

Sgt. Pepper's Lonely Hearts Club Band (Reprise) (Lennon-McCartney)   1:20
John Lennon: Maracas, Lead Guitar and Lead Vocal
Paul McCartney: Bass Guitar and Lead Vocal
George Harrison: Lead Guitar and Lead Vocal   **Ringo Starr:** Drums
Paul counts in 'one-two-three-four' to introduce the reprise of the opening track. If you listen to the counting over headphones you will hear John say 'bye' between the 'two' and 'three' of the count-in. There is no lead vocalist on this second version, everybody sings the amended lyrics. Unlike on the opening track, there are no horns here. The recording does not finish; as it fades out to the sound of an applauding audience, the acoustic guitar and piano of 'A Day In The Life' fade in.

A Day In The Life (Lennon-McCartney) 5:03
John Lennon: Acoustic Guitar, Piano* and Lead Vocal
Paul McCartney: Bass Guitar, Piano, Piano* and Lead Vocal
George Harrison: Bongos and Piano*
Ringo Starr: Drums, Maracas and Piano*
George Martin: Harmonium*
Mal Evans: Voice Counting, Alarm Clock and Piano*
Session Musicians: 41 Piece Orchestra
*Finale Only
This must be one of The Beatles' most controversial recordings. The song originally began by recounting the news from the daily papers, with a report of a car crash and subsequent death. The second news item was a report of 4,000 potholes in the roads of Blackburn that had been personally counted by a local councillor. John, having written the two segments, could not join them together, and asked Paul to fill in the middle section. Paul has been quoted as saying: 'The next bit was another song altogether but it just happened to fit. It was just me remembering what it was like to run up the road to catch a bus to school, having a smoke and going into class. We

decided: "bugger this, we're going to write a turn-on song". It was a reflection of my school days. I would have a Woodbine then, and somebody would speak and I would go into a dream. This was the only one in the album written as a deliberate provocation. A stick-that-in-your-pipe, but what we want is to turn you on to the truth rather than pot.' When the song begins it fades in from the applause of the previous track. John plays the guitar intro, with Paul joining in on piano. John's cold harsh vocal then begins. When he reaches 'I'd love to turn you on ' a 41-piece orchestra begins to play, climbing higher and higher up the musical scale until, suddenly, the noise stops and we hear the sound of an alarm clock. The lyrics continue and, for a second time repeat 'I'd love to turn you on'; the orchestra repeats its cacophonous destruction of the musical scale, reaches a climax and suddenly stops. There is then the most unearthly crash on three pianos and a harmonium. The resultant chord is drawn out for a staggering 45 seconds. The voice that can be heard counting during the 24-bar cacophonous build-up of the orchestra belongs to Mal Evans. The alarm clock was not originally intended to be included in the track, but it couldn't be removed. Paul made use of it to include the line 'woke up, fell out of bed'. The orchestral build-up was recorded four times and then dubbed one on top of the other, slightly out of synchronisation, to give a fuller sound. The three pianos and a harmonium at the end are played or struck by members of The Beatles plus George Martin. This was also recorded four times then synchronised to give an unearthly sound.

The 15,000 Hz Tone   0:08
This tone was added as a gesture from The Beatles to all the dogs in Britain so that there would be something on the LP for them too! This is included on British copies of the album only.

The Inner Groove   0:02
This two seconds of nonsense was a snippet of conversation that sounded good when edited from a recording of the party given by The Beatles after they had finished the piano parts at the end of 'A Day In The Life'. They decided they would like to fill the inner groove with something and this is what they chose.

MAGICAL MYSTERY TOUR

UK Release: 19 November 1976
US Release: 27 November 1967
Intl CD No: CDP 7 48062 2
Running Time: 36:32

Parlophone PCTC 255
Capitol MAL 2835: SMAL 2835
Producer: George Martin

SIDE ONE: Magical Mystery Tour; The Fool On The Hill; Flying; Blue Jay Way; Your Mother Should Know; I Am The Walrus.

SIDE TWO: Hello Goodbye; Strawberry Fields Forever; Penny Lane; Baby You're A Rich Man; All You Need Is Love.

The first side of this album is the sound track of the film that was originally conceived by Paul McCartney as early as March 1967 although filming didn't begin until Monday 11 September 1967. The invitation to The Beatles to appear as the British contribution to the worldwide television broadcast *Our World* in which they performed 'All You Need Is Love' that is also included on this album, caused the delay between conception and realisation of the idea.

The Beatles invited various friends and fan-club secretaries to be included in the film. Among these was their old mate Victor Spinetti who appears in the film as a recruiting sergeant. He had also appeared in The Beatles' two previous films, *A Hard Day's Night and Help!* The Beatles decided that the coach used in the film should have a special logo along the side. This logo is reproduced on the front cover of the album. The tour, on film, begins in a side street just off Marylebone Road by the London Planetarium and then continues through the West of England. In the main, the film was ad-libbed; the result was interesting though somewhat crazy. Weird characters emerge from the imaginations of The Beatles to feature in the various songs in the film, characters such as 'The Fool On The Hill', 'The Walrus', 'The Man Of A Thousand Voices' and 'The Egg Men'.

Although not made available in Britain until 1976, the album was available in the USA from 1967. It consists of the contents of the two-EP set issued in Britain on 8 December 1967 along with the A and B sides of the three singles The Beatles issued in 1967. When the album was issued in Britain, EMI did a straight pressing from the American album. This left much to be desired as three of the tracks, 'Penny Lane', 'Baby You're A Rich Man' and 'All You Need Is Love', are in fake stereo.

In 1973 EMI decided to issue a cassette version of the *Magical Mystery Tour* album. This cassette contained stereo versions of all the tracks included on the album, including a stereo version of 'Baby You're A Rich Man' that had previously been unavailable in Britain, although it was included on European pressings of the album. The cassette also includes the re-recorded version of 'All You Need Is Love' (see the *Yellow Submarine* album), although the album contains the original single version of the song. The album has the catalogue number PCTC 255 but the cassette, in addition to the usual cassette prefix of TC, has the confusing number PCS 3077, that places it between the *Rubber Soul* (PCS 3075) and *Revolver* (PCS 7009) albums.

It is interesting that The Beatles' entire 1967 record releases are contained on the *Sgt. Pepper's Lonely Hearts Club Band* and *Magical Mystery Tour* albums.

SIDE ONE
Magical Mystery Tour (Lennon-McCartney) 2:48
John Lennon: Acoustic Guitar and Backing Vocal
Paul McCartney: Bass Guitar, Piano and Lead Vocal
George Harrison: Lead Guitar and Backing Vocal   **Ringo Starr:** Drums and Tambourine
Session Musicians: Three Trumpets
The strong opening track features Paul on lead vocal and he joins John and George to sing the answer-style backing. The influences of 'Penny Lane' and 'Lovely Rita' show through on this track, with three trumpets and jazz/blues piano. The Beatles expanded their use of stereo effects on this track, placing sounds and voices to create the effect of the movement of the Magical Mystery Tour coach.

The Fool On The Hill (Lennon-McCartney) 3:00
John Lennon: Harmonica and Maracas
Paul McCartney: Piano, Recorder, Flute and Solo Vocal
George Harrison: Lead Guitar and Harmonica   **Ringo Starr:** Finger Cymbals
Paul is the solo vocalist accompanying himself on piano, double-tracked recorder and flute. John and George add harmonicas and Ringo joins in with finger cymbals. George can be heard on lead guitar in the backing. The song is in the classic McCartney ballad style and has become a standard, rating nearly as high as 'Yesterday' and 'Michelle'.

Flying (Lennon-McCartney-Harrison-Starkey)   2:16
John Lennon: Mellotron and Chanting
Paul McCartney: Assorted Guitars and Chanting
George Harrison: Assorted Guitars and Chanting   **Ringo Starr:** Drums, Maracas and Chanting
The only track to have been issued and composed by all four Beatles, this is the second of only two instrumentals ever released by them. The other was the Lennon-Harrison 1961 composition 'Cry For A Shadow'. John plays the main theme of this instrumental on a Mellotron. Paul and George add an assortment of guitars and all four Beatles produce the chanting heard later. The ending fades into an assortment of sound effects and backward-running tapes and tape loops put together by John and Ringo for this recording.

Blue Jay Way (Harrison)   3:50
John Lennon: Tambourine
Paul McCartney: Bass Guitar and Backing Vocal
George Harrison: Hammond Organ, Lead and Backing Vocal
Ringo Starr: Drums   **Session Musician:** Cello
George leaves Indian music for a while to record the story of Derek Taylor The Beatles publicist who was lost in fog in Los Angeles while trying to find Blue Jay Way where George was staying at the time. The recording fades in immediately after the previous track as if the two were joined together. This is the only track to feature phasing, an electronic effect produced by playing the recording on two tape machines slightly out of synchronisation, to produce a swirling, swishing effect. George's double-tracked lead vocals, backed mainly by himself on Hammond organ and Ringo on drums, are all phased throughout – quite an achievement, as phasing tends to slip after a while. The backing also includes a cello, various electronic sounds and backing vocals played forwards and backwards.

Your Mother Should Know (Lennon-McCartney)   2:33
John Lennon: Organ and Backing Vocal
Paul McCartney: Bass Guitar, Piano and Lead/Backing Vocal
George Harrison: Tambourine, Tabla and Backing Vocal
Ringo Starr: Drums
Paul's fascination with the 20s and 30s began to show on 'When I'm Sixty-Four' on Sgt. Pepper, when he did a very good Noel Coward impression. His fascination continues with this similar song. Paul

sings lead vocal and joins John and George for the backing vocals, the backing also includes Paul on piano, John on organ and at the end, George on an Indian tabla. The vocals start off on the left-hand channel for the first verse and switch to the right-hand channel for the second verse, then back to the left-hand channel for the third and final verse.

I Am The Walrus (Lennon-McCartney)   4:35
John Lennon: Mellotron and Lead Vocal
Paul McCartney: Bass Guitar and Backing Vocal
George Harrison: Tambourine and Backing Vocal   **Ringo Starr:** Drums
Session Musicians: Eight Violins, four Cellos and three Horns
Choir: Six Boys and Six Girls (Children of Michael Sammes Singers)
Definitely the most intriguing track The Beatles recorded. There are seven separate edits of this recording; this one features the opening riff played by John on the Mellotron repeated four times, although the British EP has the opening riff repeated six times. He is then joined by eight violins, four cellos and Ringo on drums. The nonsensical flow of John's lyrics brings to mind his two books, *In His Own Write* and *Spaniard In The Works*. Strange phrases like 'sitting on a cornflake', 'yellow matter custard', 'crabalocker fishwife', 'expert texpert chokingsmokers', 'semolina pilchard' and 'elementary penguin' seem to fit into the interwoven collage of sound that he wanted to create.

On the line 'yellow matter custard' John is joined by three horns, various voices, oscillations and discordant sounds from a radio plugged into the recording console. When the recording stops we hear a snatch of noise and oscillations from the radio, then the music starts again, this time in fake stereo. The sound is mixed into mono on the right-hand channel with the highs from the mix on the left-hand channel.

As legend goes, the radio was coming through live onto the tape and two lines spoken by two separate voices fit perfectly with the lyrics, for after John sings 'I am the egg man' the first voice says 'Are you sir?' John then continues with 'They are the egg men' and the second voice says 'A man may take you for what you are'. It was John's idea to plug the radio into the recording console, and it was him playing around with the dial that caused the noises and voices to be added to the recording. In addition to the music and the radio in the backing are six boys and girls, the children of the Michael Sammes Singers. The boys can be heard singing 'Oompah, oompah, stick it up your jumpah', and the girls are singing 'Everybody's got one.' John then tunes the radio into a Shakespeare play and at the end of the recording we hear 'Sit ye down father, rest you'.

SIDE TWO
Hello Goodbye (Lennon-McCartney)   3:24
John Lennon: Lead Guitar, Organ and Backing Vocal
Paul McCartney: Bass Guitar, Piano, Bongos, Conga Drum and Lead/Backing Vocal
George Harrison: Lead Guitar, Tambourine and Backing Vocal
Ringo Starr: Drums and Maracas   **Session Musicians:** Two Violas
This was released as a single three weeks prior to the *Magical Mystery Tour* double EP set, with 'I Am
the Walrus', a taster from the EP set, on the B side. Except for the six *Magical Mystery Tour*
recordings, this is the only song that features in the film. Paul sings lead and joins John and George for
the backing vocals. The guitars are played by John and George, and Paul plays piano and the bongos
and conga drum on the Maori finale. John also plays the organ that can be heard near the end of the
song before the Maori finale begins. Session men added the violas that crop up now and again
throughout the recording.

Strawberry Fields Forever (Lennon-McCartney)   4:05
John Lennon: Lead Guitar, Harpsichord and Solo Vocal
Paul McCartney: Bass Guitar, Piano, Bongos and Flute
George Harrison: Lead Guitar and Timpani
Ringo Starr: Drums   **Mal Evans:** Tambourine
Philip Jones: Alto Trumpet   **Session musicians:** Two Cellos and two Horns
With this song John immortalised Strawberry Fields, a Salvation Army orphanage in Liverpool, not far
from Penny Lane. He traces a slightly surrealistic trip to Strawberry Fields and reveals the confused
state of an orphan's mind; 'nothing is real'. The Beatles made two recordings of 'Strawberry Fields
Forever', and after listening to the playback John decided that he liked the first half of one recording and
the second half of the other. There was one problem – they were in different keys. John entrusted the
necessary editing to George Martin. To edit the two together, George Martin had to speed up the first
section and slow down the second so that they were approximately in the same key.
   There are two oddities on this recording of which only one has been publicised.
The first is a Morse code message, tapped out just after John sings 'Let me take you down.'
The Morse message consists of two letters, J and L. It is surprising that this has not received more
attention. The second oddity sparked off rumours of Paul McCartney's death. At the end of the recording,
John can be heard to say 'cranberry sauce'. Many people decided that John was saying 'I buried Paul.'

Penny Lane (Lennon-McCartney)   3:00
John Lennon: Piano and Harmony Vocal
Paul McCartney: Bass Guitar, Arco String Bass, Flute and Lead Vocal
George Harrison: Conga Drum and Firebell   **Ringo Starr:** Drums
George Martin: Piano   **David Mason:** Piccolo Trumpet
Philip Jones: Trumpet

Penny Lane has been known to Liverpool's residents for years as the name of a bus terminus. There is nothing particularly special about Penny Lane, it looks the same as any other road in the area, but like the Strawberry Fields Salvation Army Home, The Beatles have immortalised Penny Lane in the words of their song. Paul's reminiscence of Liverpool is finely displayed in his lyrics, although with slight surrealism.

Paul's lead vocal is backed up by John who, with George Martin, also adds piano. Besides singing lead Paul also adds string bass and a flute. The piccolo trumpet that crops up here and there was added by David Mason of the London Symphony Orchestra. Phillip Jones, who was also with the LSO, plays the trumpet on this track and also on 'Strawberry Fields Forever'.

When the record was circulated in late January 1967 to radio stations in the USA and Canada the ending had seven extra notes played by David Mason on piccolo trumpet over the final few seconds of the recording. When the record actually reached the shops those seven notes had been trimmed off. Besides making the radio station copies different, this also made them rather valuable.

Baby You're A Rich Man (Lennon-McCartney)   3:07
John Lennon: Clavioline, Piano and Lead Vocal
Paul McCartney: Bass Guitar, Piano and Harmony Vocal
George Harrison: Tambourine and Harmony Vocal   **Ringo Starr:** Drums and Maracas
Studio Engineer: Vibes

This started life as two different songs – 'One Of The Beautiful People', a song that John had written for a possible Sgt. Pepper Volume II album and 'Baby, You're A Rich Man' which was written by Paul. Although both songs were apparently recorded, neither has ever been issued in its original form. The two songs were joined together in a similar way to 'A Day In The Life' – with John singing the opening part of the song and then joining Paul and George for the 'Baby You're A Rich Man' section.

The unusual pipes-of-Pan sound is from a keyboard instrument called a clavioline. This is a rather strange device with a mind of its own and that will play only one note at a time.

John manages to play it and also the piano. Paul plays his bass guitar and adds a second piano while an obliging engineer adds some vibes. The track in its present form originally was intended for the *Yellow Submarine* film, but was hurriedly included as the B side of 'All You Need Is Love'.

All You Need Is Love (Lennon-McCartney)   3:57
John Lennon: Harpsichord and Lead Vocal
Paul McCartney: Arco String Bass, Bass Guitar and Backing Vocal
George Harrison: Violin, Lead Guitar and Backing Vocal
Ringo Starr: Drums   **George Martin:** Piano
Chorus: Includes Mick Jagger, Marianne Faithfull, Keith Richard, Gary Brooker and Keith Moon.
Session Musicians: Four Violins, two Cellos, two Trumpets, two Trombones, two Saxophones and one Accordion

The BBC invited The Beatles to represent the UK in a worldwide television broadcast called *Our World*, that was part of the Canadian EXPO 67 festival. The Beatles were to be seen recording their new single 'All You Need Is Love'. The recording was not all made live; the rhythm section was pre-recorded earlier in the day and simply played back at the time of the broadcast, although The Beatles were seen playing their guitars. All other parts including the vocals, the backing vocals and the orchestra, were recorded at the time of broadcast, before an audience of approximately 200 million people. A second recording of the song, made during rehearsals for the broadcast, is included on the *Yellow Submarine* album. The day before the broadcast, The Beatles decided that they would release 'All You Need Is Love' as soon as possible after the show. After listening to the playback, John's vocals were re-recorded and copies of the master tape were then flown all over the world and the record was on sale within weeks of being broadcast.

The Beatles asked the orchestra to dress in white dinner suits for the broadcast, and invited a few of their friends along to join in on the backing vocals including Mick Jagger, Marianne Faithfull, Keith Richard, Gary Brooker from Procol Harum and Keith Moon. As it was to be a worldwide broadcast, The Beatles wanted to have an international flavour. George Martin suggested that they use the Marseillaise, the French national anthem, for the beginning, and for the ending he included Greensleeves and Glen Miller's 'In The Mood' in its orchestral arrangement. Unfortunately, George had used Miller's own arrangement, not then out of copyright, and as soon as the record was released EMI was approached by the copyright holders.. EMI agreed to pay for the use of the arrangement and the matter was sorted out.

The initial rhythm track The Beatles recorded for 'All You Need Is Love' ran for just over ten minutes and included John playing a harpsichord, Paul an Arco string bass with a bow, George a violin and Ringo on drums. For the broadcast The Beatles played their usual instruments, except John who just sang. The orchestra, conducted by Mike Vickers, consisted of 13 musicians playing four violins, two cellos, two saxophones, two trombones, two trumpets and an accordion, even George Martin joined in on piano. At the end, John comes in with an off-key rendition of 'She Loves You'. The recording lasted for approximately six minutes, although it was later trimmed down to just under four. The broadcast took place on 25 June 1967 and the record, that was to become the international anthem for a generation, was on sale in Great Britain by 7 July 1967, and ten days later in the USA.

THE BEATLES (2 LPs)

UK Release: 22 November 1968
US Release: 25 November 1968
Intl CD No: CDS 7 46443 8
Running Time: 93:33

Apple PMC 7067-8: PCS 7067-8
Apple SWBO 101
Producer: George Martin

SIDE ONE: Back In The U.S.S.R.; Dear Prudence; Glass Onion; Ob-La-Di, Ob-La-Da; Wild Honey Pie; The Continuing Story Of Bungalow Bill; While My Guitar Gently Weeps; Happiness Is A Warm Gun.
SIDE TWO: Martha My Dear; I'm So Tired; Blackbird; Piggies; Rocky Racoon; Don't Pass Me By; Why Don't We Do It In The Road?; I Will; Julia.

SIDE THREE: Birthday; Yer Blues; Mother Nature's Son; Everybody's Got Something To Hide Except Me And My Monkey; Sexy Sadie; Helter Skelter; Long, Long, Long.
SIDE FOUR: Revolution 1; Honey Pie; Savoy Truffle; Cry Baby Cry; Revolution 9; Good Night.

This album, more widely known as The White Album although its working title was A Dolls House, was The Beatles' first album on their newly formed Apple label that had made its first appearance three months earlier on 30 August 1968 with the single 'Hey Jude/Revolution' (Apple R5722). Both tracks were recorded during the sessions for this album. With this album The Beatles appeared to return to the *Revolver* album of 1966, before their flight of fantasy into psychedelia during 1967.

Most of the 30 tracks on this double album were written during The Beatles' stay at the Maharishi Mahesh Yogi's Academy of Meditation just outside of the town of Rishikesh in northern India in early 1968. They show The Beatles' increasing ability to write and perform all types of music from hard rock 'Helter Skelter' to ballads 'Blackbird' and 'Mother Nature's Son' and a Hollywood-type number 'Goodnight', plus send-ups of previously recorded songs 'Glass Onion' and 'Revolution 1' and the nightmarish 'Revolution 9'.

The widening gap between John and Paul's writing styles begins to show on this album. John's lyrics are hard hitting and caustic, while Paul tends to write pleasant inoffensive ballads and love songs. Although these songs are jointly credited as being Lennon-McCartney compositions, the only track they did co-write on this album is 'Birthday'. From this album on, all Lennon-McCartney-credited

The BEATLES

songs can be more clearly defined as being written by the lead vocalist on the individual tracks. George Harrison, whose song-writing ability continues to progress, has four new songs on this album, 'While My Guitar Gently Weeps', 'Piggies', 'Long, Long, Long' and 'Savoy Truffle', and Ringo has one, 'Don't Pass Me By'.

At the time of recording this album, The Beatles were beginning to be disillusioned with the group; John wanted to leave and Ringo did leave for a period of two weeks but was eventually coaxed back. Following the creation of Apple The Beatles had gone from being just musicians to being businessmen. This, along with the death of Brian Epstein in 1967 and the arrival of Yoko Ono, contributed to the beginning of the end of The Beatles. The tension of continual business meetings, musical differences and John's growing interest in working with Yoko, were all contributory factors to the break-up. When the sessions for this album were eventually finished the rift between The Beatles had grown so wide that none of them had much interest in what they had recorded. The Beatles had decided to issue two albums mainly to fulfil their contract with EMI as soon as possible, so they sifted through the 32 tracks and rejected two of them. The tracks rejected were 'What's The New Mary Jane', that was continually reported as being their next single, that to date has not seen the light of day, and 'Not Guilty', that also has yet to be released.

After the elaborate Sgt. Pepper sleeve The Beatles decided to have the simplest possible plain white sleeve, hence the unofficial title of The White Album. The outer sleeve has only the title plus the catalogue number printed down the spine, with the words 'The Beatles' embossed on the front. The inner part of the sleeve gives the barest of information with song titles on one side and four black-and-white photographs of The Beatles on the other. The sleeve contains four separate colour photographs and a poster with a hodge podge of photographs, rather like a visual version of 'Revolution 9'. On the back of the poster are the complete lyrics to all the songs.

Back In The U.S.S.R. (Lennon-McCartney)   2:45
John Lennon: Six-String Bass and Backing Vocal
Paul McCartney: Lead Guitar, Piano and Lead/Backing Vocal
George Harrison: Bass Guitar and Backing Vocal   **Ringo Starr:** Drums
The opening track, originally titled 'I'm Backing The U.S.S.R.', fades in with the sound of a plane landing and goes straight into a great rock'n'roll song heavily influenced by Chuck Berry's 'Back In The U.S.A'. Paul is on lead vocals with a Beach Boys style backing from John and Paul. The lead guitar is played by Paul, as is the rocking piano. John can be heard playing a six-string bass and, for the first time on a Beatles record, George plays a bass guitar. The Beatles also add handclapping to the backing for the first time in about four years. The track ends in much the same way as it began, with the sound of an aircraft, that fades into the following track.

Dear Prudence (Lennon-McCartney)   4:00
John Lennon: Lead Guitar, Tambourine and Lead/Backing Vocal
Paul McCartney: Bass Guitar, Piano, Flugelhorn and Backing Vocal
George Harrison: Acoustic Guitar and Backing Vocal
Ringo Starr: Drums   **Mal Evans:** Tambourine
As 'Back In The U.S.S.R.' fades out to the sound of jet engines, 'Dear Prudence' fades in with the sound of a rather persistent acoustic guitar that continues throughout the recording. The gentle beginning builds up into an extravagant and interesting climax that includes a complicated drumbeat from Ringo, with Paul on bass guitar, piano and flugelhorn. The lead vocal on this recording is a multi-tracked John Lennon with a three-part backing vocal from John, Paul and George. The song could be almost made up of two songs joined together, rock song and ballad, although there is no evidence to confirm this. John's lead vocal is double-tracked for the main lyrics with a further over-dubbing in places – an extremely interesting combination. The song was written by John for Prudence Farrow, Mia Farrow's sister, while The Beatles were in India. Prudence spent most of her day meditating in spite of John's attempts to persuade her to do otherwise.

Glass Onion (Lennon-McCartney)   2:10

John Lennon: Acoustic Guitar and Solo Vocal   **Paul McCartney:** Bass Guitar, Piano and Flute
George Harrison: Lead Guitar   **Ringo Starr:** Drums and Tambourine
Session Musicians: Orchestra

Basically John's nonsensical lyrics are a series of unconnected comments that include reference to 'Strawberry Fields Forever', 'Fixing A Hole', 'The Fool On The Hill', 'Lady Madonna' and 'I Am The Walrus'. The track features an unusual combination of a 'Rain'-style drumbeat with an 'Eleanor Rigby'-style orchestration and an 'All My Loving' stop-start structure. The song sends up all those who tried to explain The Beatles' lyrics and John includes a line especially for them: 'Well, here's a clue for you all.'

Ob-La-Di, Ob-La-Da (Lennon-McCartney)   3:10

John Lennon: Maracas and Backing Vocal
Paul McCartney: Piano, Bass Guitar and Lead Vocal
George Harrison: Acoustic Guitar and Backing Vocal
Ringo Starr: Drums   **Session Musicians:** Brass

On this lively track The Beatles, having attempted many forms of music, now try their hand at reggae. Paul is on piano and lead vocals, with John and George joining in for the chorus. The recording also features some Jamaican style brass. Paul took the expression 'ob-la-di, ob-la-da life goes on, bra' from Jimmy Scott, a Jamaican friend, who had been using the expression for years and had a band called Jimmy Scott and his Ob-La-Di, Ob-La-Da Band. At the time of release of this album Paul McCartney wanted to issue this track as a single but both John and George voted against the idea.

Wild Honey Pie (Lennon-McCartney)   1:02

John Lennon: Not Present   **Paul McCartney:** Guitars, Drums and All Vocals
George Harrison: Not Present   **Ringo Starr:** Not Present

This bouncy semi-instrumental was written and performed solely by Paul. In addition to repeating the line 'honey pie' throughout the track he also plays drums, lead, bass and acoustic guitars. This was originally an experimental recording of a spontaneous sing-a-long, that Paul had thought up while The Beatles were staying in India and not intended for release. But Jane Asher, Paul's girlfriend, liked it so much that Paul edited it to its present length. The full track has yet to see the light of day.

The Continuing Story Of Bungalow Bill (Lennon-McCartney)   3:05
John Lennon: Acoustic Guitar, Organ and Lead Vocal
Paul McCartney: Bass Guitar and Backing Vocal
George Harrison: Acoustic Guitar and Backing Vocal
Ringo Starr: Drums, Tambourine and Backing Vocal
Yoko Ono: Harmony Vocal   **Chris Thomas:** Mellotron
Chorus: Includes Yoko Ono and Maureen Starkey
The track opens with a Spanish/Mexican-style acoustic guitar solo that leads straight into the sing-a-long chorus of 'Hey Bungalow Bill, what did you kill? Bungalow Bill'. The song, written by John who also sings lead, sounds rather like an updated version of 'Yellow Submarine'. It's a pleasant track with, for the first and only time on a Beatles' record, harmony vocals from Yoko Ono on the third verse and also on chorus where she is joined by Ringo's wife Maureen. The Beatles also are joined by assistant Chris Thomas who adds the Mellotron near the end. The track doesn't fade out but is linked to the following track with an 'Ey up' introduction from John.

While My Guitar Gently Weeps (Harrison)   4:46
John Lennon: Acoustic Guitar, Organ and Harmony Vocal
Paul McCartney: Bass Guitar, Piano and Harmony Vocal
George Harrison: Acoustic Guitar, Lead Guitar and Lead Vocal
Ringo Starr: Drums, Castanets and Tambourine   **Eric Clapton:** Lead Guitar
The first of four tracks written by George, who seemed at this stage to have given up using Indian instruments on Beatles recordings although he issued a solo album called *Wonderwall* consisting mainly of Indian instrumentals. Here he enlists the help of his long-time friend Eric Clapton to play the lead guitar. The lead vocal is by George, who double-tracks in part, and John and Paul join in on the chorus. The track has an extremely long fade-out that is really a showcase for Eric Clapton's lead guitar.

Happiness Is A Warm Gun (Lennon-McCartney) 2:47
John Lennon: Lead Guitar, Tambourine and Lead/Backing Vocal
Paul McCartney: Bass Guitar and Backing Vocal
George Harrison: Lead Guitar and Backing Vocal   **Ringo Starr:** Drums
This title is an interesting collage consisting of three separate songs that John had written but decided to join together into one song. The track begins as a gentle ballad with solo vocal from John who interweaves nonsensical one line comments into the lyrics. The song slowly changes into a semi-rock song that builds up with the repetitive 'Mother Superior jumped the gun'. The third and final section has John shouting out the lyrics over a bang, bang – shoot, shoot backing vocal that he recorded with Paul. John had the idea for the third section of the song after George Martin showed him an advertisement in a magazine proclaiming 'Happiness is a warm gun'.

SIDE TWO
Martha My Dear (Lennon-McCartney) 2:28
John Lennon: Bass Guitar   **Paul McCartney:** Piano and Solo Vocal
George Harrison: Lead Guitar   **Ringo Starr:** Drums
Session Musicians: Strings and Brass
This is a Paul McCartney 30s-influenced song written about his old English sheepdog. It features an orchestral/danceband backing and has a solo vocal from Paul who also plays piano.

I'm So Tired (Lennon-McCartney) 2:01
John Lennon: Acoustic Guitar, Lead Guitar, Organ and Lead Vocal
Paul McCartney: Bass Guitar and Harmony Vocal
George Harrison: Lead Guitar and Rhythm Guitar   **Ringo Starr:** Drums
Written by John about Yoko, this song features a lead vocal from John who also plays acoustic guitar and organ. Paul harmonises in places. The recording is structured in a similar way to 'Happiness Is A Warm Gun'. It starts, builds up and then stops, only to start up again. The track finishes with a few seconds of nonsensical gibberish that has been interpreted as Ringo saying 'Paul is dead, man, miss him, miss him' backwards.

Blackbird (Lennon-McCartney) 2:20
John Lennon: Not Present
Paul McCartney: Acoustic Guitar, Bongos and Solo Vocal
George Harrison: Not Present   **Ringo Starr:** Not Present
This gentle song with inoffensive lyrics has a solo vocal from Paul who double-tracks his lead vocal in part and backs it himself with an acoustic guitar. A metronomic beat is tapped out on what sounds like half of a set of bongos. Like several tracks on the album, this stops and starts up again, but here with the addition of a blackbird singing sweetly over the encore.

Piggies (Harrison) 2:04
John Lennon: Sound Effects   **Paul McCartney:** Bass Guitar
George Harrison: Acoustic Guitar and Solo Vocal   **Ringo Starr:** Tambourine
Chris Thomas: Harpsichord   **Session Musicians:** Strings
This song is a sarcastic swipe at the greedy, the piggies, always out to make money, and in particular out of The Beatles. Lead vocal is from George with double-tracking in parts. Chris Thomas plays harpsichord and the sound of grunting, snorting pigs is used to good effect.

Rocky Racoon (Lennon-McCartney) 3:33
John Lennon: Harmonium, Harmonica and Backing Vocal
Paul McCartney: Acoustic Guitar and Lead Vocal   **George Harrison:** Bass Guitar and Backing Vocal
Ringo Starr: Drums   **George Martin:** Piano
Written by Paul during one of his visits to India, this has a country/folk flavour, like his earlier 'I've Just Seen A Face', on *Help!* He sings lead vocal, and backing vocals are a three-part harmony from him, John and George. A harmonica is used, although sparingly, for the first time since the early recordings; a honky-tonk, bar-room style piano is added by George Martin and a harmonium by John.

Don't Pass Me By (Starkey)   3:52
John Lennon: Acoustic Guitar and Tambourine   **Paul McCartney:** Bass Guitar
George Harrison: Violin   **Ringo Starr:** Piano, Drums and Solo Vocal
After years of performing songs specially written for him by John and Paul, and co-writing only one song, 'What Goes On?' on *Rubber Soul*, Ringo finally sings a solo on a song he wrote in 1963, five years previously. The very bouncy backing includes a violin reputed to have been played by George Harrison, and a solid drum beat is provided by Ringo. This excellent first song from Ringo proved he too could write.

Why Don't We Do It In The Road? (Lennon-McCartney)   1:42
John Lennon: Not Present
Paul McCartney: Lead Guitar, Bass Guitar, Piano, Drums and Solo Vocal
George Harrison: Not Present   **Ringo Starr:** Not Present
A regrettably short multi-tracked solo vocal from Paul who sings and plays every instrument including piano, drums, lead and bass guitars.

I Will (Lennon-McCartney)   1:46
John Lennon: Not Present
Paul McCartney: Acoustic Guitar, Bass Guitar and Solo Vocal
George Harrison: Not Present   **Ringo Starr:** Drums, Bongos and Maracas
This ballad is also a rather short track. Paul sings solo vocal and supplies a minimum backing with an acoustic guitar. Bongos are supplied by Ringo, together with drums and maracas.

Julia (Lennon-McCartney) 2:57
John Lennon: Acoustic Guitar and Solo Vocal   **Paul McCartney:** Not Present
George Harrison: Not Present   **Ringo Starr:** Not Present
This beautiful song, written by John, with help from Yoko, is mainly about his love for his dead mother. A reference to his love for Yoko is included with the words 'ocean child' – an English translation of Yoko is 'child of the ocean'. John sings solo vocal and backs himself with two acoustic guitars.

SIDE THREE

Birthday (Lennon-McCartney) 2:40
John Lennon: Lead Guitar and Lead Vocal   **Paul McCartney:** Piano and Lead Vocal
George Harrison: Bass Guitar and Tambourine   **Ringo Starr:** Drums
Chorus: Includes Yoko Ono and Patti Harrison
This is the only track on the two albums to have been co-written by John and Paul. It is basically an up-dated, noisier re-write of the traditional 'Happy Birthday' and was written in India for Patti Harrison, George's wife, who was celebrating her birthday. It races along with a heavy drumbeat from Ringo, a persistent lead guitar riff from George and a jangling piano phased in places from Paul. The lead vocal, also from Paul, is double-tracked onto each channel of the stereo, an effect not used since *Revolver*. John sings lead in places but is mainly confined to backing with Yoko Ono and Patti Harrison.

Yer Blues (Lennon-McCartney) 4:01
John Lennon: Lead Guitar and Solo Vocal   **Paul McCartney:** Bass Guitar
George Harrison: Lead Guitar   **Ringo Starr:** Drums
This is John Lennon's send-up of the flourishing British electric blues scene of the late 60s. The music and lyrics are just as powerful as John's vocals and the stabbing, attacking lead guitar from George with Ringo's insistent drumbeat suit the track perfectly.

Mother Nature's Son (Lennon-McCartney) 2:46
John Lennon: Not Present
Paul McCartney: Acoustic Guitar, Bongos, Timpani and Solo Vocal
George Harrison: Not Present   **Ringo Starr:** Not Present
Session Musicians: Horns

Paul McCartney sets his vision of country life to pleasantly simple music. He backs his solo vocal on acoustic guitar with a secondary acoustic guitar, bongos and a very distant over-dubbed timpani. Some unobtrusive, pleasant horns are added by session musicians.

Everybody's Got Something To Hide Except Me And My Monkey (Lennon-McCartney) 2:25
John Lennon: Lead Guitar, Maracas and Lead Vocal
Paul McCartney: Bass Guitar and Backing Vocal
George Harrison: Rhythm Guitar and Firebell   **Ringo Starr:** Drums

This track was written by John in reply to a drawing depicting Yoko as a monkey sitting on his shoulders, digging long talons into his back and supposedly draining him of his talent. John dismissed it with this song, saying 'We've got nothing to hide, Yoko inspires me, she doesn't destroy my ability to write good songs'. This is a great piece of rock'n'roll with John on lead vocal and backing vocals in places from John and Paul. It features a prominent lead guitar riff and extensive use of a firebell. The song began life with the reputed working title of Come On, Come On.

Sexy Sadie (Lennon-McCartney) 3:15
John Lennon: Acoustic Guitar, Rhythm Guitar, Organ and Lead/Backing Vocal
Paul McCartney: Piano, Bass Guitar and Backing Vocal
George Harrison: Lead Guitar and Backing Vocal
Ringo Starr: Drums and Tambourine

Written by John about the Maharishi, who, during The Beatles' stay at his academy of meditation in India, had made a very non-mystical approach to Mia Farrow, proving to John that he was not all he made himself out to be. John originally intended to write the song as 'Maharishi What Have You Done, You Made A Fool of Everyone' but decided against it. The track features a lead vocal from John who joins Paul and George for the partly phased backing vocals, that produce an unusual effect. John plays acoustic guitar, Paul piano and George a distorted lead guitar.

Helter Skelter (Lennon-McCartney) 4:30
John Lennon: Bass Guitar, Lead Guitar, Saxophone and Backing Vocal
Paul McCartney: Bass Guitar, Lead Guitar and Lead Vocal
George Harrison: Rhythm Guitar and Backing Vocal
Ringo Starr: Drums   **Mal Evans:** Trumpet
This is the heaviest sound The Beatles ever produced, a sound first tried out in 1966 with tracks such
as 'Rain' and 'And Your Bird Can Sing'.

   Paul's lead vocals scream out of the speakers; the backing vocals from John and Paul add to the
overall excited sound of the recording that includes various unexplainable bleeps and squeaks. At one
point the guitars run down the musical scale and then dissolve into distorted feedback. Ringo starts
up the track again with his drums but it fades out to a few seconds of silence and the recording
seems to finish, but no, back it comes with all its heaviness and then fades slightly only to reappear
with Ringo Starr's famous statement 'I've got blisters on my fingers'. John plays saxophone and Mal
Evans, one of The Beatles' roadies, plays trumpet. This recording originally was 25 minutes long but
The Beatles realised that at that length it would take up an entire album side so it was edited to 4:30.

   After the Charles Manson murders in 1969 that reportedly were inspired, in part, by this song,
John Lennon later appeared in court to defend the recording, saying that it was simply about a
fairground slide and nothing else.

Long, Long, Long (Harrison) 3:08
John Lennon: Acoustic Guitar and Piano
Paul McCartney: Bass Guitar and Hammond Organ
George Harrison: Acoustic Guitar and Solo Vocal   **Ringo Starr:** Drums
George Harrison's third offering on the album is reminiscent of a funeral dirge. George's double-
tracked lead vocal is mixed so far back that it's difficult to hear the lyrics above the acoustic guitar.
The recording includes a very dramatic drumbeat from Ringo and features Paul playing both piano
and Hammond organ. It ends with a rather unearthly screech that sounds as though it might have
come from Yoko.

SIDE FOUR
Revolution 1 (Lennon-McCartney) 4:13
John Lennon: Lead Guitar, Acoustic Guitar and Lead/Backing Vocal
Paul McCartney: Bass Guitar, Acoustic Guitar, Piano and Backing Vocal
George Harrison: Rhythm Guitar and Backing Vocal
Ringo Starr: Drums   **Session Musicians:** Brass
This recording is a slower, almost acoustic version of the song issued as the B side of the 'Hey Jude'
single issued two or three months before the album. The double-tracked lead vocal is by John. The
track has a false start and when it does begin the lead guitar, instead of being on the right-hand
channel as it is on the faster version, is on the left-hand channel. There is a do-wop backing that makes
this track sound rather like a send-up. Additional features are a brass section and Paul playing piano.

Honey Pie (Lennon-McCartney) 2:42
John Lennon: Lead Guitar   **Paul McCartney:** Piano and Solo Vocal
George Harrison: Bass Guitar   **Ringo Starr:** Drums
Session Musicians: 15-Piece Band
Like 'When I'm Sixty-Four' and 'Your Mother Should Know' this song is influenced by the music of the
20s. Paul wrote it, sings lead vocal and plays piano. John plays lead guitar and as on several tracks of
this album George plays bass guitar. Ringo is on drums and 15 session musicians add the danceband-
type backing.

Savoy Truffle (Harrison) 2:55
John Lennon: Lead Guitar   **Paul McCartney:** Bass Guitar
George Harrison: Lead Guitar, Organ and Solo Vocal
Ringo Starr: Drums and Tambourine   **Session Musicians:** Brass
This song is dedicated to Eric Clapton's sweet tooth! George makes an uncomfortable reference to
'Ob-La-Di, Ob-La-Da' that does not fit with the other lyrics but rhymes with the line that follows. The
recording has a solid brass backing, rather reminiscent of 'Got To Get You Into My Life'.

Cry Baby Cry (Lennon-McCartney)   2:34
John Lennon: Acoustic Guitar, Piano, Organ and Solo Vocal
Paul McCartney: Bass Guitar   **George Harrison:** Lead Guitar
Ringo Starr: Drums and Tambourine   **George Martin:** Harmonium
John Lennon demonstrates his versatility on this track by playing almost every instrument. He plays
guitar, piano and organ with help from George Martin on harmonium. The guitars at the beginning are
phased and John experiments with stereo effects so that the verses appear in the centre while the
chorus appears on the left-hand channel. John was inspired to write the song by a television
commercial and his original verse was to have been 'make your mother buy' but he changed his
mind and added more nonsensical lyrics.

Can You Take Me Back (Lennon-McCartney)   0:27
John Lennon: Not Present
Paul McCartney: Acoustic Guitar, Drums, Maracas, Bongos and Solo Vocal
George Harrison: Not Present   **Ringo Starr:** Not Present
This short track links 'Cry Baby Cry' with 'Revolution 9', and possibly was originally intended to be part
of one of these songs. The lyrics are not printed on the back of the poster as are those of other songs
on the album. The solo vocal is from Paul with backing provided by an acoustic guitar, drums and
maracas presumably all played by Paul. It does not seem to be an intro to 'Revolution 9' because it
fades out completely before that track begins. It sounds rather like a first take that initially was
dismissed then included at the last moment.

Revolution 9 (Lennon-McCartney) 8:15

John Lennon: Voice, Mixing and Editing   **Paul McCartney:** Piano

George Harrison: Voice   **Ringo Starr:** Voice

Yoko Ono: Voice   **George Martin:** Mixing and Editing

What can be said about a Beatles recording that doesn't feature any music? The recording starts with a snatch of overheard conversation. Paul begins to play a piano before an anonymous voice repeats 'Number 9, Number 9, Number 9'. From here on the recording becomes a mixture of backward-running tapes, discordant sounds, laughter, snatches of conversation between John and George and crowd noises. It sounds rather like the memory of a nightmare portrayed in sound. This is one of John's experimental avant-garde recordings, many of which are featured on his *Two Virgins* album. It was created solely by John and Yoko, was rejected initially by the other three, but eventually included.

Good Night (Lennon-McCartney) 3:14

John Lennon: Not Present   **Paul McCartney:** Not Present

George Harrison: Not Present   **Ringo Starr:** Solo Vocal

Session Musicians: 30-Piece Orchestra, Harp and Choir

This was written by John specifically for Ringo and only him. The 30s, Hollywood-style backing is supplied by the George Martin orchestra with a sweet-sounding female choir. One cannot resist the feeling that this track is a Lennon send-up.

YELLOW SUBMARINE

UK Release: 17 January 1969
US Release: 13 January 1969
Intl CD No: CDP 7 46445 2
Running Time : 40:15

Apple PMC 7070: PCS 7070
Apple SW 153
Producer: George Martin

SIDE ONE: Yellow Submarine; Only A Northern Song; All Together Now; Hey Bulldog; It's All Too Much; All You Need Is Love.

SIDE TWO: Contains incidental music by George Martin and Orchestra as played in the film.

This is the soundtrack album for the feature-length cartoon film of the same name based loosely around the lyrics of *Yellow Submarine*.

The contract for the film and album, signed by Brian Epstein, stipulated that The Beatles were to supply at least three previously unreleased recordings for use in the soundtrack. The Beatles felt Brian Epstein had let them down and initially wanted nothing to do with the project but eventually decided to supply songs that would not normally have been seriously considered for release. However one song, 'Baby You're A Rich Man', originally recorded for inclusion on this album, was issued six months previously as the B side to 'All You Need Is Love' (see the *Magical Mystery Tour* album).

The four songs reluctantly supplied for use in the film: 'Only A Northern Song', 'All Together Now', 'Hey Bulldog' and 'It's All Too Much' were considered by The Beatles to be throwaway recordings. The original plan was to release the four new tracks as an EP, but after consideration it seemed that an album would sell better. Unfortunately for Beatles fans this turned out to be a one-sided Beatles album with George Martin's orchestral score of the film's incidental music on the second side. When issued in Britain, The Beatles' previous soundtrack albums, had included on their second sides tracks not used in the respective films and it was a great pity that this album was not compiled in the same way.

The film soundtrack has these six album tracks plus parts or complete recordings of 'Sgt. Pepper's Lonely Hearts Club Band', 'With A Little Help From My Friends', 'Lucy In The Sky With Diamonds', 'Within You, Without You', 'When I'm Sixty-Four', 'A Day In The Life', 'Eleanor Rigby', 'Nowhere Man', 'Baby, You're A Rich Man', 'Think For Yourself' and 'Love You To'.

SIDE ONE

Yellow Submarine (Lennon-McCartney) 2:40
John Lennon: Acoustic Guitar and Backing Vocal
Paul McCartney: Acoustic Guitar and Backing Vocal
George Harrison: Tambourine and Backing Vocal   **Ringo Starr:** Drums and Lead Vocal
Chorus: Includes George Martin, Patti Harrison, Mal Evans, Neil Aspinall and Geoff Emerick
Session Musicians: Brass Band
Previously issued on *Revolver*, this is an eternally fresh song which does not seem to have dated.

Only A Northern Song (Harrison) 3:23
John Lennon: Piano and Various Discordant Instruments
Paul McCartney: Bass Guitar and Various Discordant Instruments
George Harrison: Organ, Various Discordant Instruments and Solo Vocal
Ringo Starr: Drums and Various Discordant Instruments
This track seems to reflect George Harrison's displeasure with the project. His one-line comments are thinly linked together into what can be loosely described as a song. The ironical title was also a sarcastic jibe at the publishing company, Northern Songs. The backing is a cacophonous tune-up reminiscent of 'Tomorrow Never Knows' and 'Revolution 9'. Ringo's drums and Paul's bass guitar are the only musical parts of the backing. The organ intro is good, but gets lost amid the continuous burps and interruptions of off-key instruments. As this is a mono recording, it is difficult to tell if it continues throughout the recording. At present the track is not available in stereo.

All Together Now (Lennon-McCartney) 2:08
John Lennon: Banjo and Backing Vocal
Paul McCartney: Acoustic Guitar, Bass Guitar and Lead Vocal
George Harrison: Harmonica and Backing Vocal   **Ringo Starr:** Drums and Finger Cymbals
Paul's contribution sounds rather half-hearted. His lead vocal, with backing from John and George, seems to lack real enthusiasm, although it comes across reasonably well and is still enjoyable.

Hey Bulldog (Lennon-McCartney)   3:09
John Lennon: Piano, Lead Guitar and Lead Vocal
Paul McCartney: Bass Guitar and Harmony Vocal
George Harrison: Lead Guitar and Tambourine   **Ringo Starr:** Drums
John's sole contribution was, as he described it, 'a filler track for the album'. The recording was not intended for use in the film, as the contract demanded only three new songs, but finally it was included. John's lead vocal, without sounding over-enthusiastic, manages to give the recording power and excitement. He insisted on this title for the song rather than the more obvious 'You Can Talk To Me', although nowhere in his original lyrics was there any reference to a bulldog. He decided to include the words 'Hey Bulldog' right at the end of the song.

It's All Too Much (Harrison)   6:27
John Lennon: Lead Guitar and Harmony Vocal
Paul McCartney: Bass Guitar and Harmony Vocal
George Harrison: Lead Guitar, Organ and Lead Vocal
Ringo Starr: Drums and Tambourine   **Session Musicians:** Two Trumpets
On this, his second contribution to *Yellow Submarine*, George's lead vocals sound more enthusiastic than his first probably because it was not recorded with the project in mind. This, and the recording used in the soundtrack that has a verse not included here are reputed to have been edited from a 30-minute recording, although this has never been verified. George includes two rather odd lines. One is a line previously used in the Merseys' hit record 'Sorrow'; the second is the mysterious line in which he sings 'We are dead'.

All You Need Is Love (Lennon-McCartney)   3:47
John Lennon: Harpsichord and Lead Vocal
Paul McCartney: Arco String Bass, Bass Guitar and Backing Vocal
George Harrison: Violin, Lead Guitar and Backing Vocal   **Ringo Starr:** Drums
George Martin: Piano
Chorus: Includes Mick Jagger, Marianne Faithfull, Keith Richard, Gary Brooker and Keith Moon
Session Musicians: Four Violins, two Cellos, Trumpets, Trombones, Saxophones and an Accordion.
This is a completely different version of the track included on the *Magical Mystery Tour* album. This
recording, although using the same pre-recorded rhythm track as the single recorded during the Our
World broadcast on 25 June 1967, has a different main track and lead vocal from John. This recording
is also ten seconds shorter than the single and is in stereo whereas the single is in mono.

SIDE TWO
The George Martin Orchestra
Pepperland (Martin) 2:18; **Sea of Time** (Martin) 2:58; **Sea Of Holes** (Martin) 2:14;
Sea of Monsters (Martin) 3:35; **March of the Meames** (Martin) 2:16; **Pepperland Laid Waste**
(Martin) 2:09; **Yellow Submarine in Pepperland** (Lennon-McCartney arr. Martin) 2:10

ABBEY ROAD

UK Release: 26 September 1969
US Release: 26 September 1969
Intl CD No: CDP 7 46446 2
Running Time: 46:54

Apple PCS 7088
Apple SO 383
Producer: George Martin

SIDE ONE: Come Together; Something; Maxwell's Silver Hammer; Oh! Darling; Octopus's Garden; I Want You (She's So Heavy).

SIDE TWO: Here Comes The Sun; Because; You Never Give Me Your Money; Sun King; Mean Mr Mustard; Polythene Pam; She Came In Through The Bathroom Window; Golden Slumbers; Carry That Weight; The End; Her Majesty.

The Beatles, now on the verge of splitting up after the bad feeling created during the ill-fated Get Back sessions (see *Let It Be*), briefly settled their personal and musical differences long enough to record *Abbey Road*, their last studio album. John suspended his Peace Campaign, Paul postponed a planned holiday, George broke off other recording sessions with Billy Preston and the Radha Krishna Temple and Ringo temporarily dropped his acting career.

The tension that had grown within The Beatles since the death of Brian Epstein had now reached the point where they could no longer agree on anything, particularly their music. John's concept of *Abbey Road* was for it to be a basic rock'n'roll album like *Get Back*. Paul, however, envisaged a pop opera of different songs edited together into one long medley. In the end both got their way.

Side One of the album fulfils John's concept of individual tracks that are basically rock'n'roll. He contributes 'Come Together' and 'I Want You (She's So Heavy)', Paul his gutsy 'Oh! Darling' and 'Maxwell's Silver Hammer', while George and Ringo contribute 'Something' and 'Octopus's Garden', respectively.

Side Two has Paul's now famous pop opera of ten different songs of which only eight are listed, edited together with George's 'Here Comes The Sun' and John's 'Because' to form the 16-minute medley.

The album contains some of The Beatles' most technically perfect recordings and features some of the most intricate harmony singing the group ever recorded. A number of tracks include the use of a synthesiser, an instrument suggested by George after he had recorded the album *Electronic Sounds* using only a synthesiser. That album and his other solo venture *Wonderwall,* a soundtrack album consisting almost entirely of Indian music, showed that George's musical interests were no longer fitting into the framework of The Beatles. John, now discontented with being a Beatle, had also begun to pursue a solo career. With the help of Yoko Ono he had recorded *Two Virgins* and *Life With The Lions*, two albums consisting entirely of avant-garde sound. He had also issued a solo single, 'Give Peace A Chance', under the name of The Plastic Ono Band. He was to continue his solo career by issuing *The Wedding Album*, a third album of avant-garde sound; *Live Peace In Toronto,* a live recording of The Plastic Ono Band; and *Cold Turkey* all within weeks of the release of *Abbey Road*. Apparently John had wanted The Beatles to record 'Cold Turkey' as a new single, but neither Paul nor George were interested. John, along with Ringo, Eric Clapton and Klaus Voorman who were the first real line-up of the Plastic Ono Band, recorded 'Cold Turkey' and it was issued in direct competition with 'Something'/'Come Together' the first Beatles single to be issued in Britain from an album that had already been issued.

Abbey Road, named after the location of the recording studios where The Beatles made most of their recordings, including this one, was the first Beatles album to be issued solely in stereo. All previous Beatles albums up to and including *Yellow Submarine* had been issued in both mono and stereo. This decision was made because The Beatles felt that their music should be heard in stereo because the mono versus stereo argument of earlier years was over.

Photographed by Iain Macmillan on 8 August 1969, the sleeve of the album shows The Beatles walking across a zebra crossing in Abbey Road away from the recording studio. This, with the album's closing track 'The End', was regarded by many as being a cryptic message from The Beatles saying 'This is it, we've finished recording our final album, we're walking away and splitting up.' An announcement to that effect was to be made by Paul on 10 April 1970, almost six months after the release of this album.

SIDE ONE

Come Together (Lennon-McCartney)   4:16
Recorded: 21, 22, 23, 25, 29 and 30 July 1969, EMI Studios, Abbey Road, London
John Lennon: Rhythm Guitar, Lead Guitar, Tambourine and Lead Vocal
Paul McCartney: Bass Guitar, Electric Piano and Harmony Vocal
George Harrison: Lead Guitar and Maracas   **Ringo Starr**: Drums

Written by John, this was originally intended to be a campaign song for Timothy Leary who at one time was proposing to run for the post of Governor of California. The idea was dropped after Leary decided not to run, and John changed the style of the song. It was eventually the subject of a law suit as Maurice Levy, owner of the American music publishers Big Seven Music, who hold the publishing rights to Chuck Berry's song 'You Can't Catch Me', claimed that John had used two of the song's lines in 'Come Together'. To save months of legal arguments John apparently agreed to record, and include, 'You Can't Catch Me' and 'Sweet Little Sixteen' also Berry's compositions and published by Maurice Levy's company, on his 1975 solo album *Rock And Roll*.

 John also had another problem with the song; the BBC banned it because of a reference to Coca-Cola that they deemed to be advertising. The recording, completed in nine takes plus overdubs, features a lead vocal from John with harmonies in places from Paul. It also features two lead guitars, one played by John, the other by George.

Something (Harrison)   2:59
Recorded: 2 and 5 May, 11 and 16 July and 15 August 1969, EMI Studios, Abbey Road, London and Olympic Studios, Church Road, Barnes, London
John Lennon: Lead Guitar
Paul McCartney: Bass Guitar and Backing Vocal
George Harrison: Lead Guitar and Lead Vocal   **Ringo Starr**: Drums
Billy Preston: Piano   **Session Musicians**: 21-piece Orchestra

Recorded in 36 takes plus overdubs, this dramatic George Harrison rendition of his own song that was inspired by his wife Patti, features a lead vocal from him with occasional backing vocals from Paul. Again, the recording makes use of the twin lead guitars of Lennon and Harrison and also features Billy Preston on piano. The song uses the title of James Taylor's 'Something In The Way She Moves' as its opening line and must surely rank alongside some of the best Lennon-McCartney compositions and is one of the finest songs The Beatles ever recorded.

Maxwell's Silver Hammer (Lennon-McCartney) 3:24
Recorded: 9, 10 and 11 July and 6 August 1969, EMI Studios, Abbey Road, London
John Lennon: Acoustic Guitar and Lead Guitar
Paul McCartney: Bass Guitar, Piano, Synthesiser and Lead/Backing Vocal
George Harrison: Lead Guitar and Backing Vocal   **Ringo Starr:** Drums, Anvil and Backing Vocal
George Martin: Hammond Organ
Paul's first song on the album features himself on lead vocal with harmonies in places from George; they also get together for the backing vocals. Recorded in 21 takes plus overdubs, the truck includes Paul on piano, Ringo banging a hammer on an anvil and for the first time on the album the use of a synthesiser played by Paul. The song's final line, 'silver hammer man', features a three-part harmony from Paul, George and Ringo. The Beatles can be seen and heard rehearsing this song in the film *Let It Be.*

Oh! Darling (Lennon-McCartney) 3:28
Recorded: 20 and 26 April, 18, 22 and 23 July and 8 and 11 August 1969, EMI Studios, Abbey Road, London
John Lennon: Piano and Backing Vocal
Paul McCartney: Bass Guitar, Lead Guitar, Piano, Tambourine and Lead/Backing Vocal
George Harrison: Lead Guitar and Backing Vocal   **Ringo Starr:** Drums
Before recording the vocals for this dramatic track, Paul spent a week working at making his voice as harsh and gutsy as possible. Recorded in 26 takes with numerous overdubs, the track features John and Paul on two pianos and Paul and George overdubbed on lead guitars. The recording also features a wordless backing vocal harmony from John, Paul and George.

Octopus's Garden (Starkey) 2:49
Recorded: 26 and 29 April and 17 and 18 July 1969, EMI Studios, Abbey Road, London
John Lennon: Lead Guitar
Paul McCartney: Bass Guitar, Piano, Sound Effects and Backing Vocal
George Harrison: Lead Guitar, Sound Effects and Backing Vocal
Ringo Starr: Drums, Percussion, Sound Effects and Lead Vocal
This is the second song written by Ringo to be included on a Beatles album. The first, 'Don't Pass Me By', was included 12 months earlier on the double album *The Beatles*. Although he found it difficult to

write songs, both are bouncy with infectious chorus lines. This song is reminiscent of *Yellow Submarine*, particularly as it uses the same sound effects of water swirling around and bubbles being blown into water. Another interesting sound effect is the gargling backing vocals from Paul and George. Ringo sings lead vocals with backing from Paul and George on this track that was recorded in 32 takes. As with other tracks on this album, two lead guitars are played by John and George, and Paul can be heard playing piano.

I Want You (She's So Heavy) (Lennon-McCartney)   7:49
Recorded: 22 February, 18 and 20 April and 8 and 11 August 1969, EMI Studios, Abbey Road, London and Trident Studios, Wardour Street, London
John Lennon: Multi-tracked Lead and Rhythm Guitars, Hammond Organ, Synthesiser, White Noise Generator and Lead/Harmony Vocal
Paul McCartney: Bass Guitar and Harmony Vocal
George Harrison: Multi-tracked Lead and Rhythm Guitars, Conga Drums and Harmony Vocal
Ringo Starr: Drums
With the exception of 'Revolution 9' this is the longest recording issued by The Beatles. It is even 38 seconds longer than 'Hey Jude' that clocks in at 7:11. The track is really two separate songs, 'I Want You' and 'She's So Heavy' joined together but without a link. Each is sung in segments throughout the recording with 'I Want You' sung repeatedly, predominating, and 'She's So Heavy' inserted twice. Lead vocal and blues-style lead guitar are from John, with Paul and George harmonising here and there. The track, recorded in 35 takes with incalculable overdubs, features John and George both playing multi-tracked lead and rhythm guitars throughout. The ending features a persistent guitar riff being repeated maddeningly. John then adds a synthesiser, building up the sound seemingly forever until suddenly it stops.

SIDE TWO
Here Comes The Sun (Harrison) 3:40
Recorded: 7, 8 and 16 July and 6, 11, 15 and 19 August 1969, EMI Studios, Abbey Road, London
John Lennon: Not Present
Paul McCartney: Bass Guitar, Handclapping and Backing Vocal
George Harrison: Acoustic Guitar, Lead Guitar, Harmonium, Synthesiser, Handclapping, Lead/Backing Vocal
Ringo Starr: Drums and Handclapping   **Session Musicians:** 17-Piece Orchestra
To escape the pressure of work, George took a day off from the recording session and sat in Eric Clapton's garden on one of the first days of spring and wrote this song. It's his second song on this album, on which he also sings lead vocal. Most of the instrumentation, with the obvious exception of the orchestral overdub, is also played by George, with only the bass guitar and drums being supplied by Paul and Ringo respectively. The harmonies and backing vocals also are sung by George with help from Paul. The song, recorded in 15 takes plus overdubs, starts on the left-hand channel with an acoustic guitar and synthesiser, then floats across the stereo sound stage to the right-hand channel as George begins to sing. This recording features the same instrumental break as 'Badge', a song co-written by George Harrison and Eric Clapton and recorded by Clapton's group Cream.

Because (Lennon-McCartney) 2:45
Recorded: 1, 4 and 5 August 1969, EMI Studios, Abbey Road, London
John Lennon: Lead Guitar and Lead/Harmony Vocal
Paul McCartney: Bass Guitar and Lead/Harmony Vocal
George Harrison: Synthesiser and Lead/Harmony Vocal
Ringo Starr: Not Present   **George Martin:** Harpsichord
John got the idea for this song when he heard Yoko play Beethoven's Moonlight Sonata. John suggested that she play the chord sequence backwards, which she did. He then slightly restructured it and added lyrics. It features a close-harmony vocal from John, Paul and George with George Martin supplying the harpsichord and George adding a cleverly programmed synthesiser. Recorded in 23 takes, of which take 16 was selected as the master, the track also features John on lead guitar and Paul on bass.

You Never Give Me Your Money (Lennon-McCartney) 3:57
Recorded: 6 May and 1, 11, 15 and 31 July 1969, EMI Studios, Abbey Road, London and Olympic Studios, Church Road, Barnes, London
John Lennon: Distorted Lead Guitar and Backing Vocal
Paul McCartney: Bass Guitar, Piano, Tambourine, Chimes and Lead/Backing Vocal
George Harrison: Lead Guitar and Backing Vocal   **Ringo Starr:** Drums
This is a medley of four separate songs written by Paul. The first, 'You Never Give Me Your Money', features Paul singing solo and backing himself on piano. It was written about the boardroom squabbles at Apple and the arguments between The Beatles themselves. The second song, 'That Magic Feeling', features a honky-tonk style backing piano and Paul's vocals sound rougher, more like his Little Richard style. The third song, 'One Sweet Dream', is linked to 'That Magic Feeling' by a wordless chorus from John, Paul and George. This is another up-beat rock'n'roll song featuring Paul in fine voice. The fourth song comes in only as the track fades, John, Paul and George repeat 'One-two-three-four-five-six-seven, all good children go to heaven'. These four songs have been successfully welded together to form one. The track, recorded in 36 takes, of which take 30 was selected for use for later overdubbing, has a long fade-out overlapping the intro of the following track.

Sun King (Lennon-McCartney) 2:31
Recorded: 24, 25 and 29 July 1969, EMI Studios, Abbey Road, London
John Lennon: Rhythm Guitar, Organ and Lead/Harmony Vocal
Paul McCartney: Bass Guitar, Piano and Harmony Vocal
George Harrison: Lead Guitar and Harmony Vocal   **Ringo Starr:** Drums and Percussion
John claimed this song came to him in a dream. This might explain the lyrics that are a mixture of Spanish, Italian, French and nonsense. The sound of crickets chirping opens the track with a bluesy lead guitar played by George. John's vocals are multi-tracked for the lead and also for the backing harmonies on which he is joined by Paul and George. Recorded in 35 takes with later overdubs, this track features the same beautiful close-harmony vocals used earlier on 'Because'.

Mean Mr Mustard (Lennon-McCartney) 1:06
Recorded: 24, 25 and 29 July 1969, EMI Studios, Abbey Road, London
John Lennon: Rhythm Guitar, Organ and Lead/Harmony Vocal
Paul McCartney: Bass Guitar, Piano and Harmony Vocal
George Harrison: Electric Guitar and Harmony Vocal
Ringo Starr: Drums and Percussion
This is The Beatles getting back to the three guitars and drums of earlier years and it's rather a pity
the song didn't last a bit longer. Recorded in 35 takes together with 'Sun King', the previous song, the
track also includes an organ and piano played by John and Paul respectively. Written by John while he
was meditating in India, the song features a strong lead vocal from John in his best Liverpool accent
with harmonies in places from Paul and George.

Polythene Pam (Lennon-McCartney) 1:13
Recorded: 25, 28 and 30 July 1969, EMI Studios, Abbey Road, London
John Lennon: 12-string Acoustic Guitar, Electric Piano, Lead Vocal
Paul McCartney: Bass Guitar, Piano and Backing Vocal
George Harrison: Lead Guitar, Acoustic Guitar and Backing Vocal
Ringo Starr: Drums and Percussion
Again written by John while in India and again sung with a strong Liverpool accent, the song, recorded
in 40 takes, is about a mythical Liverpool prostitute. The backing is based around a persistent
12-string guitar riff played by John with wordless backing vocals supplied by Paul and George.

She Came In Through The Bathroom Window (Lennon-McCartney) 1:58
Recorded: 25, 28 and 30 July 1969, EMI Studios, Abbey Road, London
John Lennon: 12-string Acoustic Guitar, Electric Piano and Backing Vocal
Paul McCartney: Bass Guitar, Piano and Lead/Backing Vocal
George Harrison: Lead Guitar, Acoustic Guitar and Backing Vocal
Ringo Starr: Drums and Percussion
This song harks back to the days of The Beatles' early 60s American tours, when fans would almost
do anything to see their idols. One in particular, undaunted by the fact that The Beatles were staying
on the upper floors of a hotel, scaled a drainpipe and broke into Paul's suite through the bathroom
window. Recorded, together with the previous song, in 40 takes, the track features a lead vocal from
Paul who joins John and George for the wordless backing vocal.

Golden Slumbers (Lennon-McCartney) 1:31
Recorded: 2, 3, 4, 30 and 31 July and 15 August 1969, EMI Studios, Abbey Road, London
John Lennon: Not Present
Paul McCartney: Rhythm Guitar, Piano and Solo Vocal
George Harrison: Bass Guitar and Lead Guitar   **Ringo Starr:** Drums
Session Musicians: 30-piece Orchestra
During a stay at his father's home in Heswall, not far from Liverpool, Paul wrote this lilting melody with dramatic overtones. He took the lyrics originally from a 400-year-old poem written by Thomas Dekker from his step-sister's music book. He couldn't read the music to accompany himself on the piano so he improvised his own version. The track, recorded in 17 takes with various overdubs, features a solo vocal from Paul who accompanies himself on piano backed by George, Ringo and a 30-piece orchestra.

Carry That Weight (Lennon-McCartney) 1:37
Recorded: 2, 3, 4, 30 and 31 July and 15 August 1969, EMI Studios, Abbey Road, London
John Lennon: Not Present
Paul McCartney: Rhythm Guitar, Piano and Lead Vocal
George Harrison: Bass Guitar, Lead Guitar and Lead Vocal
Ringo Starr: Drums, Timpani and Lead Vocal   **Session Musicians:** 30-piece Orchestra
Paul McCartney reputedly wrote this song about the responsibility of keeping The Beatles together after Brian Epstein's death in 1967. The song was recorded together with 'Golden Slumbers' in 17 takes plus overdubs and is divided into three sections. It features a reprise of the second verse of 'You Never Give Me Your Money' that appears earlier on the album. The first section has a three-part harmony from Paul, George and Ringo. As mentioned, the second section is a reprise of 'You Never Give Me Your Money', and features a solo vocal from Paul. The track then returns to the original melody of 'Carry That Weight', with Paul, George and Ringo on vocals.

The End (Lennon-McCartney)   2:04
Recorded: 23 July and 5, 7, 8, 15 and 18 August 1969, EMI Studios, Abbey Road, London
John Lennon: Lead Guitar and Harmony Vocal
Paul McCartney: Bass Guitar, Lead Guitar, Piano and Lead Vocal
George Harrison: Lead Guitar and Harmony Vocal   **Ringo Starr:** Drums
Session Musicians: 30-piece Orchestra
Recorded in seven takes with numerous overdubs. Starting with a one-verse solo vocal from Paul, this track features the first and only drum solo by Ringo on a Beatles record. The 16-second solo is followed by guitar solos from John, Paul and George in that order, who also sing a monotonous 'love you' 24 times. As this section stops after just under a minute, a piano begins and Paul, with harmonies in places from John, sings the final verse. There is 20 seconds' silence before the last short track.

Her Majesty (Lennon-McCartney)   0:23
Recorded: 2 July 1969, EMI Studios, Abbey Road, London
John Lennon: Not Present
Paul McCartney: Acoustic Guitar and Solo Vocal   **George Harrison:** Not Present
Ringo Starr: Not Present
With a certain tongue-in-cheek irony, this three-take recording could be regarded as a re-written version of the British National Anthem with Paul on solo vocal and acoustic guitar. It is the last track on the last Beatles album.

HEY JUDE

UK Release: 21 May 1979
US Release: 26 February 1970
Intl CD No: None
Running Time: 32:59

Parlophone PCS 7184
Apple SW 385
Producer: George Martin

SIDE ONE: Can't Buy Me Love; I Should Have Known Better; Paperback Writer; Rain, Lady Madonna; Revolution.

SIDE TWO: Hey Jude; Old Brown Shoe; Don't Let Me Down; The Ballad Of John And Yoko.

Previously available only on import from the USA, this album eventually was released in Britain in May 1979 nearly nine years after its first appearance in the US. The album includes most of The Beatles' later singles released in 1968 and 1969 together with both sides of the 1966 single 'Paperback Writer'. Two rather odd and out of sequence inclusions are 'Can't Buy Me Love' and 'I Should Have Known Better' both from the *A Hard Day's Night* album that were included in place of 'The Inner Light' and 'Get Back' even though their respective A and B sides, 'Lady Madonna' and 'Don't Let Me Down', are included.

SIDE ONE
Can't Buy Me Love (Lennon-McCartney)   2:15
John Lennon: Rhythm Guitar
George Harrison: Lead Guitar

Paul McCartney: Bass Guitar and Solo Vocal
Ringo Starr: Drums

Previously included on the album *A Hard Day's Night*.

I Should Have Known Better (Lennon-McCartney)   2:42
John Lennon: Acoustic Guitar, Harmonica and Solo Vocal
Paul McCartney: Bass Guitar
Ringo Starr: Drums

George Harrison: Lead. Guitar

Previously included on the album *A Hard Day's Night*.

147

Paperback Writer (Lennon-McCartney) 2:25
Recorded: 13 and 14 April 1966, EMI Studios, Abbey Road, London
John Lennon: Rhythm Guitar and Backing Vocal   **Paul McCartney:** Bass Guitar and Lead Vocal
George Harrison: Lead Guitar and Backing Vocal   **Ringo Starr:** Drums

This track was recorded in two takes with one overdub during the sessions for *Revolver*, and was issued as a single on 10 June 1966, about two months prior to the release of that album. The song, written mainly by Paul, with John contributing some of the lyrics, was inspired by John Lennon's two books *In His Own Write* and *Spaniard In The Works*, and tells of Paul's wish to become a writer too. It begins with an a cappella, introduction, followed by one of the best instrumental backings on any Beatles record. The guitar sound on this record could be regarded as a foretaste of heavy metal. The lead vocal comes from Paul, who also joins John and George for the three-part harmony backing vocals, that are a combination of the title, together with a section of the French song *Frère Jacques*.

Rain (Lennon-McCartney) 2:59
Recorded: 14 and 16 April, 1966, EMI Studios, Abbey Road, London
John Lennon: Rhythm Guitar and Lead Vocal
Paul McCartney: Bass Guitar and Backing Vocal
George Harrison: Lead Guitar and Backing Vocal   **Ringo Starr:** Drums and Tambourine

Previously issued as the B side to 'Paperback Writer', this track features a stronger heavy guitar sound than the A side, making the latter sound rather tame by comparison. The sound was to influence artists such as The Who, Cream and Jimi Hendrix. The guitars attack from the beginning; Ringo's superb drumbeat accentuates the heaviness of the sound and John's laconic sententious lead vocal grinds out of the left-hand channel. At the end of this recording one line of John's vocal is played backwards: 'Rain, when the rain comes they run and hide their heads'. Note the substitution of 'When' for 'if', that is used in the main recording. Apparently, John took a copy of the master tape home and accidentally played it backwards, liked it, and included it on the final record. After this experiment, backwards-playing tapes were also included on 'I'm Only Sleeping' and 'Tomorrow Never Knows' on the *Revolver* album among others. The instrumental track that was played fast, was recorded on 14 April 1966 and then remixed with the tape running on slow/van-speed. The vocal track was added two days later on 16 April 1966 and, after eight takes, the seventh was chosen for the released stereo version.

Lady Madonna (Lennon-McCartney)   2:17
Recorded: 3 and 6 February 1968, EMI Studios, Abbey Road, London
John Lennon: Rhythm Guitar and Backing Vocal
Paul McCartney: Bass Guitar, Piano and Lead Vocal
George Harrison: Lead Guitar and Backing Vocal
Ringo Starr: Drums and Backing Vocal   **Ronnie Scott:** Tenor Saxophone
Harry Klein: Baritone Saxophone   **Bill Povey:** Tenor Saxophone
Bill Jackman: Baritone Saxophone

This was the last single issued by The Beatles on the Parlophone label in 1968 before the dream of Apple became a reality later that year. It was written and sung by Paul, who also plays piano in true rock'n'roll style, showing the influence of Little Richard and Jerry Lee Lewis. The song is rather like a rock version of his earlier 'Eleanor Rigby' song with loneliness again as the main theme. It was recorded in five takes on 3 February 1968 and completed with the saxophone backing played by Ronnie Scot, Harry Klein, Bill Povey and Bill Jackman three days later. According to various reports the saxophone segment in the middle was originally 15 to 20 seconds longer but was edited. The vocal backing, by all four Beatles, was reputed to have been achieved by them singing with their hands cupped around their mouths.

Revolution (Lennon-McCartney)   3:22
Recorded: 10-12 July 1968, EMI Studios, Abbey Road, London
John Lennon: Lead Guitar and Solo Vocal   **Paul McCartney:** Bass Guitar
George Harrison: Lead Guitar   **Ringo Starr:** Drums
Nicky Hopkins: Electric Piano

Previously issued as the B side to 'Hey Jude' The Beatles' first Apple single on 30 August 1968, this Lennon-written anti-war song written by John in India was recorded in 16 takes between 10 and 12 July 1968 and features session man Nicky Hopkins on piano. The sound of a distorted guitar, played by John, is heard at the beginning of the record to which Ringo adds an electronically compressed drumbeat to give the recording a solid heavy sound. John's lead vocals were recorded several times and rejected because he was dissatisfied with the result and eventually completed after he had lain on his back on the floor of the studio and sung them once more, finally achieving the sound he wanted.

SIDE TWO

Hey Jude (Lennon-McCartney) 7:11

Recorded: 31 July and 1 August 1968, Trident Studios, Wardour Street, London

John Lennon: Acoustic Guitar and Backing Vocal **Paul McCartney:** Piano and Lead Vocal

George Harrison: Lead Guitar and Backing Vocal **Ringo Starr:** Drums

Session Musicians: 36-Piece Orchestra

This was the A side of the first single issued by The Beatles on their own Apple label, on 30 August 1968. It was the longest single issued to that date, totalling with 'Revolution', its B side, 10 minutes 33 seconds. Written by Paul, the song had started out as Hey Jules, about John's son Julian. The Beatles first attempted to record this at Abbey Road on 29 July 1968 but moved to Trident Studios in Soho where they recorded the song in four takes on 31 July before selecting take 1 for further overdubbing on 1 August. Paul sings lead vocal and accompanies himself on piano with backing vocals from John and George. The song starts simply, the main part lasting 3 minutes 11 seconds, but builds up until it finally explodes into a four-minute fade-out, the longest on a Beatles record. The fade consists of all four Beatles plus a 36-piece orchestra rather than the 100-piece ensemble Paul had originally envisaged playing and singing along to a one-line chorus of 'na, na-na-na-na-na, na'.

Old Brown Shoe (Harrison) 3:16

Recorded: 16 and 18 April 1969, EMI Studios, Abbey Road, London

John Lennon: Rhythm Guitar

Paul McCartney: Bass Guitar, Piano and Backing Vocal

George Harrison: Lead Guitar, Hammond Organ and Lead Vocal

Ringo Starr: Drums

Originally issued as the B-side to the 1969 single 'The Ballad Of John And Yoko', this was the second George Harrison song used as the B side of a Beatles single. The first was The Inner Light on the B side of 'Lady Madonna' in 1968. It was recorded in four takes on 16 and 18 April 1969, a few days after the completion of 'The Ballad Of John And Yoko'. This, unlike the A side, features all four Beatles and is quite an up-tempo song from George, who during the previous two years had been writing either Indian mantras or slower, more doleful songs like 'While My Guitar Gently Weeps' and 'Blue Jay Way'.

Don't Let Me Down (Lennon-McCartney)   3:34
Recorded: 28 January 1969, Apple Studios, Savile Row, London
John Lennon: Lead Guitar and Lead Vocal
Paul McCartney: Bass Guitar and Harmony Vocal   **George Harrison:** Rhythm Guitar
Ringo Starr: Drums   **Billy Preston:** Organ
Previously issued as the B side to the 'Get Back' single on 11 April 1969, this recording, made within minutes of 'Get Back' on 28 January 1969, features an extremely raw lead vocal from John, with harmony vocals from Paul. The Beatles are once again joined by Billy Preston who adds to the backing and also has a solo in the middle. The lyrics to this powerful blues-influenced song, written by John with Yoko in mind, are minimal with John simply repeating the title over and over.

The Ballad Of John And Yoko (Lennon-McCartney)   2:58
Recorded: 14 April 1969, EMI Studios, Abbey Road, London
John Lennon: Acoustic Guitar, Lead Guitar, Percussion and Lead Vocal
Paul McCartney: Bass Guitar, Drums, Piano, Maracas and Harmony Vocal
George Harrison: Not Present   **Ringo Starr:** Not Present
This was released as a single on 20 May 1969 while 'Get Back' was still at No. 1. It was recorded in 11 takes. Take ten being the released version on 14 April 1969 three days after the release of 'Get Back'. The track was recorded at Abbey Road during an eight-and-a-half-hour session at which John and Paul played all the instruments. John is on lead vocal, acoustic and lead guitars and percussion, and Paul plays bass guitar, drums, piano and maracas and supplies a harmony vocal in places. The song tells the story of John and Yoko's wedding in Gibraltar the previous month and of their subsequent week-long bed-in for peace at the Amsterdam Hilton.

LET IT BE

UK Release: 8 May 1970; 6 November 1970
US Release: 18 May 1970
Intl CD No: CDP 7 46447 2
Running Time: 35:07

Apple PXS 1: PCS 7096
Apple AR 34001
Producers: George Martin and Phil Spector

SIDE ONE: Two Of Us; Dig A Pony; Across The Universe; I Me Mine; Let It Be; Maggie Mae.

SIDE TWO: I've Got A Feeling; One After 909; The Long And Winding Road; For You Blue; Get Back.

It is interesting to note that *Abbey Road* was recorded after this album. Originally *Let It Be* was called *Get Back* and was intended as the soundtrack for a television film of the same name. It was to have been the official follow-up to the double album, *The Beatles*.

The idea came from John, who wanted to record an album that was not necessarily reliant on technical tricks, overdubs or electronic wizardry. What he wanted was an album of up-to-date but basic Beatle music without studio effects. Paul suggested that they make a film showing The Beatles in the studio recording the album and so recording and filming began on 2 January 1969 and finished on 30 January 1969 with the now famous concert on the roof of the Apple Office in London's Savile Row.

The album and film were not released until a year later, they were delayed by Allen Klein, The Beatles' financial adviser. When released, the title was changed to *Let It Be*.

Klein had been called in by John against Paul's wishes to manage The Beatles' affairs, but initially proved valuable when he re-negotiated the contract with EMI to give The Beatles a higher royalty payment from their records. Now, with his eye on a better commercial proposition, he suggested that the proposed television film made in 16mm should be blown up to 35mm and marketed as a new Beatles cinema film.

As this would take time, and as the 'Get Back' single had already been released in April 1969, Klein suggested that film and album be re-scheduled and retitled 'Let It Be' and that a single of the same name be issued to promote both.

The *Get Back* album, that got as far as being pressed and sent to radio stations in the USA and Canada, was never released to record stores because Klein felt that it could be improved. Originally it

LET IT BE

consisted of: 'One After 909', 'Rocker', 'Save The Last Dance For Me', 'Don't Let Me Down', 'Dig A Pony', 'I've Got A Feeling', 'Get Back', 'For You Blue', 'Teddy Boy', 'Two Of Us', 'Maggie Mae', 'Dig It', 'Let It Be', 'The Long And Winding Road', and 'Get Back' (reprise).

Klein also wanted the live recordings of 'Get Back' and 'Don't Let Me Down' scrapped and replaced with studio recordings although the first made it through to the *Let It Be* album.

Because of the delay between recording and release of the final album, The Beatles lost interest in improving the original album, so John invited Phil Spector, who had worked with him on *Instant Karma*, and who was to work with both John and George later, to produce the album as *Let It Be*. Spector sifted through 24 hours of recorded material in which there were many different versions of each song. Eventually he salvaged the album, remixed it, and overdubbed strings on 'Let It Be', 'Across The Universe' and 'I Me Mine', and strings and a heavenly choir on 'The Long And Winding Road' to the apparent dissatisfaction of Paul McCartney who had envisioned the recording with only himself on vocals and piano, and John on bass guitar.

This was the first album since The Beatles signed with EMI for which George Martin did not have complete responsibility. Although he had produced the original recordings, the final production was left to Spector whose syrupy technique did little to hide The Beatles' sloppy playing. One wonders if he really did choose the best possible versions of each track becauses the inevitable bootlegs, such as Sweet Apple Tracks, include far better alternatives.

The album was packaged as a boxed set complete with book, exactly as had been planned for *Get Back*. It was also given the catalogue number held for the original *Get Back* album package (PXS 1). It went on sale in Britain on 8 May 1970 at £1 more than other albums, and sold poorly. After six months the album was re-issued on 6 November 1970 without the book (as PCS 7096), but because of the time lag it did not sell well although it picked up sales at Christmas.

From 96 hours of recorded film, *Let It Be* finally emerged as a 90-minute semi-documentary, about the recording of the *Get Back* album. The film is as embarrassing to watch as the album is to listen to. It shows four rather unhappy-looking individuals involved in petty squabbles. After one scene, where Paul and George are seen arguing over a guitar riff, George left for three days and filming had to be halted until he returned. It is a sad spectacle, showing the public break-up of one of the world's greatest pop groups. One can only hope that one day sufficient will be salvaged from the remaining $94\frac{1}{2}$ hours of footage to make a second movie. Certainly The Beatles were captured on film performing many rock'n'roll standards and reworkings of a number of their old songs. The most exciting surviving part of the film, shown at the end of the movie, is the impromptu concert on the roof of the Apple office in London's Savile Row. This shows the stunned and excited reaction of lunchtime shoppers and office workers in the area to the unbelievable noise of a Beatles concert drifting down from the roof to the streets below. The Beatles manage to perform five songs 'I Dig A Pony', 'I've Got A Feeling', 'One After 909', 'Don't Let Me Down' and 'Get Back' before the arrival of the police to stop the concert.

An interesting postscript is that *Get Back* was not the only album to be planned from the material that never reached the shops. There were two more that, although taken to the final stages, were never given working titles. The second was to have been re-recordings of old Beatles tracks. 'Love Me Do', 'Norwegian Wood' and 'She Said, She Said' were announced as prospective tracks. The third album was to have consisted of 14 old rock'n'roll standards without any Beatles-written songs. Tracks recorded for this included 'Shake Rattle and Roll', 'Lawdy Miss Clawdy', 'Blue Suede Shoes' and 'Tracks Of My Tears'.

It is also interesting to document the events that followed *Let It Be*. After the recording sessions for *Abbey Road* finished in August 1969, Paul and Ringo began work on their first solo albums. John and George had already done so. Ringo's first solo album, *Sentimental Journey,* a run-through of 12 standards, was issued on 27 March 1970 and Paul McCartney's album, *McCartney*, a selection of left-over Beatles songs and instrumentals, was issued on 17 April 1970, a few weeks prior to the release of the *Let It Be* album. John, George and Ringo were not pleased that Paul was about to issue a solo album in competition with a Beatles album. He could not be persuaded otherwise even though Ringo was sent by John to try to change his mind. On 10 April 1970, exactly one week prior to the release of the McCartney album, Paul announced that he was leaving The Beatles, a statement that shook and saddened all Beatles fans. Many also thought that Paul's statement was a little too well timed to tie in with the release of his first solo album.

After Paul left the group John, George and Ringo considered recruiting bass player Klaus Voormann and forming The Ladders. This line-up did get together once in 1973 with Billy Preston when they recorded the track 'I'm The Greatest' for Ringo's solo album *Ringo* (Apple PCTC 252).

SIDE ONE
Two Of Us (Lennon-McCartney) 3:33
John Lennon: Acoustic Guitar and Lead Vocal
Paul McCartney: Acoustic Guitar and Lead Vocal   **George Harrison**: Lead Guitar
Ringo Starr: Drums

Just before this track begins a snatch of studio conversation is included and John proclaims 'I dig a pygmy by Charles Hawtrey and the Deaf Aids – Phase one, in which Doris gets her oats.' 'Two Of Us' was written by Paul as a duet for himself and John, possibly as a reaction to the arrival of Yoko Ono who was claiming all of John's attention. When the song was originally recorded it was called 'On Our Way Home'. After the *Get Back* album was scrapped Paul gave the song to one of Apple's latest signings, a New York trio called Mortimer, who recorded the song under its original title in May 1969. The recording, produced by Paul, never appeared and nothing has been heard of Mortimer since.

The track is a close harmony duet between John and Paul who also play acoustic guitars with Paul soloing in places. George adds lead guitar with Ringo on drums and revives memories of the three-guitars-and-drums sound of the early 60s. The song is featured twice in the film *Let It Be;* first, in rehearsal, slightly up-tempo when John and Paul ad-lib the lyrics, and secondly when they play the complete song that is the version issued on this album.

Dig A Pony (Lennon-McCartney) 3:55
John Lennon: Lead Guitar and Lead Vocal
Paul McCartney: Bass Guitar and Harmony Vocal
George Harrison: Rhythm Guitar   **Ringo Starr**: Drums
Billy Preston: Organ

The first of the four live recordings taken from the 30 January 1969 rooftop concert included on the album, this was written by John as two separate songs, 'All I Want Is You' and 'Dig A Pony'. When the track listing for the *Get Back* album was announced, this track was called 'All I Want Is You', but when the album was compiled the title was changed to 'Dig A Pony'. It has a false start then a lead vocal from John with harmonies from Paul. The lyrics sound as if they could have been made up on the spot. John makes references to the Rolling Stones and Johnny and The Moondogs – one of The Beatles' earlier names. At the end of the recording John can be heard complaining that his hands are cold. The recording sounds rough both in instrumentation and in the falsetto harmonies from John and Paul.

It should be noted that the album's American sleeve lists this track as 'I Dig A Pony'.

Across The Universe (Lennon-McCartney) 3:51
John Lennon: Acoustic Guitar, Lead Guitar and Lead Vocal
Paul McCartney: Piano   **George Harrison:** Tamboura and Maracas
Ringo Starr: Drums and Tomtoms
Session Musicians: (Overdubbed) 35-Piece Orchestra and 14-Piece Choir
The original recording of this song that appeared on the charity album *No One's Gonna Change Our World* (Regal Starline SRS 5018) and that now appears on *Past Masters – Volume Two* (Parlophone BPM 2), is a far superior version. Unfortunately Phil Spector's heavenly choir and slushy orchestra, overdubbed on to this version in April 1970, have destroyed the original simplicity of the song. This recording is slightly slower than the original, as if it has been deliberately slowed down from its recorded speed, and unfortunately this gives John's voice a whining quality. The original recording featured backing vocals from Paul and George and two female singers (see Past Masters – Volume Two); these are not included on this version.

I Me Mine (Harrison) 2:25
John Lennon: Not Present
Paul McCartney: Bass Guitar, Electric Piano and Backing Vocal
George Harrison: Acoustic Guitar, Lead Guitar, Organ and Lead/Backing Vocal
Ringo Starr: Drums
Session Musicians: (Overdubbed) 35-Piece Orchestra
Recorded on 3 January 1970 at the first of two final recording sessions by The Beatles. Although John Lennon was absent this was the last song ever recorded by them. Bearing a distinct resemblance to Harrison's earlier 'Savoy Truffle' on *The White Album*, it opens with a dramatic organ from George who also plays acoustic guitar, Paul on electric piano and Ringo on drums. The vocals are mainly a solo from George but are supplemented by backing from Paul on the chorus. This track, like the preceding 'Across The Universe', also has an overdubbed 35-piece orchestra, but thankfully Phil Spector has not mixed them too far forward.

Dig It (Lennon-McCartney-Starkey-Harrison) 0:51

John Lennon: Bass Guitar and Solo Vocal   **Paul McCartney:** Piano
George Harrison: Lead Guitar   **Ringo Starr:** Drums
Billy Preston: Organ

The original recording of this track lasts for nearly 12 and a half minutes but only a mere 51 seconds is included here, although an extract lasting nearly four minutes was included on the *Get Back* album. This short extract fades in with John singing odd, unconnected lines held together with the insistent chorus of 'dig it'. As the track fades John announces 'That was "Can you dig it" by Georgie Wood, now we'd like to do Ark The Angels Come" '; 'Let It Be' then begins.

Let It Be (Lennon-McCartney) 4:01

John Lennon: Bass Guitar
Paul McCartney: Piano, Maracas and Lead/Harmony Vocal
George Harrison: Lead Guitar and Harmony Vocal   **Ringo Starr:** Drums
Billy Preston: Organ   **Session Musicians:** Brass and Cellos

Sounding rather like a choirboy singing a hymn at a requiem mass, Paul leads The Beatles through this song, that originally was recorded on 31 January 1969 during the ill-fated *Get Back* sessions.

This and the version released as a single on 6 March 1970 (Apple R5833) are, in effect, the same basic recording. They both originate from the same eight-track master tape that contains two lead-guitar tracks one of which was an overdub. When Phil Spector was asked to produce an album from the *Get Back* tapes he used the original recording of this – together with the sloppy lead guitar – and remixed the track entirely. In doing so he ruined the original arrangement and his mixing is disastrous. Near the end Paul's vocal battles with George's lead guitar that has been mixed too far forward.

Maggie Mae (Trad. Arr. Lennon-McCartney-Harrison-Starkey) 0:39

John Lennon: Acoustic Guitar and Lead Vocal
Paul McCartney: Acoustic Guitar and Harmony Vocal
George Harrison: Bass Guitar and Harmony Vocal   **Ringo Starr:** Drums

Here, The Beatles interpret a traditional old Liverpool song. John is on lead vocal with Paul and George harmonising. John and Paul play acoustic guitars and Ringo, drums. The Beatles quite often did short renditions of songs like this to warm up their recording sessions. This is one of only a few such tracks to be released (see *The Unreleased Tracks*).

SIDE TWO

I've Got A Feeling (Lennon-McCartney) 3:38

John Lennon: Lead Guitar and Lead Vocal   **Paul McCartney:** Bass Guitar and Lead Vocal
George Harrison: Rhythm Guitar   **Ringo Starr:** Drums
Billy Preston: Organ

The second live recording on the album taken from the rooftop concert on 30 January 1969 sounds as rough as the previous live track, 'Dig A Pony', on side one. George's heavily distorted rhythm guitar provides the intro. The verses are split between John and Paul with Paul on lead vocal for the first two. John leads on the second two and finally there is an interesting interchange between stereo channels, with Paul on the left, repeating the first two verses, and John on the right-hand channel, repeating the third and fourth verses.

One After 909 (Lennon-McCartney) 2:52

John Lennon: Lead Guitar and Lead Vocal   **Paul McCartney:** Bass Guitar and Lead Vocal
George Harrison: Rhythm Guitar   **Ringo Starr:** Drums
Billy Preston: Organ

This is one of John's earliest songs that he revived especially for the *Get Back* project. Again this is a rough-sounding recording, also taken from the rooftop concert. The vocals are a duet between John and Paul with John singing solo for one verse.

   At the end of the track John goes into an off-the-cuff rendition of 'Danny Boy', not credited on either record label or sleeve.

The Long And Winding Road (Lennon-McCartney) 3:40

John Lennon: Bass Guitar   **Paul McCartney:** Piano and Solo Vocal
George Harrison: Lead Guitar   **Ringo Starr:** Drums
Session Musicians: (Overdubbed) 35-Piece Orchestra and 14-Piece Choir

Paul McCartney's ballad is overlaid with Spector's choirs and orchestras. Originally, Paul backed himself on piano while John, George and Ringo supplied a gentle accompaniment.

For You Blue (Harrison)   2:33

John Lennon: Steel Guitar

Paul McCartney: Bass Guitar and Piano

George Harrison: Acoustic Guitar and Solo Vocal

Ringo Starr: Drums

Prior to this track another snatch of studio chat can be heard from John: 'The Queen says no to pot-smoking FBI members.' Musically this is quite good, but at the same time it still seems like a rehearsal recording. It features a lead vocal from George, who also plays acoustic guitar, with John on a steel guitar, Paul on bass and Ringo on drums. Although The Beatles' music changed between 1962 and 1970 the return to a basic four-instrument sound is quite evident on this recording. Curiously, although this track is called 'For You Blue', the title is not mentioned anywhere in the lyrics.

Get Back (Lennon-McCartney)   3:09

John Lennon: Lead Guitar and Harmony Vocal

Paul McCartney: Bass Guitar and Lead Vocal

George Harrison: Rhythm Guitar

Ringo Starr: Drums

Billy Preston: Organ

The recording starts with Paul saying 'Rosetta, Oh Rosetta' that prompts John to launch into 'Sweet Rosetta Fart, she thought she was a cleaner, but she was a frying pan'. Although this is a live recording, the quality is comparable with the studio version that was issued as a single instead of this one as planned. The track features a lead vocal from Paul, who wrote the song, with harmonies in places from John. This recording omits the final verse of the song that is included on the studio version. The track ends with John saying poignantly 'I'd like to say "thank you" on behalf of the group and ourselves. I hope we've passed the audition.'

THE BEATLES 1962-1966 (2 LPs)

UK Release: 20 April 1973
US Release: 2 April 1973
Intl CD No: To be released
Running Time: 61:26

Apple PCSP 717
Apple SKBO 3403
Producer: George Martin

Side One
Please Please Me   2:00
She Loves You   2:18
All My Loving   2:04

Love Me Do   2:1
From Me To You   1:55
I Want To Hold Your Hand   2:24
Can't Buy Me Love   2:15

Side Two
A Hard Day's Night   2:32
Eight Days A Week   2:43
Ticket To Ride   3:03

And I Love Her   2:27
I Feel Fine   2:19
Yesterday   2:04

Side Three
James Bond Theme (Norman) 0:16*
You've Got To Hide Your Love Away   2:08
Day Tripper   2:37
Norwegian Wood (This Bird Has Flown)   2:00

Help!   2:16
We Can Work It Out   2:10
Drive My Car   2:25

Side Four
Nowhere Man   2:40
In My Life   2:23
Paperback Writer   2:25
Yellow Submarine   2:40

Michelle   2:42
Girl   2:26
Eleanor Rigby   2:11

The George Martin Orchestra (U.S. copies only)   All Lennon-McCartney songs except where stated.

The Beatles / 1962-1966

THE BEATLES 1967-1970 (2 LPs)

UK Release: 20 April 1973
US Release: 2 April 1973
Intl CD No: To be released
Running Time: 98:51

Apple PCSP 718
Apple SK.BO 3404
Producers: George Martin and Phil Spector

Side One

Strawberry Fields Forever   4:05
Sgt. Pepper's Lonely Hearts Club Band   1:59
Lucy In The Sky With Diamonds   3:25
All You Need Is Love   3:57

Penny Lane   3:00
With A Little Help From My Friends   2:46
A Day In The Life   5:03

Side Two

I Am The Walrus   4:35
The Fool On The Hill   3:00
Lady Madonna   2:17
Revolution   3:22

Hello Goodbye   3:24
Magical Mystery Tour   2:48
Hey Jude   7:11

Side Three

Back In The U.S.S.R.   2:45
Ob-La-Di, Ob-La-Da   3:10
Don't Let Me Down   3:34
Old Brown Shoe (Harrison)   3:16

While My Guitar Gently Weeps (Harrison)   4:46
Get Back   3:11
The Ballad of John And Yoko   2:58

Side Four

Here Comes The Sun (Harrison)   3:04
Something (Harrison)   2:59
Let It Be   3:50
The Long And Winding Road   3:40**

Come Together   4:16
Octopus's Garden (Starkey)   2:49
Across The Universe   3:51* *

Produced by George Martin/Phil Spector; all others produced by George Martin.
All Lennon-McCartney songs except where stated.

164

The Beatles / 1967-1970

Although it was three years after the *Let It Be* album of May 1970 before the next Beatles album was released, it was worth waiting for. It was not one album but four, compiling The Beatles' greatest hits, selected by themselves. Although its release was planned to combat the ever-growing numbers of bootleg compilations it is excellent, nonetheless. The four albums, as the titles suggest, trace The Beatles' recording history from the first single 'Love Me Do' in 1962 to 1970 and 'Let It Be'. All The Beatles' No. 1 hit songs are included, plus all the A sides of the singles and a fair selection of tracks from almost every LP released. Every one of the 54 tracks is Beatle-written, either by Lennon and McCartney, George Harrison or Ringo Starr. In a way, it is sad that one or two of the 24 non-Beatle-written tracks were not included, but as they wrote so many highly commercial songs, there just wasn't room for any songs they didn't write. Similarly, although The Beatles' solo material was also considered, there was not sufficient space.

The first double album, *The Beatles 1962-1966*, contains all the A sides of The Beatles' singles issued on Parlophone up to the end of 1966, plus a selection of album tracks from the same period, namely, 'All My Loving' from *With The Beatles*, 'Eight Days A Week' from *Beatles For Sale*, 'Yesterday' from *Help!* and 'Norwegian Wood' and 'Michelle' from *Rubber Soul*. These two albums consist solely of Lennon-McCartney songs.

The second double album, *The Beatles 1967-1970*, compiles the remaining A sides of singles, plus a further selection of album tracks issued during that period. Of the 28 tracks, three 'While My Guitar Gently Weeps', 'Old Brown Shoe' and 'Something' are written by George Harrison. 'Octopus's Garden' is written by Ringo and the remaining 24 tracks are written by Lennon and McCartney.

The sleeves of these two double albums show two photographs, of The Beatles in the same pose taken eight years apart. The first is that used in 1963 for the *Please Please Me* album; the second, taken in 1969, had been planned for the unreleased *Get Back* album. It was good that this was not scrapped as the two make an effective pair. They differ in their coloured borders, the first is red, the second blue, reputedly picked by The Beatles for their Liverpool fans to show the colours of Liverpool's two football clubs, Liverpool and Everton. In the late 1970s when coloured vinyl records became popular, these two double albums were re-issued on coloured vinyl, the first on red, the second on blue. To date, these are the only Beatles albums available in Britain on coloured vinyl, although other albums are available elsewhere in the world in varying colours. Because of this they have the additional letters R and B for Red and Blue in their catalogue number prefixes. They make interesting but expensive additions if the black vinyl copies have already been acquired.

ROCK AND ROLL MUSIC (2 LPs)

UK Release: 11 June 1976
US Release: 7 June 1976
Intl CD No: None
Running Time: 72:44

Parlophone PCSP 719
Capitol SKBO 11537
Producers: George Martin and Phil Spector

SIDE ONE: Twist And Shout; I Saw Her Standing There; You Can't Do That; I Wanna Be Your Man; I Call Your Name; Boys; Long Tall Sally.
SIDE TWO: Rock And Roll Music; Slow Down; Kansas City/Hey Hey Hey Hey; Money; Bad Boy; Matchbox; Roll Over Beethoven.

SIDE THREE: Dizzy Miss Lizzy; Any Time At All; Drive My Car; Everybody's Trying To Be My Baby; The Night Before; I'm Down; Revolution.
SIDE FOUR: Back In The U.S.S.R.; Helter Sketler; Taxman; Got To Get You Into My Life; Hey Bulldog; Birthday; Get Back.

After the release of the four-album set, but prior to the release of this album, The Beatles' contract expired and in 1976 EMI decided to re-issue every Beatles single at the same time! This caused chaos in the British record charts. No less than six reached the top 40: 'Help' (37), 'Strawberry Fields Forever' (32), 'Paperback Writer' (23), 'Hey Jude' (12), 'Get Back' (28) and a specially issued single of 'Yesterday' (8). As could be expected, other record companies were irate because it was spoiling the chances of newer artists.

Decca Records, the Rolling Stones record company throughout the 60s, replied by re-promoting Rolling Stones singles with advertisements stating 'The Rolling Stones singles are, and always have been available: none has ever been deleted'. Although this seemed like a Battle of the Giants created by the two record companies of the 60s, none of the Rolling Stones' singles was to make it into the top 40 in 1976 although their new single 'Fool To Cry' (RS 19131) issued on their own label, reached No. 6 on 1 May 1976.

It seemed hopeful that after the re-release of the old Beatles singles some of the unreleased tracks would then be issued. Instead, the idea for this album, *Rock and Roll Music*, came from Bhaskar Menon, the head of Capitol Records in the U.S.A. After trying unsuccessfully to contact one or all of The Beatles for approval of the track listing for this new double album, Menon eventually

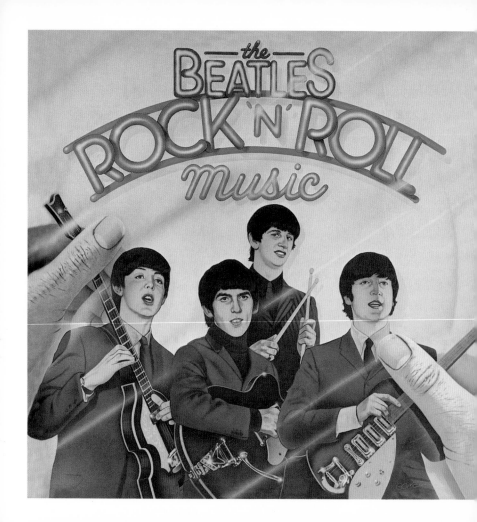

gave up and contacted George Martin, their producer. When Martin was told of the plan to release this compilation of old Beatles tracks as a new album he flew to the Hollywood offices of Capitol.

After hearing some of the older tracks with bad background noise and poor stereo Martin was appalled at the prospect of their reissue and set about filtering and remixing every track included on this album. On some of the older tracks, such as 'Twist and Shout' and 'I Saw Her Standing There', he reversed the stereo and brought the vocal track away from the edge into the centre, adding a slight echo for a more modern sound. He also filtered out the bass from the rhythm track and also placed that in the centre of the stereo sound stage and with the aid of filters and equalisers, gave the recordings a crisper sound.

When he had finished his work, Martin took a copy of the revised tapes back to EMI Records in Britain. The company was horrified because The Beatles had issued official instructions that the tapes must not be 'touched, added to, edited or mutilated in any way'. EMI Records took this edict rather too literally, assuming. that if they were to be re-issued, the tapes should be exactly as originally recorded. Thus George Martin's remixed and filtered versions of the original tracks were not included on the *Rock and Roll Music* album when it was released in Britain.

However, In 1980, EMI Records relented and decided to issue the remixed recordings. They split the two albums, put them into new sleeves after receiving numerous complaints about the original sleeves and issued them on the Music For Pleasure label as *Rock and Roll Music, Volumes 1 and 2* (MFP 50506 and 50507). These two albums are worth buying if only to compare the original recordings with the remixes.

The following track listing, complete with timings, applies to both the original double album *and* the two remixed Music For Pleasure albums *Rock and Roll Music Volumes 1 and 2* (MFP50506 and 50507) issued in 1980.

Side One

Twist And Shout (Medley-Russell) 2:32
I Saw Her Standing There 2:50
You Can't Do That 2:33
I Wanna Be Your Man 1:59
I Call Your Name 2:02
Boys (Goffin-King) 2:24
Long Tall Sally (Johnson-Penniman-Blackwell) 1:58

Side Two

Rock and Roll Music (Berry) 2:02
Slow Down (Williams) 2:54
Kansas City (Leiber-Stoller)/Hey
Hey Hey Hey (Penniman) 2:30
Money (Bradford-Gordy) 2:47
Bad Boy (Williams) 2:17
Matchbox (Perkins) 1:37
Roll Over Beethoven (Berry) 2:44

Side Three

Dizzy Miss Lizzy (Williams) 2:51
Any Time At All 2:10
Drive My Car 2:25
Everybody's Trying To Be My Baby (Perkins) 2:24
The Night Before 2:33
I'm Down 2:30
Revolution 3:22

Side Four

Back In the U.S.S.R. 2:45
Helter Skelter 4:30
Taxman (Harrison) 2:36
Got To Get You Into My Life 2:31
Hey Bulldog 3:09
Birthday 2:40
Get Back 3:09*

Produced by George Martin and Phil Spector; all others produced by George Martin.
All Lennon-McCartney songs except where stated.

THE BEATLES AT
THE HOLLYWOOD BOWL

UK Release: 6 May 1977
US Release: 2 May 1977
Intl CD No: To be released
Producers: Voyle Gilmore and George Martin

Parlophone EMTV 4
Capitol SMAS 11638

Running Time: 33:50

SIDE ONE: Twist And Shout; She's A Woman; Dizzy Miss Lizzy; Ticket To Ride; Can't Buy Me Love; Things We Said Today; Roll Over Beethoven.

SIDE TWO: Boys; A Hard Day's Night; Help!; All My Loving; She Loves You; Long Tall Sally.

The release of a live album by The Beatles recorded at the Hollywood Bowl had been announced in the music press at various times during the 1970s. In 1972 it was announced that a recording would be released to combat the increasing number of bootleg albums appearing on the market. Eighteen months later the release of an album was announced again. Details were given that the album would be a live recording of the Hollywood Bowl concert on 23 August 1964, with the following tracks:

Side One: Twist And Shout; You Can't Do That; All My Loving; She Loves You; Things We Said Today; Roll Over Beethoven.

Side Two: Can't Buy Me Love; If I Fell; I Want To Hold Your Hand; Boys; A Hard Day's Night; Long Tall Sally.

However, once again the album did not appear.

In 1977 the release of a live album by The Beatles was announced yet again. This time it was to include some of the recordings from the 1964 concert with some from a second concert held on 29 August 1965. The album did appear this time and was worth waiting for. The excitement of a Beatles concert is captured perfectly, complete with the sound of 17,000 screaming Beatles fans, the only disadvantage being that because of the noise, the album is neither technically nor musically perfect. Of the 13 tracks, six 'All My Loving', 'She Loves You', 'Things We Said Today', 'Roll Over Beethoven', 'Boys' and 'Long Tall Sally' are from the 1964 concert. The remaining seven 'Twist and

Shout', 'She's A Woman', 'Dizzy Miss Lizzy', 'Ticket To Ride', 'Can't Buy Me Love', 'A Hard Day's Night', and 'Help!' are from the 1965 concert. They have been edited together successfully by George Martin to make a highly enjoyable live album.

Because the original recordings were made on old-fashioned three-track machines, it was necessary to transfer them onto 16-track tape before George Martin and Geoff Emerick, his studio engineer, could filter, equalise and edit them. The major problem was that with continual use the tape heads of these old machines overheated and melted the magnetic tape. The resourceful Martin hit on the idea of using hair dryers blowing cold air to cool down the tape heads.

As a postscript, it is interesting to note that the biggest concert ever given by The Beatles was neither of these Hollywood Bowl concerts but one given two weeks previously at New York's Shea Stadium on 15 August 1965 before 65,000 fans. It was recorded and also filmed. Nine months after the concert, on 1 May 1966, the BBC premiered the film on British television. Unlike the recording of the Hollywood Bowl Concert, the Shea Stadium Concert has never been officially released, although it is available on bootleg albums.

Side One: 17:57
Twist And Shout
  (Medley-Russell) 1:20
She's A Woman 2:45
Dizzy Miss Lizzy (Williams) 3:00
Ticket To Ride 2:18
Can't Buy Me Love 2:08
Things We Said Today 2:07
Roll Over Beethoven (Berry) 2:10

Side Two: 15:53
Boys (Dixon-Farrell) 1:57
A Hard Day's Night 2:30
Help! 2:16
All My Loving 1:55
She Loves You 2:10
Long Tall Sally (Johnson-Penniman-
Blackwell) 1:54

All Lennon-McCartney songs except where stated.

LOVE SONGS (2 LPs)

UK Release: 28 November 1977
US Release: 24 November 1977
Intl CD No: None
Running Time: 59:25

Parlophone PCSP 721
Capitol SKBL 11711
Producers : George Martin and Phil Spector

SIDE ONE: Yesterday; I'll Follow The Sun; I Need You; Girl; In My Life; Words Of Love; Here, There And Everywhere.
SIDE TWO: Something; And I Love Her; If I Fell; I'll Be Back; Tell Me What You See; Yes It Is.

SIDE THREE: Michelle; It's Only Love; You're Going To Lose That Girl; Every Little Thing; For No One; She's Leaving Home.
SIDE FOUR: The Long And Winding Road; This Boy; Norwegian Wood (This Bird Has Flown); You've Got To Hide Your Love Away; I Will; P. S. I Love You.

This album is mainly a compilation of tracks previously available on other Beatles albums. The only two not previously issued on British albums are 'This Boy' and 'Yes It Is' and these are simply mono recordings re-channelled into fake stereo, even though 'This Boy' is available in stereo on a Canadian single.

The album was issued just in time for Christmas 1977, so sales were guaranteed to a certain extent. In addition to taking Christmas buyers for a ride, the record also exploited dedicated fans and collectors who always bought Beatles albums. To add insult to injury there were many other tracks available that would have made a far better compilation album. One good feature of the album package is the inclusion of the 1967 Richard Avedon poster.

Side One

Yesterday 2:04
I'll Follow The Sun 1:46
I Need You (Harrison) 2:28
Girl 2:26
Words Of Love (Holly) 2:10
Here, There And Everywhere 2:29

Side Two

Something (Harrison) 2:59
And I Love Her 2:27
If I Fell 2:16
I'll Be Back 2:22
Tell Me What You See 2:35
Yes It Is 2:40

Side Three

Michelle 2:42
It's Only Love 1:53
You're Going To Lose That Girl 2:18
Every Little Thing 2:01
In My Life 2:23
For No One 2:03
She's Leaving Home 3:24

Side Four

The Long And Winding Road 3:40*
This Boy 2:11
Norwegian Wood (This Bird Has Flown) 2:00
You've Got To Hide Your Love Away 2:08
I Will 1:46
P. S. I Love You 2:02

*Produced by George Martin/Phil Spector. All others produced by George Martin.
All Lennon-McCartney songs except where stated.

THE BEATLES COLLECTION

UK Release: 15 December 1978
US Release: None
Producers: George Martin and Phil Spector

Parlophone/Apple BC 13
Intl CD No: See Individual Albums
Running Time: See Individual Albums

A boxed set containing the following albums; *Please Please Me; With The Beatles; A Hard Day's Night; Beatles For Sale; Help!; Rubber Soul; Revolver; Sgt. Pepper's Lonely Hearts Club Band; The Beatles; Yellow Submarine; Abbey Road; Let It Be; The Beatles Rarities.*

This collection of the main Beatles albums as a boxed set was inevitable. Unfortunately, it is by no means a complete collection of The Beatles' recordings issued by EMI/Parlophone between 1962 and 1970. Rather it is a collection of The Beatles' studio albums issued by EMI in Britain during that period. Curiously, *A Collection of Beatles Oldies* is excluded, although included is a brand new album *The Beatles' Rarities*, a collection of B sides from singles, plus a few tracks not previously available on British Beatles albums.

As usual with a collection of this sort, there are a few gaps. The main omissions are *Magical Mystery Tour, Hey Jude* and *The Beatles At The Hollywood Bowl,* plus a number of other tracks available on *The Beatles 1962-1966* and *The Beatles 1967-1970.*

Overall it is a good collection for either young Beatles fans buying for the first time or older fans who would like to renew their Beatles albums. For the serious collector, who has bought everything issued since 1962, the only thing of interest is the box.

The Beatles Collection comes neatly packaged in a dark blue box with the title and the four Beatles' autographs printed in gold on the front. It consists of the stereo versions of the 12 studio albums, plus *The Beatles Rarities* album.

Please Please Me (PCS 3042)
With The Beatles (PCS 3045)
A Hard Day's Night (PCS 3058)
Beatles For Sale (PCS 3062)
Help! (PCS 3071)
Rubber Soul (PCS 3075)
Revolver (PCS 7009)

Sgt. Pepper's Lonely Hearts Club
  Band (PCS 7027)
The Beatles (PCS 7067/8)
Yellow Submarine (PCS 7070)
Abbey Road (PCS 7088)
Let It Be (PCS 7096)
The Beatles Rarities (PSLP 261)

The Beatles collection

THE BEATLES "RARITIES"

UK Release: October 1979
US Release: None
Producer: George Martin

Parlophone PSLP 261 : PCM 1001
Intl CD No: None
Running Time: 43:29

SIDE ONE: Across The Universe; Yes It Is; This Boy; The Inner Light; I'll Get You; Thank You Girl; Komm, Gib Mir Deine Hand; You Know My Name (Look Up The Number); Sie Liebt Dich.

SIDE TWO: Rain; She's A Woman; Matchbox; I Call Your Name; Bad Boy; Slow Down; I'm Down; Long Tall Sally.

Originally included as a free addition to the 1978 boxed set, *The Beatles Collection*, this album was issued separately in 1979 after EMI had received complaints that the only way of obtaining this free album was to pay for the box and its duplicate copies of Beatles albums. For most British fans the only rare tracks are 'Across The Universe', previously available only on the now-deleted charity album *No One's Gonna Change Our World,* and the German-language versions of 'She Loves You' and 'I Want To Hold Your Hand', previously unavailable in Britain. The sleeve notes proclaim the remaining 14 tracks, that are a collection of B sides and EP tracks, were not available on earlier British Beatles albums. In fact eight of the 17 tracks were previously available: 'Long Tall Sally', 'I Call Your Name', 'Slow Down', 'Matchbox' and 'I'm Down' are on the *Rock and Roll Music* album; 'Yes It Is' and 'This Boy' on *Love Songs*; and 'Rain' on the *Hey Jude* album.

Although the album contains very little in the way of rare tracks, it is an intelligent compilation of some of the material previously available only on B sides, EPs and foreign releases.

Beatles fans who play this album expecting to find long-awaited stereo versions of tracks will be disappointed. Only four of the 17 tracks 'Across The Universe', 'Komm, Gib Mir Deine Hand', 'Sie Liebt Dich', and 'Bad Boy', are in stereo. The remaining 13, of which four, 'Long Tall Sally', 'I Call Your Name', 'Slow Down' and 'Matchbox' that were issued as the Long Tall Sally EP, are the original mono mixes issued as B sides to various singles.

As a collection of B sides and EP tracks together with three actual rarities, this album is a good start towards making some rare and semi-rare tracks available and is certainly cheaper than buying all the singles and trying to track down copies of long-deleted records. But an album of real rarities would have been a much more exciting prospect.

The Beatles "Rarities"

Across The Universe
Yes It Is
This Boy
The Inner Light
I'll Get You
Thank You Girl
Komm, Gib Mir Deine Hand
You Know My Name (Look Up The Number)
Sie Liebt Dich
Rain
She's A Woman
Matchbox
I Call Your Name
Bad Boy
Slow Down
I'm Down
Long Tall Sally

SIDE ONE
Across The Universe (Lennon-McCartney) 3:41
Recorded: 4 and 8 February 1968, EMI Studios, Abbey Road, London
John Lennon: Acoustic Guitar, Lead Guitar and Lead/Backing Vocal
Paul McCartney: Piano and Harmony/Backing Vocal
George Harrison: Tamboura, Maracas and Backing Vocal
Ringo Starr: Tomtoms   **Lizzie Bravo:** Backing Vocal
Gayleen Pease: Backing Vocal

Recorded in eight takes on 4 and 8 February 1968 during the same period as 'Lady Madonna', this was considered as a possible rival for the March 1968 single, but 'Lady Madonna' was chosen instead.

Shortly after being rejected in favour of 'Lady Madonna', this was given to the World Wildlife Fund who included it on the charity album *No One's Gonna Change Our World* that was released on 12 December 1969 (Regal Starline SRS 5013). A different mix that was minus the sound effects and a considerable amount of the original backing but with an orchestral and choral backing appeared some four months later on the *Let It Be* album.

The track begins with the sound of birds that was added for the purposes of the charity album that flies across the stereo sound stage. When it fades the track proper begins, featuring John singing lead vocal on his own song with Paul harmonising in places. The backing vocals were added by two young women, Lizzie Bravo and Gayleen Pease, who were waiting outside the studios to see The Beatles. Paul invited them in to add a falsetto harmony to John's lead vocal.

The lyrics to this song are some of John's most imaginative, with his incessant chorus line 'Nothing's gonna change my world' accentuating their dreamy effect.

Yes It Is (Lennon-McCartney) 2:40
Recorded: 16 February 1965, EMI Studios, Abbey Road, London
John Lennon: Acoustic Guitar and Lead Vocal   **Paul McCartney:** Bass Guitar and Backing Vocal
George Harrison: Lead Guitar and Backing Vocal   **Ringo Starr:** Drums

The B side to 'Ticket To Ride' that was included on the *Help!* album, this beautiful ballad was released on 9 April 1965. It was recorded in 14 takes on 16 February 1965 and written by John. The song is very reminiscent of his earlier 'This Boy' and features a similar three-part harmony from John, Paul and George, with John singing solo in parts. The whining guitar in the backing is played by George who achieved the effect with a volume/tone control pedal with which he had been experimenting at the time.

This Boy (Lennon-McCartney)   2:11
Recorded: 17 October 1963, EMI Studios, Abbey Road, London
John Lennon: Acoustic Guitar and Lead Vocal
Paul McCartney: Bass Guitar and Harmony Vocal
George Harrison: Lead Guitar and Harmony Vocal   **Ringo Starr**: Drums
This track was originally released in 1963 as the B side to The Beatles' multimillion seller 'I Want To
Hold Your Hand'. 'This Boy' was recorded at the same 17 October 1963 session as 'I Want To Hold
Your Hand', and also went to 17 takes before the 15th was finally chosen for release.

The song is dominated by a close three-part harmony from John, Paul and George, with an
extremely powerful solo vocal from John. For the film *A Hard Day's Night,* George Martin produced an
orchestral version of this that was retitled 'Ringo's Theme' and used in the film as the soundtrack to a
section featuring Ringo who, among other things, is seen walking along the banks of the River
Thames.

The Inner Light (Harrison)   2:36
Recorded: (Instrumental Track) 12 January 1968, EMI Studios, Bombay, India
(Vocal Track) 6 and 8 February 1968, EMI Studios, Abbey Road, London
John Lennon: Backing Vocal   **Paul McCartney**: Backing Vocal
George Harrison: Lead Vocal   **Ringo Starr**: Not Present
Session Musicians: All Instruments
Issued originally in 1968 as the B side of 'Lady Madonna', this was George's first song to be released
on a Beatles single. It is the last of three Beatles tracks by George Harrison featuring almost entirely
Indian instrumentation. The previous two were 'Love You To', included on *Revolver*, and 'Within You,
Without You', featured on *Sgt. Pepper's Lonely Hearts Club Band*. The instrumental track was
recorded in five takes on 12 January 1968 at EMI studios in Bombay, India. It features some of India's
virtuoso musicians and was made during the recording of George's *Wonderwall* album. The vocal
track, that includes a brief backing from John and Paul, and was overdubbed nearly a month later on
6 and 8 February 1968 at Abbey Road. Extracts from a Japanese poem by Roshi, translated into
English by R. H. Bluth, formed the basis of George's lyrics for this interesting and introspective song.

I'll Get You (Lennon-McCartney)   2:04
Recorded: 1 July 1963, EMI Studios, Abbey Road, London
John Lennon: Rhythm Guitar, Harmonica and Lead Vocal
Paul McCartney: Bass Guitar and Harmony Vocal
George Harrison: Lead Guitar and Harmony Vocal   **Ringo Starr:** Drums
Originally considered as an A side for the follow-up to 'From Me To You', this was released in 1963 as the B side to 'She Loves You'. The song is reminiscent of 'She Loves You' with the opening 'Oh yeah' and the duet by John and Paul on lead vocals. John's overdubbed harmonica is prominent at the beginning and ending but is mixed back during the rest of the track. The take details of this and 'She Loves You', are unknown. This is because the studio master was erased shortly after the session. That also accounts for the lack of stereo versions of both these tracks.

Thank You Girl (Lennon-McCartney)   2:01
Recorded: 5 and 13 March 1963, EMI Studios, Abbey Road, London
John Lennon: Acoustic Guitar, Harmonica and Lead Vocal
Paul McCartney: Bass Guitar and Lead Vocal   **George Harrison:** Lead Guitar
Ringo Starr: Drums
This exciting track dates back to April 1963 when it was originally released as the B side of The Beatles' third Parlophone single 'From Me To You'. It has a predominant harmonica from John and the usual John and Paul lead vocal duet featured on most of their 1963 singles. The recording was completed in 13 takes on 5 March 1963 and some additional edit sections were recorded on 13 March 1963.

Komm, Gib Mir Deine Hand (Lennon-McCartney-Nicolas-Heilmer)   2:24
Recorded: (Instrumental Track) 17 October 1963, EMI Studios, Abbey Road, London
(Vocal Track) 29 January 1964, Pathé Marconi Studios, Paris, France
John Lennon: Rhythm Guitar and Lead Vocal   **Paul McCartney:** Bass Guitar and Lead Vocal
George Harrison: Lead Guitar   **Ringo Starr:** Drums
The German-language versions of 'I Want To Hold Your Hand' and 'She Loves You' were not recorded, as many thought, as a tribute to The Beatles' early days in Hamburg, but in answer to a request from EMI in Germany who wanted authentic versions for the German market. The Beatles were far from enthusiastic about the idea but George Martin eventually persuaded them to record the tracks in the

EMI studios in Paris where they were at the time. The two recordings subsequently were released in Germany as a double-A-sided single on 5 March 1964 (Odeon 2267 1). The German lyrics of both songs were written by two German songwriters, one of whom was present at the recording session to ensure that the songs were sung with the correct accent.

For this version of the song The Beatles used the original backing track that was used for the English version and, in 11 takes, added the new German vocals plus hand-claps.

You Know My Name (Look Up The Number) (Lennon-McCartney)   4:20
Recorded: 17 May, 7 and 8 June 1967 and 30 April 1969, EMI Studios, Abbey Road, London
John Lennon: Maracas and Lead Vocal
Paul McCartney: Piano, Bass Guitar and Lead Vocal
George Harrison: Vibraphone and Backing Vocal   **Ringo Starr**: Drums, Bongos and Lead Vocal
Mal Evans: Backing Vocal   **Brian Jones**: Alto Saxophone

This intriguing off-beat track began life on 17 May 1967 shortly after the Sgt. Pepper album had been completed, when a section of the backing track was recorded. On 7 and 8 June 1967 further sections were recorded and these were then edited together on 9 June of the same year to form a final master track. Following that, it was abandoned. On 30 April 1969, John and Paul resurrected it and added the vocals and the sound effects together with Mal Evans, but again it was shelved. On 26 November 1969 John edited the track down from its original six minutes to its current length of just under four and a half minutes and planned to issue it, together with 'What's The New Mary Jane', another unreleased Beatles track, as a single under the banner of The Plastic Ono Band. At the last minute, despite being given the catalogue number App 1002 and a release date of 5 December 1969, it was withdrawn without explanation.

The track finally emerged on 6 March 1970 when it was issued as the B side of the 'Let It Be' single. One of the interesting points concerning that release is that the catalogue number of Apple 1002 is stamped in the run-off groove.

The lyrics to this Lennon-conceived track are basically a repetition of the title with various additional comments and sound effects thrown in for good measure. The jazz piano is supplied by Paul McCartney and the saxophone solo by Brian Jones of the Rolling Stones.

Despite being planned as a Plastic Ono Band release, this track is the B side to The Beatles' final single, therefore it is interesting to note that right at the end of the track, the final comment is 'Goodbye'.

Sie Liebt Dich (Lennon-McCartney-Nicolas-Montague) 2:18
Recorded: 29 January 1964, Pathé Marconi Studios, Paris, France
John Lennon: Rhythm Guitar and Lead Vocal   **Paul McCartney:** Bass Guitar and Lead Vocal
George Harrison: Lead Guitar and Harmony Vocal   **Ringo Starr:** Drums
This German-language version of 'She Loves You' shares the same basic history as 'Komm, Gib Mir Deine Hand'. But unlike that track that used the backing track from 'I Want To Hold Your Hand', 'Sie Liebt Dich' is a brand-new recording. The Beatles were unable to use the backing track to 'She Loves You' for 'Sie Leibt Dich' because the original studio master had been erased. Instead they had to make a completely new recording.

SIDE TWO
Rain (Lennon-McCartney) 2:59
Recorded: 14 and 16 April 1966, EMI Studios, Abbey Road, London
John Lennon: Rhythm Guitar and Lead Vocal
Paul McCartney: Bass Guitar and Backing Vocal
George Harrison: Lead Guitar and Backing Vocal   **Ringo Starr:** Drums and Tambourine
Originally released as the B side to 'Paperback Writer' on 10 June 1966, this track was included together with 'Paperback Writer' on the *Hey Jude* album in 1970.

She's A Woman (Lennon-McCartney) 2:57
Recorded: 8 October 1964, EMI Studios, Abbey Road, London
John Lennon: Rhythm Guitar
Paul McCartney: Bass Guitar Piano and Solo Vocal
George Harrison: Lead Guitar   **Ringo Starr:** Drums and Percussion
This great chunk of syncopated rock'n'roll, written and sung by Paul in his best rock'n'roll style, was recorded in seven takes and originally issued as the B side of 'I Feel Fine' on 27 November 1964.

Matchbox (Perkins) 1:37
Recorded: 1 June 1964, EMI Studios, Abbey Road, London

John Lennon: Rhythm Guitar	**Paul McCartney:** Bass Guitar
George Harrison: Lead Guitar	**Ringo Starr:** Drums and Solo Vocal
George Martin: Piano	

This was recorded in five takes during the same session as 'Slow Down' and released as part of the *Long Tall Sally* EP. Ringo gives a rousing rendition of this 1957 Carl Perkins song that was recorded with Perkins present although he did not participate.

I Call Your Name (Lennon-McCartney) 2:02
Recorded: 1 March 1964, EMI Studios, Abbey Road, London

John Lennon: Rhythm Guitar and Solo Vocal	**Paul McCartney:** Bass Guitar
George Harrison: Lead Guitar	**Ringo Starr:** Drums

This was originally written for Billy J. Kramer and The Dakotas, who recorded and issued it as the B side to 'Bad To Me', another Lennon-McCartney composition. When John who wrote it, discovered it had been buried on a B side he decided that The Beatles should also record and issue it. So with John on lead vocals The Beatles recorded the song that has a similar feel, both musically and vocally, to John's later 'You Can't Do That', in seven takes. The released version was an edit of takes five and seven of the seven takes recorded during the same session that produced 'Long Tall Sally'. Like 'Long Tall Sally', this was issued as part of the American album *The Beatles Second* on 10 April 1964, and then in Britain on 19 June 1964 as part of the *Long Tall Sally* EP.

Bad Boy (Williams) 2:17
Recorded: 10-11 May 1965, EMI Studios, Abbey Road, London
John Lennon: Rhythm Guitar, Hammond Organ and Solo Vocal

Paul McCartney: Bass Guitar and Electric Piano	**George Harrison:** Lead Guitar
Ringo Starr: Drums and Tambourine	

This was originally issued as part of the American album *Beatles VI* on 14 June 1965 and later included on the British album *A Collection Of Beatles Oldies* released on 9 December 1966. The recording was completed in four takes and features a solo vocal from John and a very enthusiastic backing from the rest of The Beatles. This and another Larry Williams song 'Dizzy Miss Lizzy' that was recorded during the same session, were the last two songs apart from the rather short rendition of 'Maggie Mae' on *Let It Be* issued by The Beatles that they did not write themselves.

Slow Down (Williams) 2:54
Recorded: 1 and 4 June 1964, EMI Studios, Abbey Road, London
John Lennon: Rhythm Guitar and Solo Vocal   **Paul McCartney**: Bass Guitar
George Harrison: Lead Guitar   **Ringo Starr**: Drums
George Martin: Piano

Released as part of the *Long Tall Sally* EP on 19 June 1964, this track was partially recorded during six takes on 1 June and completed on 4 June. It features John on lead vocal and is an extremely enthusiastic rendition of this little-known Larry Williams song. It is the first of three Williams songs The Beatles recorded and released.

I'm Down (Lennon-McCartney) 2:30
Recorded: 14 June 1965, EMI Studios, Abbey Road, London
John Lennon: Hammond Organ and Backing Vocal   **Paul McCartney**: Bass Guitar and Lead Vocal
George Harrison: Lead Guitar and Backing Vocal   **Ringo Starr**: Drums and Bongos

This is The Beatles at their rock'n'roll best! This superb McCartney-written track, similar in style to Little Richard's 'Long Tall Sally', was originally issued on 23 July 1965 as the B side of 'Help!' and was included on the album of the same name. The recording, completed in seven takes, rattles along at an incredible pace with Paul shouting out the lyrics in true Little Richard style while John hammers away at the Hammond organ. Unbelievably, this recording was made during the same session that produced 'Yesterday'.

Long Tall Sally (Johnson-Penniman-Backwell) 1:58
Recorded: 1 March 1964, EMI Studios, Abbey Road, London
John Lennon: Rhythm Guitar   **Paul McCartney**: Bass Guitar and Solo Vocal
George Harrison: Lead Guitar   **Ringo Starr**: Drums
George Martin: Piano

This Little Richard song, originally released as part of the American album *The Beatles Second* on 10 April 1964 and then in Britain on 19 June 1964 as the title track of an EP, provides Paul with a perfect vehicle for his voice. Here, his solo vocal sounds just as enthusiastic and spontaneous as John's does on the classic 'Twist And Shout'. In fact, like 'Twist And Shout', this was recorded in one take. The Beatles had used both songs for years during their live performances that invariably opened with 'Twist And Shout' and closed with 'Long Tall Sally' – a format they were to continue to use for their later, large-scale concert performances.

THE BEATLES BALLADS

UK Release: 20 October 1980
US Release: None
Producers: George Martin and Phil Spector

Parlophone PCS 7214
Intl CD No: None
Running Time: 58:29

SIDE ONE: Yesterday; Norwegian Wood (This Bird Has Flown); Do You Want To Know A Secret; For No One; Michelle; Nowhere Man; You've Got To Hide Your Love Away; Across The Universe; All My Loving; Hey Jude.

SIDE TWO: Something; The Fool On The Hill; Till There Was You; The Long And Winding Road; Here Comes The Sun; Blackbird; And I Love Her; She's Leaving Home; Here, There And Everywhere; Let It Be.

Most of these tracks appear on *Love Songs*. Although a better compilation album than *Love Songs*, it contains nothing new, no previously unreleased tracks or even stereo versions of former mono recordings. A remixed version of 'Norwegian Wood' is included with the backing track now on the right-hand channel instead of on the left and the vocals mixed into the centre. Also, someone in the depths of EMI seems to have confused and reversed the stereo on 'Yesterday', 'You've Got To Hide Your Love Away', 'She's Leaving Home' and 'Here, There and Everywhere'.

The possible permutations of material for compilation albums boggle the mind. We have had the rock'n'roll music, the love songs, and on this album the ballads. Presumably one album still to be compiled is *The Songs The Beatles Didn't Write*. After all, there are 24 of them. There could be four separate albums: John Lennon and The Beatles, Paul McCartney and The Beatles, George Harrison and The Beatles, and Ringo Starr and The Beatles. This is not such a ridiculous idea when you consider that the album *The Best of George Harrison* (Parlophone PAS 10011) has on side one 'Something', 'If I Needed Someone', 'Here Comes The Sun', 'Taxman', 'Think For Yourself', 'For You Blue' and 'While My Guitar Gently Weeps'.

THE BEATLES BALLADS

20 ORIGINAL TRACKS

Side One

Yesterday 2:04
Norwegian Wood (This Bird Has Flown) 2:00
Do You Want To Know A Secret 1:55
For No One 2:03
Michelle 2:42
Nowhere Man 2:40
You've Got To Hide Your Love Away 2:08
Across The Universe 3:41
All My Loving 2:04
Hey Jude 7:11

Side Two

Something (Harrison) 2:59
The Fool On The Hill 3:00
Till There Was You (Wilison) 2:12
The Long And Winding Road* 3:40
Here Comes The Sun (Harrison) 3:40
Blackbird 2:20
And I Love Her 2:27
She's Leaving Home 3:24
Here, There And Everywhere 2:29
Let It Be 3:50

Produced by George Martin/Phil Spector. All others produced by George Martin.
All Lennon-McCartney songs except where stated.

REEL MUSIC

UK Release: 12 March 1982
US Release: 12 March 1982
Producers: George Martin and Phil Spector

Parlophone PCS 7218
Capitol SV 12199
Running Time: 42:03

SIDE ONE: A Hard Day's Night; t Should Have Known Better; Can't Buy Me Love; And I Love Her; Help!; You've Got To Hide Your Love Away; Ticket To Ride; Magical Mystery Tour.

SIDE TWO: I Am The Walrus; Yellow Submarine; All You Need Is Love; Let It Be; Get Back; The Long And Winding Road.

Rock and Roll Music, Love Songs, The Beatles Ballads, now we have a further compilation, *Reel Music,* a selection of songs from The Beatles' films.

The album features four songs from *A Hard Day's Night,* three from *Help!,* two from *Magical Mystery Tour,* two from *Yellow Submarine* and three from *Let It Be.* Unfortunately, from the way the album is arranged, there is no real sense of flow to *Reel Music.* For a Beatles album to have 'Ticket To Ride' followed by 'Magical Mystery Tour', and 'I Am The Walrus' followed by 'Yellow Submarine' suggests some peculiar criteria for selection of tracks.

The album cover, that depicts The Beatles in their five different roles as film stars arriving at a cinema, reflects the album's contents and indicates a rapidly produced piece of merchandise.

The sleeve notes consist of a six-paragraph potted history of The Beatles and their film career. These words are aimed mainly at new, young Beatles fans, many not even born when the fab four broke up. For the fans' benefit, the sleeve also credits the individual Beatles as composers, the first album to do so since *With The Beatles* in 1963.

The album is complete with a 12-page Souvenir Program that contains a brief resumé of each of the five Beatles movies along with selected stills. The inner sleeve has a further selection of stills and other photographs.

Following the 1981-2 worldwide success of the Stars-on-45 medley by the Dutch Beatles soundalike group Starsound, a medley that contained some very believable John Lennon-sounding vocals, Capitol Records decided to put together their own Beatle medley using original Beatles master tapes. The record, entitled *The Beatles Movie Medley,* contains excerpts from 'Magical Mystery Tour', 'All You Need

Is Love', 'You've Got To Hide Your Love Away', 'I Should Have Known Better', 'A Hard Day's Night', 'Ticket To Ride' and 'Get Back'. The recording was issued as a single (Capitol B-5107) on 30 March 1982.

The editing, that is questionable, was carried out by John Palladino of Capitol Records. Unfortunately, the inclusion of 'You've Got To Hide Your Love Away' within the medley seems to spoil the rhythm of the medley as a whole, which has a running time of three minutes 56 seconds.

When the first promotional copies of this record were pressed, the B side contained an edited press conference interview from 1964, but when the record reached the stores, the B side had been changed to 'I'm Happy Just To Dance With You'.

In Britain, EMI Records decided that the editing of Beatles recordings was unacceptable and withheld release of the record but still allocated it a catalogue number just in case. Demand for imported copies of the US record was so high that EMI conceded and eventually issued it on 25 May 1982 (Parlophone R6055).

Side One
A Hard Day's Night 2:32
I Should Have Known Better 2:42
Can't Buy Me Love 2:15
And I Love Her 2:27
Help! 2:16
You've Got To Hide Your Love Away 2:08
Ticket To Ride 3:03
Magical Mystery Tour 2:48

Side Two
I Am The Walrus 4:35
Yellow Submarine 2:40
All You Need Is Love 3:47
Let It Be 4:01*
Get Back 3:09*
The Long And Winding Road 3:40*

*Poduced by George Martin and Phil Spector. All others produced by George Martin.

THE BEATLES BOX

UK Release: 27 October 1980
US Release: None
Producers: George Martin and Phil Spector

Parlophone/World Records SM 701-8
Intl CD No: None
Running Time: See Individual Albums

Track listings for the eight albums in the box are given on the following pages.

This collection is a must for any Beatles fan or collector. A masterpiece, it spans the entire recording career of The Beatles from 'Love Me Do' to 'Let It Be' and is even better than *The Beatles 1962-66* and *The Beatles 1967-70* albums.

The eight albums that make up *The Beatles Box* contain 124 tracks of what can be definitively classed as The Beatles' greatest hits. It is a tribute to the group's achievement as there cannot be many artists whose greatest hits would fill eight albums. Another good point is that *The Beatles Box* consists of eight new albums, not re-packages like *The Beatles Collection* issued in 1978. Among the 124 tracks are ten of particular interest.

The first is the original single version of 'Love Me Do' with Ringo on drums. This is not the version included on the *Please Please* Me album. 'All My Loving' in this version was previously only available on the German album *Beatles Greatest* (Odeon SMO 83991) and features a five-tap hi-hat intro. It makes its first appearance on a British Beatles album here. 'And I Love Her', as heard here, was previously unavailable in Britain but was on the German album *Something New* (Odeon 1C 072-04 600). The final riff is repeated here six times whereas on the album *A Hard Day's Night* it is repeated only four times. 'She's A Woman' was previously available in Britain only in mono. This is the stereo version that had been available only on the East Asian/Australian album *The Beatles Greatest Hits Vol. 2* (Parlophone LPEA 1002). 'I Feel Fine' is the much talked about whispering version previously included on the album *The Beatles 1962-66*. It is the same stereo recording as on the album *A Collection Of Beatles Oldies* but includes two seconds of mysterious whisperings at the beginning. 'Day Tripper' is a different stereo mix from that available on the album *A Collection Of Beatles Oldies*, previously available only on the American album *Yesterday... And Today* (Capitol ST 2553), it has the guitar intro mixed into the left-hand channel instead of across the stereo stage. 'Paperback Writer' is the re-mixed version from *Hey Jude* with the stereo channels reversed and the backing vocals mixed further forward than on *A Collection Of Beatles Oldies*. 'Penny Lane' in this version was previously unavailable anywhere in the world. It was distributed to radio stations in America and Canada prior to the release of the single. It features seven extra piccolo trumpet notes played over the ending of the recording that had been edited out by the time the record reached the stores. 'Baby, You're A Rich Man' is in stereo for the first time in Britain. 'I Am The Walrus', previously unavailable anywhere in the world in this format, is included in full, combining the oddities of three previous versions. The British single features the organ intro repeated four times, the stereo version on the *Magical Mystery Tour* two-EP set, six times, and the American single with the organ intro repeated four times also has a few extra beats in the middle between the lines 'I'm crying' and 'Yellow matter custard'. These are missing from both British versions but are combined here.

Other tracks of interest are the stereo version of 'Long Tall Sally', 'I Call Your Name', 'Matchbox', 'Slow Down' and 'I'm Down'. Previously included on the rather messy compilation album *Rock and Roll Music*, these five tracks are presented here in a far superior way. On record six, 'All You Need Is Love' is the original mono single not the re-recorded version from *Yellow Submarine*. 'Get Back', 'Let It Be' and 'Across The Universe' are the recordings from the album *Let It Be*, and not, in the case of the first two, the versions released as singles.

The eight albums, complete with individual sleeve notes, come packaged in a cardboard box looking rather like a wooden crate. This album set is available only through World Records, EMI's mail-order division.

The Beatles BOX – RECORD 1
Parlophone/World Records 5M701
Producer: George Martin
Running Time: 31:57
Side One
Love Me Do 2:22
P.S. I Love You 2:02
I Saw Her Standing There 2:50
Please Please Me 2:00
Misery 1:43
Do You Want To Know A Secret 1:55
A Taste Of Honey (Marlow-Scott) 2:02
Twist And Shout (Medley-Russell) 2:32

Side Two
From Me To You 1:55
Thank You Girl 2:01
She Loves You 2:18
It Won't Be Long 2:11
Please Mister Postman (Holland) 2:34
All My Loving 2:07
Roll Over Beethoven (Berry) 2:44
Money (Bradford-Gordy) 2:47
All Lennon-McCartney songs except where stated.

The Beatles BOX – RECORD 2
Parlophone/World Records 5M702
Producer: George Martin
Running Time: 38:13
Side One
I Want To Hold Your Hand 2:24
This Boy 2:11
Can't Buy Me Love 2:15
You Can't Do That 2:33
A Hard Day's Night 2:32
I Should Have Known Better 2:42
If I Fell 2:16
And I Love Her 2:36

Side Two
Things We Said Today 2:35
I'll Be Back 2:22
Long Tall Sally (Johnson-Penniman-Blackwell) 1:58
I Call Your Name 2:02
Matchbox (Perkins) 1:37
Slow Down (Williams) 2:54
She's A Woman 2:57
I Feel Fine 2:19

The Beatles BOX – RECORD 3
Parlophone/World Records SM703
Producer: George Martin
Running Time: 38:12
Side One
Eight Days A Week 2:43
No Reply 2:15
I'm A Loser 2:31
I'll Follow The Sun 1:46
Mr Moonlight (Johnson) 2:35
Every Little Thing 2:01
I Don't Want To Spoil The Party 2:33
Kansas City (Lieber-Stoller)/
Hey Hey Hey Hey (Penniman) 2:30

Side Two
Ticket To Ride 3:03
I'm Down 2:30
Help! 2:16
The Night Before 2:33
You've Got To Hide Your Love Away 2:08
I Need You (Harrison) 2:28
Another Girl 2:02
You're Going To Lose That Girl 2:18
All Lennon-McCartney songs except where stated.

The Beatles BOX – RECORD 4
Parlophone/World Records SM704
Producer: George Martin
Running Time: 38:49
Side One
Yesterday 2:04
Act Naturally (Morrison-
  Russell) 2:27
Tell Me What You See 2:35
It's Only Love 1:53
You Like Me Too Much (Harrison) 2:34
I've Just Seen A Face 2:04
Day Tripper 2:37
We Can Work It Out 2:10

Side Two
Michelle 2:42
Drive My Car 2:25
Norwegian Wood (This Bird Has Flown) 2:00
You Won't See Me 3:19
Nowhere Man 2:40
Girl 2:26
I'm Looking Through You 2:20
In My Life 2:23

The Beatles BOX – RECORD 5
Parlophone/World Records SM7OS
Producer: George Martin
Running Time: 34:13
Side One
Paperback Writer 2:25
Rain 2:59
Here, There And Everywhere 2:29
Taxman (Harrison) 2:36
I'm Only Sleeping 2:58
Good Day Sunshine 2:08
Yellow Submarine 2:40

Side Two
Eleanor Rigby 2:11
And Your Bird Can Sing 2:02
For No One 2:03
Dr. Robert 2:14
Got To Get You Into My Life 2:31
Penny Lane 3:00
Strawberry Fields Forever 4:05

The Beatles BOX – RECORD 6
Parlophone/World Records SM706
Producer: George Martin
Running Time: 47:07
Side One
Sgt. Pepper's Lonely Hearts Club Band 1:59
With A Little Help From My Friends 2:46
Lucy In The Sky With Diamonds 3:25
Fixing A Hole 2:33
She's Leaving Home 3:24
Being For The Benefit Of Mr.Kite 2:36
A Day In The Life 5:03

Side Two
When I'm Sixty-Four 2:38
Lovely Rita 2:43
All You Need Is Love 3:57
Baby, You're A Rich Man 3:07
Magical Mystery Tour 2:48
The Fool On The Hill 3:00
I Am The Walrus 4:35

All Lennon-McCartney songs except where stated.

The Beatles BOX – RECORD 7
Parlophone/World Records SM707
Producer: George Martin
Running Time: 48:17
Side One

Hello Goodbye   3:24
Lady Madonna   2:17
Hey Jude   7:11
Revolution   3:22
Back In The U.S.S.R.   2:45
Ob-La-Di, Ob-La-Da   3:10
While My Guitar Gently Weeps
  (Harrison)   4:46

Side Two

The Continuing Story Of Bungalow Bill   3:05
Happiness Is A Warm Gun   2:47
Martha My Dear   2:28
I'm So Tired   2:01
Piggies (Harrison)   2:04
Don't Pass Me By (Starkey)   3:52
Julia   2:57
All Together Now   2:08

All Lennon-McCartney songs except where stated.

The Beatles BOX – RECORD 8
Parlophone/World Records SM708
Producers: George Martin and Phil Spector
Running Time: 52:11
Side One

Get Back   3:09
Don't Let Me Down   3:34
The Ballad Of John And Yoko   2:58
Across The Universe   3:51
For You Blue (Harrison)   2:33
Two Of Us   3:33
The Long And Winding Road   3:40
Let it Be   4:01

Side Two

Come Together   4:16
Something (Harrison)   2:59
Maxwell's Silver Hammer   3:24
Octopus's Garden (Starkey)   2:49
Here Comes The Sun (Harrison)   3:04
Because   2:45
Golden Slumbers   1:31
Carry That Weight   1:37
The End   2:04
Her Majesty   0:23

THE SONGS LENNON AND McCARTNEY GAVE AWAY

UK Release: 9 April 1979
US Release: None
Producer: Various (See individual tracks)

EMI Nut 18
Intl CD No: None
Running Time: 46:14

SIDE ONE: I'm The Greatest (Ringo Starr); One And One Is Two (The Strangers with Mike Shannon); From A Window (Billy J. Kramer and The Dakotas); Nobody I Know (Peter and Gordon); Like Dreamers Do (The Applejacks); I'll Keep You Satisfied (Billy J. Kramer and The Dakotas); Love Of The Loved (Cilla Black); Woman (Peter and Gordon); Tip Of My Tongue (Tommy Quickly); I'm In Love (The Fourmost)

SIDE TWO: Hello Little Girl (The Fourmost); That Means A Lot (P.J. Proby); It's For You (Cilla Black); Penina (Carlos Mendes); Step Inside Love (Cilla Black); World Without Love (Peter and Gordon); Bad To Me (Billy J. Kramer and The Dakotas); I Don't Want To See You Again (Peter and Gordon); I'll Be On My Way (Billy J. Kramer and The Dakotas); Catcall (The Chris Barber Band).

During their career as the main song writers for The Beatles, John Lennon and Paul McCartney wrote a number of songs that they gave away to other artists, many of whom were old friends from Liverpool. Among those friends were Billy J. Kramer and The Dakotas who are featured on four songs: 'From A Window', 'I'll Keep You Satisfied', 'Bad To Me' and 'I'll Be On My Way'; Cilla Black with 'Love Of The Loved', 'It's For You' and 'Step Inside Love'; and The Fourmost with 'Hello Little Girl' and 'I'm In Love'.

Curiously, the first song that Lennon and McCartney gave away – 'I'll Be On My Way', recorded by Billy J. Kramer in 1963, is also the only song The Beatles officially recorded for the BBC on 4 April 1963.

Although recordings by John Lennon, Paul McCartney or The Beatles exist of the other songs that are featured on this album, most, if not all, were recorded as demonstration recordings for the artists who were to eventually record the song.

Only one song on this album does not come from The Beatles' collective recording career, 'I'm The Greatest', a song written by John Lennon that he gave to Ringo for his 1973 album, *Ringo*. The 19 remaining tracks performed by ten other artists were given away during The Beatles' career from

The SONGS LENNON AND McCARTNEY Gave Away

By the Original Artists

1962 to 1969. Most were not written specifically for the artists who recorded them with the exceptions of 'Step Inside Love' that was written for Cilla Black by Paul McCartney in 1968, and the Peter and Gordon recordings on the album, that were also written for them by McCartney.

Seven other John Lennon and/or Paul McCartney songs given away between 1963 and 1969 and recorded by other artists are mentioned at the end of the album listing here. These are relevant although they do not appear on the album.

SIDE ONE

I'm The Greatest (John Lennon)   3:23

Ringo Starr
UK Release: 9 November 1973
US Release: 2 November 1973
Producer: Richard Perry
John Lennon: Piano and Harmony Vocal
George Harrison: Lead Guitar
Klaus Voormann: Bass Guitar

Apple PCTC 252 (LP Ringo)
Apple SWAL 3413 (LP Ringo)

Paul McCartney: Not Present
Ringo Starr: Drums and Lead Vocal
Billy Preston: Organ

This is the only song on the album that does not come from The Beatles' collective recording career, but it is also the only recording on this album that almost could be termed a Beatles recording. As can be seen from the line-up that, incidentally, John Lennon thought about putting together in 1970, the only Beatle missing here is Paul McCartney.

Written by John Lennon for Ringo's 1973 album, *Ringo*, the lyrics refer to, among other things, The Beatles, Sgt. Pepper and Yoko Ono. The music has snatches reminiscent of 'I Want You (She's So Heavy)', 'Golden Slumbers', 'Being For The Benefit of Mr. Kite', 'Revolution' and 'Cry Baby Cry'.

One And One Is Two (Lennon-McCartney) 2:10
The Strangers with Mike Shannon
UK Release: 8 May 1964
US Release: None

Phillips BF 1335
Producer: Unknown

From A Window (Lennon-McCartney) 1:55
Billy J. Kramer and The Dakotas
UK Release: 17 July 1964
US Release: 12 August 1964
Producer: George Martin

Parlophone R5156
Imperial 66051

Nobody I Know (Lennon-McCartney) 2:27
Peter and Gordon
UK Release: 27 May 1964
US Release: 15 June 1964
Producer: John Burgess

Columbia DB 7292
Capitol 5211

Like Dreamers Do (Lennon-McCartney) 2:30
The Applejacks
UK Release: 5 May 1964
US Release: 6 July 1964
Producer: Mike Smith

Decca F11916
London 9681

I'll Keep You Satisfied (Lennon-McCartney) 2:04
Billy J. Kramer and The Dakotas
UK Release: 1 November 1963
US Release: 11 November 1963
Producer: George Martin

Parlophone R5073
Liberty 55643

Love Of The Loved (Lennon-McCartney) 2:00
Cilla Black
UK Release: 27 September 1963
US Release: None

Parlophone R5065
Producer: George Martin

Woman (Paul McCartney as B. Webb) 2:21
Peter and Gordon
UK Release: 11 February 1966
US Release: 10 January 1966
Producer: John Burgess

Columbia DB 7834
Capitol 5579

Tip Of My Tongue (Lennon-McCartney) 2:02
Tommy Quickly
UK Release: 30 July 1963
US Release: None

Piccadilly 7N 35137
Producer: Les Reed

I'm In Love (Lennon-McCartney) 2:07
The Fourmost
UK Release: 15 November 1963
US Release: 10 February 1964
Producer: George Martin

Parlophone R5078
Atco 6285

SIDE TWO

Hello Little Girl (Lennon-McCartney) 1:50
The Fourmost
UK Release: 30 August 1963
US Release: 15 November 1963
Producer: George Martin

Parlophone R5056
Atco 6280

That Means A Lot (Lennon-McCartney) 2:31
P. J. Proby
UK Release: 17 September 1965   **Liberty LBF 10215**
US Release: 23 August 1965   **Liberty LST 7421** (LP P. J. Proby)
Producer: Ron Richards

It's For You (Lennon-McCartney) 2:20
Cilla Black
UK Release: 31 July 1964   **Parlophone R5162**
US Release: 17 August 1964   **Capitol 5258**
Producer: George Martin

Penina (Paul McCartney) 2:36
Carlos Mendes
UK Release: None: Portugal only, July 1969   **Parlophone QMSP 16459**
US Release: None   **Producer:** Unknown

Step Inside Love (Lennon-McCartney) 2:20
Cilla Black
UK Release: 8 March 1968   **Parlophone R5674**
US Release: 6 May 1968   **Bell 726**
Producer: George Martin

World Without Love (Lennon-McCartney) 2:38
Peter and Gordon
UK Release: 28 February 1964   **Columbia DB 7225**
US Release: 27 April 1964   **Capitol 5175**
Producer: Norman Newell

Bad To Me (Lennon-McCartney) 2:18
Billy J. Kramer and The Dakotas
UK Release: 26 July 1963   **Parlophone R5049**
US Release: 23 September 1963   **Liberty 55626**
Producer: George Martin

I Don't Want To See You Again (Lennon-McCartney) 1:59
Peter and Gordon
UK Release: 11 September 1964   **Columbia DB 7356**
US Release: 21 September 1964   **Capitol 5272**
Producer: Norman Newell

I'll Be On My Way (Lennon-McCartney) 1:38
Billy J. Kramer and The Dakotas
UK Release: 26 April 1963   **Parlophone R5023**
US Release: 10 June 1963   **Liberty 55586**
Producer: George Martin

Catcall (Paul McCartney) 3:05
The Chris Barber Band
UK Release: 20 October 1967   **Marmalade 598-005**
US Release: None
Producers: Chris Barber, Giorgio Gomelsky, Reggie King

The seven songs, written by John Lennon and/or Paul McCartney, and recorded by other artists up to the end of 1969, but not included on this album, are:

Theme From The Family Way (Paul McCartney) 2:05
The George Martin Orchestra
UK Release: 23 December 1966   **United Artists UP 1165**
US Release: None   **Producer:** George Martin

Love In The Open Air (Paul McCartney) 2:18
The George Martin Orchestra
UK Release: 23 December 1966   **United Artists UP 1165**
US Release: 24 April 1967   **United Artists UA 50148**
Producer: George Martin

Thingumybob (Paul McCartney) 1:51
John Fosters and Sons Ltd. Black Dyke Mills Band
UK Release: 6 September 1968   **Apple 4**
US Release: 28 August 1968   **Apple 1800**
Producer: Paul McCartney

Goodbye (Lennon-McCartney) 2:23
Mary Hopkin
UK Release: 28 March 1969   **Apple 10**
US Release: 7 April 1969   **Apple 1806**
Producer: Paul McCartney

Give Peace A Chance (Lennon-McCartney) 4:49
The Plastic Ono Band
UK Release: 4 July 1969   **Apple 13**
US Release: 7 July 1969   **Apple 1809**
Producers: John Lennon and Yoko Ono

Cold Turkey (John Lennon) 4:59
The Plastic Ono Band
UK Release: 24 October 1969   **Apple 1001**
US Release: 20 October 1969   **Apple 1813**
Producers: John Lennon and Yoko Ono

Come And Get It (Paul McCartney) 2:21
Badfinger
UK Release: 5 December 1969   **Apple 20**
US Release: 12 January 1970   **Apple 1815**
Producer: Paul McCartney

THE
AMERICAN
ALBUMS

MEET THE BEATLES

Capitol ST 2047
Release Date: 20 January 1964

Producer: George Martin
Running Time: 26:43

SIDE ONE: I Want To Hold Your Hand; I Saw Her Standing There; This Boy; It Won't Be Long; All I've Got To Do; All My Loving.

SIDE TWO: Don't Bother Me; Little Child; Till There Was You; Hold Me Tight; I Wanna Be Your Man; Not A Second Time.

After rejecting The Beatles for almost a year, Capitol Records put together this first official American Beatles album. Previously, Beatles records issued on Parlophone in the UK, were on a variety of record labels in the USA such as Vee Jay, Tollie and Swan. When Beatlemania swept America, Capitol, fully aware that they had rejected The Beatles, were desperate to take up the option of issuing their records.

Meet The Beatles, has a similar jacket to the British album *With The Beatles*, and contains nine of the 14 tracks from that album plus 'I Saw Her Standing There' from *Please Please Me* and The Beatles' latest British single at the time, 'I Want To Hold Your Hand/This Boy'. Capitol issued 'I Want To Hold Your Hand' with the B side 'I Saw Her Standing There' as a single from this album.

Side One

I Want To Hold Your Hand 2:24
(See *A Collection Of Beatles Oldies* Album PCS 7016)
I Saw Her Standing There 2:50
(See *Please Please Me Album* PCS 3042)
This Boy 2:11
(See *British Rarities Album* PCM 1001)
It Won't Be Long 2:11
(See *With The Beatles* Album PCS 3045)
All I've Got To Do 2:05
(See *With The Beatles Album* PCS 3045)
All My Loving 2:04
(See *With The Beatles* Album PCS 3045)
All Lennon-McCartney songs except where stated.

Side Two

Don't Bother Me (Harrison) 2:28
(See *With The Beatles* Album PCS 3045)
Little Child 1:46
(See *With The Beatles* Album PCS 3045)
Till There Was You (Willson) 2:12
(See *With The Beatles* Album PCS 3045)
Hold Me Tight 2:30
(See *With The Beatles* Album PCS 3045)
I Wanna Be Your Man 1:59
(See *With The Beatles* Album PCS 3045)
Not A Second Time 2:30
(See *With The Beatles* Album PCS 3045)

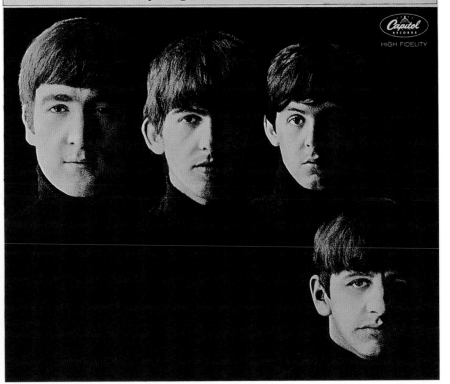

THE BEATLES' SECOND ALBUM

Capitol ST 2020
Release Date: 10 April 1964

Producer: George Martin
Running Time: 26:12

SIDE ONE: Roll Over Beethoven; Thank You Girl; You Really Got A Hold On Me; Devil In Her Heart; Money; You Can't Do That.

SIDE TWO: Long Tall Sally; I Call Your Name; Please Mr. Postman; Ill Get You; She Loves You.

Within four months of issuing *Meet The Beatles*, Capitol Records, now fully aware of the surge of Beatlemania in America, issued this album that includes the remaining five tracks from *With The Beatles*. Along with 'You Can't Do That', the B side of 'Can't Buy Me Love' that was Capitol Records' latest Beatles single and was also to be included on the soundtrack and album of *A Hard Day's Night*, 'She Loves You' and 'I'll Get You' that were both previously issued as a single by Swan Records for which Capitol had not acquired the rights, 'Long Tall Sally' and 'I Call Your Name' that had been issued on the EP *Long Tall Sally* in Britain and the stereo recording of 'Thank You Girl' that was yet to be issued in Britain.

Side One

Roll Over Beethoven (Berry) 2:44
(See *With The Beatles* Album PCS 3045)
Thank You Girl 2:01
(See *British Rarities* Album PCM 1001)
You Really Got A Hold On Me (Robinson) 2:58
(See *With The Beatles* Album PCS 3045)
Devil In Her Heart (Drapkin) 2:23
(See *With The Beatles* Album PCS 3045)
Money (Bradford- Gordy) 2:47
(See *With The Beatles* Album PCS 3045)
You Can't Do That 2:33
(See British *A Hard Day's Night* Album PCS 3058)
All Lennon-McCartney songs except where stated.

Side Two

Long Tall Sally (Johnson-Penniman-Blackwell) 1:5
(See *British Rarities* Album PCM 1001)
I Call Your Name 2:02
(See *British Rarities* Album PCM 1001)
Please Mr. Postman (Holland) 2:34
(See *With The Beatles* Album PCS 3045)
I'll Get You 2:04
(See *British Rarities* Album PCM 1001)
She Loves You 2:18
(See *A Collection Of Beatles Oldies* Album PCS 7016)

THE BEATLES'
SECOND ALBUM

ELECTRIFYING BIG-BEAT PERFORMANCES BY ENGLAND'S
Paul McCartney, John Lennon, George Harrison and Ringo Starr

featuring
SHE
LOVES YOU
and
ROLL OVER
BEETHOVEN

A HARD DAY'S NIGHT

United Artists UAS 6366
Release Date: 26 June 1964

Producer: George Martin
Running Time: 29:21

SIDE ONE: A Hard Day's Night; Tell Me Why; I'll Cry Instead; (I Should Have Known Better); I'm Happy Just To Dance With You; (And I Love Her).

SIDE TWO: I Should Have Known Better; If I Fell; And I Love Her; (Ringo's Theme – This Boy); Can't Buy Me Love; (A Hard Day's Night).

The Beatles' first movie soundtrack album bears little resemblance to the British album of the same name, although it does include all the new material used in the film plus George Martin's orchestral contributions. The seven new songs heard in the film are spread between the two album sides whereas they are all on side one of the British album with 'I'll Cry' Instead that was dropped from the film at the last minute.

Side One

A Hard Day's Night   2:28
(See British *A Hard Day's Night* Album PCS 3058)
Tell Me Why   2:04
(See British *A Hard Day's Night* Album PCS 3058)
I'll Cry Instead   2:06
(See British *A Hard Day's Night* Album PCS 3058)
I Should Have Known Better*   2:16
I'm Happy Just To Dance With You   1:59
(See British *A Hard Day's Night* Album PCS 3058)
And I Love Her*   3.42

Side Two

I Should Have Known Better   2:42
(See British *A Hard Day's Night* Album PCS 3058)
If I Fell   2:16
(See British *A Hard Day's Night* Album PCS 3058)
And I Love Her   2:27
(See British *A Hard Day's Night* Album PCS 3058)
Ringo's Theme (This Boy)*   3:06
Can't Buy Me Love   2:15
(See British *A Hard Day's Night* Album PCS 30358)
A Hard Day's Night*   2:00

* The George Martin Orchestra

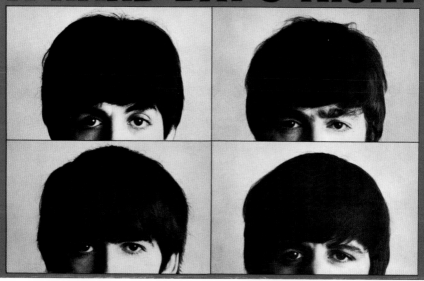

stereo

THE BEATLES • A HARD DAY'S NIGHT • UNITED ARTISTS UAS 6366

UNITED ARTISTS RECORDS

ORIGINAL MOTION PICTURE SOUND TRACK

THE BEATLES

A HARD DAY'S NIGHT

SOMETHING NEW
SOMETHING NEW

THE BEATLES

HIGH FIDELITY

THINGS WE SAID TODAY
ANY TIME AT ALL
WHEN I GET HOME
SLOW DOWN
MATCHBOX
KOMM, GIB MIR DEINE HAND

...plus the hit vocals from the
Motion Picture "A Hard Day's Night"
A United Artists' Release

I'LL CRY INSTEAD
TELL ME WHY
AND I LOVE HER
I'M HAPPY JUST TO DANCE WITH YOU
IF I FELL

SOMETHING NEW

Capitol STBO 2222
Release Date: 23 November 1964

Producers: Gary Usher and Roger Christian
Running Time: 49:54

SIDE ONE: I'll Cry Instead; Things We Said Today; Any Time At All; When I Get Home; Slow Down; Matchbox.

SIDE TWO: Tell Me Why; And I Love Her; I'm Happy Just To Dance With You; If I Fell; Komm, Gib Mir Deine Hand.

Although this album claims to be something new, five of the 11 tracks were previously issued on the American album *A Hard Day's Night*. Of the remaining six tracks, three have been extracted from the British album *A Hard Day's Night*, while 'Slow Down' and 'Matchbox' come from the British EP *Long Tall Sally*. The final track, 'Komm, Gib Mir Deine Hand', is the German language version of 'I Want To Hold Your Hand', that although issued in both Germany and America, was not issued in Britain until 1978 on the *Rarities* album.

Side One

I'll Cry Instead 1:44
(See British *A Hard Day's Night* Album PCS 3058)
Things We Said Today 2:35
(See British *A Hard Day's Night* Album PCS 3058)
Any Time At All 2:10
(See British *A Hard Day's Night* Album PCS 3058)
When I Get Home 2:14
(See British *A Hard Day's Night* Album PCS 3058)
Slow Down (Williams) 2:54
(See British *Rarities* Album PCM 1001)
Matchbox (Perkins) 1:37
(See British *Rarities* Album PCM 1001)

Side Two

Tell Me Why 2:04
(See British *A Hard Day's Night* Album PCS 3058)
And I Love Her 2:27
(See British *A Hard Day's Night* Album PCS 3058)
I'm Happy Just To Dance With You 1:59
(See British *A Hard Day's Night* Album PCS 3058)
If I Fell 2:16
(See British *A Hard Day's Night* Album PCS 3058)
Komm, Gib Mir Deine Hand
(Lennon-McCartney-Nicolas-Helimer) 2:24
(See *British Rarities* Album PCM 1001)

All Lennon-McCartney songs except where stated.

THE BEATLES' STORY

Capitol STBO 2222
Release Date: 23 November 1964

Producers: Gary Usher and Roger Christian
Running Time: 49:54

SIDE ONE: On Stage With The Beatles; How Beatlemania Began; Beatlemania In Action; Man Behind The Beatles – Brian Epstein; John Lennon; Who's A Millionaire?
SIDE TWO: Beatles Will Be Beatles; Man Behind The Music – George Martin; George Harrison.

SIDE THREE: A Hard Day's Night – Their First Film; Paul McCartney; Sneaky Haircuts And More About Paul.
SIDE FOUR: The Beatles Look At Life; 'Victims' Of Beatlemania, Beatle Medley; Ringo Starr; Liverpool And All The World!

Many Beatles interview albums appeared in the USA during 1964, and Capitol Records put together this biography in sound of The Beatles. It gives an approximate 50-minute history of The Beatles, from their beginnings in Liverpool as The Quarrymen and their days in Hamburg, to their eventual worldwide success. It is compiled and narrated by John Babcock in association with Al Wiman and Roger Christian of radio station KFWB, Hollywood, California, and is produced by Gary Usher and Roger Christian with the exception of the brief snatches of Beatles records produced by George Martin.

Overall, the album is a rather glossy biography of The Beatles and includes interviews with them and some of their hysterical fans after the 1964 Hollywood Bowl concert that is where the live recording of 'Twist And Shout' on side four comes from. Interspersed with the interviews and narration are 14 Beatles recordings that are not credited on the album's jacket or record label. In addition to 'Twist and Shout' the remaining tracks are: 'I Want To Hold Your Hand', 'Slow Down', 'This Boy', 'You Can't Do That', 'If I Fell', 'A Hard Day's Night', 'And I Love Her', 'Things We Said Today', 'I'm Happy Just To Dance With You', 'Little Child', 'Long Tall Sally', 'She Loves You; Boys'.

Throughout the album the narrators give brief biographies of each of The Beatles, also of Brian Epstein their manager and George Martin their record producer. They try to explain Beatlemania but somehow don't succeed. Even so the album does manage to capture the spirit and excitement of Beatlemania in America at the height of The Beatles' success.

Side One

On Stage With The Beatles   1:03
How Beatlemania Began   1:18
Beatlemania in Action   2:24
Man Behind The Beatles – Brian Epstein   3:01
John Lennon   4:24
Who's A Millionaire?   0:43

Side Two

Beatles Will Be Beatles   7:37
Man Behind The Music – George Martin   0:47
George Harrison   4:43

Side Three

A Hard Day's Night – Their First Movie   3:45
Paul McCartney   1:55
Sneaky Haircuts and More About Paul   3:38

Side Four

The Beatles Look At Life   1:51
Victims Of Beatlemania   1:21
Beatle Medley   3:36
Ringo Starr   6:19
Liverpool And All The World!   1:09

BEATLES '65

Capitol ST 2228
Release Date: 15 December 1964

Producer: George Martin
Running Time: 25:10

SIDE ONE: No Reply; I'm A Loser; Baby's In Black; Rock And Roll Music; I'll Follow The Sun; Mr. Moonlight; Honey Don't.

SIDE TWO: I'll Be Back; She's A Woman; I Feel Fine; Everybody's Trying To Be My Baby.

The first side of this album is in essence side one of the British album *Beatles For Sale* without the last track, 'Kansas City'. The second side contains two further tracks from *Beatles For Sale*: 'Honey Don't' and 'Everybody's Trying To Be My Baby', along with the 13th and remaining track from the British album *A Hard Day's Night*, 'I'll Be Back', plus: 'I Feel Fine' and 'She's A Woman', issued as a single a week after the release of this album.

Side One
No Reply 2:15
(See *Beatles For Sale* Album PCS 3062)
I'm A Loser 2:31
(See *Beatles For Sale* Album PCS 3062)
Baby's In Black 2:02
(See *Beatles For Sale* Album PCS 3062)
Rock and Roll Music (Berry) 2:02
(See *Beatles For Sale* Album PCS 3062)
I'll Follow The Sun 1:46
(See *Beatles For Sale* Album PCS 3062)
Mr. Moonlight (Johnson) 2:35
(See *Beatles For Sale* Album PCS 3062)

Side Two
Honey Don't (Perkins) 2:56
(See *Beatles For Sale* Album PCS 3062)
I'll Be Back 2:22
(See British *A Hard Day's Night* Album PCS 3058)
She's A Woman 2:57
(See *British Rarities* Album PCM 1001)
I Feel Fine 2:20
(See *A Collection of Beatles Oldies* Album PCS 7016)
Everybody's Trying To Be My Baby (Perkins) 2:24
(See *Beatles For Sale* Album PCS 3062)

All Lennon-McCartney songs except where stated.

GREAT NEW HITS BY JOHN · PAUL · GEORGE · RINGO

BEATLES '65

HIGH FIDELITY

I FEEL FINE · SHE'S A WOMAN · NO REPLY · I'M A LOSER · ROCK AND ROLL MUSIC · I'LL FOLLOW THE SUN ·
HONEY DON'T · I'LL BE BACK · BABY'S IN BLACK · EVERYBODY'S TRYING TO BE MY BABY · MR. MOONLIGHT

THE EARLY BEATLES

Capitol ST 2309
Release Date: 22 March 1965

Producer: George Martin
Running Time: 25:31

SIDE ONE: Love Me Do; Twist And Shout; Anna (Go To Him); Chains; Boys; Ask Me Why.

SIDE TWO: Please Please Me; P. S. I Love You; Baby It's You; A Taste Of Honey; Do You Want To Know A Secret.

Because Capitol Records rejected The Beatles in 1963, Veejay Records issued an album called *Introducing The Beatles*. When Beatlemania reached its peak at the end of 1964, Capitol acquired the rights of the Veejay recordings and issued this album that is a rather truncated version of the British album *Please Please Me*, without 'I Saw Her Standing There' that was already on Capitol's *Meet The Beatles* album and without 'Misery' and 'There's A Place' that was not to be issued on a Capitol album until 1980.

Side One
Love Me Do   2:19
(See *Please Please Me* Album PCS 3042)
Twist And Shout (Medley-Russell)   2:32
(See *Please Please Me* Album PCS 3042)
Anna (Go To Him) (Alexander)   2:56
(See *Please Please Me* Album PCS 3042)
Chains (Goffin-King)   2:21
(See *Please Please Me* Album PCS 3042)
Boys (Dixon-Farrell)   2:24
(See *Please Please Me* Album PCS 3042)
Ask Me Why   2:24
(See *Please Please Me* Album PCS 3042)

Side Two
Please Please Me   2:00
(See *Please Please Me* Album PCS 3042)
P. S. I Love You   2:02
(See *Please Please Me* Album PCS 3042)
Baby It's You (David-Bacharach-Williams)   2:36
(See *Please Please Me* Album PCS 3042)
A Taste Of Honey (Marlow-Scott)   2:02
(See *Please Please Me* Album PCS 3042)
Do You Want To Know A Secret   1:55
(See *Please Please Me* Album PCS 3042)

All Lennon-McCartney songs except where stated.

CAPITOL FULL DIMENSIONAL STEREO

The Early BEATLES

ELEVEN OF THEIR 1964
AMERICAN HIT RECORDINGS
NOW ON CAPITOL

LOVE ME DO · TWIST AND SHOUT · ANNA · CHAINS · BOYS · ASK ME WHY · PLEASE PLEASE ME
· P.S. I LOVE YOU · BABY IT'S YOU · DO YOU WANT TO KNOW A SECRET · A TASTE OF HONEY ·

(NEW IMPROVED *FULL DIMENSIONAL* STEREO)

BEATLES VI

THE WORLD'S MOST POPULAR FOURSOME! JOHN · PAUL · GEORGE · RINGO

YOU LIKE ME TOO MUCH · TELL ME WHAT YOU SEE · BAD BOY · DIZZY MISS LIZZIE · EIGHT DAYS A WEEK · YES IT IS
WORDS OF LOVE · KANSAS CITY · I DON'T WANT TO SPOIL THE PARTY · EVERY LITTLE THING · WHAT YOU'RE DOING

RECORDED IN ENGLAND

Capitol
RECORDS

BEATLES VI

Capitol ST 2358
Release Date: 14 June 1965

Producer: George Martin
Running Time: 27:24

SIDE ONE: Kansas City/Hey Hey Hey Hey;
Eight Days A Week; You Like Me Too Much;
Bad Boy; I Don't Want To Spoil The Party;
Words Of Love.

SIDE TWO: What You're Doing; Yes It Is;
Dizzy Miss Lizzy; Tell Me What You See; Every
Little Thing.

With Beatlemania still at its height in America, Capitol Records came up with *Beatles VI*, a compilation of the remaining six tracks left over from the British album *Beatles For Sale*, plus three tracks pulled from the British *Help!* album. They also put 'Yes It Is' the B side of the current single 'Ticket To Ride' on this album, leaving the A side that is featured in the film *Help!* for that album. The only curio on this album is 'Bad Boy', that although recorded in 1965, was not released in Britain until some 18 months later when it was included on the album *A Collection Of Beatles Oldies*.

Side One

Kansas City (Leiber-Stoller)/
  Hey Hey Hey Hey (Penniman) 2:30
(See *Beatles For Sale* Album PCS 3062)
Eight Days A Week 2:43
(See *Beatles For Sale* Album PCS 3062)
You Like Me Too Much (Harrison) 2:34
(See British *Help!* Album PCS 3071)
Bad Boy (Williams) 2:17
(See *A Collection of Beatles Oldies* Album PCS 7016)
I Don't Want To Spoil The Party 2:23
(See *Beatles For Sale* Album PCS 3062)
Words Of Love (Holly) 2:10
(See *Beatles For Sale* Album PCS 3062)

Side Two

What You're Doing 2:30
(See *Beatles For Sale* Album PCS 3062)
Yes It Is 2:40
(See *British Rarities* Album PCM 1001)
Dizzy Miss Lizzy (Williams) 2:51
(See British *Help!* Album PCS 3071)
Tell Me What You See 2:35
(See British *Help!* Album PCS 3071)
Every Little Thing 2:01
(See *Beatles For Sale* Album PCS 3062)

All Lennon-McCartney songs except where stated.

HELP!

Capitol SMAS 2386
Release Date: 13 August 1965

Producer: George Martin
Running Time: 28:40

SIDE ONE: (The James Bond Theme); Help!; The Night Before; (From Me To You Fantasy); You've Got To Hide Your Love Away; I Need You; (In The Tyrol).

SIDE TWO: Another Girl; (Another Hard Day's Night); Ticket To Ride; (The Bitter End/You Can't Do That; You're Going To Lose That Girl; (The Chase).

The soundtrack of The Beatles' second movie includes the new songs specially written for the film and also the incidental music played by the George Martin Orchestra. When this album was released in the USA many fans were annoyed to find that it had been issued as an expensive de-luxe package but included only seven Beatles tracks. On the sleeve, the four photographs of The Beatles have been inadvertently rearranged so that the semaphore message spells out a nonsensical H-P-E-L!. Also, unlike the British track listing, this album cover offers the version 'You're Gonna Lose That Girl'; this spelling occurs elsewhere only on Record 3 of *The Beatles Box.*

Side One

The James Bond Theme (Norman)* 0:16
Help! 2:16
(See British *Help!* Album PCS 3071)
The Night Before 2:33
(See British *Help!* Album PCS 3071)
From Me To You Fantasy* 2:03
You've Got To Hide Your Love Away 2:08
(See British *Help!* Album PCS 3071)
I Need You (Harrison) 2:28
(See British *Help!* Album PCS 3071)
In The Tyrol (Wagner-Arr. Thorne)* 2:21

Side Two

Another Girl 2:02
(See British *Help!* Album PCS 3071)
Another Hard Day's Night* 2:28
Ticket To Ride 3:03
(See British *Help!* Album PCS 3071)
The Bitter End (Thorne)/You Can't Do That 2:20
You're Going to Lose That Girl 2:18
(See British *Help!* Album PCS 3071)
The Chase (Thorne)* 2:24

* The George Martin Orchestra. All Lennon-McCartney songs except where stated.

NEW IMPROVED FULL DIMENSIONAL STEREO

ORIGINAL MOTION PICTURE SOUNDTRACK

THE BEATLES

HELP!

HELP! · THE NIGHT BEFORE · YOU'VE GOT TO HIDE YOUR LOVE AWAY · I NEED YOU
ANOTHER GIRL · TICKET TO RIDE · YOU'RE GONNA LOSE THAT GIRL
And Exclusive Instrumental Music From the Picture's Soundtrack

RUBBER SOUL

Capitol ST 2442
Release Date: 6 December 1965

Producer: George Martin
Running Time: 28:46

SIDE ONE: I've Just Seen A Face; Norwegian Wood (This Bird Has Flown); You Won't See Me; Think For Yourself; The Word; Michelle.

SIDE TWO: It's Only Love; Girl; I'm Looking Through You; In My Life; Wait; Run For Your Life.

Although the title and sleeve of the American *Rubber Soul* album are the same as the British, the contents are different. The American *Help!* album had used only seven tracks from the British album, leaving four over, so two of these 'I've Just Seen A Face' and 'It's Only Love' were included on the American *Rubber Soul* plus ten tracks from the British *Rubber Soul*. The remaining two tracks from the British *Help!* and four from *Rubber Soul* were issued on *Yesterday and Today* yet another album by Capitol.

Side One
I've Just Seen A Face   2:04
(See British *Help!* Album PCS 3071)
Norwegian Wood (This Bird Has Flown)   2:00
(See British *Rubber Soul* Album PCS 3075)
You Won't See Me   3:19
(See British *Rubber Soul* Album PCS 3075)
Think For Yourself (Harrison)   2:16
(See British *Rubber Soul* Album PCS 3075)
The Word   2:42
(See British *Rubber Soul* Album PCS 3075)
Michelle   2:42
(See British *Rubber Soul* Album PCS 3075)

Side Two
It's Only Love   1:53
(See British *Help!* Album PCS 3071)
Girl   2:26
(See British *Rubber Soul* Album PCS 3075)
I'm Looking Through You   2:27
(See British *Rubber Soul* Album PCS 3075)
In My Life   2:23
(See British *Rubber Soul* Album PCS 3075)
Wait   2:13
(See British *Rubber Soul* Album PCS 3075)
Run For Your Life   2:21
(See British *Rubber Soul* Album PCS 3075)

All Lennon-McCartney songs except where stated.

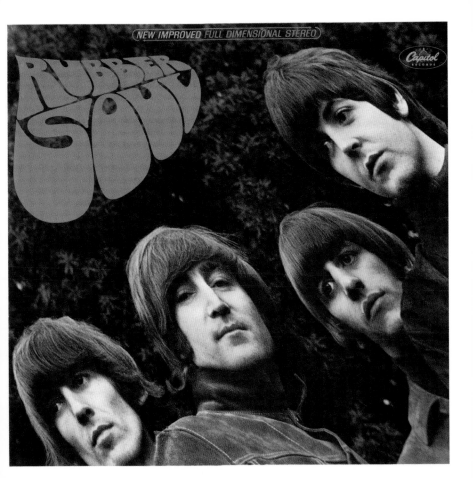

YESTERDAY AND TODAY

Capitol ST 2553
Release Date: 20 June 1966

Producer: George Martin
Running Time: 26:40

SIDE ONE: Drive My Car; I'm Only Sleeping; Nowhere Man; Dr. Robert; Yesterday; Act Naturally.

SIDE TWO: And Your Bird Can Sing; If I Needed Someone; We Can Work It Out; What Goes On?; Day Tripper.

When Capitol Records revealed that they intended to release this album, The Beatles decided to register a protest against the way their albums had been butchered, and were photographed for the sleeve dressed in butchers' aprons, holding pieces of meat and decapitated baby dolls; see the inner photograph on US *Rarities* sleeve for details. The public outcry was so great that this sleeve was withdrawn, the present sleeve quickly printed and substituted, and the album reissued. Because so many of the original sleeves had been printed, many simply had the new photograph pasted over the offending one. These examples are now quite valuable.

Tracks include 'Yesterday' and 'Act Naturally' from *Help!*, 'Drive My Car', 'Nowhere Man', 'If I Needed Someone' and 'What Goes On?' from *Rubber Soul*, plus three tracks originally planned for *Revolver* and included on the British *Revolver* album: 'I'm Only Sleeping', 'Dr. Robert', and 'And Your Bird Can Sing'. To complete the album Capitol included 'We Can Work It Out' and 'Day Tripper' that was issued as a double-A-sided single, six months before this album was released.

Side One
Drive My Car 2:24
(See British *Rubber Soul* Album PCS 3075)
I'm Only Sleeping 2:58
(See British *Revolver* Album PCS 7009)
Nowhere Man 2:40
(See British *Rubber Soul* Album PCS 3075)
Dr. Robert 2:14
(See British *Revolver* Album PCS 7009)

Side Two
And Your Bird Can Sing 2:02
(See British *Revolver* Album PCS 7009)
If I Needed Someone (Harrison) 2:19
(See British *Rubber Soul* Album PCS 3075)
We Can Work It Out 2:10
(See *A Collection Of Beatles Oldies* Album PCS 7016)
What Goes On? (Lennon-McCartney-Starkey) 2:44
(See British *Rubber Soul* Album PCS 3075)

Yesterday 2:04
(See British *Help!* Album PCS 3071)
Act Naturally (Morrison-Russell) 2:27
(See British *Help!* Album PCS 3071)

Day Tripper 2:37
(See *A Collection Of Beatles Oldies*
Album PCS 7016)
All Lennon–McCartney songs except where stated.

REVOLVER

Capitol ST 2576
Producers: George Martin
Release Date: 8 August 1966

SIDE ONE: Taxman; Eleanor Rigby; Love You To; Here, There And Everywhere; Yellow Submarine; She Said, She Said.

SIDE TWO: Good Day Sunshine; For No One; I Want To Tell You; Got To Get You Into My Life; Tomorrow Never Knows.

This is the first Beatles album to be issued in the USA bearing any resemblance to its UK equivalent. With the exception of three tracks included on *Yesterday And Today*, the tracks on this album are the same as on the British album. All subsequent albums except *Rarities* had identical American and British editions.

Side One

Taxman (Harrison) 2:36
(See British *Revolver* Album PCS 7009)
Eleanor Rigby 2:11
(See British *Revolver* Album PCS 7009)
Love You To (Harrison) 3:00
(See British *Revolver* Album PCS 7009)
Here, There And Everywhere 2:29
(See British *Revolver* Album PCS 7009)
Yellow Submarine 2:40
(See British *Revolver* Album PCS 7009)
She Said, She Said 2:39
(See British *Revolver* Album PCS 7009)

Side Two

Good Day Sunshine 2:08
(See British *Revolver* Album PCS 7009)
For No One 2:03
(See British *Revolver* Album PCS 7009)
I Want To Tell You (Harrison) 2:30
(See British *Revolver* Album PCS 7009)
Got To Get You Into My Life 2:31
(See British *Revolver* Album PCS 7009)
Tomorrow Never Knows 3:00
(See British *Revolver* Album PCS 7009)

All Lennon-McCartney songs except where stated.

RARITIES

Capitol SHAL 12060
Release Date: 24 March 1980

Producer: George Martin
Running Time: 41:04

SIDE ONE: Love Me Do; Misery; There's A Place; Sie Liebt Dich; And I Love Her; Help!; I'm Only Sleeping; I Am The Walrus.

SIDE TWO: Penny Lane; Helter Skelter; Don't Pass Me By; The Inner Light; Across The Universe; You Know My Name (Look Up The Number); Sgt. Pepper Inner Groove.

When Capitol Records in America informed EMI that they intended to release a *Rarities* album; EMI assumed they meant the album as included in the box-set *The Beatles Collection*; so EMI also decided t release it as a separate album on 29 October 1979, changing the catalogue number from PSLP 261 to PCM 1001. However Capitol's plans differed somewhat from the album that EMI had compiled. What Capitol had planned and what they released was an album of tracks that were rare in America. Almost the entire contents of the British *Rarities* album were already included on American albums, so Capitol saw very little point in releasing that album in America. What they did was to collect together those tracks not previously included on albums along with various rarities from around the world.

Although previously released in America, the tracks included here that make their first appearance c a US album are 'Misery', 'There's A Place', 'Sie Liebt Dich', 'The Inner Light' and 'You Know My Name'.

Of the remaining ten tracks, seven 'Love Me Do', 'Help!', 'I'm Only Sleeping', 'Helter Skelter', 'Don't Pass Me By', 'Across The Universe' and 'Sgt. Pepper Inner Groove', originate from British releases; while the version of 'And I Love Her' included here was originally included on the German version of the albun *Something New* (Odeon IC 072-04 600). The remaining two tracks, 'I Am The Walrus' and 'Penny Lane', are newly created versions edited together from other versions. In the case of 'I Am The Walrus', this was edited together using the British stereo version and editing in a few extra beats that originally appeared only on the US single. The version of 'Penny Lane' included here also was edited together using the British stereo version plus a few extra notes on a piccolo trumpet that had been included on a mono version of promotional copies distributed to radio stations in America and Canada.

What Capitol released was an album rather more worthy of the title *Rarities* than the album released in Britain by EMI that was basically a compilation of Beatle B sides.

THE BEATLES RARITIES

Side One

Love Me Do   2:22
(See *Please Please Me* Album PC 3042)
Misery   1:43
(See *Please Please Me* Album PCS 3042)
There's A Place   1:44
(See *Please Please Me* Album PCS PCS 7067-8)
Sie Liebt Dich (Lennon-McCartney-Nicolas-
Montague) 2:18
(See *Past Masters – Vol 1* Album BPM 1)
And I Love Her   2:36
(See *British A Hard Day's Night* Album PCS 3058)

Help!   2:16
(See British *Help!* Album PCS 3071)
I'm Only Sleeping   2:58
(See British *Revolver* Album PCS 7027)
I Am The Walrus   4:35
(See *Magical Mystery Tour* Album PCTC 255)

All Lennon-McCartney songs except where stated

Side Two

Penny Lane   3:00
(See *Magical Mystery Tour* Album PCTC 255)
Helter Skelter   3.38
(See *The Beatles* Album (PCS 7067-8)
Don't Pass Me By (Starkey)   3:45
(See *The Beatles* Album (PCS 7067-8)
The Inner Light (Harrison)   2.36

(See *Past Masters – Vol 2* Album BPM 2)
Across the Universe   3.41
(See *Past Masters – Vol 2* Album BPM 2)
You Know My Name (Look Up The Number)   4.20
(See *Past Masters – Vol 2* Album BPM 2)
Sgt. Pepper Inner Groove   0.02
(See *Sgt. Pepper* Album PCS 7009)

20 GREATEST HITS

Capitol SV 12245
Release Date: 18 October 1982

Producers: George Martin and Phil Spector
Running Time: 58:59

SIDE ONE: She Loves You; Love Me Do; I Want To Hold Your Hand; Can't Buy Me Love; A Hard Day's Night; I Feel Fine; Eight Days A Week; Ticket To Ride; Help!; Yesterday; We Can Work It Out; Paperback Writer.

SIDE TWO: Penny Lane; All You Need Is Love; Hello Goodbye; Hey Jude; Get Back; Come Together; Let It Be; The Long And Winding Road.

The release of a Beatles greatest hits album in both the UK and USA must pose a minor problem for the compilers. Do they compile an international greatest hits album or compile albums tailor-made for the individual market concerned? For this album Capitol in America and Parlophone in Britain decided on the latter and, using the Billboard charts, Capitol compiled an album of The Beatles' American greatest hits. Some of the recordings included on this American album are not on the British version and vice versa. Included here are 'Eight Days A Week', 'Yesterday', 'Penny Lane', 'Come Together', 'Let It Be' and 'The Long And Winding Road', in place of 'From Me To You', 'Day Tripper', 'Yellow Submarine', 'Eleanor Rigby', 'Lady Madonna' and 'The Ballad of John And Yoko' that are included on the British version. 'Eight Days A Week', 'Yesterday' and 'The Long And Winding Road' were issued as singles, unlike in Britain. Together with the rest of the tracks on this version of the album that, unlike the British version, cover the whole of The Beatles' Parlophone recording career from 1962 to 1970, they all reached No. 1 in the Billboard singles chart.

One interesting inclusion on the American album is a shorter version of 'Hey Jude' that fades out just over two minutes earlier than the full version and clocks in at five minutes five seconds.

The sleeves of both British and American albums are very similar except that the British sleeve has the album contents printed across the top.

Following the release of this album, Capitol also reissued 'Love Me Do' on 12 November 1982 and not 10 October, as was expected, to tie in with its British re-release. Originally 'Love me Do' had been issued by Tollie Records (Tollie 9008) on 27 April 1964.

Side One

She Loves You   2:18
(See *Past Masters – Vol 1* Album (BPM 1)
Love Me Do   2:19
(See *Beatles For Sale* Album PCS3042)
I Want To Hold Your Hand   2:24
(See *Past Masters – Vol 1* Album BPM 1)
Can't Buy Me Love   2:15
(See British *A Hard Day's Night* Album PCS 3058)
A Hard Day's Night   2:32
(See British *A Hard Day's Night* Album PCS 3058)

I Feel Fine   2:19
(See *Past Masters – Vol 1* Album BPM 1)
Eight Days A Week   2:43
(See *Please Please Me* Album PCS 3062)
Ticket To Ride   3:03
(See British *Help!* Album PCS 3071)
Help!   2:16
(See British *Help!* Album PCS 3071)
Yesterday   2:04
(See British *Help!* Album PCS 3071)
We Can Work It Out   2:10
(See *Past Masters – Vol 2* BPM 2)
Paperback Writer   2:25
(See *Past Masters – Vol 2* BPM 2)

Side Two

Penny Lane   3:00
(See *Magical Mystery Tour* Album PCTC 255)
All You Need Is Love   3:47
(See *Magical Mystery Tour* Album PCTC 235)
Hello Goodbye   3:42
(See *Magical Mystery Tour* Album PCTC 255)
Hey Jude   5:05
(See *Past Masters – Vol 2* Album BPM 2)

Get Back   3:11
(See *Past Masters –– Vol 2* Album BPM 2)
Come Together   4:16
(See *Abbey Road* Album PCS 7088)
Let It Be   3:50
(See *Let It Be* Album PCS 7096)
*The Long And Winding Road   3:40
(See *Let It Be* Album PCS 7096)

*Produced by George Martin/Phil Spector. All others produced by George Martin.

20
GREATEST HITS

THE
BEATLES

IN THE BEGINNING

US Release: 7 November 2000
Running Time: 40.17

Polydor 549268
Producer: Bert Kaempfert

Ain't She Sweet; Cry for a Shadow; Let's Dance; My Bonnie; Take Out Some Insurance On Me, Baby; What'd I Say; Sweet Georgia Brown; When The Saints Go Marching In; Ruby Baby; Why; Nobody's Child; Ya Ya (Parts 1 & 2)

Although these tracks have been re-issued and repackaged many times, this is a completely re-mastered set – with a much-improved sound – of the the Beatles' early recording sessions in Hamburg, Germany. The tracks feature John, Paul, George and drummer Pete Best on their own and backing vocalist Tony Sheridan as The Beatles, plus four numbers recorded by Sheridan with 'The Beat Brothers'.

Ain't She Sweet (Yellen-Ager)   2.12
The Beatles
Recorded: 22-23 June 1961, Hamburg (see *The Beatles First*, Polydor 823 701-2)
Cry For A Shadow (Harrison-Lennon)   2.23
The Beatles
Recorded: 22-23 June 1961, Hamburg (see *The Beatles First*, Polydor 823 701-2)
Let's Dance (Lee)   2.33
Tony Sheridan & The Beat Brothers
Recorded: 18 October 1962, Hamburg (see *The Beatles First*, Polydor 823 701-2)
My Bonnie (Pratt)   2.42
The Beatles with Tony Sheridan
Recorded: 22-23 June 1961, Hamburg (see *The Beatles First*, Polydor 823 701-2)
Take Out Some Insurance On Me, Baby (aka If You Love Me Baby) (Singleton-Hall)   2.53
The Beatles with Tony Sheridan
Recorded: 24 June 1961, Hamburg (see *The Beatles First*, Polydor 823 701-2)

What'd I Say (Charles) 2.39
Tony Sheridan & The Beat Brothers
Recorded: 31 January 1963, Hamburg (see *The Beatles First,* Polydor 823 701-2)
Sweet Georgia Brown (Bernie-Pinkard-Casey) 2.05
The Beatles with Tony Sheridan
Recorded: 21 December 1961, Hamburg (see *The Beatles First,* Polydor 823 701-2)
When The Saints Go Marching In (Trad. arr Sheridan) 3.18
The Beatles with Tony Sheridan
Recorded: 22-23 June 1961, Hamburg (see *The Beatles First*, Polydor 823 701-2)
Ruby Baby (Leiber-Stoller) 2.52
Tony Sheridan & The Beat Brothers
Recorded: 31 January 1963, Hamburg (see *The Beatles First*, Polydor 823 701-2)
Why (Can't You Love Me Again) (Crompton-Sheridan) 2.58
The Beatles with Tony Sheridan
Recorded: 22-23 June 1961, Hamburg (see *The Beatles First*, Polydor 823 701-2)
Nobody's Child (Foree-Coben) 3.55
The Beatles with Tony Sheridan
Recorded: 22-23 June 1961, Hamburg (see *The Beatles First*, Polydor 823 701-2)
Ya Ya (Parts 1 & 2) (Robinson-Dorsey-Lewis) 5.08
Tony Sheridan & The Beat Brothers
Recorded: 28 August 1962, Hamburg (see *The Beatles First*, Polydor 823 701-2)

FURTHER BRITISH ALBUMS

20 GREATEST HITS

UK Release: 18 October 1982
US Release: None
Producer: George Martin

Parlophone PCTC 260 20
Intl CD No: None
Running Time: 56:12

SIDE ONE: Love Me Do; From Me To You; She Loves You; I Want To Hold Your Hand; Can't Buy Me Love; A Hard Day's Night; I Feel Fine; Ticket To Ride; Help!; Day Tripper; We Can Work It Out.

SIDE TWO: Paperback Writer; Yellow Submarine; Eleanor Rigby; All You Need Is Love; Hello Goodbye; Lady Madonna; Hey Jude; Get Back; The Ballad Of John And Yoko.

Issued on 18 October 1982, two weeks after the re-release of 'Love Me Do', this album contains the A sides of The Beatles' 17 British No. 1 singles starting with 'From Me To You' released in 1963 and going through to 1969 and 'The Ballad Of John And Yoko'. The three remaining tracks included are 'Day Tripper' and 'Eleanor Rigby' (two B sides) together with 'Love Me Do'.

Originally, this was planned as a double album called *The Beatles Greatest Hits* and was to have contained the A sides of every one of the 26 Beatles singles issued on Parlophone in Britain. The album got as far as the test-pressing stage and was even given a catalogue number (EMTVS 34), but at the last moment was scrapped in favour of a single album to tie in with the American release. Although both albums use the same title, they have somewhat differing contents; the American album also includes a shorter version of 'Hey Jude' not featured on the British album (see page 147).

The sleeve is not as cheap looking as some previously produced and is basically the same for both albums and is also the first Beatles album sleeve ever to feature recording dates, release dates and chart positions achieved.

For the anniversary re-release of 'Love Me Do' on 4 October 1982, almost exactly 20 years to the day of its first release, EMI Records pressed the record with a red Parlophone label similar to the one used on the original release, and issued it in a special picture sleeve. They even used the original catalogue number (R4949). Unfortunately, the only thing not original about the record is the recording. As is widely known, there are two versions of 'Love Me Do', the original single version

LOVE ME DO • FROM ME TO YOU • SHE LOVES YOU • I WANT TO HOLD YOUR HAND • CAN'T BUY ME LOVE • A HARD DAY'S NIGHT
I FEEL FINE • TICKET TO RIDE • HELP • DAY TRIPPER • WE CAN WORK IT OUT • PAPERBACK WRITER • YELLOW SUBMARINE
ELEANOR RIGBY • ALL YOU NEED IS LOVE • HELLO GOODBYE • LADY MADONNA • HEY JUDE • GET BACK • THE BALLAD OF JOHN & YOKO

20 GREATEST HITS

THE BEATLES

that features Ringo Starr on drums and the album version that features session drummer Andy White. It is the latter that was used on the re-issued single.

The record was also issued as a limited edition picture disc (RP4949) and following the release of this album, also was issued as a 12-inch single (12R4949) on 1 November 1982. This, unlike the ordinary single, does contain the original version of 'Love Me Do' together with the album version and the single's original B side, 'PS I Love You'.

'Love Me Do' was to become The Beatles' second Top 10 hit of 1982 when it reached No. 4 in the British charts, its highest previous position had been No. 17. The Beatles' Movie Medley, issued earlier in the year, had reached No. 10, not bad for a group that had split up some 12 years previously.

Side One
Love Me Do 2:19
From Me To You 1:55
She Loves You 2:18
I Want To Hold Your Hand 2:24
Can't Buy Me Love 2:15
A Hard Day's Night 2:32
I Feel Fine 2:19
Ticket To Ride 3:03
Help! 2:16
Day Tripper 2:37
We Can Work It Out 2:10

Side Two
Paperback Writer 2:25
Yellow Submarine 2:40
Eleanor Rigby 2:11
All You Need Is Love 3:47
Hello Goodbye 3:24
Lady Madonna 2:17
Hey Jude 7:11
Get Back 3:11
The Ballad Of John And Yoko 2:58

TRIBUTE TO THE CAVERN

UK Release: 26 April 1984
US Release: None
Producers: George Martin and Walter J. Ridley

Parlophone CAV 1
Intl CD No: None
Running Time: 38:30

SIDE ONE:
Bad To Me (Billy J. Kramer and The Dakotas);
Hello Little Girl (The Fourmost);
You'll Never Walk Alone (Gerry and The Pacemakers);
Hippy Hippy Shake (The Swinging Blue Jeans);
Little Children (Billy J. Kramer and The Dakotas);
You're No Good (The Swinging Blue Jeans);
It's For You (Cilla Black);
Ferry 'Cross The Mersey (Gerry and The Pacemakers).

SIDE TWO:
Love Me Do;
I Saw Her Standing There;
Twist And Shout;
She Loves You;
Money;
I Want To Hold Your Hand;
Can't Buy Me Love;
A Hard Day's Night.

This custom-pressed album is available exclusively at the Cavern Club in Mathew Street, Liverpool and was produced for the club by EMI to celebrate its rebuilding and re-opening on 26 April 1984.

After many years of almost no interest on the part of Liverpool City Council in recognising the city's most famous sons, the local commercial radio station, Radio City, decided to lead the way by buying up an enormous amount of Beatles memorabilia and opening Beatle City in Seel Street, where in the early 60s, Allan Williams, The Beatles' first manager, had The Blue Angel Club.

Prior to the opening of Beatle City, The Liverpool Beatles Appreciation Society, a group of fans including many original Cavern Club members, had been campaigning to have a statue or some other form of permanent tribute erected in the city. Impressed by their enthusiasm, the Liverpool-based Royal Insurance Company decided to build Cavern Walks on the original site of the Cavern Club.

Opened in 1984, Cavern Walks contains a rebuilt Cavern Club located slightly farther up Mathew Street than the original plus a shopping arcade complete with a bronze statue of The Beatles. Following that, in early 1985, the British-born entertainer Tommy Steele presented the people of Liverpool with a bronze statue of Eleanor Rigby for which he charged the City of Liverpool half a sixpence, the title of a successful musical that starred Steele. This statue is sited in Stanley Street just

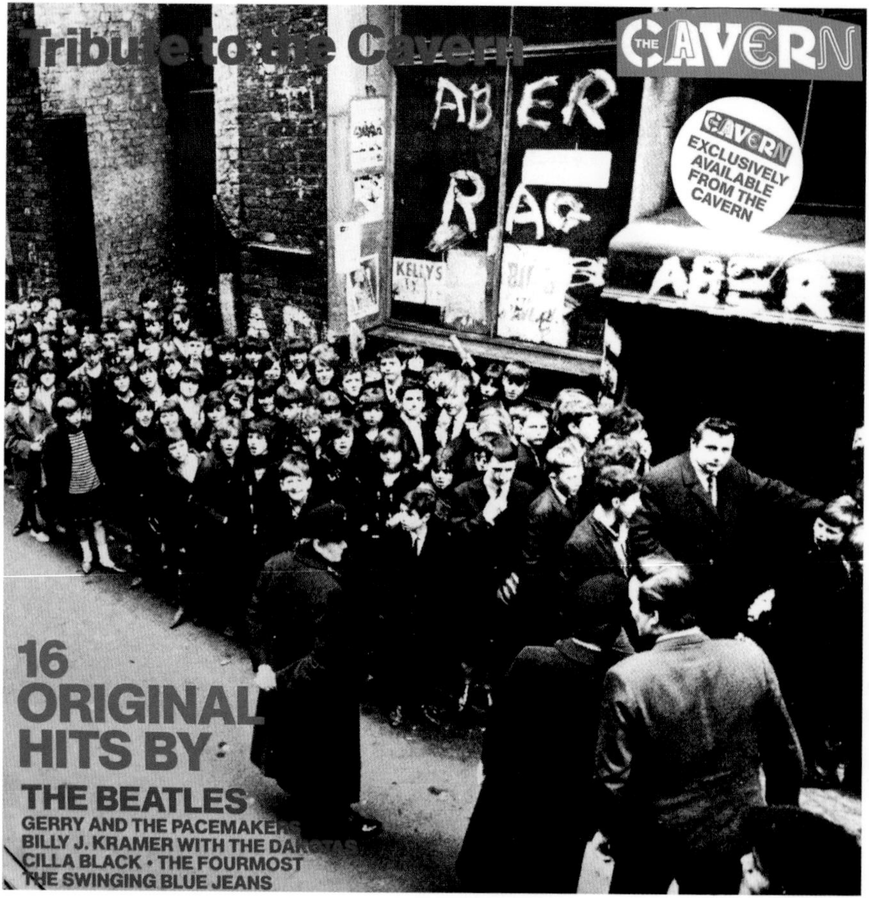

Tribute to the Cavern

THE CAVERN

AB ER
RAG

KELLYS

AB R

CAVERN
EXCLUSIVELY
AVAILABLE
FROM THE
CAVERN

16
ORIGINAL
HITS BY :

THE BEATLES
GERRY AND THE PACEMAKERS
BILLY J. KRAMER WITH THE DAKOTAS
CILLA BLACK · THE FOURMOST
THE SWINGING BLUE JEANS

around the corner from the Cavern Club. Since then, The Beatles Shop in Mathew Street has also opened, selling mainly Beatles records and memorabilia and records by other Merseyside artists.

This album almost could be called The Greatest Hits of Merseybeat, as it contains some of the most famous recordings to emerge from that era. Besides The Beatles tracks that are featured on side two, it also includes other Merseybeat artists such as Gerry and The Pacemakers and Cilla Black.

One of the other interesting aspects of this album is the inclusion of sleeve notes written by Tony Barrow who wrote the sleeve notes for a number of The Beatles' early albums and EPs.

Side One

Bad To Me   2:18
  Billy J. Kramer and The Dakotas
Hello Little Girl   1:50
  The Fourmost
You'll Never Walk Alone   2:40
  (Rodgers-Hammerstein II)
  Gerry and The Pacemakers
Hippy Hippy Shake   1:44*
  (Romero)
  The Swinging Blue Jeans
Little Children   2:47
  (Shuman-McFarland)
  Billy J Kramer and The Dakotas
You're No Good   2:16*
  (C. Ballard Jnr)
  The Swinging Blue Jeans
It's For You   2:20
  Cilla Black

Ferry 'Cross The Mersey   2:38
  (Marsden)
  Gerry and The Pacemakers

Side Two

Love Me Do   2:19
I Saw Her Standing There   2:50
Twist And Shout   2:32
  (Medley-Russell)
She Loves You   2:18
Money (Bradford-Gordy)   2:47
I Want To Hold Your Hand   2:24
Can't Buy Me Love   2:15
A Hard Day's Night   2:32

All Lennon-McCartney songs except where stated.

Only The Beatles...

SMMC 151

JOHN   PAUL   GEORGE   RINGO   JOHN   PAUL   GEORGE   RINGO

JOHN   PAUL   GEORGE   RINGO   JOHN   PAUL   GEORGE   RINGO

SIDE ONE
LOVE ME DO
TWIST AND SHOUT
SHE LOVES YOU
THIS BOY
EIGHT DAYS A WEEK
ALL MY LOVING

SIDE TWO
TICKET TO RIDE
YES IT IS
OB-LA-DI OB-LA-DA
LUCY IN THE SKY WITH DIAMONDS
AND I LOVE HER
STRAWBERRY FIELDS FOREVER

ONLY THE BEATLES . . .

UK Release: 30 June 1986
US Release: None
Producer: George Martin

Parlophone SMMC 151 (Cassette only)
Intl CD No: None
Running Time: 33:10

SIDE ONE: Love Me Do; Twist And Shout; She Loves You;This Boy; Eight Days A Week; All My Loving.

SIDE TWO: Ticket To Ride; Yes It Is; Ob-La-Di Ob-La-Da; Lucy In The Sky With Diamonds; And I Love Her; Strawberry Fields Forever.

Available by mail order only from Heineken, this cassette was backed by newspaper advertisements in the British press and was available only for a short time before being quickly withdrawn due to objections by The Beatles.

The cassette features 12 tracks, includes the previously unreleased stereo version of 'Yes It Is'. Among the remaining tracks is the original single version of 'Love Me Do' together with a further ten tracks from various points in The Beatles' career. Despite the claims on the inlay card, the version of 'This Boy' included is not a previously unreleased stereo version, but the reprocessed stereo version previously available on *Love Songs* and other compilations. The unreleased stereo version, at present remains unreleased. However, the stereo version as released on singles in Australia and Canada in 1976 was included on the 1988 album *Past Masters / Volumes One and Two*.

Its short-lived and limited availability makes this cassette a much sought-after collector's item.

Side One
Love Me Do   2:22
Twist And Shout   2:32
(Medley-Russell)
She Loves You   2:18
This Boy   2:11
Eight Days A Week   2:43
All My Loving   2:04

Side Two
Ticket To Ride   3:03
Yes It Is   2:40
Ob-La-Di, Ob-La-Da   3:10
Lucy In The Sky With
Diamonds   3:25
And I Love Her   2:27
Strawberry Fields Forever   4:05

All Lennon-McCartney songs except where stated.

THE BEATLES

PAST MASTERS · VOLUME ONE

PAST MASTERS – VOLUME ONE

UK Release: 7 March 1988
US Release: 7 March 1988
Intl CD No: CDP 7 90043 2
Running Time: 42:30

Parlophone BPM 1
Capitol: C129 90043
Producer: George Martin

SIDE ONE: Love Me Do; From Me To You; Thank You Girl; She Loves You; I'll Get You; I Want To Hold Your Hand; This Boy; Komm, Gib Mir Deine Hand; Sie Liebt Dich.

SIDE TWO: Long Tall Sally; I Call Your Name; Slow Down; Matchbox; I Feel Fine; She's A Woman; Bad Boy; Yes It Is; I'm Down.

Following the worldwide release by EMI of The Beatles' original studio albums on compact disc, they have collected together in this and the accompanying volume, the remaining studio material not included on those albums. Twenty-five of the 33 tracks on these two albums originally were issued on singles in Britain. A further two, Komm, Gib Mir Deine Hand and Sie Liebt Dich originally were issued as a single in Germany in 1964. Four others: 'Long Tall Sally', 'I Call Your Name', 'Slow Down' and 'Matchbox', originate from the 1964 *Long Tall Sally* EP; while 'Bad Boy' was issued as part of the 1966 album *A Collection Of Beatles Oldies* and 'Across The Universe' originally was included on the charity album *No One's Gonna Change Our World* issued in 1969.

This first album covers the early days from 'Love Me Do' through to the heady days of the Beatlemania years of 1964-5, and contains the material that wasn't destined for British albums at the time. Among the contents of this album is the original version of 'Love Me Do' with Ringo on drums, together with both the A and B sides of a further four singles 'From Me To You', 'She Loves You', 'I Want To Hold Your Hand' and 'I Feel Fine', together with their respective B sides of 'Thank You Girl', 'I'll Get You', 'This Boy' and 'She's A Woman'. Other tracks on this album are 'Komm, Gib Mir Deine Hand' and 'Sie Liebt Dich', the German-language versions of 'I Want To Hold Your Hand' and 'She Loves You', that were originally issued in Germany as a single in 1964. 'Long Tall Sally' and 'I Call Your Name' were originally part of the 1964 American album *The Beatles Second*. These, together with 'Slow Down' and 'Matchbox', were later issued in Britain as the *Long Tall Sally* EP. 'Bad Boy' originates from the 1965 American album *Beatles VI* and was later to be included on the 1966 British album *A Collection Of Beatles Oldies*. Finally are included 'Yes It Is' and 'I'm Down', that were the B sides of 'Ticket To Ride' and 'Help!' respectively and were included on the *Help!* album. They are the only B sides on this album not accompanied by their respective A sides.

As previously mentioned, this album contains the original version of 'Love Me Do' with Ringo on drums, and is the first of a number of tracks included here that originally were quite rare. The version of 'This Boy' is the true stereo version originally available only on singles issued in Australia (Parlophone A8l03) and Canada (Capitol 72144), and it makes its first appearance on an album here. 'She's A Woman' again in stereo, originates from the 1967 Australian album *Greatest Hits Volume 2* (Parlophone PCSO 7534). 'Yes It Is', in its stereo form, was issued in Britain in 1986 as part of the *Only The Beatles* cassette (Parlophone SMMC 151). Finally, 'I'm Down', in its stereo form, originally was issued as part of the Japanese *Help!* EP (Odeon EAS 30006). With the exception of 'I'm Down', these stereo versions have been given their first international release on this album.

In collecting together these tracks for these two albums, EMI have finally produced compilations that w be extremely welcome among Beatles fans worldwide. Having these and the rest of The Beatles' collection available on compact disc is like having your own personal copy of The Beatles' studio master tapes.

These albums are worthy additions to any Beatles record collection and, in the case of the CD collection, are essential as they finally tidy up the studio material not included on the original albums.

SIDE ONE
Love Me Do (Lennon-McCartney)   2:22
Recorded: 4 September 1962, EMI Studios, Abbey Road, London
John Lennon: Harmonica and Lead Vocal   **Paul McCartney:** Bass Guitar and Lead Vocal
George Harrison: Acoustic Guitar and Harmony Vocal
Ringo Starr: Drums

This is the original version featuring Ringo on drums and not the version included on the *Please Please Me* album that features session drummer Andy White. This version comes from The Beatles' first official recording session with EMI that took place on 4 September 1962 three months after George Martin had firs given them a recording test on 6 June 1962. During that period Ringo had replaced Pete Best on drums.

The recording was completed in approximately 15 takes and is dominated by John's harmonica. The main lead vocals are a duet from John and Paul with John singing solo at various times. The lyric are rather sparse but with the dominant harmonica and John's asthmatic-sounding Liverpudlian vocals it is still an excellent first effort from very nervous Beatles.

It is this version that was issued as a single together with 'PS I Love You' on 5 October 1962. It entered the charts the following week and eventually achieved its highest position at No. 17. In 1982 it was reissued to celebrate its 20th anniversary: on that occasion it reached No. 4.

From Me To You (Lennon-McCartney)   1:55
Recorded: 5 March 1963, EMI Studios, Abbey Road, London
John Lennon: Rhythm Guitar, Harmonica and Lead Vocal
Paul McCartney: Bass Guitar and Lead Vocal
George Harrison: Lead Guitar and Harmony Vocal   **Ringo Starr:** Drums
With this, the follow-up single to 'Please Please Me' and The Beatles' second No. 1, they began to prove that they had both musical and song-writing ability. According to some charts 'Please Please Me' reached only No. 2, and 'From Me To You' was their first No. 1 single. If it were, it began a string of 11 consecutive No. 1 singles, a record that has not been equalled to date.

Like so many of The Beatles' early recordings the lead vocal is shared by John and Paul with George joining in here and there and on chorus. The recording also makes very effective use of John's harmonica.

This song was reputed to have been written on 28 February 1963 after John and Paul had read the letters column From You To Us in the *New Musical Express* during a coach journey from York to Shrewsbury while they were on tour as the support act with Helen Shapiro.

During the early 60s The Beatles had their own BBC radio show, some episodes were called From Us To You that featured a reworded recording of 'From Me To You'.

Thank You Girl (Lennon-McCartney)   2:01
Recorded: 5 and 13 March 1963, EMI Studios, Abbey Road, London
John Lennon: Acoustic Guitar, Harmonica and Lead Vocal
Paul McCartney: Bass Guitar and Lead Vocal   **George Harrison:** Lead Guitar
Ringo Starr: Drums
This exciting track dates back to April 1963 when it was originally released as the B side of The Beatles' third Parlophone single 'From Me To You'. It has a predominant harmonica from John, and the usual John and Paul lead-vocal duet that featured on most of their 1963 singles. The recording was completed in 13 takes on 5 March 1963 and some additional edit sections were recorded on 13 March 1963.

She Loves You (Lennon-McCartney)   2:18
Recorded: 1 July 1963, EMI Studios, Abbey Road, London
John Lennon: Rhythm Guitar and Lead Vocal   **Paul McCartney:** Bass Guitar and Lead Vocal
George Harrison: Lead Guitar and Harmony Vocal   **Ringo Starr:** Drums
This is the A side of The Beatles' fourth single, issued on Parlophone in Britain on 23 August 1963,
featuring the usual lead-vocal duet from John and Paul. The song includes the famous catchy chorus line
of yeah, yeah, yeah and the equally famous oooo that previously was used in 'I Saw Her Standing There'
on the *Please Please Me* album. If 'Love Me Do', 'Please Please Me' and 'From Me To You' had not
convinced people that The Beatles had staying-power, the catchy chorus line and excitement generated
by 'She Loves You' surely must have done so.

I'll Get You (Lennon-McCartney)   2:04
Recorded: 1 July 1963, EMI Studios, Abbey Road, London
John Lennon: Rhythm Guitar, Harmonica and Lead Vocal
Paul McCartney: Bass Guitar and Harmony Vocal
George Harrison: Lead Guitar and Harmony Vocal   **Ringo Starr:** Drums
Originally considered as an A side for the follow-up to 'From Me To You', this was released in 1963 as
the B side to 'She Loves You'. The song is reminiscent of 'She Loves You' with the opening Oh yeah and
the duet by John and Paul on lead vocals. John's overdubbed harmonica is prominent at the beginning
and ending but is mixed back during the rest of the track. The take details of this and 'She Loves You',
are unknown. This is because the studio master was erased shortly after the session. This also accounts
for the lack of stereo versions of both these tracks.

I Want To Hold Your Hand (Lennon-McCartney)   2:24
Recorded: 17 October 1963, EMI Studios, Abbey Road, London
John Lennon: Rhythm Guitar and Lead Vocal   **Paul McCartney:** Bass Guitar and Lead Vocal
George Harrison: Lead Guitar and Harmony Vocal   **Ringo Starr:** Drums
As a single, this record sold over 15 million copies worldwide. In fact, prior to its release in Britain on 29
November 1963, there were advance orders approaching one million copies. On its release in Britain it
entered the charts at No. 1 where it remained for six weeks. This was the record that in 1964 gave birth
to Beatlemania in America where it sold nearly five million copies and opened up the American market
for other British artists.

The recording opens with John's rhythm guitar, a sound that builds up to an intense pitch and then almost explodes as John and Paul begin their lead-vocal duet. For the chorus line John and Paul are joined by George and all three add excited hand-clapping to make this one of their most powerful early recordings.

Recorded in 17 takes on 17 October 1963, this was The Beatles' first four-track recording. This enabled George Martin to produce a rather better stereo image than the previous two-track recordings of earlier sessions.

This Boy (Lennon-McCartney)   2:11
Recorded: 17 October 1963, EMI Studios, Abbey Road, London
John Lennon: Acoustic Guitar and Lead Vocal
Paul McCartney: Bass Guitar and Harmony Vocal
George Harrison: Lead Guitar and Harmony Vocal   **Ringo Starr:** Drums

This track originally was released in 1963 as the B side to The Beatles' multi-million seller 'I Want To Hold Your Hand'. 'This Boy' was recorded at the same 17 October 1963 session as 'I Want To Hold Your Hand', and also went to 17 takes before the 15th was finally chosen for release.

The song is dominated by a close three-part harmony from John, Paul and George, with an extremely powerful solo vocal from John. For the film *A Hard Day's Night*, George Martin produced an orchestral version that was retitled *Ringo's Theme* and used in the film as the soundtrack to a section featuring Ringo who is seen walking along the banks of the River Thames.

Komm, Gib Mir Deine Hand (Lennon-McCartney-Nicolas-Helimer)   2:24
Recorded: (Instrumental Track) 17 October 1963, EMI Studios, Abbey Road, London
(Vocal Track) 29 January 1964, Pathé Marconi Studios, Paris, France
John Lennon: Rhythm Guitar and Lead Vocal   **Paul McCartney:** Bass Guitar and Lead Vocal
George Harrison: Lead Guitar   **Ringo Starr:** Drums

The German-language versions of 'I Want To Hold Your Hand' and 'She Loves You' were not recorded, as many thought, as a tribute to The Beatles' early days in Hamburg, but in answer to a request from EMI in Germany who wanted authentic versions for the German market. The Beatles were far from enthusiastic about the idea but George Martin eventually persuaded them to record the tracks in the EMI studios in Paris where they were at the time. The two recordings subsequently were released in Germany as a double-A-sided single on 5 March 1964 (Odeon 22671). The German lyrics of both songs were written by two German songwriters, one of whom was present at the recording session to ensure that the songs were sung with the correct accent.

For this version of the song The Beatles used the original English version backing track and, in 11 takes, added the new German vocals plus hand-claps.

Sie Liebt Dich (Lennon-McCartney-Nicolas-Montague) 2:18
Recorded: 29 January 1964, Pathé Marconi Studios, Paris, France
John Lennon: Rhythm Guitar and Lead Vocal   **Paul McCartney:** Bass Guitar and Lead Vocal
George Harrison: Lead Guitar and Harmony Vocal   **Ringo Starr:** Drums
This German-language version of 'She Loves You' shares the same basic history as 'Komm, Gib Mir Deine Hand'. But unlike 'Komm, Gib Mir Deine Hand' that used the backing track from 'I Want To Hold Your Hand', 'Sie Liebt Dich' is a brand-new recording. The Beatles were unable to use the backing track to 'She Loves You' for 'Sie Liebt Dich' because the original studio master had been erased.

SIDE TWO
Long Tall Sally (Johnson-Penniman-Blackwell) 1:58
Recorded: 1 March 1964, EMI Studios, Abbey Road, London
John Lennon: Rhythm Guitar   **Paul McCartney:** Bass Guitar and Solo Vocal
George Harrison: Lead Guitar   **Ringo Starr:** Drums
George Martin: Piano
This Little Richard song, originally released as part of the American album *The Beatles Second* on 10 April 1964 and then in Britain on 19 June 1964 as the title track of an EP, provides Paul with a perfect vehicle for his voice. Here, his solo vocal sounds just as enthusiastic and spontaneous as John's does on the classic 'Twist And Shout'. In fact, like 'Twist And Shout', this was recorded in one take. The Beatles had used both songs for years during their live performances that invariably opened with this song and closed with 'Long Tall Sally' a format they were to continue to use for their later, large-scale concert performances.

I Call Your Name (Lennon-McCartney)   2:02
Recorded: 1 March 1964, EMI Studios, Abbey Road, London
John Lennon: Rhythm Guitar and Solo Vocal   **Paul McCartney:** Bass Guitar
George Harrison: Lead Guitar   **Ringo Starr:** Drums

This was written originally for Billy J. Kramer and The Dakotas, who recorded and issued it as the B side to 'Bad To Me' another Lennon-McCartney composition. John wrote it and when he discovered it had been buried on a B side he decided that The Beatles should also record and issue it. So with John on lead vocals The Beatles recorded the song in seven takes, the released version being an edit of takes 5 and 7. During the same session, 'Long Tall Sally' was produced. Like 'Long Tall Sally', 'I Call Your Name' was issued as part of the American album *The Beatles Second* on 10 April 1964, and in Britain on 19 June 1964 on the *Long Tall Sally* EP

Slow Down (Williams)   2:54
Recorded: 1 and 4 June 1964, EMI Studios, Abbey Road, London
John Lennon: Rhythm Guitar and Solo Vocal   **Paul McCartney:** Bass Guitar
George Harrison: Lead Guitar   **Ringo Starr:** Drums
George Martin: Piano

Released as part of the *Long Tall Sally* EP on 19 June 1964, this track was partly recorded during six takes on 1 June and completed on 4 June. It features John on lead-vocal and is an extremely enthusiastic rendition of this little-known Larry Williams song. It is the first of three Williams songs The Beatles recorded and released.

Matchbox (Perkins)   1:37
Recorded: 1 June 1964, EMI Studios, Abbey Road, London
John Lennon: Rhythm Guitar   **Paul McCartney:** Bass Guitar
George Harrison: Lead Guitar   **Ringo Starr:** Drums and Solo Vocal
George Martin: Piano

This was recorded in five takes during the same session as 'Slow Down' and released as part of the *Long Tall Sally* EP. Ringo gives a rousing rendition of this 1957 Carl Perkins song that was recorded with Perkins present although he did not participate.

I Feel Fine (Lennon-McCartney)   2:19
Recorded: 18 October 1964, EMI Studios, Abbey Road, London
John Lennon: Rhythm Guitar, Lead Guitar and Lead Vocal
Paul McCartney: Bass Guitar and Backing Vocal
George Harrison: Lead Guitar and Backing Vocal   **Ringo Starr:** Drums
With advance orders of three quarters of a million copies, this was issued as a single on 27 November 1964 as the follow-up to 'A Hard Day's Night'. It was The Beatles' eighth single and sixth consecutive No. 1. The recording, that was completed in nine takes, opens with a single note of feedback that goes into the riff around which the song is constructed. This was the first time feedback had been used on a record and it gave ideas to many musicians like Jimi Hendrix who later used feedback as a musical note and not just as a noise. Theories at the time about the sound at the beginning of the record included the idea of an amplified humming bee. In fact The Beatles did not use any pre-recorded sound effects until two years later in 1966. The lead vocal is from John, with Paul and George joining him on the chorus. Paul and George also sing a wordless vocal backing.

She's A Woman (Lennon-McCartney)   2:57
Recorded: 8 October 1964, EMI Studios, Abbey Road, London
John Lennon: Rhythm Guitar
Paul McCartney: Bass Guitar, Piano and Solo Vocal
George Harrison: Lead Guitar   **Ringo Starr:** Drums and Percussion
This great chunk of syncopated rock'n'roll, written and sung by Paul in his best rock'n'roll style, was recorded in seven takes and issued originally as the B side of 'I Feel Fine' on 27 November 1964.

Bad Boy (Williams)   2:17
Recorded: 10-11 May 1965, EMI Studios, Abbey Road, London
John Lennon: Rhythm Guitar, Hammond Organ and Solo Vocal
Paul McCartney: Bass Guitar and Electric Piano   **George Harrison:** Lead Guitar
Ringo Starr: Drums and Tambourine
This was issued originally as part of the American album *Beatles VI* on 14 June 1965 and later included on the British album *A Collection Of Beatles Oldies* released on 9 December 1966. The recording was completed in four takes and features a solo vocal from John and a very enthusiastic backing from the rest of The Beatles. This and another Larry Williams song, 'Dizzy Miss Lizzy' that was recorded during

the same session, were the last two songs issued by The Beatles during their collective career that they did not write themselves apart from the rather short rendition of 'Maggie Mae' on *Let It Be*.

Yes It Is (Lennon-McCartney)   2:40
Recorded: 16 February 1965, EMI Studios, Abbey Road, London
John Lennon: Acoustic Guitar and Lead Vocal
Paul McCartney: Bass Guitar and Backing Vocal
George Harrison: Lead Guitar and Backing Vocal   **Ringo Starr:** Drums
The B side to 'Ticket To Ride' that was released on 9 April 1965, this beautiful ballad was recorded in 14 takes on 16 February 1965. Written by John, the song is very reminiscent of his earlier 'This Boy' and features a similar three-part harmony from John, Paul and George, with John singing solo in parts. The whining guitar in the backing is played by George who achieved the effect with a volume/tone control pedal with which he had been experimenting at the time.

I'm Down (Lennon-McCartney)   2:30
Recorded: 14 June 1965, EMI Studios, Abbey Road, London
John Lennon: Rhythm Guitar, Hammond Organ and Backing Vocal
Paul McCartney: Bass Guitar and Lead Vocal   **George Harrison:** Lead Guitar and Backing Vocal
Ringo Starr: Drums and Bongos
This is The Beatles at their rock'n'roll best! This superb McCartney-written track, similar in style to Little Richard's 'Long Tall Sally', originally was issued on 23 July 1965 as the B side of *Help!* that was included on the album of the same name. The recording was completed in seven takes and rattles along at an incredible pace with Paul shouting out the lyrics in true Little Richard style while John hammers away at the Hammond organ. Unbelievably, this recording was made during the same session that produced 'Yesterday'.

PAST MASTERS – VOLUME TWO

UK Release: 7 March 1988
US Release: 7 March 1988
Intl CD No: CDP 7 90044 2
Running Time: 51:03

Parlophone BPM 2
Capitol: C12P 90044
Producer: George Martin

SIDE ONE: Day Tripper; We Can Work It Out; Paperback Writer; Rain; Lady Madonna; The Inner Light; Hey Jude; Revolution.

SIDE TWO: Get Back; Don't Let Me Down; The Ballad Of John And Yoko; Old Brown Shoe; Across The Universe; Let It Be; You Know My Name (Look Up The Number).

With the release of the *Rubber Soul* album in late 1965, together with the 'We Can Work It Out'/'Day Tripper' single, The Beatles were slowly moving away from the three-minute pop single towards a more progressive though still highly commercial form of music that was to culminate in 1967 with the release of the *Sgt. Pepper's Lonely Hearts Club Band* album.

In 1966, prior to the release of Sgt. Pepper, The Beatles were beginning to experiment in the studio with sound effects, backwards-running tapes and other such studio wizardry. Examples of their early experimentation can be found on the *Revolver* album. One further example from the same period, 'Rain' that was not included on *Revolver,* is included on this album. It features one of John Lennon's weirdest vocal performances when, just near the end, he can be heard singing backwards.

With more than a little help from George Martin, by 1967 The Beatles had almost perfected the use of studio effects, many of which were used to great effect on both the Sgt. Pepper album and the *Magical Mystery Tour* EPs. During 1967 The Beatles issued three singles: 'Penny Lane'/'Strawberry Fields Forever', 'All You Need Is Love'/'Baby, You're A Rich Man' and 'Hello Goodbye'/'I Am The Walrus'. These, together with the tracks from the *Magical Mystery Tour* EPs, were issued as an album in America and subsequently have been issued as a compact disc and are not included on this album.

In 1968, after the psychedelia of Sgt. Pepper, The Beatles returned to rock'n'roll with 'Lady Madonna', that they followed up with their most popular single, 'Hey Jude', on the newly founded Apple label. 'Hey Jude' was a record among records, it was the longest single to have been issued up to that date, it clocks in at an amazing seven minutes 11 seconds and despite its running time remains one of pop music's all-time classics.

THE BEATLES

PAST MASTERS · VOLUME TWO

During 1969 The Beatles issued two singles that were not included on albums at the time. The first, 'Get Back'/'Don't Let Me Down', was originally to have been two tracks from the *Get Back* album that The Beatles attempted to record during January 1969 at Apple Studios in Savile Row. The album eventually was abandoned, but the single was released on 11 April 1969.

After their brief stay at Apple The Beatles returned to Abbey Road to record their second single of 1969, 'The Ballad Of John And Yoko'/'Old Brown Shoe'. The A side was recorded by John and Paul during an eight-and-a-half-hour session on 14 April 1969 and 'Old Brown Shoe' that features all four Beatles, was recorded two days later. Both titles were issued as a single on 30 May 1969.

Following the release of the *Abbey Road* album, EMI issued a charity album called *No One's Gonna Change Our World* (Regal Starline SRS 5013) in December 1969. This album featured 'Across The Universe', a track that The Beatles had recorded almost two years earlier in February 1968. Over the years that version has become known as the Wildlife Version and is the only track included here not to have originated from a single.

1970 saw the release of *Let It Be*, The Beatles' final single and album. Almost the entire album had been taken from the *Get Back* sessions of January 1969 and remixed by Phil Spector. Though still from the same sessions, the single differs from the album version quite considerably and is George Martin's original mix, issued on 6 March 1970.

Aside from the tracks already mentioned, this second album also contains 'Paperback Writer' that together with 'Rain' was issued as a single in June 1966; 'The Inner Light', the B side to the March 1968 single 'Lady Madonna'; 'Revolution' that was the upside of The Beatles' first Apple single 'Hey Jude' in August 1968; and, finally, 'You Know My Name' the B side to their final single 'Let It Be' in March 1970.

SIDE ONE
Day Tripper (Lennon-McCartney) 2:37
Recorded: 16 October 1965, EMI Studios, Abbey Road, London
John Lennon: Rhythm Guitar, Tambourine and Lead Vocal
Paul McCartney: Bass Guitar and Lead Vocal
George Harrison: Lead Guitar and Harmony Vocal   **Ringo Starr:** Drums
This track was issued with 'We Can Work It Out' as a double-A-sided single on 3 December 1965; the same day also saw the release of the *Rubber Soul* album. It was written mainly by John with Paul contributing some of the lyrics. The lyrics are reminiscent of the earlier 'Ticket To Ride' and the title is similar. It was recorded in three takes on 16 October 1965 and features a lead vocal duet between John and Paul with George joining them for the harmony sections. It entered the British charts at No. 1 on its release where it stayed for five weeks, selling over one million copies before the end of the month.

We Can Work It Out (Lennon-McCartney) 2:10
Recorded: 20 and 29 October 1965, EMI Studios, Abbey Road, London
John Lennon: Harmonium and Harmony Vocal   **Paul McCartney:** Bass Guitar and Lead Vocal
George Harrison: Acoustic Guitar and Tambourine   **Ringo Starr:** Drums
This could be classified as The Beatles' first-ever peace song. It predated 'All You Need Is Love' by two years and 'Give Peace A Chance' by four years. Released as the follow-up to 'Help!' in 1965 this is The Beatles' 11th Parlophone single and their ninth No. 1. By 1965 The Beatles had progressed from the beat group sound of some of their early 1963-4 singles to a more technically and musically proficient group of musicians. Lead vocal on this is by Paul, with John joining in for the chorus and also playing harmonium. At various times the recording lapses into a slow waltz but then picks up again for the verses. John later used the same style for the instrumental break in the middle of 'Being For The Benefit Of Mr. Kite' on *Sgt. Pepper's Lonely Hearts Club Band*. Paul's optimistic main lyrics are countered by John's realism with the verse beginning 'Life is very short'. John did a similar thing with Paul's 'Getting Better' on Sgt. Pepper. The main part of the track was recorded in two takes on 20 October and completed with an overdub on 29 October.

Paperback Writer (Lennon-McCartney)   2:25
Recorded: 13 and 14 April 1966, EMI Studios, Abbey Road, London
John Lennon: Rhythm Guitar and Backing Vocal   **Paul McCartney:** Bass Guitar and Lead Vocal
George Harrison: Lead Guitar and Backing Vocal   **Ringo Starr:** Drums
This track was recorded in two takes with one overdub during the sessions for *Revolver* and was issued as a single on 10 June 1966, some two months prior to that album. The song, written mainly by Paul with John contributing some of the lyrics, was inspired by John Lennon's two books *In His Own Write* and *Spaniard In The Works*, and tells of Paul's wish to become a writer too. It begins with an a cappella introduction, followed by one of the best instrumental backings on any Beatles record. The guitar sound on this record could be regarded as a foretaste of heavy metal. The lead vocal comes from Paul, who also joins John and George for the three-part harmony backing vocals that are a combination of the title, together with a section of the French song 'Frère Jacques'.

Rain (Lennon-McCartney)   2:59
Recorded: 14 and 16 April 1966, EMI Studios, Abbey Road, London
John Lennon: Rhythm Guitar and Lead Vocal
Paul McCartney: Bass Guitar and Backing Vocal
George Harrison: Lead Guitar and Backing Vocal   **Ringo Starr:** Drums and Tambourine
Previously issued as the B side to 'Paperback Writer', this track features a stronger heavy guitar sound than the A side, making the latter sound by comparison rather tame. The sound was to influence artists such as The Who, Cream and Jimi Hendrix. The guitars attack from the beginning; Ringo's superb drumbeat accentuates the heaviness of the sound and John's laconic sententious lead vocal grinds out of the left-hand speaker. At the end of this recording one line of John's vocal is played backwards: 'Rain, when the rain comes they run and hide their heads' note the substitution of 'when' for 'if', that is used in the main recording. Apparently, John took a copy of the master tape home and accidentally played it backwards, liked it, and included it on the final record. After this experiment, backwards-playing tapes were also included on 'I'm Only Sleeping' and 'Tomorrow Never Knows' on the *Revolver* album. The instrumental track to this, that was played fast, was recorded on 14 April 1966 and then remixed with the tape running on slow/van-speed. The vocal track was added two days later on 16 April 1966 and, after eight takes, the seventh was chosen for the released stereo version.

Lady Madonna (Lennon-McCartney)   2:17
Recorded: 3 and 6 February 1968, EMI Studios, Abbey Road, London
John Lennon: Rhythm Guitar and Backing Vocal
Paul McCartney: Bass Guitar, Piano and Lead Vocal   **George Harrison:** Lead Guitar and Backing Vocal
Ringo Starr: Drums and Backing Vocal   **Ronnie Scott:** Tenor Saxophone
Harry Klein: Baritone Saxophone   **Bill Povey:** Tenor Saxophone
Bill Jackman: Baritone Saxophone

This was the last single issued by The Beatles on the Parlophone label in 1968 before the dream of Apple became a reality later that year. It was written and sung by Paul, who also plays piano in true rock'n'roll style, showing the influence of Little Richard and Jerry Lee Lewis, among others. The song is rather like a rock version of his earlier 'Eleanor Rigby' with loneliness again as the main theme. It was recorded in five takes on 3 February 1968 and completed with the saxophone backing played by Ronnie Scott, Harry Klein, Bill Povey and Bill Jackman three days later. According to various reports, the saxophone segment in the middle was originally 15 to 20 seconds longer, but was edited. The vocal backing, by all four Beatles, was reputed to have been achieved by them singing with their hands cupped around their mouths.

The Inner Light (Harrison)   2:36
Recorded: (Instrumental Track) 12 January 1968, EMI Studios, Bombay, India
     (Vocal Track) 6 and 8 February 1968, EMI Studios, Abbey Road, London
John Lennon: Backing Vocal   **Paul McCartney:** Backing Vocal
George Harrison: Lead Vocal   **Ringo Starr:** Not Present
Session Musicians: All Instruments

Originally Issued in1968 as the B side of 'Lady Madonna', this was George's first song to be released on a Beatles single. It is the last of three Beatles tracks by George Harrison featuring almost entirely Indian instrumentation. The previous two were 'Love You To', included on *Revolver*, and 'Within You, Without You', featured on *Sgt. Pepper's Lonely Hearts Club Band*. The instrumental track was recorded in five takes on 12 January 1968 at EMI Studios in Bombay, India with some of India's virtuoso musicians, during the recording of George's *Wonderwall* album. The vocal track includes a brief backing from John and Paul and was overdubbed nearly a month later on 6 and 8 February 1968 at Abbey Road. Extracts from a Japanese poem by Roshi, translated into English by R. H. Bluth, formed the basis of George's lyrics for this interesting and introspective song.

Hey Jude (Lennon-McCartney) 7:11
Recorded: 31 July and 1 August 1968, Trident Studios, Wardour Street, London
John Lennon: Acoustic Guitar and Backing Vocal   **Paul McCartney:** Piano and Lead Vocal
George Harrison: Lead Guitar and Backing Vocal   **Ringo Starr:** Drums
Session Musicians: 36-Piece Orchestra

The A side of the first single issued by The Beatles on their own Apple label on 30 August 1968, this was the longest single issued to that date, totalling with its B side 'Revolution', 10 minutes 33 seconds. Written by Paul, the song had started out as 'Hey Jules', about Johns son Julian. The Beatles first attempted to record this at Abbey Road on 29 July 1968 but moved to Trident Studios in Soho where they recorded the song in four takes on 31 July, finally selecting take 1 for further overdubbing on 1 August. Paul sings lead vocal and accompanies himself on piano with backing vocals from John and George. The song starts simply, the main part lasting 3 minutes 11 seconds, but builds up until it finally explodes into a four-minute fade-out, the longest on a Beatles record. The fade consists of all four Beatles plus a 36-piece orchestra, rather than the hundred that Paul originally had envisaged playing and singing along to a one-line chorus of na, na-na-na-na-na, na.

Revolution (Lennon-McCartney) 3:22
Recorded: 10-12 July 1968, EMI Studios, Abbey Road, London
John Lennon: Lead Guitar and Solo Vocal   **Paul McCartney:** Bass Guitar
George Harrison: Lead Guitar   **Ringo Starr:** Drums
Nicky Hopkins: Electric Piano

Previously issued as the B side to 'Hey Jude' The Beatles' first Apple single on 30 August 1968, this anti war song was written by John in India. It was recorded in 16 takes between 10 and 12 July 1968 and features session man Nicky Hopkins on piano. The sound of a distorted guitar, played by John, is heard at the beginning of the record, to which Ringo then adds an electronically compressed drumbeat, giving the recording a solid heavy sound. Although recorded several times and rejected because he was dissatisfied with the result, John's lead vocals were eventually completed after he had lain on his back on the floor of the studio and sung them once more as an experiment, finally achieving the sound he had wanted.

SIDE TWO

Get Back (Lennon-McCartney)   3:11

Recorded: 28 January 1969, Apple Studios, Savile Row, London

John Lennon: Lead Guitar and Harmony Vocal   **Paul McCartney:** Bass Guitar and Lead Vocal
George Harrison: Rhythm Guitar   **Ringo Starr:** Drums
Billy Preston: Organ

After the technical wizardry of the previous couple of years The Beatles decided to 'Get Back' to the simplicity of earlier years and make an album featuring straight performances: no orchestras, no tricks and no overdubs.

After numerous unnumbered recording takes that had begun five days earlier, The Beatles finally selected this take that was recorded live without any overdubs on 28 January 1969, for release as a surprise single on 11 April 1969. Copies of the single were sent to Radio 1 without any prior announcement of its impending release, for broadcast on Easter Sunday 6 April 1969, DJs Alan Freeman and John Peel duly obliging. After hearing the broadcast, The Beatles hurriedly remixed the record the following day and it was in the shops by the Friday of that week. The following Tuesday, 15 April 1969, The Beatles took out a quarter-page advert in the *Daily Mirror* to announce the release of the 'Get Back'/'Don't Let Me Down single' that described it as 'The Beatles as nature intended'. It then went on to describe the single as 'the first Beatles record that is as live as can be in this electronic age'.

Originally the title track of an album, the song features a lead vocal from Paul who also wrote it with harmonies in places from John.

The Beatles also had decided to 'Get Back' to the basic three-guitars-and-drums line-up of their first recordings. No studio trickery, no overdubs, just The Beatles, but with one addition – Billy Preston, who was brought in to supply the organ for which he was to receive a gold disc. Preston also can be heard playing both on the following track and on the *Let It Be* album. The rather different version of this as featured on the *Let It Be* album was recorded on 27 January 1969.

Don't Let Me Down (Lennon-McCartney)   3:34
Recorded: 28 January 1969, Apple Studios, Savile Row, London
John Lennon: Lead Guitar and Lead Vocal
Paul McCartney: Bass Guitar and Harmony Vocal
George Harrison: Rhythm Guitar   **Ringo Starr:** Drums
Billy Preston: Organ

Previously issued as the B side to the 'Get Back' single on 11 April 1969, this recording, made within minutes of 'Get Back' on 28 January 1969, features an extremely raw lead vocal from John, with harmony vocals from Paul. The Beatles are once again joined by Billy Preston who adds to the backing and also has a solo in the middle. The lyrics to this powerful blues-influenced song, written by John with Yoko in mind, are minimal, with John simply repeating the title over and over.

The Ballad Of John And Yoko (Lennon-McCartney)   2:58
Recorded: 14 April 1969, EMI Studios, Abbey Road, London
John Lennon: Acoustic Guitar, Lead Guitar, Percussion and Lead Vocal
Paul McCartney: Bass Guitar, Drums, Piano, Maracas and Harmony Vocal
George Harrison: Not Present   **Ringo Starr:** Not Present

This was released as a single on 20 May 1969 while 'Get Back' was still at No. 1. It was recorded at Abbey Road during an eight-and-a-half-hour session in 11 takes, take ten being the version that was released on April 1969, just three days after the release of 'Get Back'. John and Paul played all the instruments heard. John is on lead vocal, acoustic and lead guitars and percussion, and Paul plays bass guitar, drums, piano and maracas, supplying a harmony vocal in places. The song tells the story of John and Yoko's wedding in Gibraltar the previous month and their subsequent week-long bed-in for peace at the Amsterdam Hilton.

Old Brown Shoe (Harrison) 3:16
Recorded: 16 and 18 April 1969, EMI Studios, Abbey Road, London
John Lennon: Rhythm Guitar and Backing Vocal
Paul McCartney: Bass Guitar, Piano and Backing Vocal
George Harrison: Lead Guitar, Hammond Organ and Lead Vocal
Ringo Starr: Drums
Originally issued as the B side to the 1969 single 'The Ballad Of John And Yoko', this was the second George Harrison song used as the B side of a Beatles single. The first was 'The Inner Light' on the B side of 'Lady Madonna' in 1968. It was recorded in four takes between 16 and 18 April 1969, a few days after the completion of 'The Ballad Of John And Yoko'. Unlike the A side, this features all four Beatles and is quite an up-tempo song from George who during the previous two years had been writing either Indian mantras or slower, more doleful songs like 'While My Guitar Gently Weeps' and 'Blue Jay Way'.

Across The Universe (Lennon-McCartney) 3:41
Recorded: 4 and 8 February 1968, EMI Studios, Abbey Road, London
John Lennon: Acoustic Guitar, Lead Guitar, Organ and Lead/Backing Vocal
Paul McCartney: Piano and Harmony/Backing Vocal
George Harrison: Tamboura, Maracas and Backing Vocal
Ringo Starr: Tomtoms
Lizzie Bravo: Backing Vocal   **Gayleen Pease:** Backing Vocal
Recorded in eight takes on 4 and 8 February 1968 during the same period as 'Lady Madonna', this was considered as a possible rival for the March 1968 single, but 'Lady Madonna' was chosen instead.

   Shortly after being rejected in favour of 'Lady Madonna', this was given to the World Wildlife Fund who included it on the charity album *No One's Gonna Change Our World* that was released on 12 December 1969 (Regal Starline SRS 5013). A different mix of the recording minus the sound effects and a considerable amount of the original backing appeared with an orchestral and choral backing about four months later on the *Let It Be* album.

   The track begins with the sound of birds that was added for the charity album that flies across the stereo sound stage. When it fades the track proper begins, featuring John singing lead vocal on his own song, with Paul harmonising in places. The backing vocals were added by two young women,

Lizzie Bravo and Gayleen Pease, who were waiting outside to see The Beatles. They were invited into the studio by Paul to add the falsetto harmony to John's lead vocal.

The lyrics to this song are some of John's most imaginative, with his incessant chorus line 'Nothing's gonna change my world' accentuating their dreamy effect.

Let It Be (Lennon-McCartney)   3:50
Recorded: 31 January and 30 April 1969 and 4 January 1970, Apple Studios, Savile Row, London and EMI Studios, Abbey Road, London
John Lennon: Bass Guitar
Paul McCartney: Piano, Maracas and Lead/Harmony Vocal
George Harrison: Lead Guitar and Harmony Vocal   **Ringo Starr:** Drums
Billy Preston: Organ   **Session Musicians:** Brass and Cellos
From 'Love Me Do' to 'Let It Be' was a very long and often winding road for The Beatles who, after a collective career spanning more than 15 years that began in the clubs of Liverpool and Hamburg in the late 50s and finally ended in disarray, bowed out with this, their final single.

Sounding rather like a choirboy singing a hymn at a requiem mass, Paul leads The Beatles through this song that was recorded on 31 January 1969 during the ill-fated 'Get Back' sessions.

This and the version included on the *Let It Be* album are, in effect, the same basic recording. They both originate from the same eight-track master tape that contains two lead guitar tracks, one each for the two versions. The lead guitar heard on this version was overdubbed by George during what turned out to be The Beatles' final recording session, at which John wasn't present, on 4 January 1970. The lead guitar heard on the album version is the original, recorded during the 'Get Back' Sessions.

'Let It Be', together with 'You Know My Name', was issued as a single on 6 March 1970.

You Know My Name (Look up the number) (Lennon-McCartney) 4:20
Recorded: 17 May, 7 and 8 June 1967 and 30 April 1969, EMI Studios, Abbey Road, London
John Lennon: Maracas and Lead Vocal
Paul McCartney: Piano, Bass Guitar and Lead Vocal
George Harrison: Vibraphone and Backing Vocal   **Ringo Starr:** Drums, Bongos and Lead Vocal
Mal Evans: Backing Vocal   **Brian Jones:** Alto Saxophone

This intriguing off-beat track began life on 17 May 1967 shortly after the Sgt. Pepper album had been completed, when a section of the backing track was recorded. On 7 and 8 June 1967 further sections were recorded and these were then edited together on 9 June of the same year to form a final master track. Following that, it was abandoned. On 30 April 1969, John and Paul resurrected it and added the vocals and the sound effects, together with Mal Evans, but again it was shelved. On 26 November 1969 John edited the track down from its original six minutes to its current length of just under four and a half minutes and planned to issue it, together with 'What's The New Mary Jane' another unreleased Beatles track, as a single under the banner of The Plastic Ono Band. At the last minute, despite being given the catalogue number Apple 1002 and a release date of 5 December 1969, it was withdrawn without explanation.

The track finally emerged on 6 March 1970 when it was issued as the B side of the 'Let It Be' single. One of the interesting points concerning that release is that the catalogue number of Apple 1002 is stamped in the run-off groove.

The lyrics to this Lennon-conceived track are basically a repetition of the title, with various additional comments and sound effects thrown in for good measure. The jazz piano is supplied by Paul McCartney and the saxophone solo by Brian Jones of the Rolling Stones.

Despite being planned as a Plastic Ono Band release, this track is the B side to The Beatles' final single and also the last track on this album. It is interesting to note that, right at the end of the track, the final comment is 'Goodbye'.

LIVE AT THE BBC

UK Release: 30 November 1994
US Release: 6 December 1994
Running Time: 132.21

Apple 31796
Apple CD: 7243 8 31796 2 6
Producer: Various

CD DISC 1 (vinyl Side A): Beatles Greetings [Speech]; From Us To You; Riding On A Bus [Speech]; I Got A Woman; Too Much Monkey Business; Keep Your Hands Off My Baby; I'll Be On My Way; Young Blood; A Shot Of Rhythm And Blues; Sure To Fall (In Love With You); Some Other Guy; Thank You Girl; Sha La La La La! [Speech]; Baby It's You; That's All Right (Mama); Carol; Soldier Of Love
(vinyl Side B): A Little Rhyme [Speech]; Clarabella; I'm Gonna Sit Right Down And Cry (Over You); Crying, Waiting, Hoping; Dear Wack! [Speech]; You Really Got A Hold On Me; To Know Her Is To Love Her; A Taste Of Honey; Long Tall Sally; I Saw Her Standing There; The Honeymoon Song; Johnny B. Goode; Memphis, Tennessee; Lucille; Can't Buy Me Love; From Fluff To You [Speech]; Till There Was You

CD DISC 2 (vinyl Side C): Crinsk Dee Night [Speech]; A Hard Day's Night; Have A Banana! [Speech]; I Wanna Be Your Man; Just A Rumour [Speech]; Roll Over Beethoven; All My Loving; Things We Said Today; She's A Woman; Sweet Little Sixteen; 1822! [Speech]; Lonesome Tears In My Eyes; Nothin' Shakin'; The Hippy Hippy Shake; Glad All Over; I Just Don't Understand; So How Come (No One Loves Me); I Feel Fine
(vinyl Side D): I'm A Loser; Everybody's Trying To Be My Baby; Rock And Roll Music; Ticket To Ride; Dizzy Miss Lizzy; Kansas City/Hey-Hey-Hey-Hey!; Set Fire To That Lot! [Speech]; Matchbox; I Forgot To Remember To Forget; Love These Goon Shows! [Speech]; I Got To Find My Baby; Ooh! My Soul; Ooh! My Arms [Speech]; Don't Ever Change; Slow Down; Honey Don't; Love Me Do

The first album to appear on the Apple label in over two decades, these 56 songs were recorded when The Beatles appeared on BBC Radio, many of them specifically on their own programme *Pop Go The Beatles* that was broadcast every Tuesday at 5pm through the summer of 1963. Other BBC shows they appeared on, and represented on the double CD album, include *Easy Beat, Top Gear* and the well-remembered *Saturday Club*. The bulk of the material was from the group's vast repertoire of non-original material that typified their stage act when they played long sets in

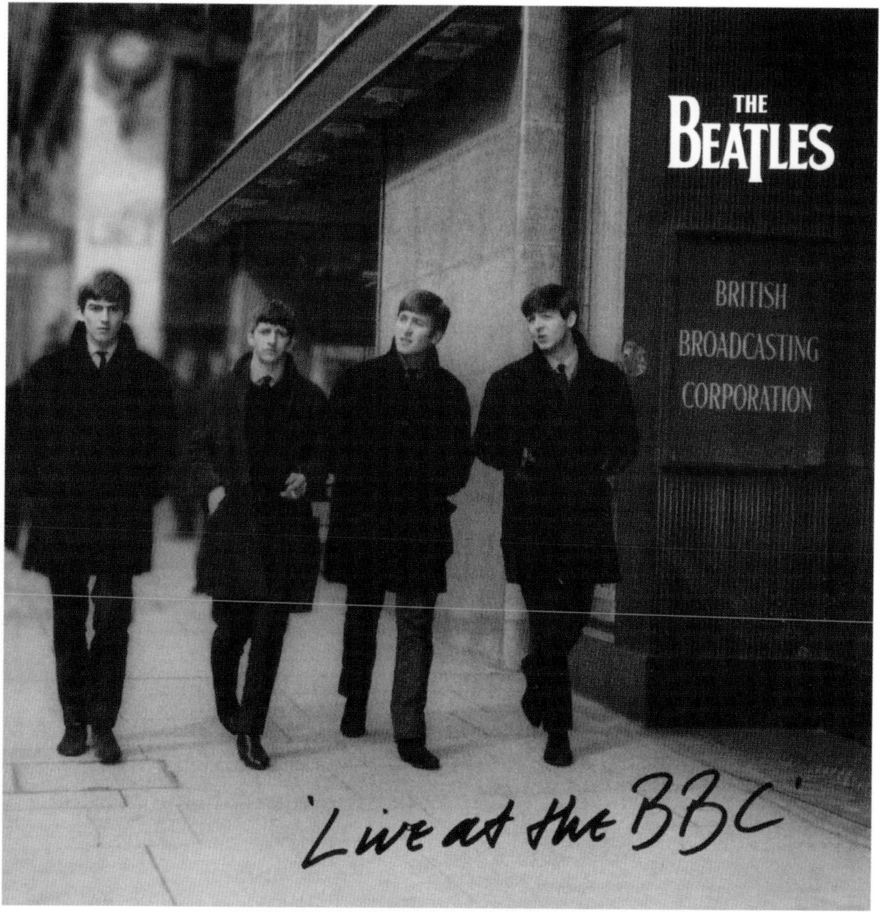
THE BEATLES
BRITISH
BROADCASTING
CORPORATION
'Live at the BBC'

Hamburg and Liverpool, only a tiny proportion of which saw its way onto their studio recordings in the 60s.

The cover photo was taken outside the BBC Paris Theatre in London's Lower Regent Street. The back photograph was actually a paste-in job using the same background but a different shot of The Beatles.

By the time of the collection's release in 1994, Capitol in America had stopped pressing vinyl so had to lease it to Specialty Records. Only 250,000 were pressed, making the US vinyl release something of a collector's item.

DISC 1:
Beatles Greetings 0.13 [speech]
Transmitted: 3 November 1963, The Public Ear
Recorded: 9 October 1963   **Presenter:** Tony Hall
Part of a documentary programme charting the group's rise to fame in which The Beatles mockingly introduce themselves to the listeners ('I'm John and I play the guitar, and sometimes I play the fool').

From Us To You (Lennon-McCartney) 0.27
Lead Vocals: John Lennon, Paul McCartney
Transmitted: Various dates 1964, From Us To You
Recorded: 28 February 1964   **Producer:** Bryant Marriott
An adaptation of The Beatles' third single, used as the title and signature tune for three specials broadcast on the Easter, Whitsun and August Bank Holidays during 1964.

Riding On A Bus 0.53 [speech]
Transmitted: 26 November 1964, Top Gear
Recorded: 17 November 1964   **Presenter:** Brian Matthew
Producer: Bernie Andrews
Presenter Brian Matthew interviewed The Beatles many times during the Beatlemania years. Here he quizzes them about aspects of life that become more difficult with fame, like riding on a bus.

I Got A Woman (Charles)   2.48
Vocal: John Lennon
Transmitted: 13 August 1963, Pop Go The Beatles
Recorded: 16 July 1963   **Producer:** Terry Henebery
A Ray Charles original from 1954, John almost certainly first heard the song when it appeared on Elvis' debut album in 1956, Presley having recorded it at the same session as his first smash 'Heartbreak Hotel'.

Too Much Monkey Business (Berry)   2.05
Vocal: John Lennon
Transmitted: 10 September1963, Pop Go The Beatles
Recorded: 3 September 1963   **Producer:** Ian Grant
There are no less than eight Chuck Berry numbers on this collection, indicative of the influence the seminal rocker had on the group – particularly on George Harrison as lead guitarist, though John sings all but one of the numbers.

Keep Your Hands Off My Baby (Goffin-King)   2.30
Lead Vocal: John Lennon
Transmitted: 26 January 1963, Saturday Club
Recorded: 22 January 1963   **Producer:** Bernie Andrews
From The Beatles' debut on the prestigious *Saturday Club* programme, before they had really hit the big time with 'Please Please Me', right at the beginning of 1963. By the end of the year they would be the biggest name in the country, and just 18 months away from being the biggest name in the world.

I'll Be On My Way (Lennon-McCartney)   1.57
Harmony Vocals: John Lennon/George Harrison/Paul McCartney
Transmitted: 24 June 1963, Side By Side
Recorded: 4 April 1963   **Producer:** Bryant Marriott
A decidedly Buddy Holly influence shows here on a Lennon-McCartney number that The Beatles never released themselves, but gave to Billy J Kramer and the Dakotas as the B side for their debut single.

Young Blood (Leiber-Stoller-Pomus) 1.56
Lead Vocal: George Harrison
Transmitted: 11 June 1963, Pop Go The Beatles
Recorded: 1 June 1963   **Producer:** Terry Henebery
The song that The Beatles played at their famously failed audition for Decca Records early in
1962, written by ace rock'n'roll composers Jerry Leiber and Mike Stoller and featured as the
B side to the Coasters 1957 hit 'Searchin'.

A Shot Of Rhythm And Blues (Thompson) 2.14
Lead Vocal: John Lennon
Transmitted: 27 August 1963, Pop Go The Beatles
Recorded: 1 August 1963   **Producer:** Terry Henebery
Typical of The Beatles pre-fame repertoire, this is a cover of an American rhythm-and-blues
B side by Arthur Alexander. It was the flip of his 1962 hit 'You Better Move On'. Like the better-
known 'Twist And Shout', this was an opportunity for John Lennon to flex his R&B vocal muscles.

Sure To Fall (In Love With You) (Perkins-Claunch-Cantrell) 2.07
Lead Vocal: Paul McCartney
Transmitted: 18 June1963, Pop Go The Beatles
Recorded: 1 June 1963   **Producer:** Terry Henebery
Some real down-home harmonies with Paul leading, showing the group's penchant for rockabilly
and country music with a Carl Perkins favourite.

Some Other Guy (Leiber-Stoller-Barrett) 2.00
Lead Vocal: John Lennon
Transmitted: 23 June 1963, Easy Beat
Recorded: 19 June 1963   **Producer:** Ron Belchier
Recorded by Richie Barrett in 1962, this song was a great favourite among the Merseyside
groups at the time. The Beatles were seen performing the number at the Cavern Club in
Liverpool in a local Granada Television film made in August 1962 and broadcast in October,
a week or so after the release of their first single 'Love Me Do'.

Thank You Girl (Lennon-McCartney)   2.01
Lead Vocals: Paul McCartney, John Lennon
Transmitted: 23 June 1963, Easy Beat
Recorded: 19 June 1963   **Producer:** Ron Belchier
The flip-side of their third single 'From Me To You'. The *Easy Beat* show was recorded in front of a live audience at the Playhoues Theatre, London, as is clearly evident from the sound of screaming fans on this and the previous track.

Sha La La La La!   0.27 [speech]
Transmitted: 11 June 1963, Pop Go The Beatles
Recorded: 1 June 1963   **Presenter:** Lee Peters
Producer: Terry Henebery
More Beatle banter as Lee Peters, the presenter of the first four *Pop Go The Beatles* shows, almost introduces the next song as 'Sha La La La' before being corrected, and goaded by John in his famous James Mason impersonation voice.

Baby It's You (David-Bacharach-Williams)   2.43
Lead Vocal: John Lennon
Transmitted: 11 June 1963, Pop Go The Beatles
Recorded: 1 June 1963   **Producer:** Terry Henebery
One of the stand-out tracks on their stand-out debut album *Please Please Me*, the familiar 'Sha la la la la' bringing in the Burt Bacharach-Hal David classic. It had been a Top 10 hit in the summer of 1962 for The Shirelles.

That's All Right (Mama) (Crudup)   2.53
Vocal: Paul McCartney
Transmitted: 16 July 1963, Pop Go The Beatles
Recorded: 2 July 1963   **Producer:** Terry Henebery
Written by blues man Arthur 'Big Boy' Crudup, this song is notable for being the very first single release by Elvis Presley in 1954, back in his days at Sun Records. Paul had been singing it with John and Co since their skiffle days as the Quarrymen.

Carol (Berry) 2.34
Vocal: John Lennon
Transmitted: 16 July 1963, Pop Go The Beatles
Recorded: 2 July 1963   **Producer:** Terry Henebery
Another Chuck Berry item that John takes in his stride with characteristic confidence, and one of the many otherwise unreleased songs by The Beatles that appear on this collection.

Soldier Of Love (Cason-Moon) 1.59
Lead Vocal: John Lennon
Transmitted: 16 July 1963, Pop Go The Beatles
Recorded: 2 July 1963   **Producer:** Terry Henebery
A fairly obscure track previously recorded by Arthur Alexander, whose 'Shot Of Rhythm And Blues' appears earlier on the disc, and whose 'Anna' John Lennon covered on the *Please Please Me* album.

A Little Rhyme 0.25 [speech]
Transmitted: 16 July 1963, Pop Go The Beatles
Recorded: 2 July 1963
Presenter: Rodney Burke   **Producer:** Terry Henebery
It was a feature of *Pop Go The Beatles* that the boys read out requests sent in by listeners. Here John reads out a little rhyme from the upper third in a school in Hemel Hempstead, asking the group to 'Brighten up our lives at school'.

Clarabella (Pingatore) 2.39
Vocal: Paul McCartney
Transmitted: 16 July 1963, Pop Go The Beatles
Recorded: 2 July 1963   **Producer:** Terry Henebery
Paul with one of his archetypal rock'n'roll screamers, with John on harmonica. It was part of The Beatles regular stage repertoire in the early years, and dated from the mid-50s.

I'm Gonna Sit Right Down And Cry (Over You) (Thomas-Biggs)   2.01
Lead Vocal: John Lennon
Transmitted: 6 August 1963, Pop Go The Beatles
Recorded: 16 July 1963   **Producer:** Terry Henebery
Another song that The Beatles would have first heard via Elvis' debut album. It can also be heard on *The Beatles Historic Sessions* (see page 31) where it appeared on a live recording made at The Star Club, Hamburg, in December 1962.

Crying, Waiting, Hoping (Holly)   2.09
Lead Vocal: George Harrison
Transmitted: 6 August 1963, Pop Go The Beatles
Recorded: 16 July 1963   **Producer:** Terry Henebery
Another number – this one by Buddy Holly – that The Beatles also recorded in their audition for Decca Records on New Year's Day, 1962. The song was recorded by Holly in his New York apartment only a few weeks before his death in a plane crash in February 1959.

Dear Wack!   0.42 [speech]
Transmitted: 24 August 1963, Saturday Club
Recorded: 30 July 1963   **Presenter:** Brian Matthew
Producer: Bernie Andrews
A request from *Saturday Club* listeners in Nottingham that John reads out accompanied (presumably) by George on guitar.

You Really Got A Hold On Me (Robinson)   2.37
Lead Vocals: John Lennon, George Harrison
Transmitted: 24 August 1963, Saturday Club
Recorded: 30 July 1963   **Producer:** Bernie Andrews
Featured on *With The Beatles* released in November 1963, this is The Beatles' cover of the Smokey Robinson & The Miracles classic. The Beatles would record the song four times for the BBC during the summer of 1963.

To Know Her Is To Love Her (Spector) 2.49
Lead Vocal: George Harrison
Transmitted: 6 August 1963, Pop Go The Beatles
Recorded: 16 July 1963   **Producer:** Terry Henebery
When Phil Spector was still at high school he formed The Teddy Bears and cut this song as 'To Know Him Is To Love Him' that went to No. 1 in the US charts and to No. 2 in the UK in 1958. Spector would re-produce The Beatles' final album *Let It Be* amid much controversy within the band themselves.

A Taste Of Honey (Marlow-Scott) 1.57
Lead Vocal: Paul McCartney
Transmitted: 23 July 1963, Pop Go The Beatles
Recorded: 10 July 1963   **Producer:** Terry Henebery
'A waste of money' The Beatles used to chorus when they sang this live in the Cavern and elsewhere, a contemporary standard that the group included on *Please Please Me*. The song had been a minor US hit for American soul stylist Lennie Welch the previous year.

Long Tall Sally (Johnson-Penniman-Blackwell) 1.52
Vocal: Paul McCartney
Transmitted: 13 August 1963, Pop Go The Beatles
Recorded: 16 July 1963   **Producer:** Terry Henebery
In June 1964 The Beatles released 'Long Tall Sally' on an EP of the same name, but the Little Richard barn-stormer had been a crowd-pleasing part of their stage act since the Hamburg days.

I Saw Her Standing There (Lennon-McCartney) 2.31
Lead Vocal: Paul McCartney
Transmitted: 20 October 1963, Easy Beat
Recorded: 16 October 1963   **Producer:** Ron Belchier
This sensational Paul McCartney-led opener to *Please Please Me* was no less potent an item on their second appearance before the studio audience on *Easy Beat*.

The Honeymoon Song (Theodorakis-Sansom) 1.39
Vocal: Paul McCartney
Transmitted: 6 August 1963, Pop Go The Beatles
Recorded: 16 July 1963   **Producer:** Terry Henebery
Paul's romantic side comes over on this treatment of a theme tune ballad from the 1959 film *Honeymoon*. It was written by the Greek composer Mikis Theodorakis, who would find even greater success with his music for *Zorba The Greek* in 1964.

Johnny B. Goode (Berry) 2.51
Vocal: John Lennon
Transmitted: 15 February 1964, Saturday Club
Recorded: 7 January 1964   **Producer:** Bernie Andrews
George Harrison leads in with the classic Chuck Berry guitar lick before John takes over on vocals – 'Go, Johnny, go!'.

Memphis, Tennessee (Berry) 2.12
Vocal: John Lennon
Transmitted: 30 July 1963, Pop Go The Beatles
Recorded: 10 July 1963   **Producer:** Terry Henebery
According to the album notes, Berry's melancholy classic was recorded by The Beatles for the BBC five times, including one for their debut broadcast in March 1962. It also featured on their Decca audition tapes recorded 1 January 1962.

Lucille (Collins-Penniman) 1.49
Vocal: Paul McCartney
Transmitted: 5 October 1963, Saturday Club
Recorded: 7 September 1963   **Producer:** Bernie Andrews
Brian Matthew introduces this rocker as a Paul McCartney tribute to the Everly Brothers, who happened to be on the same edition of Saturday Club and had enjoyed a hit with the song. But it's the Little Richard original that's clearly the inspiration for Paul's dynamic performance.

Can't Buy Me Love (Lennon-McCartney) 2.06
Vocal: Paul McCartney
Transmitted: 30 March 1964, From Us To You
Recorded: 28 February 1964   **Producer:** Bryant Marriott
'Can't Buy Me Love' was The Beatles' current hit, it had hit the chart at No. 1 just the week before when the first of the Bank Holiday *From Us To You* shows was broadcast on Easter Monday 1964.

From Fluff To You   0.28 [speech]
Transmitted: 30 March 1964, From Us To You
Recorded: 28 February 1964   **Presenter:** Alan Freeman
Producer: Bryant Marriott
Also out the previous week was John Lennon's book *In His Own Write*, and while presenter Alan 'Fluff' Freeman asks Paul about his musical heroes, John insists on shouting 'what about my book?'

Till There Was You (Wilson)   2.13
Vocal: Paul McCartney
Transmitted: 30 March 1964, From Us To You
Recorded: 28 February 1964   **Producer:** Bryant Marriott
This ballad, that originated in the stage and film musical *The Music Man*, was a 1961 hit for Peggy Lee. It had been recorded already by The Beatles at the Decca auditions, live at the Star Club Hamburg and on their second Parlophone album *With The Beatles*.

DISC 2:

Crinsk Dee Night   1.04 [speech]
Transmitted: 16 July 1964, Top Gear
Recorded: 14 July 1964   **Presenter:** Brian Matthew
Producer: Bernie Andrews
From the first edition of the late night show *Top Gear*. Presenter Brian Matthew talks to
The Beatles about movie acting – their film *A Hard Day's Night* had just been released.

A Hard Day's Night (Lennon-McCartney)   2.24
Lead Vocal: John Lennon
Transmitted: 16 July 1964, Top Gear
Recorded: 14 July 1964   **Producer:** Bernie Andrews
As is pointed out in the booklet that accompanies the CD, the piano break in the middle has
been lifted from the single and cut into the BBC session recording. According to producer
Bernie Andrews this was because George Martin, who played piano in the studio version, was
supposed to take part but never made it.

Have A Banana!   0.21 [speech]
Transmitted: 16 July 1964, Top Gear
Recorded: 14 July 1964   **Presenter:** Brian Matthew
Producer: Bernie Andrews
As 'A Hard Days Night' fades, the voices of Matthew and The Beatles come in, 'to prove that we
weren't playing the record there'. No mention of the piano solo though!

I Wanna Be Your Man (Lennon-McCartney)   2.09
Lead Vocal: Ringo Starr
Transmitted: 30 March 1964, From Us To You
Recorded: 28 February 1964   **Producer:** Bryant Marriott
Not as convincing as the studio version that appeared on *With The Beatles*, Ringo's vocal
contribution is supported by harmonies from Paul and John on the chorus.

Just A Rumour   0.20 [speech]
Transmitted: 30 March 1964, From Us To You
Recorded: 28 February 1964   **Presenter:** Alan Freeman
Producer: Bryant Marriott
Another item from *From Us To You* broadcast on Easter Monday 1964, Alan Freeman's brief intro
with George taking us into 'Roll Over Beethoven'.

Roll Over Beethoven (Berry)   2.15
Vocal: George Harrison
Transmitted: 30 March 1964, From Us To You
Recorded: 28 February 1964   **Producer:** Bryant Marriott
Also from *With The Beatles*, this Chuck Berry number had been one of the highlights of Beatle
performances, especially with dedicated George fans.

All My Loving (Lennon-McCartney)   2.04
Lead Vocal: Paul McCartney
Transmitted: 30 March 1964, From Us To You
Recorded: 28 February 1964   **Producer:** Bryant Marriott
One of the strongest tracks from *With The Beatles*. On the radio recording Paul's voice is just as
assured and George's rockabilly-tinged guitar break just as masterful as on the album.

Things We Said Today (Lennon-McCartney)   2.18
Lead Vocal: Paul McCartney
Transmitted: 16 July 1964, Top Gear
Recorded: 14 July 1964   **Producer:** Bernie Andrews
Although recorded for the *Top Gear* programme, the voiceover at the beginning of the track is
Brian Matthew on a show distributed overseas by the BBC Transcription Service on LPs called
Top Of The Pops.

She's A Woman (Lennon-McCartney)   3.14
Vocal: Paul McCartney
Transmitted: 26 November 1964, Top Gear
Recorded: 17 November 1964   **Producer:** Bernie Andrews
Released as the B side to 'I Feel Fine' the day after this *Top Gear* broadcast, this is a fine piece of McCartney rock'n'roll with the usual whoops and yells, and some understated rockabilly licks from George.

Sweet Little Sixteen (Berry)   2.20
Vocal: John Lennon
Transmitted: 23 July 1963, Pop Go The Beatles
Recorded: 10 July 1963   **Producer:** Terry Henebery
Possibly Chuck Berry's finest piece of pop poetry, and a lyrical as well as a musical inspiration to The Beatles. They'd been playing it for years, as this effortless version suggests, with George and John in full flight.

1822!   0.10 [speech]
Transmitted: 23 July 1963, Pop Go The Beatles
Recorded: 10 July 1963   **Producer:** Terry Henebery
An almost-formal announcement by John Lennon introducing the next number, before he reverts to his usual nonsense – 'recorded in 1822' – and Goonish voices.

Lonesome Tears In My Eyes (J and D Burnette-Burlison-Mortimer)   2.36
Vocal: John Lennon
Transmitted: 23 July 1963, Pop Go The Beatles
Recorded: 10 July 1963   **Producer:** Terry Henebery
A piece of Latin-tinged rockabilly with Ringo on tom-tom percussion and George's guitar in Tex-Mex mode. Composers Johnny and Dorsey Burnette, along with bass player Paul Burlison, were the Rock'n'Roll Trio, legendary among aficionados of 50s rockabilly.

Nothin' Shakin' (Fontaine-Calacrai-Lampert-Gluck) 2.59
Vocal: George Harrison
Transmitted: 23 July 1963, Pop Go The Beatles
Recorded: 10 July 1963   **Producer:** Terry Henebery
Previously appearing on the tapes recorded live at Hamburg's Star Club, George covers a slice o
vintage rockabilly from Eddie Fontaine, who had a minor hit with the number and appeared in *T*
Girl Can't Help It, the best rock'n'roll film of the 50s.

The Hippy Hippy Shake (Romero) 1.49
Vocal: Paul McCartney
Transmitted: 30 July 1963, Pop Go The Beatles
Recorded: 10 July 1963   **Producer:** Terry Henebery
It's rockin' Paul with another Merseybeat standard. Originally recorded by Chan Romero in 1959
it hit No. 2 in the UK charts via Liverpool outfit The Swinging Blue Jeans in 1964.

Glad All Over (Bennett-Tepper-Schroeder) 1.51
Vocal: George Harrison
Transmitted: 30 August 1963, Pop Go The Beatles
Recorded: 16 July 1963   **Producer:** Terry Henebery
More rockabilly from George Harrison, this time with a song made famous by veteran Carl Perki

I Just Don't Understand (Wilkin-Westeberry) 2.46
Vocal: John Lennon
Transmitted: 30 August 1963, Pop Go The Beatles
Recorded: 16 July 1963   **Producer:** Terry Henebery
The Swedish-American film actress Ann-Margret had a minor hit with this waltz-time song in 19
John taking it on with gusto.

So How Come (No One Loves Me) (Bryant)   1.53
Harmony Vocal: Paul McCartney, John Lennon, George Harrison
Transmitted: 23 July 1963, Pop Go The Beatles
Recorded: 10 July 1963   **Producer:** Terry Henebery
Some close harmony vocalising in the style of the Everly Brothers who featured it on their 1961
album *A Date With The Everly Brothers.*

I Feel Fine (Lennon-McCartney)   2.12
Lead Vocal: John Lennon
Transmitted: 26 November 1964, Top Gear
Recorded: 17 November 1964   **Producer:** Bernie Andrews
Classic Beatles pop, complete with a compulsive guitar riff. Not to mention the feed-back intro
that took a few takes to get the same effect as on the single!

I'm A Loser (Lennon-McCartney)   2.32
Lead Vocal: John Lennon
Transmitted: 26 November 1964, Top Gear
Recorded: 17 November 1964   **Producer:** Bernie Andrews
More marvellous Lennon-McCartney songwriting, this *Top Gear* version sounds every bit as good
as the album track, with tight vocal harmonies, George's country-light guitar and John's
harmonica.

Everybody's Trying To Be My Baby (Perkins)   2.20
Vocal: George Harrison
Transmitted: 26 December 1964, Saturday Club
Recorded: 25 November 1964   **Producer:** Bernie Andrews
One of two Carl Perkins songs on *Beatles For Sale*, released on 4 December 1964, here
recorded at the Beeb for the Boxing Day edition of *Saturday Club*.

Rock And Roll Music (Berry) 2.00
Vocal: John Lennon
Transmitted: 26 December 1964, Saturday Club
Recorded: 25 November 1964   **Producer:** Bernie Andrews
John, as usual, roars into Chuck Berry material. It doesn't have the bonus of the piano played by
John, Paul and George Martin all at once as on the *Beatles For Sale* track, but it's still riveting stuff.

Ticket To Ride (Lennon-McCartney) 2.56
Lead Vocal: John Lennon
Transmitted: 6 June 1965, The Beatles Invite You To Take A Ticket To Ride
Recorded: 26 May 1965   **Producer:** Keith Bateson
The Beatles Invite You To Take A Ticket To Ride was the last BBC special featuring the group, in fact it
was their final performance on the network. It was well-timed as a prelude to their movie *Help!* that
was released in August 1965, 'Ticket To Ride', their most recent single, being featured in the film.

Dizzy Miss Lizzy (Williams) 2.42
Vocal: John Lennon
Transmitted: 6 June 1965, The Beatles Invite You To Take A Ticket To Ride
Recorded: 26 May 1965   **Producer:** Keith Bateson
The final track on their forthcoming *Help!* album, this Larry Williams song is a familiar vehicle for
John's rock'n'roll shouting.

Kansas City/Hey-Hey-Hey-Hey! (Leiber-Stoller/Penniman) 2.37
Lead Vocal: Paul McCartney
Transmitted: 6 August 1963, Pop Go The Beatles
Recorded: 16 July 1963   **Producer:** Terry Henebery
As included on *Beatles For Sale* at the end of the following year, Paul doing his Little Richard bit
in this tried-and-tested medley.

Set Fire To That Lot!   0.27 [speech]
Transmitted: 30 July 1963, Pop Go The Beatles
Recorded: 10 July 1963   **Presenter**: Rodney Burke
Producer: Terry Henebery
Ringo gets a rare chance to speak on one of the request spots, bringing in the next number.

Matchbox (Perkins)   1.57
Vocal: Ringo Starr
Transmitted: 30 July 1963, Pop Go The Beatles
Recorded: 10 July 1963   **Producer**: Terry Henebery
This Carl Perkins song from 1957 was sung by John on The Beatles' first recording of this, made live from the Hamburg Star Club, but it had become a Ringo feature spot by the time they laid it down for the *Long Tall Sally* EP.

I Forgot To Remember To Forget (Kesler-Feathers)   2.08
Vocal: Paul McCartney
Transmitted: 18 May 1964, 'From Us To You'
Recorded: 1 May 1964   **Producer**: Bryant Marriott
Another piece of vintage Elvis, with Paul McCartney very much on a country kick.

Love These Goon Shows!   0.26 [speech]
Transmitted: 11 June 1963, Pop Go The Beatles
Recorded: 1 June 1963   **Presenter**: Lee Peters
Producer: Terry Henebery
John explains to presenter Lee Peters that he's playing a blues harp, not harmonica, on the next song.

I Got To Find My Baby (Berry)   1.55
Vocal: John Lennon
Transmitted: 11 June 1963, Pop Go The Beatles
Recorded: 1 June 1963   **Producer:** Terry Henebery
One of the lesser-known Chuck Berry items among the eight that John tackles in the course of these recordings.

Ooh! My Soul (Penniman)   1.36
Vocal: Paul McCartney
Transmitted: 27 August 1963, Pop Go The Beatles
Recorded: 1 August 1963   **Producer:** Terry Henebery
This 1958 Top 40 US hit for Little Richard gets the full rock'n'roll treatment from Paul.

Ooh! My Arms   0.35 [speech]
Transmitted: 27 August 1963, Pop Go The Beatles
Recorded: 1 August 1963   **Presenter:** Rodney Burke
Producer: Terry Henebery
Another corny link during *Pop Go The Beatles*, this edition being recorded at the Playhouse Theatre in Manchester.

Don't Ever Change (Goffin-King)   2.02
Harmony Vocals: Paul McCartney, John Lennon, George Harrison
Transmitted: 27 August 1963, Pop Go The Beatles
Recorded: 1 August 1963   **Producer:** Terry Henebery
Written by songwriters supreme Gerry Goffin and Carole King, 'Don't Ever Change' had been a UK Top 5 hit for the Crickets in 1962.

Slow Down (Williams) 2.36
Vocal: John Lennon
Transmitted: 20 August 1963, Pop Go The Beatles
Recorded: 16 July 1963   **Producer:** Terry Henebery
Not one of his big hits, but 'Slow Down' was certainly one of Larry Williams' best. And The Beatles take here is certainly on a par with the version they recorded nearly a year later for the *Long Tall Sally* EP in June 1964.

Honey Don't (Perkins) 2.11
Vocal: John Lennon
Transmitted: 3 September, 1963, Pop Go The Beatles
Recorded: 1 August 1963   **Producer:** Ian Grant
Many Beatle fans will associate this Carl Perkins song with Ringo as he covered it on *Beatles for Sale*, but in live shows previously it had always been a vehicle for John, who sings it here.

Love Me Do (Lennon-McCartney) 2.29
Lead Vocals: Paul McCartney, John Lennon
Transmitted: 23 July 1963, Pop Go The Beatles
Recorded: 10 July 1963   **Producer:** Terry Henebery
The Beatles debut single was a must-play item in all the group's stage shows through late 1962 and the Beatlemania year of 1963, the boys performing it nine times on BBC broadcasts.

ANTHOLOGY 1

UK Release: 21 November 1995
US Release: 21 November 1995
Running Time: 122.58
Remix Engineer: Geoff Emerick

Apple 34445
Apple CD: 7243 8 34445 2 6
Producer: George Martin

CD DISC 1 (vinyl Side A): Free As A Bird; "We were four guys … that's all"; That'll Be The Day; In Spite Of All The Danger; "Sometimes I'd borrow … those still exist"; Hallelujah, I Love Her So; You'll Be Mine; Cayenne; "First of all … it didn't do a thing here"; My Bonnie; Ain't She Sweet; Cry For A Shadow
(vinyl Side B): "Brian was a beautiful guy … he presented us well"; "I secured them an audition … a Beatle drink even then"; Searchin'; Three Cool Cats; The Sheik Of Araby; Like Dreamers Do; Hello Little Girl; "Well, the recording test … by my artists"; Besame Mucho; Love Me Do; How Do You Do It; Please Please Me
(vinyl Side C): One After 909 (sequence); One After 909 (complete); Lend Me Your Comb; I'll Get You; "We were performers … in Britain"; I Saw Her Standing There; From Me To You; Money (That's What I Want); You Really Got A Hold On Me; Roll Over Beethoven

CD DISC 2 (vinyl Side D): She Loves You; Till There Was You; Twist And Shout; This Boy; I Want To Hold Your Hand; "Boys, what I was thinking … " Moonlight Bay; Can't Buy Me Love
(vinyl Side E): All My Loving; You Can't Do That; And I Love Her; A Hard Day's Night; I Wanna Be Your Man; Long Tall Sally; Boys; Shout; I'll Be Back (Take 2); I'll Be Back (Take 3)
(vinyl Side F): You Know What To Do; No Reply (demo); Mr. Moonlight; Leave My Kitten Alone; No Reply; Eight Days A Week (sequence); Eight Days A Week (complete); Kansas City/Hey-Hey-Hey-Hey!

The *Anthology* releases had their origin in a series of TV documentaries tracing the story of The Beatles through vintage interview footage, performance material, news film and interviews with Paul, George and Ringo specifically recorded for the films. In addition previously unknown interview material with John Lennon was used. The whole project was overseen by the three ex-Beatles, and Yoko One in respect of newly-aired John Lennon items. The series was broadcast

in Britain on the ITV network from 19 November 1965 for an hour a week until Christmas Eve. It was aired in America on ABC as a five-hour mini-series over the three nights of 19, 20 and 21 November. The entire documentary was later released on video with additional material not seen on TV, running to 10 hours in total, the whole set being released on DVD on 1 April 2003.

The first *Anthology* CD and vinyl set was released just two days after the TV series came on the air, on 21 November 1995, followed by *Anthology 2* and *3* in March and October 1996. The subsequent long-awaited book, *The Beatles Anthology*, was published in October 2000. This included interviews with all four band members, much of which had been culled from the TV series, and many rare photographs and memorabilia.

Anthology 1 was hailed as the first official Beatles bootleg, containing as it did within its 55 songs, 33 that had already appeared on bootlegs over the years. But the overall package is far richer than any one bootleg. It includes unreleased versions of songs from EMI, Polydor and Decca archives, live material from radio and TV broadcasts and interview snippets that draw an intimate perspective on the material.

Particularly important tracks include demos by the Quarrymen (incredibly low-fi), some home taping by Paul, John, George and Stuart Sutcliffe, five songs from their Decca audition including two previously unheard Lennon/McCartney originals, and an early version of 'Love Me Do' with Pete Best on drums. There's also some live material from Sweden that proves John Lennon's assertion that when it came to straight rock'n'roll, there was nobody around to beat them. In addition, there are lots of studio stops and starts interspersed with snatches of conversation that cast a candid spotlight on The Beatles in their first amazing flush of creativity.

The album spent ten weeks in the British Record Retailer chart, peaking at No. 2, while in the United States it topped the Billboard listing for three weeks running. In America it sold over a million copies in its first week, and over four million by the end of the second!

DISC 1
Free As A Bird

(Original composition Lennon, Beatles version Lennon-McCartney-Harrison-Starr) 4.23
Recorded: c 1977, New York City/February, March 1994, Sussex, England
Producers: John Lennon, Paul McCartney, George Harrison, Richard Starkey, Jeff Lynne
Engineer: Geoff Emerick

Recorded by John Lennon as a demo in his New York home circa 1977. When the tape was given to Paul, George and Ringo it resulted in the first Beatles sessions since 1970. The recording took place in Paul's Mill Studios in Sussex, with Jeff Lynne co-producing. John's original cassette tape was expanded into a 48-track recording with the regular Beatles instrumental back-up and augmented vocals from Paul, George and Ringo. Released as a single at the end of the following year, it went to No. 2 in the UK charts. In the US it spent 11 weeks in the singles chart, peaking at No. 6, and earning a Gold Disc in July 1996.

"We were four guys...that's all" 0.13 [speech]
Recorded: 8 December 1970, New York City

A snippet from John Lennon's famous "We were just a band who made it very, very big" quote speaking to Jann Wenner of *Rolling Stone* magazine.

That'll Be The Day (Allison-Holly-Petty) 2.07
Recorded: Spring/summer 1958, Phillips Sound Recording Service, Liverpool
Engineer: Percy F Phillips

Percy Phillips had a small recording facility set up in his house at 38 Kensington, Liverpool, and the Quarrymen were among many young hopefuls who paid their 17s 6d (87.5 pence) for him to create an acetate of their sound. The now priceless one and only copy of this historic recording featuring John, Paul, George and fellow-Quarrymen John Lowe (piano) and Colin Hanton (drums), belongs to Paul McCartney. A snatch of this has appeared on many bootlegs after Paul played a segment on a TV programme in 1984, but this is the only time the full number has been released.

In Spite Of All The Danger (McCartney-Harrison)   2.44
Recorded: Spring/summer 1958, Phillips Sound Recording Service, Liverpool
Engineer: Percy F Phillips
Written by Paul and George, John takes the lead – as he did on Buddy Holly's 'That'll Be The Day' – on the Quarrymen's other acetate track, edited here from the original's three minutes 25 seconds.

"Sometimes I'd borrow...those still exist"   0.17 [speech]
Recorded: 3 November 1994, London
Paul talks to writer Mark Lewisohn about how the early Beatles would record numbers on a borrowed Grundig home tape machine.

Hallelujah, I Love Her So (Charles)   1.13
Recorded: Spring/summer 1960, Liverpool
The first of three home recordings made in Paul's house with Paul, John and George on guitars and Stuart Sutcliffe on bass. These are the only known recordings made while Sutcliffe was in the group. They had no regular drummer at the time.

You'll Be Mine (Lennon-McCartney)   1.38
Recorded: Spring/summer 1960, Liverpool
Paul sings lead, as on the previous Ray Charles song, on this jokey number in which The Beatles mimic the Ink Spots' vocal group style with a characteristically bizarre middle passage spoken by John.

Cayenne (McCartney)   1.13
Recorded: Spring/summer 1960, Liverpool
A moody instrumental penned by Paul. All these home tapings had appeared in poor-quality bootlegs but after Paul McCartney acquired the source tapes in 1995 these cleaned up versions were available for the first time.

"First of all ... it didn't do a thing here"   0.07 [speech]
Recorded: 27 October 1962, Port Sunlight, Cheshire.
Paul McCartney talking about their days backing Tony Sheridan in Hamburg. It was part of an interview for hospital radio, conducted backstage at Hume Hall in Port Sunlight, Cheshire, one of The Beatles' regular early venues.

My Bonnie (Trad. arr. Sheridan)   2.42
Recorded: 22 June 1961, Hamburg
Producer: Bert Kaempfert   **Engineer:** Karl Hinze
The best-known of the five or six numbers The Beatles recorded with singer Tony Sheridan, released on a single as The Beat Brothers. The line-up consisted of Sheridan on vocals and guitar, George Harrison and John Lennon on guitars, Paul McCartney on bass and on drums Pete Best who had joined the group in August 1960.

Ain't She Sweet (Ager-Yellen)   2.13
Recorded: 22 June 1961, Hamburg
Producer: Bert Kaempfert   **Engineer:** Karl Hinze
Part of the same Hamburg recording session. Sheridan doesn't feature here, the lead vocals on this 20s pop song being handled by John Lennon.

Cry For A Shadow (Harrison-Lennon)   2.22
Recorded: 22 June 1961, Hamburg
Producer: Bert Kaempfert   **Engineer:** Karl Hinze
The third Hamburg track, all of which have appeared many time before on 'early Beatles' compilations. This is a George Harrison instrumental much in the style popularised bt The Shadows at the time – hence the title?

"Brian was a beautiful guy...he presented us well"   0.10 [speech]
Recorded: October 1971, New York City
John talks about Brian Epstein to journalist David Wigg. Broadcast on the BBC Radio 1 programme *Scene And Heard* in November 1971.

"I secured them an audition...a Beatle drink even then"   0.18 [speech]
Recorded: 13 October 1964, EMI Studios, London
Producer: George Martin   **Engineer:** Stuart Eltham
Brian Epstein reading from his autobiography *A Cellarful Of Noise*; he hoped to record enough for an album, but the project was never completed. Here he tells how he set up an audition with Decca Records.

Searchin' (Leiber-Stoller) 2.59
Recorded: 1 January 1962, Decca Sudios, London
Producer: Mike Smith
This Coasters song and the four that follow were from 15 that The Beatles recorded during their famous Decca audition – infamous in retrospect, because the company turned them down.

Three Cool Cats (Leiber-Stoller) 2.25
Recorded: 1 January 1962, Decca Sudios, London
Producer: Mike Smith
Another Coasters comedy item from the pens of Gerry Leiber and Mike Stoller. This was a great favourite from The Beatles' stage act at the trime, handled here by George Harrison.

The Sheik Of Araby (Smith-Wheeler-Snyder) 1.43
Recorded: 1 January 1962, Decca Sudios, London
Producer: Mike Smith
More knock-about rock, a corny show-biz number full of mock-Arabian cliches

Like Dreamers Do (Lennon-McCartney) 2.35
Recorded: 1 January 1962, Decca Sudios, London
Producer: Mike Smith
An early Lennon-McCartney original. John and Paul were writing songs together from early in their musical partnership, but this was one they never recorded for commercial release. It was taken into the Top 20 by the Applejacks in 1964.

Hello Little Girl (Lennon-McCartney) 1.40
Recorded: 1 January 1962, Decca Sudios, London
Producer: Mike Smith
Another original that The Beatles never recorded once contracted to EMI. Instead it went to fellow Epstein signees The Fourmost who made the No. 9 spot with it in 1963.

"Well, the recording test…by my artists" 0.32 [speech]
Recorded: 16 October 1964, EMI Studios, London
Producer: George Martin   **Engineer:** Stuart Eltham
More of Brian Epstein from his autobiography, relating how, after being rejected by Decca, he decided to give himself another 24 hours to find a record company for The Beatles.

Besame Mucho (Velasquez-Skylar) 2.37
Recorded: 6 June 1962, EMI Studios, London
Producer: George Martin   **Engineer:** Norman Smith
From the group's first EMI session, at which they ran through several numbers and taped four. Of those, only two survive, including this item from their current stage act.

Love Me Do (Lennon-McCartney) 2.31
Recorded: 6 June 1962, EMI Studios, London
Producer: George Martin   **Engineer:** Norman Smith
At the same session that had Pete Best on drums, they also recorded a version of 'Love Me Do' that famously would become their debut single after they recorded it again (twice) in September. The tape, having being thought lost, was found at the back of a cupboard by Judy, George Martin's wife, in 1994.

How Do You Do It (Murray) 1.57
Recorded: 4 September 1962, EMI Studios, London
Producer: George Martin   **Engineer:** Norman Smith
None of the songs recorded on 6 June 1962 was thought to be worth releasing, and the next time The Beatles appeared in the EMI studios was with their new drummer, Ringo Starr, on 4 September. Here George Martin suggested a Mitch Murray song for the A side of their first single 'How Do You Do It'. They duly recorded but discarded this song in favour of 'Love Me Do'. The Murray song of course became a huge hit for Epstein's second signing, Gerry and the Pacemakers.

Please Please Me (Lennon-McCartney) 1.59
Recorded: 4 September 1962, EMI Studios, London
Producer: George Martin   **Engineer:** Norman Smith
A first version of what would be The Beatles' second single and first big hit. For the session George Martin brought in studio drummer Andy White. This version also differs from the eventual master recording with Ringo, in that the familiar harmonica part is missing.

One After 909 (sequence) (Lennon-McCartney) 2.23
Recorded: 5 March 1963, EMI Studios, London
Producer: George Martin   **Engineer:** Norman Smith
A sequence of extracts from Takes 3, 4 and 5, in which there are various false starts including some amusing banter regarding Paul's lost plectrum.

One After 909 (complete) (Lennon-McCartney) 2.55
Recorded: 5 March 1963, EMI Studios, London
Producer: George Martin   **Engineer:** Norman Smith
Takes 4 and 5 edited into what have could have been a master track. However, the song would not appear for another six years when it was recorded for the *Let It Be* album.

Lend Me Your Comb (Twomey-Wise-Weisman) 1.49
Recorded: 2 July 1963, BBC Maida Vale Studios, London
Producer: Terry Henebery
This is from one of numerous sessions The Beatles recorded for the BBC in their *Pop Go The Beatles* series of programmes, broadcast in 15 half-hour editions between 4 June and 24 September 1963. As is evident on the *Live At The BBC* collection, most of the numbers featured on the show were not originals – 'Lend Me Your Comb' is from a 1956 Carl Perkins single – but drawn from their huge repertoire that featured in their stage performances at the time.

I'll Get You (Lennon-McCartney) 2.08
Recorded: 13 October 1963, the London Palladium, London
Recorded from a live performance on the weekly TV variety show Val Parnell's *Sunday Night At The London Palladium*, this was their first appearance on the top-rated show. The reaction of female fans in the audience to their ten-minute spot on the programme was apparently what triggered the phrase Beatlemania in the British press.

"We were performers...in Britain" 0.12 [speech]
Recorded: 8 December 1970, New York City
John talking to Rolling Stone's Jann Wenner, modestly claiming there was 'nobody to touch us' when it came to straight rock'n'roll. This was almost certainly true.

I Saw Her Standing There (Lennon-McCartney) 2.48
Recorded: 24 October 1963, Karlsplansstudion, Stockholm.
Producer: Klas Burling   **Engineer:** Hans Westman
The Beatles broke big in Sweden almost as soon as they had in Great Britain, and the national Sveriges Radio network gave them their own 25-minute programme that was broadcast on 11 November 1963. The opening 'I Saw Her Standing There' suggests that John's assessment above was spot-on.

From Me To You (Lennon-McCartney) 2.05
Recorded: 24 October 1963, Karlsplansstudion, Stockholm.
Producer: Klas Burling   **Engineer:** Hans Westman
At the end of 'I Saw Her Standing There' Paul introduces 'From Me To You' to rapturous screams and applause. Having already appeared on bootlegs, the Swedish programme has often been considered The Beatles' finest recorded live performance.

Money (That's What I Want) (Gordy-Bradford) 2.52
Recorded: 24 October 1963, Karlsplansstudion, Stockholm.
Producer: Klas Burling   **Engineer:** Hans Westman
John roars through 'Money' just like he did at the Cavern and elsewhere, an era that was sadly coming to an end even at this early point in The Beatles' career.

You Really Got A Hold On Me (Robinson)   2.58
Recorded: 24 October 1963, Karlsplansstudion, Stockholm.
Producer: Klas Burling   **Engineer:** Hans Westman
This Miracles' classic is introduced by John. Technically, the Swedish radio recordings stand up to the studio versions very well.

Roll Over Beethoven (Berry)   2.21
Recorded: 24 October 1963, Karlsplansstudion, Stockholm.
Producer: Klas Burling   **Engineer:** Hans Westman
George Harrison sounds in his element with this Chuck Berry favourite. The last three of these five Swedish airshots would appear on *With The Beatles*, The Beatles next studio album, released four weeks later.

DISC 2
She Loves You (Lennon-McCartney)   2.50
Recorded: 4 November 1963, Prince of Wales Theatre, London
The autumn of Beatlemania reached a peak of media coverage when The Beatles made their memorable appearance on the Royal Command Peformance, also referred to as the Royal Variety Show. 'She Loves You' had been the biggest of The Beatles UK hits through the previous frantic months since 'Please Please Me', and with its 'Yeah, yeah, yeah' became a trademark of the group.

Till There Was You (Wilson)   2.54
Recorded: 4 November 1963, Prince of Wales Theatre, London
Paul's 'Sophie Tucker' joke at the end of the previous track goes down well with the crowd as he launches into his ballad from The Music Man stage musical. Over the end applause, John introduces the closing 'Twist And Shout', with his famous crack about the audience in the more expensive seats rattling their jewellery.

Twist And Shout (Russell, Medley) 3.05
Recorded: 4 November 1963, Prince of Wales Theatre, London
Broadcast on BBC TV and radio on Sunday 10 November (many UK homes still didn't have television in 1963), the Royal Command Performance set the seal on The Beatles being all-round national favourites in Britain. This track ends with the house band riding out with what sounds like a swing version of the 'Twist And Shout' theme.

This Boy (Lennon-McCartney) 2.22
Recorded: 2 December 1963, ATV Studios, Borehamwood, Hertfordshire
When The Beatles appeared on the British TV series The Morecambe and Wise Show, it confirmed their status as family entertainers – for the moment at least. The 35-minute programme, hosted by the country's top comedy act of the period, was not broadcast until 18 April 1964.

I Want To Hold Your Hand (Lennon-McCartney) 2.36
Recorded: 2 December 1963, ATV Studios, Borehamwood, Hertfordshire
'This Boy' and 'I Want To Hold Your Hand' were, at the time of recording, the B and A sides of The Beatles' chart-topping single that was released a few days before and became their fourth hit single 1963.

"Boys, what I was thinking..." 2.05 [speech]
Recorded: 2 December 1963, ATV Studios, Borehamwood, Hertfordshire
As was traditional on Morcambe and Wise's TV shows, their guests appeared in at least one comedy routine with them, and The Beatles were no exception.

Moonlight Bay (Madden, Wenrich) 0.49
Recorded: 2 December 1963, ATV Studios, Borehamwood, Hertfordshire
After the wisecracks, the group were joined by Ernie Wise – all five now in straw boaters and striped jackets – for a rendition of the oldie 'Moonlight Bay', while Eric Morcambe re-appeared in Beatle wig and collarless Beatle jacket shouting 'yeah yeah yeah', 'twist and shout' and other Beatle catch-phrases.

Can't Buy Me Love (Lennon-McCartney)   2.10
Recorded: 29 January 1964, Pathé Marconi, Paris
A much bluesier version than the final master that was released as The Beatles' sixth single in March 1964, this was part of preliminary rough takes recorded at EMI's Pathé Marconi studio in Paris while The Beatles were playing a series of concerts at the Olympia concert hall in the French capital.

All My Loving (Lennon-McCartney)   2.19
Recorded: 9 February 1964, CBS television studios, New York City
Almost drowned in screams, this was The Beatles' first song on their debut appearance on The Ed Sullivan TV Show. They performed five numbers during the show that went out live to an estimated 73 million viewers, and changed popular music history.

You Can't Do That (Lennon-McCartney)   2.42
Recorded: 25 February 1964, EMI Studios, London.
Producer: George Martin   **Engineer:** Norman Smith
Take 6 of 'You Can't Do That', on which John provides a guide vocal for what was an attempt at a basic track. The final master was Take 9.

And I Love Her (Lennon-McCartney)   1.52
Recorded: 25 February 1964, EMI Studios, London.
Producer: George Martin   **Engineer:** Norman Smith
The first complete studio run-through of 'And I Love Her', with a fuller group sound to the final master that didn't matrerialise in the studio until a couple of days later.

A Hard Day's Night (Lennon-McCartney)   2.43
Recorded: 16 April 1964, EMI Studios, London.
Producer: George Martin   **Engineer:** Norman Smith
The first recorded run-through of the number that was never intended as a final version – hence the laughter at the end – with a guitar break where eventually there would be George Martin's memorable piano part.

I Wanna Be Your Man (Lennon-McCartney)   1.47
Recorded: 19 April 1964, IBC Studios, London
Producer: Jack Good   **Engineer:** Terry Johnson
With pioneering pop TV producer Jack Good at the helm, The Beatles recorded a TV special for
Associated Rediffusion called *Around The Beatles*. By this time 'I Wanna Be Your Man' had
appeared as the Ringo track on *With The Beatles*, and as the second single from the Rolling
Stones.

Long Tall Sally (Johnson-Penniman-Blackwell)   1.45
Recorded: 19 April 1964, IBC Studios, London
Producer: Jack Good   **Engineer:** Terry Johnson
A suitably frenetic Paul vocal, this Little Richard perennial that differs from the version recorded
for EMI on 1 March 1964, on this version there is no piano.

Boys (Dixon-Farrell)   1.49
Recorded: 19 April 1964, IBC Studios, London
Producer: Jack Good   **Engineer:** Terry Johnson
'Boys' another Ringo special, didn't appear in the final version of the TV programme so the
recording appeared for the first time on this album.

Shout (Isley-Isley-Isley)   1.31
Recorded: 19 April 1964, IBC Studios, London
Producer: Jack Good   **Engineer:** Terry Johnson
The fourth track from the *Around The Beatles* show, the Isley Brothers' 'Shout' never featured
on any of The Beatles' singles or albums, so this version is unique. The 1959 barnstormer that
The Beatles had included in their early repertoire, was popularised in the UK via Lulu's 1964 hit
single.

I'll Be Back (Take 2) (Lennon-McCartney)   1.12
Recorded: 1 June 1964, EMI Studios, London.
Producer: George Martin   **Engineer:** Norman Smith
Finishing the second (non-soundtrack) side of *A Hard Day's Night*, The Beatles were in the studio for three days from I June 1964. Here we hear John's original concept of the song in 3/4 waltz time that falls to bits towards the end.

I'll Be Back (Take 3) (Lennon-McCartney)   1.57
Recorded: 1 June 1964, EMI Studios, London.
Producer: George Martin   **Engineer:** Norman Smith
The song is now in the familiar 4/4 time, as it appeared on the closing track of *A Hard Day's Night*, although the master version used was Take 16.

You Know What To Do (Harrison)   1.58
Recorded: 3 June 1964, EMI Studios, London.
Producer: George Martin   **Engineer:** Norman Smith
A previously unissued song by George Harrison, incorporating vocal, bass, guitar and tambourine tracks. Ringo was indisposed, having been taken ill with tonsilitis that morning.

No Reply (demo) (Lennon-McCartney)   1.46
Recorded: 3 June 1964, EMI Studios, London.
Producer: George Martin   **Engineer:** Norman Smith
'No Reply' eventually would be recorded on 30 September 1964 and appear as the opener on the album *Beatles For Sale*, but on this demo John delivers it in a jumpy, albeit ragged, style.

Mr. Moonlight (Johnson)   2.47
Recorded: 14 August 1964, EMI Studios, London.
Producer: George Martin   **Engineer:** Norman Smith
An evocative version of the 1962 Dr Feelgood number that would appear on *Beatles For Sale*. There, the instrumental break was on organ, here it's a quirky bit of George Harrison trickery on the guitar.

Leave My Kitten Alone (John-Turner-McDougal)   2.56
Recorded: 14 August 1964, EMI Studios, London.
Producer: George Martin   **Engineer:** Norman Smith
Another track that remained in obscurity and unissued until this collection. It's a strident John-led version of Little Willie John's R&B hit from 1959.

No Reply (Lennon-McCartney)   2.29
Recorded: 30 September 1964, EMI Studios, London.
Producer: George Martin   **Engineer:** Norman Smith
What the CD notes refer to as a stepping stone version of the song that takes it from the demo of almost four months earlier to its final take on 30 September, Take 8. This was Take 2, and the boys seem to have got it.

Eight Days A Week (sequence) (Lennon-McCartney)   1.25
Recorded: 6 October 1964, EMI Studios, London.
Producer: George Martin   **Engineer:** Norman Smith
These incomplete outtakes Takes, 1, 2 and 4, show how the intro to 'Eight Days A Week' evolved in the studio.

Eight Days A Week (complete) (Lennon-McCartney)   2.47
Recorded: 6 October 1964, EMI Studios, London.
Producer: George Martin   **Engineer:** Norman Smith
A complete take (Take 5) that has a significantly different intro, ending and harmonies to the master used that was Take 13.

Kansas City/Hey-Hey-Hey-Hey! (Leiber-Stoller/Penniman)   2.44
Recorded: 18 October 1964, EMI Studios, London.
Producer: George Martin   **Engineer:** Norman Smith
The final issued version was in fact Take 1, and this (Take 2) simply couldn't compete with the one-off that appeared on *Beatles For Sale*. The medley of the two songs originally was conceived by 'Hey-Hey-Hey-Hey!' composer/singer Little Richard back in 1959.

ANTHOLOGY 2

UK Release: 18 March 1996
US Release: 19 March 1994
Running Time: 127.58
Remix Engineer: Geoff Emerick

Apple 34448
Apple CD: 7243 8 34448 2 3
Producer: George Martin

CD DISC 1 (vinyl Side A): Real Love; Yes It Is; I'm Down; You've Got To Hide Your Love Away; If You've Got Trouble; That Means A Lot; Yesterday; It's Only Love
(vinyl Side B): I Feel Fine; Ticket To Ride; Yesterday; Help!; Everybody's Trying To Be My Baby; Norwegian Wood (This Bird Has Flown); I'm Looking Through You; 12-Bar Original
(vinyl Side C): Tomorrow Never Knows; Got To Get You Into My Life; And Your Bird Can Sing; Taxman; Eleanor Rigby (strings only); I'm Only Sleeping (rehearsal); I'm Only Sleeping (Take 1); Rock And Roll Music; She's A Woman

CD DISC 2 (vinyl Side D): Strawberry Fields Forever (demo sequence); Strawberry Fields Forever (Take 1); Strawberry Fields Forever (Take 7 and edit piece); Penny Lane; A Day In The Life; Good Morning Good Morning; Only A Northern Song
(vinyl Side E): Being For The Benefit Of Mr. Kite! (Takes 1 And 2); Being For The Benefit Of Mr. Kite! (Take 7); Lucy In The Sky With Diamonds; Within You Without You (instrumental); Sgt. Pepper Lonely Hearts Club Band (Reprise); You Know My Name (Look Up The Number)
(vinyl Side F): I Am The Walrus; The Fool On The Hill (demo); Your Mother Should Know; The Fool On The Hill (Take 4); Hello, Goodbye; Lady Madonna; Across The Universe

Intended for release in February 1996, *Anthology 2* was delayed because of a last-minute change of mind by Paul McCartney. He decided he wanted 'I'm Down' to be moved from the sixth track to the third, presumably because this would be a more effective opener than 'That Means A Lot'. Apparently EMI had to be compensated for thousands of cassette jackets and CD booklets that had been printed ready for the release.

Like the opener to *Anthology 1*, 'Free As A Bird', the first track 'Real Love' is a new Beatles item adding Paul, George and Ringo to a previously unheard John Lennon demo tape. After that

the set ranges from the beginning of 1965 through to February 1968, and again tells The Beatles story chronologically with alternative takes, outtakes and so on. There are also a number of new mixes created from basic takes that in some ways get away from the archival 'authenticity' that was the core of the project.

Highlights include four live tracks recorded for a summer TV show broadcast from Blackpool, some amazing demo and alternate material of 'Strawberry Fields Forever', a very psychedelic version of 'And Your Bird Can Sing' and the first take of 'Tomorrow Never Knows' that is quite different to the track on *Revolver*.

The collection entered the British album chart at No.1 on 30 March 1996, remaining at the top for just one week but staying in the chart for a further 11 weeks, three months in all. It spent just one week at the top of the US Billboard chart but stayed in that listing for 37 weeks from 6 April 1996. it went on to sell over two million copies in America.

DISC 1
Real Love (Lennon) 3.54
Recorded: 1979, New York City/February 1995, Sussex, England
Producers: Jeff Lynne, John Lennon, Paul McCartney, George Harrison, Ringo Starr
Engineer: Geoff Emerick, Jon Jacobs

As with 'Free As A Bird' recorded a year earlier, in 1995 Paul, George and Ringo got together with Jeff Lynne as co-producer at Paul's Mill studios in rural Sussex to complete another unfinished John Lennon recording. Not long before his death John had made a casette tape demo of 'Real Love' in his New York apartment, adding a drum machine beat and a second vocal track. Yoko Ono gave the tape to the three ex-Beatles in 1994, and at the sessions they added vocal backing tracks, guitars, bass and drums. Paul recorded two bass tracks, the second on the upright double bass that Bill Black had used on Elvis Presley's 1956 recording of 'Heartbreak Hotel'.

Yes It Is (Lennon-McCartney) 1.50
Recorded: 16 February 1965, EMI Studios, London
Producer: George Martin   **Engineer:** Norman Smith
This is a breakdown of Take 2 edited (at 1:02) into the master version Take 14, that has had a newly remixed and edited version.

I'm Down (Lennon-McCartney) 2.54
Recorded: 14 June 1965, EMI Studios, London
Producer: George Martin   **Engineer:** Norman Smith
Take 1 of what would become the B side of 'Help!' on July 1965, an equally energetic alternative to the master version released that was Take 7.

You've Got To Hide Your Love Away (Lennon-McCartney) 2.45
Recorded: 18 February 1965, EMI Studios, London
Producer: George Martin   **Engineer:** Norman Smith
The track starts with John's count-in and a false start from Take 1, some studio chat off Take 2, and the complete Take 5. Take 5 was without the flute overdub that featured on the only other complete take, the master Take 9.

If You've Got Trouble (Lennon-McCartney)
Recorded: 18 February 1965, EMI Studios, London
Producer: George Martin   **Engineer:** Norman Smith
Previously unreleased, though often bootlegged, this was to have been Ringo's vocal contribution to *Help!* The recording never came together satisfactorily so it was decided to ditch it in favour of 'Act Naturally' as the Ringo track.

That Means A Lot (Lennon-McCartney) 2.26
Recorded: 20 February 1965, EMI Studios, London
Producer: George Martin   **Engineer:** Norman Smith
Another song planned for *Help!* that never saw the light of day. After working on the number for five hours plus a further stab at it on 30 March, they jettisoned the song, giving it to singer PJ Proby whose version made the UK Top 30 in September 1965.

Yesterday (Lennon-McCartney)   2.34
Recorded: 14 June 1965, EMI Studios, London
Producer: George Martin   **Engineer:** Norman Smith
The string quartet that distinguishes this Beatles classic was overdubbed onto Take 2, so this first take is the only version with just Paul's voice and his acoustic guitar. At the start we can also hear Paul giving the chord changes to George, though the latter never appeared on any take of the number.

It's Only Love (Lennon-McCartney)   1.59
Recorded: 15 June 1965, EMI Studios, London
Producer: George Martin   **Engineer:** Norman Smith
With just acoustic guitar, bass, drums and Lennon's voice, this (Take 2) is without the overdubbed lead guitar by George Harrison that we hear on the master, Take 6.

I Feel Fine (Lennon-McCartney)   2.15
Recorded: 1 August 1965, ABC Theatre, Blackpool
This and the next three tracks were from six that The Beatles played on the UK television show *Blackpool Night Out*.

Ticket To Ride (Lennon-McCartney)   2.45
Recorded: 1 August 1965, ABC Theatre, Blackpool
Broadcast live every Sunday through the summer of 1965 from 9.10 to 10.05pm, this was the group's second and final performance on *Blackpool Night Out*.

Yesterday (Lennon-McCartney)   2.43
Recorded: 1 August 1965, ABC Theatre, Blackpool
This was the first stage performance of 'Yesterday', a song that would prove far more popular than anybody could have predicted.

Help! (Lennon-McCartney)   2.54
Recorded: 1 August 1965, ABC Theatre, Blackpool
The stage debut of 'Help!' and The Beatles' only British TV appeance to promote the single – not to mention the new film and album of the same name.

Everybody's Trying To Be My Baby (Perkins) 2.46
Recorded: 15 August 1965, Shea Stadium, New York City
When the now-legendary Shea Stadium concert was shown as a special on BBC TV entitled *The Beatles At Shea Stadium* on 1 March 1966, George's performance of this Carl Perkins song had been edited out, but remained on the soundtrack of the original film footage,

Norwegian Wood (This Bird Has Flown) (Lennon-McCartney) 1.59
Recorded: 12 October 1965, EMI Studios, London
Producer: George Martin   **Engineer:** Norman Smith
According to the *Anthology 2* notes, this take, Take 1, was marked 'best' on the tape box and clearly intended as the master until the group recorded it again on 21 October. So here on Take 1, courtesy of George Harrison, is the first time a sitar was heard on a pop recording.

I'm Looking Through You (Lennon-McCartney) 2.53
Recorded: 24 October 1965, EMI Studios, London
Producer: George Martin   **Engineer:** Norman Smith
Again, initially considered a master take (Take1), this was superseded by a remake a couple of weeks later (Take 4) when the two 'Why, tell me why' choruses were added.

12-Bar Original (Lennon-McCartney-Harrison-Starr) 2.54
Recorded: 4 November 1965, EMI Studios, London
Producer: George Martin   **Engineer:** Norman Smith
A previously unissued instrumental, their first since signing with EMI in 1962, this is an edited version of the six-minute-plus take that features The Beatles and George Martin on harmonium.

Tomorrow Never Knows (Lennon-McCartney) 3.14
Recorded: 6 April 1966, EMI Studios, London
Producer: George Martin   **Engineer:** Geoff Emerick
Take 1 (recorded under a working title 'Mark I') or The Beatles' revolutionary sound-collage that would, in Take 3, become the final track of *Revolver* their seventh album.

Got To Get You Into My Life (Lennon-McCartney) 2.54
Recorded: 7 April 1966, EMI Studios, London
Producer: George Martin   **Engineer:** Geoff Emerick
A totally different version (Take 5) from the one that appeared on *Revolver* that by Take 9 had evolved with a radically amended arrangement and alternative lyrics.

And Your Bird Can Sing (Lennon-McCartney) 2.14
Recorded: 20 April 1966, EMI Studios, London
Producer: George Martin   **Engineer:** Geoff Emerick
Another instance of a version of a song (Take 2) that was considered the master for a while, until on 26 April it was re-recorded with a new arrangement.

Taxman (Harrison) 2.32
Recorded: 21 April 1966, EMI Studios, London
Producer: George Martin   **Engineer:** Geoff Emerick
The main difference between this version of George's witty *Revolver* opener (Take 11) and the Take 12 master, is the clean ending instead of the repeated guitar break, and backing vocals singing 'anybody got a bit of money' instead of the familiar 'Mr Wilson, Mr Heath'.

Eleanor Rigby (strings only) (Lennon-McCartney) 2.06
Recorded: 28 April 1966, EMI Studios, London
Producer: George Martin   **Engineer:** Geoff Emerick
This is just the double string quartet (four viotns, two violas and two cellos) on Take 14 of the classic that was mixed with the overdubbed vocals for the master version.

I'm Only Sleeping (rehearsal) (Lennon-McCartney) 0.41
Recorded: 29 April 1966, EMI Studios, London
Producer: George Martin   **Engineer:** Geoff Emerick
A snatch of an instrumental rehearsal on which we hear a vibraphone with a guitar and drums that survived on the tape after most of it was recorded over by five proper takes.

I'm Only Sleeping (Take 1) (Lennon-McCartney)   2.59
Recorded: 29 April 1966, EMI Studios, London
Producer: George Martin   **Engineer:** Geoff Emerick
The initial take of the five mentioned above. Take 11 of a session recorded two days earlier
ended up as the master used on *Revolver*.

Rock And Roll Music (Berry)   1.39
Recorded: 30 June 1966, Budokan Hall, Tokyo
This live version of the Chuck Berry song was recorded during two shows taped by the
Japanese televison company NTV.

She's A Woman (Lennon-McCartney)   2.55
Recorded: 30 June 1966, Budokan Hall, Tokyo
Recorded the same night as 'Rock And Roll Music'. The Japanese shows were part of a five-date
stint in Tokyo, not long before The Beatles gave up touring completely.

DISC 2
Strawberry Fields Forever (demo sequence) (Lennon-McCartney)   1.42
Recorded: mid-November, 1966, Kenwood, Weybridge, Surrey
John Lennon recorded solo demo versions of 'Strawberry Fields' at his home in Weybridge
before taking them to The Beatles next recording session at EMI on 24 November 1966.

Strawberry Fields Forever (Take 1) (Lennon-McCartney)   2.34
Recorded: 24 November 1966, EMI Studios, London
Producer: George Martin   **Engineer:** Geoff Emerick
Taken from the initial session, this early version of 'Strawberry Fileds' has a different
arrangement and order of lyrics to that of the master that would not emerge until a month later
after many re-recordings, overdubs and takes.

Strawberry Fields Forever (Take 7 and edit piece) (Lennon-McCartney)   4.14
Recorded: 29 November/9 December 1966, EMI Studios, London
Producer: George Martin   **Engineer:** Geoff Emerick
After five days this song had undergone some radical changes. The first minute of the final
master was from Take 7, here released in full for the first time, along with an edit piece that
includes Lennon intoning 'cranberry sauce' – it was approaching Christmas – that was
unintelligible on the released mix.

Penny Lane (Lennon-McCartney)   3.13
Recorded: 29 and 30 December 1966/4,5,6,9,10,12 and 17 January 1967,
EMI Studios, London
Producer: George Martin   **Engineer:** Geoff Emerick
A completely remixed version of this song was recorded specifically for this album with
elements from various takes that went into the original master broken down and restructured.
A telling illustration of how almost the same components can result in a radically different end
product when re-arranged in this way.

A Day In The Life (Lennon-McCartney)   5.04
Recorded: 19 and 29 January/10 February 1967, EMI Studios, London
Producer: George Martin   **Engineer:** Geoff Emerick
Another composite mix created for *Anthology 2* utilising unreleased outtakes from 'A Day In The
Life'. Oddities include John muttering 'sugar plum fairy, sugar plum fairy' near the beginning, and
assistant Mal Evans counting out one of the long gaps that later would be filled by the climactic
orchestral sequences at the end.

Good Morning Good Morning (Lennon-McCartney)   2.40
Recorded: 8 and 16 February 1967, EMI Studios, London
Producer: George Martin   **Engineer:** Geoff Emerick
This is Take 8 of 'Good Morning Good Morning', the basic track of which was recorded on
8 February 1967 with John's vocal overdubbed on the 16th, and was assumed to be the master
for some time. However, what ended up on Sgt. Pepper was, after a series of overdubs, Take 11.

Only A Northern Song (Harrison)   2.44
Recorded: 13 and 14 February/20 April 1967, EMI Studios, London
Producer: George Martin   **Engineer:** Geoff Emerick
'Only A Northern Song' originally was intended to go on the Sgt. Pepper, but ended up on the *Yellow Submarine* soundtrack album in 1969. This mix is Take 3, the basic track from 13 February 1967 with bass and guitar added later, plus unused vocal tracks overdubbed.

Being For The Benefit Of Mr. Kite! (Takes 1 and 2) (Lennon-McCartney)   1.06
Recorded: 17 and 20 February 1967, EMI Studios, London
Producer: George Martin   **Engineer:** Geoff Emerick
The first two takes of 'Mr Kite', both of which broke down almost immediately.

Being For The Benefit Of Mr. Kite! (Take 7) (Lennon-McCartney)   2.33
Recorded: 17 and 20 February 1967, EMI Studios, London
Producer: George Martin   **Engineer:** Geoff Emerick
This take constituted the basis for the final master take invoving George Martin on harmonium and a crossfaded calliope (a fairground pipe organ) effects tape.

Lucy In The Sky With Diamonds (Lennon-McCartney)   3.06
Recorded: 1 and 2 March 1967, EMI Studios, London
Producer: George Martin   **Engineer:** Geoff Emerick
More remixing for the *Anthology 2* release, this time Take 6 is overdubbed with the tamboura from Take 7 and vocals from Take 8 to produce an alternative 'Lucy' that throws little new light on the production of the original.

Within You Without You (Instrumental) (Harrison)   5.27
Recorded: 15, 16 and 22 March/3 April 1967, EMI Studios, London
Producer: George Martin   **Engineer:** Geoff Emerick
Basically a remix of the instrumental tracks without George's vocal. The Indian instrumentals, on tamboura, tabla, dilruba and swaramandal were recorded on the March dates, the violins, cellos and George's sitar were added on 3 April.

Sgt. Pepper's Lonely Hearts Club Band (Reprise) (Lennon-McCartney)   1.27
Recorded: 1 April 1967, EMI Studios, London
Producer: George Martin   **Engineer:** Geoff Emerick
A basic track with no overdubs, just Paul McCartney's guide vocal.

You Know My Name (Look Up The Number) (Lennon-McCartney)   5.44
Recorded: 17 May/7 and 8 June 1967/30 April 1969, EMI Studios, London
Producer: George Martin (1967 recordings), Chris Thomas (1969)
Engineer: Geoff Emerick (1967 recordings), Jeff Jarratt (1969)
A full version of the 1970 flipside to 'Let It Be', recorded over a two-year period. This is the full version that John edited down to four minutes-plus for the single and is in stereo for the first time.

I Am The Walrus (Lennon-McCartney)   4.02
Recorded: 5 September 1967, EMI Studios, London
Producer: George Martin   **Engineer:** Geoff Emerick
This is Take 16 of John Lennon's surrealistic classic. It is the basic track before all the amazing effects and George Martin's string and backing vocal arrangements were added.

The Fool On The Hill (demo) (Lennon-McCartney)   2.48
Recorded: 6 September 1967, EMI Studios, London
Producer: George Martin   **Engineer:** Geoff Emerick
A studio-recorded demo by Paul McCartney on piano and vocals, on which even the lyrics have yet to be finalised.

Your Mother Should Know (Lennon-McCartney)   3.02
Recorded: 16 September 1967, EMI Studios, London
Producer: George Martin   **Engineer:** Ken Scott
This was Take 27 and the master was Take 52 of Paul's composition that features harmonium, a honky-tonk style piano and vocals.

The Fool On The Hill (Take 4) (Lennon-McCartney)   3.45
Recorded: 25 September 1967, EMI Studios, London
Producer: George Martin   **Engineer:** Ken Scott
Paul still hadn't finished the lyrics when this take was made, that added recorder, drums and
the lead vocal to the previous day's three takes.

Hello, Goodbye (Lennon-McCartney)   3.18
Recorded: 2 and 19 October 1967, EMI Studios, London
Producer: George Martin   **Engineer:** Ken Scott
This is Take 16 of 'Hello Goodbye', an intermediate version that would require more overdubs
before the final master (Take 22) was achieved.

Lady Madonna (Lennon-McCartney)   2.22
Recorded: 3 and 6 February 1968, EMI Studios, London
Producer: George Martin
Engineer: Ken Scott (3 February), Geoff Emerick (6 February)
Another remix specifically created for the *Anthology* album, from Takes 3 and 4 of the original
'Lady Madonna' sessions.

Across The Universe (Lennon-McCartney)   3.28
Recorded: 3 February 1968, EMI Studios, London
Producer: George Martin   **Engineer:** Ken Scott
An alternative take (Take 2) of one of John Lennon's under-acknowledged works, that would
appear in its finished form on a charity compilation LP in 1970, then in a version remixed by Phil
Spector on the *Let It Be* album later that year.

ANTHOLOGY 3

UK Release: 28 October 1996
US Release: 29 October 1996
Running Time: 145.36
Remix Engineer: Geoff Emerick

Apple 34451
Apple CD: 7243 8 34451 2 7
Producer: George Martin

CD DISC 1 (Vinyl Side A): A Beginning (Instrumental); Happiness Is A Warm Gun; Helter Skelter; Mean Mr. Mustard (Demo); Polythene Pam (Demo); Glass Onion (Demo); Junk (Demo); Piggies (Demo); Honey Pie (Demo); Don't Pass Me By; Ob-La-Di, Ob-La-Da; Good Night
(vinyl Side B): Cry Baby Cry; Blackbird; Sexy Sadie; While My Guitar Gently Weeps; Hey Jude; Not Guilty; Mother Nature's Son
(vinyl Side C): Glass Onion; Rocky Raccoon; What's The New Mary Jane; Step Inside Love/Los Paranoias; I'm So Tired; I Will; Why Don't We Do It In The Road; Julia

CD DISC 2 (vinyl Side D): I've Got A Feeling; She Came In Through The Bathroom Window; Dig A Pony; Two Of Us; For You Blue; Teddy Boy; Medley: Rip It Up/Shake, Rattle And Roll/Blue Suede Shoes
(vinyl Side E): The Long And Winding Road; Oh! Darling; All Things Must Pass; Mailman, Bring Me No More Blues; Get Back (Live!); Old Brown Shoe; Octopus's Garden; Maxwell's Silver Hammer
(vinyl Side F): Something; Come Together; Come And Get It; Ain't She Sweet; Because; Let It Be; I Me Mine; The End

The third in the *Antholgy* series ranges from May 1968 and the recording of The Beatles through to 1970 and the final tracks recorded by the group. In the collection there's a high proportion of material that had never appeared before in any context; of the 50 tracks, only 17 had even appeared on bootlegs.

Highlights include demos recorded by all four Beatles at George Harrison's home at Esher, an alternative 'Get Back' recorded on the roof of the Apple offices, George's own acoustic demos of songs including 'Something' and 'When My Guitar Gently Weeps' and part of the legendary 12-minute 'Helter Skelter' jam, though it had to be cut down to under five.

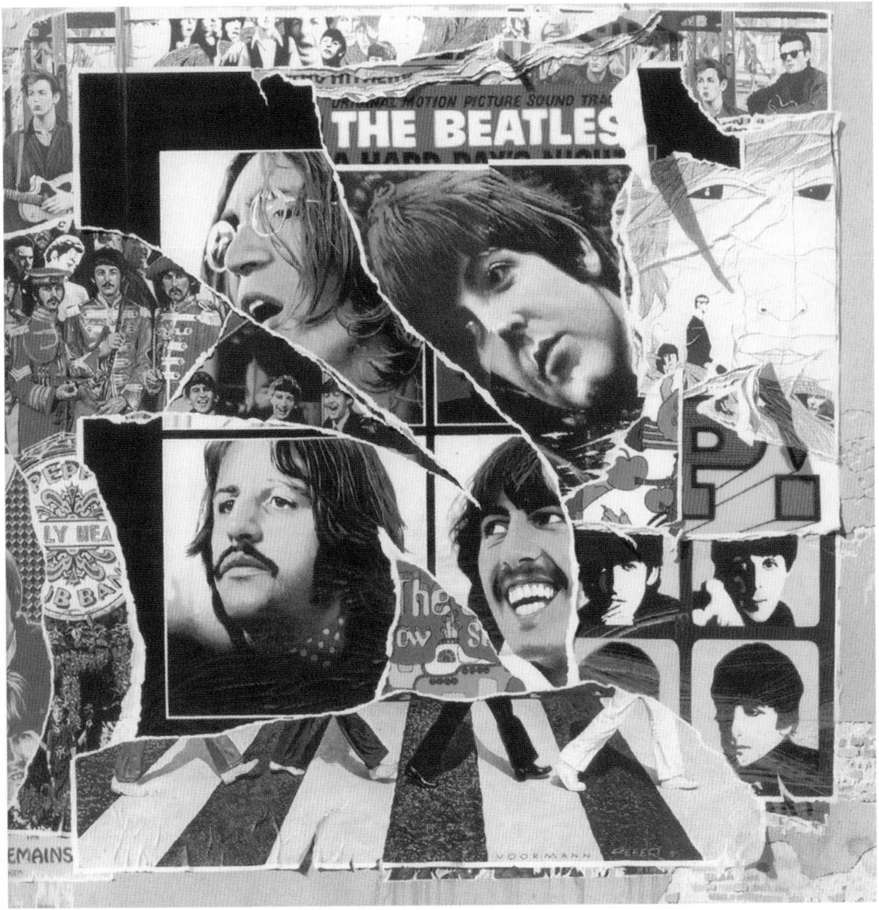
MOTION PICTURE SOUND TRA
THE BEATLES
EMAINS
VOORMANN

Candid moments are captured from the *Let It Be* sessions when The Beatles decided to record everything without overdubs and such like, while the nine-part vocals on *Abbey Road*'s 'Because' is an amazing example of what the group and George Martin could achieve with technology.

The album spent 11 weeks in the British LP chart, peaking at No. 4. Iin the United States it occupied the No. 1 spot for the first week of the four months it was in the best-sellers. During that time it sold over one-and-a-half million copies in America.

DISC 1

A Beginning (Martin)   0.50
Recorded: 22 July 1968, EMI Studios, London
Producer: George Martin   **Engineer:** Ken Scott
A lyrical-sounding George Martin orchestral arrangement that was intended as an introduction to Ringo's song 'Don't Pass Me By' but never utilised. It was recorded during the same session that provided the orchestration for 'Good Night' that closed *The Beatles* (the *White Album*).

Happiness Is A Warm Gun (Lennon-McCartney)   2.14
Recorded: May 1968, Esher, Surrey
Part of the legendary demos recorded at George Harrison's house in Esher. The Beatles gathered there at the end of May 1968 to run though their latest composition in preparation for what would be their next album, *The Beatles*.

The final song 'Happiness Is A Warm Gun' comprised three separate Lennon themes, 'I Need A Fix', 'Mother Superior Jumped The Gun'. and 'Happiness Is A Warm Gun'. The first two appear here.

Helter Skelter (Lennon-McCartney)   4.37
Recorded: 18 July 1968, EMI Studios, London
Producer: George Martin   **Engineer:** Ken Scott
The Beatles taped three extended versions of 'Helter Skelter' in preparation for their next album, and this jam-session take (Take 2) originally ran to an amazing 12 minutes 35 seconds. It's been edited down here to a more modest 4.37 and is distinctive by having a much more intense Delta-blues feel than the final master version.

Mean Mr. Mustard (Lennon-McCartney)   1.57
Recorded: May 1968, Esher, Surrey
An Esher demo, written by John Lennon that wasn't developed for the *White* album. It was produced at EMI in 1969 for The Beatles' final recorded LP *Abbey Road*.

Polythene Pam (Lennon-McCartney)   1.26
Recorded: May 1968, Esher, Surrey
Another John song that ended up as a track on *Abbey Road*.

Glass Onion (Lennon-McCartney)   1.51
Recorded: May 1968, Esher, Surrey
John hadn't finished the lyrics when this demo was laid down at Esher, hence the nonsense lyrics halfway through this Beatles try-out.

Junk (McCartney)   2.24
Recorded: May 1968, Esher, Surrey
A Paul McCartney song that was never to be included on any Beatles record until this collection but a similar acoustic version did appear on *McCartney* Paul's first solo album.

Piggies (Harrison)   2.01
Recorded: May 1968, Esher, Surrey
A double-tracked demo by George that ended up on the *White* album with slightly altered lyrics.

Honey Pie (Lennon-McCartney)   1.19
Recorded: May 1968, Esher, Surrey
Paul double-tracked this one, again the version on *The Beatles* having amended lyrics.

Don't Pass Me By (Starr)   2.42
Recorded: 5 and 6 June 1968, EMI Studios, London
Producer: George Martin   **Engineer:** Geoff Emerick
An alternative to the master used on *The Beatles*, Ringo's first solo song composition wthout the addition of the country fiddle part.

Ob-La-Di, Ob-La-Da (Lennon-McCartney) 2.56
Recorded: 3,4 and 5 July 1968, EMI Studios, London
Producer: George Martin   **Engineer:** Geoff Emerick
Featuring overdubs of sessions musicians, three saxophones and conga drums. This remained unissued in favour of a complete re-make the following week.

Good Night (Lennon-McCartney) 2.37
Recorded: 28 June, 22 July 1968, EMI Studios, London
Producer: George Martin
Engineer: Geoff Emerick (June session), Ken Scott (July session)
A rehearsal that happened to be recorded rather than an actual take. As it came to a premature close it has been segued into the final master here with the orchestral part that was added by George Martin nearly a month later

Cry Baby Cry (Lennon-McCartney) 2.46
Recorded: 16 July 1968, EMI Studios, London
Producer: George Martin   **Engineer:** Geoff Emerick
Take 1 of the John Lennon song that was completed with a basic master (Take 12) five hours later at the same session.

Blackbird (Lennon-McCartney) 2.18
Recorded: 11 June 1968, EMI Studios, London
Producer: George Martin   **Engineer:** Geoff Emerick
A perfectly viable version of Paul's solo acoustic performance, this take (Take 4) might possibly have been used had it not been for some intrusive background noise. In the event, Take 32 clinched it, with a second guitar track and the familiar bird sound effects.

Sexy Sadie (Lennon-McCartney) 4.06
Recorded: 19 July 1968, EMI Studios, London
Producer: George Martin   **Engineer:** Ken Scott
A slower version than the eventual master take, this recording fades out at the end on account of the coda to the song having not yet been written in its final form.

While My Guitar Gently Weeps (Harrison)   3.27
Recorded: 25 July 1968, EMI Studios, London
Producer: George Martin   **Engineer:** Ken Scott
An early acoustic take with an organ played by Paul and a verse that was left out of later versions. This song was to be famously augmented by a lead guitar track by Eric Clapton.

Hey Jude (Lennon-McCartney)   4.21
Recorded: 29 July 1968, EMI Studios, London   **Engineer:** Ken Scott
A simplified version (Take 2) of what would become an epic. Here we have Paul on live piano and vocals, live drums, acoustic and electric guitars. The magnificent final master, Take 26, would be laid down four days later.

Not Guilty (Harrison)   3.22
Recorded: 8,9 and 12 August 1968, EMI Studios, London
Producer: George Martin   **Engineer:** Ken Scott
The Beatles went to great lengths with this George number, making over 100 takes, this was Take 102, it was left off *The Beatles* for which it was intended and didn't appear until 1979 when George recorded an acoustic re-make for the album *George Harrison*.

Mother Nature's Son (Lennon-McCartney)   3.17
Recorded: 9 August 1968, EMI Studios, London
Producer: George Martin   **Engineer:** Ken Scott
An early, wistful and completely solo acoustic version from Paul that stands up on its own perfectly.

Glass Onion (Lennon-McCartney)   2.08
Recorded: 11,12,13, 16 and 26 September 1968, EMI Studios, London
Producer: Chris Thomas   **Engineer:** Ken Scott
Before the master version of 'Glass Onion' was completed with George Martin's string arrangement, John Lennon had laid down this mix with various sound effects he had accumulated over the previous few days.

Rocky Raccoon (Lennon-McCartney) 4.12
Recorded: 15 August 1968, EMI Studios, London
Producer: George Martin   **Engineer:** Ken Scott
What begins by sounding like it might be a master take (that was eventually Take 10), this
Take 8 soon descends into light-hearted scat-singing.

What's The New Mary Jane (Lennon-McCartney) 6.12
Recorded: 14 August 1968, EMI Studios, London
Producer: George Martin   **Engineer:** Ken Scott
A John-and-George recording with double-tracked piano and double-tracked guitar, this song
would never appear on the *White Album* as intended despite John's vocals on typically
surrealistic lyrics plus sound effects by Yoko Ono and assistant Mal Evans.

Step Inside Love (Lennon-McCartney);
Los Paranoias (Lennon-McCartney-Harrison-Starr) 2.30
Recorded: 16 September 1968, EMI Studios, London
Producer: Chris Thomas   **Engineer:** Ken Scott
A humorous bit of jamming, starting with Paul running through the song he'd written for Cilla
Black the previous year as a theme for her TV series *Cilla* that had its first airing at the beginning
of 1968.

I'm So Tired (Lennon-McCartney) 2.14
Recorded: 8 October 1968, EMI Studios, London
Producer: George Martin   **Engineer:** Ken Scott
A collage of various takes (3, 6 and 9) that culminated in Take 14 being taped live with a small
amount of overdubbing as the master for the *White album*.

I Will (Lennon-McCartney) 1.55
Recorded: 16 September 1968, EMI Studios, London
Producer: Chris Thomas   **Engineer:** Ken Scott
A first run-through of 'I Will' with Paul on vocal and acoustic guitar, and John and Ringo providing
some light percussion.

Why Don't We Do It In The Road (Lennon-McCartney) 2.15
Recorded: 9 October 1968, EMI Studios, London
Engineer: Ken Townsend
An engagingly sparse solo take (Take 4) of 'Why Don't We Do It In The Road' that ended up much heavier with the master take (Take 5) for *The Beatles*.

Julia (Lennon-McCartney) 1.57
Recorded: 13 October 1968, EMI Studios, London
Producer: George Martin   **Engineer**: Ken Scott
An interesting take on John's ballad, concentrating on the acoustic guitar track in which he breaks off to discuss how it's going with Paul who's talking to him from the studio control room.

DISC 2
I've Got A Feeling (Lennon-McCartney) 2.49
Recorded: 23 January 1969, Apple Studios, London
Producer: George Martin   **Engineer**: Glyn Johns
A tough take on the rocker that would appear on *Let It Be* in 1970. The sessions that made up the album were all live with no overdubs, at The Beatles' new Apple Studios at 3 Savile Row, London, and included on some tracks, like this one, the American keyboard player Billy Preston.

She Came In Through The Bathroom Window (Lennon-McCartney) 3.36
Recorded: 22 January 1969, Apple Studios, London
Engineer: Glyn Johns
At this stage 'She Came In Through The Bathroom Window' was intended for *Let It Be* that was tentatively titled Get Back, but it eventually appeared as part of the medley track on *Abbey Road* that was recorded in July 1969.

Dig A Pony (Lennon-McCartney) 4.18
Recorded: 22 January 1969, Apple Studios, London
Engineer: Glyn Johns
One of several run-throughs of 'Dig A Pony' for *Let It Be*. On the album version, the 'all I want is' vocals and the beginning and end were mixed out.

Two Of Us (Lennon-McCartney)   3.27
Recorded: 24 January 1969, Apple Studios, London
Engineer: Glyn Johns
Paul and John in a close-harmony duet. The live take is not vastly different from the one that appeared on the *Let It Be* album.

For You Blue (Harrison)   2.22
Recorded: 25 January 1969, Apple Studios, London
Producer: George Martin   **Engineer:** Glyn Johns
A 12-bar blues from George recorded live, the main difference between this and the released version was a lead vocal re-recorded by George in January 1970.

Teddy Boy (McCartney)   3.18
Recorded: 24 and 28 January 1969, Apple Studios, London
Engineer: Glyn Johns
A song from Paul that never saw the light of day on any Beatles album but which he recorded for *McCartney* his first solo album that was released in April 1970.

Medley: Rip It Up/Shake Rattle And Roll/Blue Suede Shoes
(Blackwell-Marascalco/Calhoun/Perkins)   3.10
Recorded: 26 January 1969, Apple Studios, London
Producer: George Martin
Engineer: Glyn Johns
The Beatles never lost their energetic love for vintage rock'n'roll songs, and here they jam along with Billy Preston on organ on classics made famous by Little Richard, Joe Turner, Bill Haley, Carl Perkins and not forgetting Elvis, respectively.

The Long And Winding Road (Lennon-McCartney)   3.40
Recorded: 31 January 1969, Apple Studios, London
Producer: George Martin   **Engineer:** Glyn Johns
The live take that eventually appeared on *Let It Be* with orchestral and choral over-dubs courtesy of Phil Spector, similar to the take released in its pure form on the *Let It Be... Naked* album in 2003.

Oh! Darling (Lennon-McCartney)   4.08
Recorded: 27 January 1969, Apple Studios, London
Producer: George Martin   **Engineer**: Glyn Johns
Another song that was intended for *Let It Be*, only to be re-recorded for *Abbey Road* later in the year. At the end of what becomes a free-wheeling jam, John makes an announcement of a more personal nature.

All Things Must Pass (Harrison)   3.05
Recorded: 25 February 1969, EMI Studios, London
Engineer: Ken Scott
A delightful demo version of the song that George would not commit to a master tape for another year and a half, after which it would appear on his debut solo album *All Things Must Pass* in late 1970.

Mailman, Bring Me No More Blues (Roberts-Katz-Clayton)   1.55
Recorded: 29 January 1969, Apple Studios, London
Producer: George Martin   **Engineer**: Glyn Johns
A loping, laid back run-through of an old Buddy Holly B side, with lead vocal by John. The Beatles had already paid tribute to Holly on *Beatles For Sale*, with 'Words Of Love', and John would do so again with 'Peggy Sue' on his 1975 album *Rock'n'Roll* .

Get Back (Lennon-McCartney)   3.08
Recorded: 30 January 1969, Apple rooftop, London
Producer: George Martin   **Engineer**: Glyn Johns
The third performance of 'Get Back' during The Beatles' celebrated appearance on the roof of their Apple offices in London's smart Savile Row. During this take the police arrived to tell them to stop, hence some timely ad-libbing by Paul.

Old Brown Shoe (Harrison) 3.02
Recorded: 25 February 1969, EMI Studios, London
Engineer: Ken Scott
Another George demo recorded at the Abbey Road studios on 25 February 1969 with various overdubbed guitar passages on top of his basic vocal and piano. The full group version of the song was recorded in April, and appeared as the B side to the single 'The Ballad of John And Yoko'.

Octopus's Garden (Starkey) 2.49
Recorded: 26 April 1969, EMI Studios, London
Producer: The Beatles   **Engineer:** Jeff Jarratt
Ringo sings a guide vocal while playing drums on this early take (Take 2) of the *Abbey Road* track without all the sound effects and backing vocals of the master (Take 32), though with a spoken interjection at the end lifted from Take 8.

Maxwell's Silver Hammer (Lennon-McCartney) 3.49
Recorded: 9 July 1969, EMI Studios, London
Producer: George Martin   **Engineer:** Phil McDonald
An *Abbey Road* song minus various overdubs, including the anvil effect, with a guide vocal by Paul that he would re-record when they got the best instrumental take.

Something (Harrison) 3.18
Recorded: 25 February 1969, EMI Studios, London
Engineer: Ken Scott
George Harrison's most famous song, here recorded for the first time during George's demo sessions on his 26th birthday, 25 February 1969. The live guitar and vocal take includes a counter melody that was dropped from the definitive version that appeared on *Abbey Road* and launched hundreds of cover versions.

Come Together (Lennon-McCartney)   3.40
Recorded: 21 July 1969, EMI Studios, London
Producer: George Martin   **Engineer:** Geoff Emerick, Phil McDonald
A near-perfect first take of John Lennon's hypnotic *Abbey Road* song, with bass, guitar and drums plus John's handclapping and his vocals minus the echo that would characterise the final master.

Come And Get It (McCartney)   2.29
Recorded: 24 July 1969, EMI Studios, London
Producer: George Martin   **Engineer:** Phil McDonald
A Paul demo on which he sang and played piano, then overdubbed maracas, drums and bass guitar in that order. It was specifically for Apple's new signing, the Iveys, whose version of the song Paul would produce just over a week later. The Iveys changed their name to Badfinger before it was released to become a Top 5 hit.

Ain't She Sweet (Ager-Yellen)   2.08
Recorded: 24 July 1969, EMI Studios, London
Producer: George Martin   **Engineer:** Geoff Emerick
A bit of studio busking, with John vocalising on the oldie that they had already recorded back in 1961 in Hamburg. This version owes more to a 1956 Gene Vincent recording than their previous interpretation.

Because (Lennon-McCartney)   2.23
Recorded: 1 and 4 August 1969, EMI Studios, London
Producer: George Martin   **Engineers:** Geoff Emerick, Phil McDonald
An amazing a capella version, the accompaniment having been removed in the mix, of John, Paul and George's three-part harmonies multiplied by three via overdubs to achieve a nine-voice effect.

Let It Be (Lennon-McCartney)   4.05
Recorded: 25 January 1969, Apple Studios, London
Producer: George Martin   **Engineer:** Glyn Johns
This was an early rendition of Paul's song made six days before they recorded the master plus some comments from John culled from the 31 January session.

I Me Mine (Harrison)   1.47
Recorded: 3 January 1970, EMI Studios, London
Producer: George Martin   **Engineer:** Phil McDonald
Recorded with just George, Paul and Ringo as John was on holiday, a fact obliquely referred to in George's opening remarks. This track is an early run-through of the number during the rehearsal period of the *Get Back/Let It Be* film-and-recording project.

The End (Lennon-McCartney)   2.50
Recorded: 23 July, 5,7,8,15 and 18 August 1969, EMI Studios, London;
Final chord: 22 February 1967, EMI Studios, London.
Producer: George Martin
Engineers: Geoff Emerick, Phil McDonald, final chord Geoff Emerick
The final full track on The Beatles' final album, this is a new mix that brings in more of the guitar sound, with Paul, George and John taking it in turns to play two bars each of the guitar solo.
Plus there's the final chord dubbed from the 'A Day In The Life' session of February 1967.

YELLOW SUBMARINE SONGTRACK

UK Release: 13 September 1999
US Release: 14 September 1999
Running Time: 45.40
Vinyl: Apple 521 4811
CD: Apple 521 4812
Producers: George Martin/Peter Cobbin

Vinyl: Side A: Yellow Submarine; Hey Bulldog; Eleanor Rigby; Love You To; All Together Now; Lucy In The Sky With Diamonds; Think For Yourself; Sgt. Pepper's Lonely Hearts Club Band; With A Little Help From My Friends
Side B: Baby, You're A Rich Man; Only A Northern Song; All You Need Is Love; When I'm Sixty-Four; Nowhere Man; It's All Too Much

CD: Yellow Submarine; Hey Bulldog; Eleanor Rigby; Love You To; All Together Now; Lucy In The Sky With Diamonds; Think For Yourself; Sgt. Pepper's Lonely Hearts Club Band; With A Little Help From My Friends; Baby, You're A Rich Man; Only A Northern Song; All You Need Is Love; When I'm Sixty-Four; Nowhere Man; It's All Too Much

When *Yellow Submarine* was first released in January 1969, coinciding with the animated cartoon film, the only Beatles tracks were on side one. There were just six of them – 'Yellow Submarine', 'Only A Northern Song', 'All Together Now', 'Hey Bulldog', 'It's All Too Much' and 'All You Need Is Love' – and only four of them were new. Side two was devoted entirely to George Martin's musical score for the movie.

Thirty years later it was decided to restore the film, digitalising the soundtrack in the process, and the songtrack album is a result of that remastering. Released in 1999, it was the first collection of Beatles songs to get a digital remix, but more significantly it dispensed with the film score that had appeared on side two and included instead most of the other songs featured in the film that hadn't appeared on the earlier LP. The only songs in the movie that don't appear

here are 'Within You Without You' and 'A Day In The Life', the latter omitted because EMI didn't want to include too many songs from the Sgt. Pepper album.

But it's the re-mixing that makes this collection stand out. When The Beatles recorded the originals they had access only to four-track tape machines, so all the voices, instruments and other effects were compressed onto those four tracks. By the end of the 90s, digital technology and 24, 32 or even 48-track recording common in the industry, made it possible for The Beatles' material to be remastered, in many cases bringing out hidden depths. And the most obvious difference to the listener when comparing these tracks to the originals is the absence of the quirky left-right stereo panning that had some of the vocals on one side only. The new mixes presented the vocals squarely in the middle and the instruments spread out around the voices rather than in their individual positions in the sound picture.

When The Beatles' back catalogue was first remixed for release on CD in the 80s, producer George Martin supervised the whole project with a view to retaining the original sound so far as possible. But by the time of *Yellow Submarine* songtrack Martin had retired, and Peter Cobbin a young engineer, was brought in for the remix.

The album went into the UK LP charts on 25 September 1999, staying there for five weeks and peaking at No. 8. In the United States meanwhile, Capitol Records decided to limit the release to CDs and cassettes, so fans wanting vinyl had to buy copies imported from England. It hit the Billboard Top 20 at 15, staying in the chart for 15 weeks, and after less than two months had sold over half a million copies in America.

Yellow Submarine (Lennon-McCartney)   2.38
Original Release: Revolver, 1966
Ringo sounds centre stage, unlike on the original mix, and there's more depth to the many sound effects.

Hey Bulldog (Lennon-McCartney)   3.11
Original Release: Yellow Submarine, 1969
This newly mixed version of the rocker, one of the fim's originals, reveals Paul McCartney's bass playing as sensational.

Eleanor Rigby (Lennon-McCartney)   2.04
Original Release: Revolver, 1966
The impact of the string quartet sound is even more stunning than previously.

Love You To (Harrison)   2.57
Original Release: Revolver, 1966
George's Indian-instrument backing is better defined in this mix, we can hear what individual players are doing for the first time.

All Together Now (Lennon-McCartney)   2.09
Original Release: Yellow Submarine, 1969
The hand clapping and percussion take on a whole new dynamic, while John and Paul's vocals coalesce where before they were separate.

Lucy In The Sky With Diamonds (Lennon-McCartney)   3.27
Original Release: Sgt. Pepper's Lonely Hearts Club Band, 1967
The nearest to the sound of the original track on the whole album.

Think For Yourself (Harrison)   2.17
Original Release: Rubber Soul, 1965
The Beatles' basic line-up as it sounded for real, with vocals, rhythm section and guitars distinct in their own right, but marvellously integrated at the same time.

Sgt. Pepper's Lonely Hearts Club Band (Lennon-McCartney)   2.00
Original Release: Sgt. Pepper's Lonely Hearts Club Band, 1967
The slightly awkward segue between the 'Sgt. Pepper' intro and 'A Little Help' is tightened up here with Paul and Ringo both positioned in the middle, making for an easier move from one song to the other.

With A Little Help From My Friends (Lennon-McCartney)   2.44
Original Release: Sgt. Pepper's Lonely Hearts Club Band, 1967
Not that big a difference here, apart from Ringo singing from the centre.

Baby, You're A Rich Man (Lennon-McCartney)   2.59
Original Release: Single (B Side to 'All You Need Is Love'), 1967
Always considered one of the Beatle's minor efforts, this B side to the iconic 'All You Need Is Love' sounded a bit messy round the edges. But the rich stero mix here puts it into a different league.

Only A Northern Song (Harrison)   3.23
Original Release: Yellow Submarine, 1969
Another song that previously sold short in the mono mix, here reveals hidden depths.

All You Need Is Love (Lennon-McCartney)   3.46
Original Release: Single, 1967
How to improve on a Beatles classic, the horns, the strings, everything sounds just that much better here.

When I'm Sixty-Four (Lennon-McCartney)   2.38
Original Release: Sgt. Pepper's Lonely Hearts Club Band, 1967
More from Sgt. Pepper, and another track that needed little improvement.

Nowhere Man (Lennon-McCartney)   2.41
Original Release: Rubber Soul, 1965
From the same album as 'Think For Yourself', again the simpler Beatles line up of earlier years makes for less to play with production-wise, but the sound is certainly crisper and the stereo effect less contrived.

It's All Too Much (Harrison)   6.24
Original Release: Yellow Submarine, 1969
A complex recording that benefits from more precise, sharper definition all round.

1

UK Release: 13th November 2000
US Release: 14 November 2000
Running Time: 79:10
Producer: Various

Apple UK 29325
Apple CD: 7243 5 29970 2

Vinyl: Side A: Love Me Do; From Me To You; She Loves You; I Want To Hold Your Hand; Can't Buy Me Love; A Hard Day's Night; I Feel Fine; Eight Days A Week
Side B: Ticket To Ride; Help!; Yesterday; Day Tripper; We Can Work It Out; Paperback Writer; Yellow Submarine; Eleanor Rigby
Side C: Penny Lane; All You Need Is Love; Hello, Goodbye; Lady Madonna; Hey Jude
Side D: Get Back; The Ballad Of John And Yoko; Something; Come Together; Let It Be; The Long And Winding Road

CD: Love Me Do; From Me To You; She Loves You; I Want To Hold Your Hand; Can't Buy Me Love; A Hard Day's Night; I Feel Fine; Eight Days A Week; Ticket To Ride; Help!; Yesterday; Day Tripper; We Can Work It Out; Paperback Writer; Yellow Submarine; Eleanor Rigby; Penny Lane; All You Need Is Love; Hello, Goodbye; Lady Madonna; Hey Jude; Get Back; The Ballad Of John And Yoko; Something; Come Together; Let It Be; The Long And Winding Road

Surprising though it may seem, when *1* was released in November 2000 it was the first single-disc compilation of Beatles hits since *20 Greatest Hits* 18 years earlier, and the first new composition to be released on CD. The idea was simple, a collection of all The Beatles' No. 1 hits in the UK and America. Although the majority of their singles topped the charts in both countries, the first and last tracks on the compilation illustrated how this was not always the case. 'Love Me Do' reached only No. 17 when it was released in the UK in 1962, but by the time it came out in the US in 1964 the group could do no wrong and it shot to the pole position. Likewise their final American chart topper – 'A Long And Winding Road' – wasn't actually released in Britain as a single.

In its vinyl version the album included the four celebrated portraits of the group by photographer Richard Avedon and a 24" by 36" poster of 126 different singles picture sleeves, while the CD came with a 32-page booklet with a foreword by George Martin and a page of picture covers of each of the singles.

The collection turned out to be the best-selling greatest hits album ever. In the UK, no compilation of The Beatles had reached No.1, not even the Red and Blue albums, but *1* went to the top of the chart as soon as it was released. In the first week it sold more than a third of a mllion copies in Britain, 59,000 in the first day and in two weeks over half a million. It stayed in the UK album chart for nearly a year, the first nine weeks at No. 1.

The album's performance in America was even more phenomenal. It sold over half a million in its first week, five million after a month and eight million in a year. Billboard called it 'Album of the Year' and honoured The Beatles as 'Number One Group for 2001' even though they had disbanded over 30 years earlier! Worldwide the collection topped the charts in 34 different contries, and sold a staggering total of 23 million copies in its first two months!

All the details below are for the UK as the original release territory unless otherwise stated.

Love Me Do (Lennon-McCartney) 2.19
Original Release: Parlophone R4949
Producer: George Martin

Original Release Date: 5 October 1962
UK No. 17 (1962), No.4 (1982)
US No. 1 for one week

From Me To You (Lennon-McCartney) 1.55
Original Release: Parlophone R4983
Producer: George Martin

Original Release Date: 12 April 1963
UK No. 1 for seven weeks. US Not charted

She Loves You (Lennon-McCartney) 2.21
Original Release: Parlophone R5055
Producer: George Martin

Original Release Date: 28 August 1963
UK No. 1 for six weeks
US No. 1 for two weeks

I Want To Hold Your Hand (Lennon-McCartney) 2.25
Original Release: Parlophone R5084
Producer: George Martin

Original Release Date: 29 November 1963
UK No. 1 for five weeks
US No. 1 for seven weeks

Can't Buy Me Love (Lennon-McCartney) 2.11
Original Release: Parlophone R5114
Producer: George Martin

Original Release Date: 16 March 1964
UK No. 1 for three weeks.
US No. 1 for five weeks

A Hard Day's Night (Lennon-McCartney) 2.33
Original Release: Parlophone R5160
Producer: George Martin

Original Release Date: 10 July 1964
UK No. 1 for three weeks
US No. 1 for two weeks

I Feel Fine (Lennon-McCartney) 2.18
Original Release: Parlophone R5200
Producer: George Martin

Original Release Date: 23 November 1964
UK No. 1 for five weeks
US No. 1 for three weeks

Eight Days A Week (Lennon-McCartney) 2.43
Original Release: Capitol 5371 (US)
Producer: George Martin

Original Release Date: 15 February 1965
UK No single release
US No. 1 for two weeks

Ticket To Ride (Lennon-McCartney) 3.10
Original Release: Parlophone R5265
Producer: George Martin

Original Release Date: 9 April 1965
UK No. 1 for three weeks
US No. 1 for one week

Help! (Lennon-McCartney) 2.19
Original Release: Parlophone R5305
Producer: George Martin

Original Release Date: 19 July 1965
UK No. 1 for 3 weeks
US No. 1 for 3 weeks

Yesterday (Lennon-McCartney) 2.05
Original Release: Capitol 5498 (US)
Producer: George Martin

Original Release Date: 13 September 1965
UK No. 8 (1976)
US No. 1 for 4 weeks

Day Tripper (Lennon-McCartney) 2.47
Original Release: Parlophone R5389
Producer: George Martin

Original Release Date: 3 December 1965
UK No. 1 for five weeks. US No. 5

We Can Work It Out (Lennon-McCartney) 2.15
Original Release: Parlophone R5389
Producer: George Martin

Original Release Date: 3 December 1965
UK No. 1 for five weeks
US No. 1 for three weeks

Paperback Writer (Lennon-McCartney) 2.18
Original Release: Parlophone R5452
Producer: George Martin

Original Release Date: 30 May 1966
UK No. 1 for two weeks.
US No. 1 for two weeks

Yellow Submarine (Lennon-McCartney) 2.37
Original Release: Parlophone R5489
Producer: George Martin

Original Release Date: 5 August 1966
UK No. 1 for four weeks
US No. 2 for one week

Eleanor Rigby (Lennon-McCartney) 2.06
Original Release: Parlophone R5489
Producer: George Martin

Original Release Date: 5 August 1966
UK No. 1 for four weeks. US No. 11

Penny Lane (Lennon-McCartney) 2.59
Original Release: Parlophone R5570
Producer: George Martin

Original Release Date: 17 February 1967
UK No. 2; US No. 1 for one week

All You Need Is Love (Lennon-McCartney) 3.47
Original Release: Parlophone R5620
Producer: George Martin

Original Release Date: 7 July 1967
UK No. 1 for three weeks
US No. 1 for one week

Hello, Goodbye (Lennon-McCartney) 3.27
Original Release: Parlophone R5655
Producer: George Martin

Original Release Date: 24 November 1967
UK No. 1 for seven weeks
US No. 1 for three weeks

Lady Madonna (Lennon-McCartney) 2.17
Original Release: Parlophone R5675
Producer: George Martin
Original Release Date: 15 March 1968
UK No. 1 for two weeks. US No. 4

Hey Jude (Lennon-McCartney) 7.03
Original Release: Apple R5722
Producer: George Martin
Original Release Date: 30 August 1968
UK No. 1 for two weeks
US No. 1 for nine weeks

Get Back (Lennon-McCartney) 3.11
Original Release: Apple R5777
Producer: George Martin/Phil Spector
Original Release Date: 11 April 1969
UK No. 1 for six weeks
US No. 1 for five weeks

The Ballad Of John And Yoko (Lennon-McCartney) 2.59
Original Release: Apple R5786
Producer: George Martin
Original Release Date: 30 May 1969
UK No. 1 for three weeks. US No. 8

Something (Harrison) 3.00
Original Release: Apple R5814
Producer: George Martin
Original Release Date: 6 October 1969
UK No. 4. US No. 1 for one week

Come Together (Lennon-McCartney) 4.17
Original Release: Apple R5814
Producer: George Martin
Original Release Date: 6 October 1969
UK No. 4. US No. 1 for one week

Let It Be (Lennon-McCartney) 3.50
Original Release: Apple R5833
Producer: George Martin/Phil Spector
Original Release Date: 6 March 1970
UK No. 2. US No. 1 for two weeks

The Long And Winding Road (Lennon-McCartney) 3.37
Original Release: Apple 2832 (US)
Producer: George Martin/Phil Spector
Original Release Date: 11 May 1970
UK No single release. US No. 1 for two weeks

Let It Be... Naked

UK Release: 17 November 2003
Running Times: 34.58/21.56 (bonus disc)
Producers: Paul Hicks, Guy Massey, Allan Rouse

US Release: 17 November 2003
Apple CD: 07243 595713 2 4

CD: (vinyl Side 1): Get Back; Dig A Pony; For You Blue; The Long And Winding Road; Two Of Us; I've Got A Feeling
(vinyl Side 2): One After 909; Don't Let Me Down; I Me Mine; Across The Universe; Let It Be
Bonus Disc: Fly On The Wall

From the time of its release, *Let It Be* was regarded as an aberration by many of those closely involved in its creation because of the involvement of Phil Spector in the final production process after the basic album had been recorded. Paul McCartney was most displeased, given that he wasn't a party to Spector being involved in the first place.

Most prominently Spector added orchestrations to numbers where they didn't previously feature, and George Martin was another who was appalled by what had been done to the tracks that he'd originally produced. "I thought the orchestral work on it was totally uncharacteristic," said George Martin. "We had established a particular style of music over the years, generally overlaid music on most Beatles tracks, and I felt that what Phil Spector had done was not only uncharacteristic, but wrong. I was totally disappointed with what happened to *Let It Be*."

Over 30 years later, *Let It Be... Naked* was advertised as "*Let It Be* as it was meant to be", promising the original album as envisaged prior to Spector's involvement. In fact it was a brand-new mix of the orignal tapes, produced by Paul Hicks, Guy Massey and Allan Rouse, all of whom had been involved in the *Anthology* and *Yellow Submarine* songtrack projects.

Using Pro-Tools, one of the recording industry's music-manipulation computer utilities, they were able to clean each track of unwanted background noise and repair various mistakes. By editing in sections from other takes they created entirely new master versions.

As part of the cleaning-up process, the brief jamming sequences and bits of humorous banter disappeared from the album, but this is more than compensated for by the 'Fly On The Wall' bonus disc. Along with a new running order, the album also includes a sensational version of

LET IT BE... NAKED

THE BEATLES

'Don't Let Me Down' that was missed out from the original. On its first week of release, *Let It Be... Naked* entered the UK album chart at No. 7, staying in the Top 50 for another four weeks.

Get Back (Lennon-McCartney) 2.34
Recorded: 27 January 1969, Apple Studios, London
Producer: George Martin   **Engineer:** Glyn Johns
 'Get Back' ended the original *Let It Be* album, with John' saying 'I hope we pass the audition', dubbed on from the rooftop recording on 30 January. Now it opens the set, with a very crisp mix but without the fade out or ad-lib.

Dig A Pony (Lennon-McCartney) 3.38
Recorded: 30 January 1969, Apple rooftop, London
Producer: George Martin   **Engineer:** Glyn Johns
The only track that appears in the same place that it occupied on the original album, for *Naked* it loses the false start and end conversation.

For You Blue (Harrison) 2.27
Recorded: 25 January 1969, Apple Studios, London
Producer: George Martin   **Engineer:** Glyn Johns
With the drums coming forward and the rhythm guitar moved back, this makes for a much more distinct mix than previously.

The Long And Winding Road (Lennon-McCartney) 3.34
Recorded: 31 January 1969, Apple Studios, London
Producer: George Martin   **Engineer:** Glyn Johns
Not quite the original version minus the Phil Spector strings, this is actually the next take (Take 19) that was used in the *Let It Be* film documentary.

Two Of Us (Lennon-McCartney)   3.21
Recorded: 31 January 1969, Apple Studios, London
Producer: George Martin   **Engineer:** Glyn Johns
A clearer mix than the original, but otherwise an almost identical sound.

I've Got A Feeling (Lennon-McCartney)   3.30
Recorded: 30 January 1969, Apple rooftop, London
Producer: George Martin   **Engineer:** Glyn Johns
A sensational track and a different take from the one on the album with a really hard sound
and a great mix, and the band sounding totally energised.

One After 909 (Lennon-McCartney)   2.44
Recorded: 30 January 1969, Apple rooftop, London
Producer: George Martin   **Engineer:** Glyn Johns
Again, a clearer mix than the original that brings out the best in the performance.

Don't Let Me Down (Lennon-McCartney)   3.18
Recorded: 30 January 1969, Apple rooftop, London
Producer: George Martin   **Engineer:** Glyn Johns
Another rooftop recording that never appeared on the orignal *Let It Be* album but came
out as the B side to the 'Get Back' single.

I Me Mine (Harrison)   2.21
Recorded: 3 January 1970, EMI Studios, London
Producer: George Martin   **Engineer:** Phil McDonald
A newly edited extended version rather than the Phil Spector extension and a cleaner mix.

Across The Universe (Lennon-McCartney)   3.38
Recorded: 4 February 1968, EMI Studios, London
Producer: George Martin   **Engineer:** Ken Scott
From the original master made in 1968 but without the Phil Spector 1970 overdubs, this is
a much more intense and emotional treatment of John Lennon's vocal.

Let It Be (Lennon-McCartney) 3.53
Recorded: 31 January 1969, Apple Studios, London
Producer: George Martin   **Engineer:** Glyn Johns
The original take but without the Phil Spector elements. Simpler, better and nearer to the truth.

Bonus Disc: Fly On The Wall
Recorded: January 1969, Apple Studios, London
Compiled and edited: Kevin Howlett   **Technical assistant:** Brian Thompson
The 'Fly On The Wall' bonus disc is a collage of outtakes from the January 1969 Apple sessions, as The Beatles were rehearsing and recording. In between snippets of songs we get pieces of conversation, The Beatles talking about their immediate plans, the proposed *Let It Be* film documentary, and of course the music.

The music items in the list below are followed by their duration.

Conversation
Sun King (0.17)
Don't Let Me Down (0.35)
Conversation
One After 909 (0.09)
Conversation
Because I Know You Love Me So (1.32)
Conversation
Don't Pass Me By (0.03)
Taking A Trip To Carolina (0.19)
John's Piano Piece (0.18)
Conversation
Child Of Nature (0.24)
Back In The USSR (0.09)
Conversation
Every Little Thing (0.09)
Don't Let Me Down (1.01)
Conversation

All Things Must Pass (0.21)
Conversation
She Came In Through The Bathroom Window (0.05)
Conversation
Paul's Piano Piece (1.01)
Conversation
Get Back (0.15)
Conversation
Two Of Us (0.22)
Maggie Mae (0.22)
Fancy My Chances With You (0.27)
Conversation
Can You Dig It? (0.31)
Conversation
Get Back (0.32)
Conversation

THE CAPITOL ALBUMS Vol 1 [Box Set]

UK Release: 15 November 2004
Parlophone (UK): B0006840ES
Total Running Time: 203.46

US Release: 16 November 2004
Capitol (US): B00065XJ48
Producer: George Martin

DISC 1 (stereo)**:** I Want To Hold Your Hand; I Saw Her Standing There; This Boy; It Won't Be Long; All I've Got To Do; All My Loving; Don't Bother Me; Little Child; Till There Was You; Hold Me Tight; I Wanna Be Your Man; Not A Second Time
(original mono): I Want To Hold Your Hand; I Saw Her Standing There; This Boy; It Won't Be Long; All I've Got To Do; All My Loving; Don't Bother Me; Little Child; Till There Was You; Hold Me Tight; I Wanna Be Your Man; Not A Second Time (disc running time: 53.26)

DISC 2 (stereo)**:** Roll Over Beethoven; Thank You Girl; You Really Got A Hold On Me; Devil In Her Heart; Money; You Can't Do That; Long Tall Sally; I Call Your Name; Please Mr. Postman; I'll Get You; She Loves You
(original mono:) Roll Over Beethoven; Thank You Girl; You Really Got A Hold On Me; Devil In Her Heart; Money; You Can't Do That; Long Tall Sally; I Call Your Name; Please Mr. Postman; I'll Get You; She Loves You (disc running time: 48.26)

DISC 3 (stereo)**:** I'll Cry Instead; Things We Said Today; Any Time At All; When I Get Home; Slow Down; Matchbox; Tell Me Why; And I Love Her; I'm Happy Just To Dance With You; If I Fell; Komm, Gib Mir Deine Hand (I Want To Hold Your Hand)
(original mono): I'll Cry Instead; Things We Said Today; Any Time At All; When I Get Home; Slow Down; Matchbox; Tell Me Why; And I Love Her; I'm Happy Just To Dance With You; If I Fell; Komm, Gib Mir Deine Hand (I Want To Hold Your Hand); (disc running time: 49.34)

DISC 4 (stereo)**:** No Reply; I'm A Loser; Baby's In Black; Rock And Roll Music; I'll Follow The Sun; Mr. Moonlight; Honey Don't; I'll Be Back; She's A Woman; I Feel Fine; Everybody's Trying To Be My Baby (original mono); No Reply; I'm A Loser; Baby's In Black; Rock And Roll Music; I'll Follow The Sun; Mr. Moonlight; Honey Don't; I'll Be Back; She's A Woman; I Feel Fine; Everybody's Trying To Be My Baby (disc running time: 52.20)

357

For the first time on CD, The Beatles' first four US Capitol albums are presented in both their stereo and mono versions. Each disc in the handsomely packaged box set represents the American original – *Meet The Beatles, The Beatles' Second Album, Something New* and *Beatles '65* – with the added bonus of each track being repeated in the original order in the original mono mix. For American fans this is an important release because previous CD re-issues of the albums often differed in their track listings, and were released only in the mono versions. For British record collectors it presents many numbers that were originally available only on singles, and again, usually just in mono. Compiled from the American master tapes, the special packaging includes the original album cover artwork, and a collector's booklet with some rare photographs, written by The Beatles' historian Mark Lewisohn.

DISC 1
(all tracks composed by Lennon-McCartney unless otherwise stated)
I Want to Hold Your Hand 2:24
(see *A Collection Of Beatles Oldies* Parlophone PMC 7016: PCS 7016)
I Saw Her Standing There 2:50 (see *Please Please Me* Parlophone PMC 1202: PCS 3042)
This Boy 2:11 (see *With The Beatles* Parlophone PMC 1206: PCS 3045)
It Won't Be Long 2:11 (see *With The Beatles* Parlophone PMC 1206: PCS 3045)
All I've Got to Do 2:05 (see *With The Beatles* Parlophone PMC 1206: PCS 3045)
All My Loving 2:04 (see *With The Beatles* Parlophone PMC 1206: PCS 3045)
Don't Bother Me 2:28 (see *With The Beatles* Parlophone PMC 1206: PCS 3045)
Little Child 1:46 (see *With The Beatles* Parlophone PMC 1206: PCS 3045)
Till There Was You (Wilson) 2:12 (see *With The Beatles* Parlophone PMC 1206: PCS 3045)
Hold Me Tight 2:30 (see *With The Beatles* Parlophone PMC 1206: PCS 3045)
I Wanna Be Your Man 1:59 (see *With The Beatles* Parlophone PMC 1206: PCS 3045)
Not a Second Time 2:03 (see *With The Beatles* Parlophone PMC 1206: PCS 3045)

DISC 2

(all tracks composed by Lennon-McCartney unless otherwise stated)

Roll over Beethoven (Berry) 2:44 (see *With The Beatles* Parlophone PMC 1206: PCS 3045)
Thank You Girl 2:01 (see *Rock and Roll Music* Parlophone PCSP 719)
You've Really Got a Hold on Me (Robinson) 2:58
(see *With The Beatles* Parlophone PMC 1206: PCS 3045)
Devil in Her Heart (Dropkin) 2:23 (see *With The Beatles* Parlophone PMC 1206: PCS 3045)
Money (That's What I Want) (Bradford, Gordy) 2:47
(see *With The Beatles* Parlophone PMC 1206: PCS 3045)
You Can't Do That 2:23 (see *A Hard Day's Night* Parlophone PMC 1230: PCS 3058)
Long Tall Sally (Blackwell, Johnson) 1.58 (see *Rock and Roll Music* Parlophone PCSP 719)
I Call Your Name (see *Rock and Roll Music* Parlophone PCSP 719)
Mr. Postman (Bateman, Dobbins, Garrett) 2:34
(see *With The Beatles* Parlophone PMC 1206: PCS 3045)
I'll Get You 2:04
She Loves You 2:19 (see *A Collection Of Beatles Oldies* Parlophone PMC 7016: PCS 7016)

DISC 3

(all tracks composed by Lennon-McCartney unless otherwise stated)

I'll Cry Instead 2:04 (see *A Hard Day's Night* Parlophone PMC 1230: PCS 3058)
Things We Said Today 2:35 (see *A Hard Day's Night* Parlophone PMC 1230: PCS 3058)
Any Time at All 2:10 (see *A Hard Day's Night* Parlophone PMC 1230: PCS 3058)
When I Get Home 2:14 (see *A Hard Day's Night* Parlophone PMC 1230: PCS 3058)
Slow Down (Williams) 2:54
Matchbox (Perkins) 1:37
Tell Me Why 2:06 (see *A Hard Day's Night* Parlophone PMC 1230: PCS 3058)
And I Love Her 2:28 (see *A Hard Day's Night* Parlophone PMC 1230: PCS 3058)
I'm Happy Just to Dance With You 1:56
(see *A Hard Day's Night* Parlophone PMC 1230: PCS 3058)
If I Fell 2:19 (see *A Hard Day's Night* Parlophone PMC 1230: PCS 3058)
Komm, Gib Mir Deine Hand (I Want To Hold Your Hand) 2:24

DISC 4

(all tracks composed by Lennon-McCartney unless otherwise stated)

No Reply   2:15   (see *Beatles For Sale* Parlophone PMC 1240: PCS 3062)

I'm a Loser   2:31   (see *Beatles For Sale* Parlophone PMC 1240: PCS 3062)

Baby's in Black   2:02   (see *Beatles For Sale* Parlophone PMC 1240: PCS 3062)

Rock And Roll Music (Berry)   2:02   (see *Beatles For Sale* Parlophone PMC 1240: PCS 3062)

I'll Follow the Sun   1:46   (see *Beatles For Sale* Parlophone PMC 1240: PCS 3062)

Mr. Moonlight (Johnson)   2:35   (see *Beatles For Sale* Parlophone PMC 1240: PCS 3062)

Honey Don't (Perkins)   2:56   (see *Beatles For Sale* Parlophone PMC 1240: PCS 3062)

I'll Be Back   2:22   (see *A Hard Day's Night* Parlophone PMC 1230: PCS 3058)

She's a Woman   2:57

I Feel Fine   2:20   (see *A Collection Of Beatles Oldies* Parlophone PMC 7016: PCS 7016)

Everybody's Trying to Be My Baby (Perkins)   2:24

(see *Beatles For Sale* Parlophone PMC 1240: PCS 3062)

THE
CHRISTMAS
ALBUMS

FROM THEN TO YOU

UK Release: 18 December 1970
Intl CD No: To be released
Running Time: 43:58

Apple LYN 2154 (Fan Club Only)
Producers: George Martin and The Beatles

SIDE ONE: The Beatles Christmas Record;
Another Beatles Christmas Record; The
Beatles Third Christmas Record; The Beatles
Fourth Christmas Record.

SIDE TWO: Christmas Time Is Here Again!;
The Beatles 1968 Christmas Record;
The Beatles Seventh Christmas Record.

FROM THEN TO YOU

Sincere Good Wishes
for
Christmas and the New Year
from

John *Paul*
George *Ringo*

The Official
Beatles Fan Club

THE BEATLES CHRISTMAS ALBUM

SIDE ONE: The Beatles Christmas Record;
Another Beatles Christmas Record;
The Beatles Third Christmas Record;
The Beatles Fourth Christmas Record.

SIDE TWO: Christmas Time Is Here Again;
The Beatles 1968 Christmas Record;
The Beatles Seventh Christmas Record.

In the summer of 1963, with the popularity of The Beatles steadily growing and the fan club membership rapidly expanding, the volume of letters and enquiries became more difficult for fan-club secretaries, Fred Kelly and Bettina Rose, to handle and still maintain individual contact with the members.

With the membership standing at 25,000, Tony Barrow, the PR and Publicity Manager of NEMS Enterprises that also supervised The Beatles' Fan Club and ensured that all members got their money's worth and were kept up to date about The Beatles, came up with the idea of a Christmas record containing a personal message from The Beatles to their most devoted fans.

The first record, scripted by Tony Barrow, and originally intended as a one off, was sent out during the first week of December 1963 to an unsuspecting 28,000 fan club members. The response was so great that the following year fan-club membership more than doubled to over 65,000 and Beatlemania was well and truly under way. The Beatles, having taken it for granted that Barrow's original idea was to be an annual event, recorded a further special message, a tradition that was to continue until 1969.

Interest in these special fan-club records became so great that each year the British music papers would review the records as though they had gone on general sale but unfortunately for a lot of non-fan club members, they didn't. Radio stations also would beg for preview copies and play them with equal enthusiasm.

The idea of the Merry Christmas and thank you style of message on the first record continued through to the 1965 record. In 1966 The Beatles – always innovators – decided to be a bit different. That year their record, entitled 'Pantomime: Everywhere It's Christmas', contained just that – a pantomime!

The record centres around the idea that everywhere it's Christmas at the end of every year and it contains three new songs: the title track plus 'Orowanyna' and 'Please Don't Bring Your Banjo Back'. For the 1967 record The Beatles continued in their Goonish style of humour, this time centring the situation around a visit to BBC Broadcasting House, and again the record contains songs unavailable elsewhere.

In 1968 the enthusiastic banter of the earlier records and the lunacy of the 1966 and 1967 recordings had all but disappeared, to be replaced by a growing feeling of animosity between The Beatles. For both

THE
BEATLES
CHRISTMAS
ALBUM

the 1968 and 1969 Christmas records The Beatles recorded their contributions separately and entrusted the job of producing a finished record to Kenny Everett, who edited the separate pieces together.

With no new material for Christmas 1970, the fan club compiled the previous seven Christmas records into an album entitled *From Then To You* that was sent to every member of the fan club as that year's Christmas record. In America, where the singles hadn't been issued, the album was retitled *The Beatles Christmas Album*. The American version also features a far superior sleeve, similar in style to the sleeve of the *A Hard Day's Night* album. This, unlike the British sleeve that uses the cover of the 1963 Christmas record, shows each of The Beatles at various stages of their career, with four group photographs also taken at various times throughout the 60s.

The original flexi-disc singles that were made by Lyntone Recordings, together with both pressings of the album that contains all seven flexi-discs, include a whole host of songs unavailable on any other Beatles record. They are now extremely valuable collector's items.

SIDE ONE
The Beatles Christmas Record   5:00
Recorded: 17 October 1963, EMI Studios, Abbey Road, London
John Lennon: Talking and Singing   **Paul McCartney:** Talking and Singing
George Harrison: Talking and Singing   **Ringo Starr:** Talking and Singing

This record was recorded in a single afternoon session after The Beatles had completed 'I Want To Hold Your Hand' and 'This Boy' that became their biggest-selling single and was to break all records worldwide and also help establish Beatlemania in America.

Originally they worked from a script written for them by Tony Barrow, but this was quickly abandoned as both the recording and the ad-libbing progressed.

The finished recording, produced by George Martin, was then sent out to members of the fan club on 6 December 1963 (Lyntone LYN 492).

The track opens with John singing the first of many re-worded versions of 'Good King Wenceslas'; he then launches into his scripted speech that he quickly abandons with 'Hello, this is John speaking with his voice.' He goes on to say what a good year it's been and mentions topping the bill at the London Palladium and also being invited to perform at The Royal Variety Command Performance at which point he starts to whistle 'God Save The Queen' with the rest of The Beatles joining in. He continues with his very laboured speech and finishes off with a further re-worded version of 'Good King Wenceslas'.

Paul, who follows, comments that The Beatles much prefer making records to performing live and also mentions that they have been recording all day before starting to record this. Having been performing live for at least five years by this point in their career, Paul's comments are perfectly understandable. John then launches into a further version of 'Good King Wenceslas', this time in German!

Following that little bout of lunacy Ringo comes next and, prompted by Paul, wishes everyone a merry Christmas and then begins to sing 'Good King Wenceslas' as a jazz number. George, who follows, thanks the fan club secretaries including the non-existent Ann Collingham and finishes off with his version of 'Good King Wenceslas'. The track comes to a close with a re-worded version of 'Rudolph the Red-Nosed Reindeer' that comes out as 'Rudolph the Red-Nosed Ringo', Had a very shiny nose, When everybody picked it...' and finally ends with all four Beatles saying 'Merry Christmas everybody'.

Another Beatles Christmas Record   4:05
Recorded: 26 October 1964, EMI Studios, Abbey Road, London
John Lennon: Piano, Lead Vocal and Talking   **Paul McCartney:** Harmony Vocal and Talking
George Harrison: Harmony Vocal and Talking   **Ringo Starr:** Harmony Vocal and Talking
This recording, originally released on 18 December 1964 (Lyntone LYN 757), opens with a wildly out-of-tune 'Jingle Bells' and continues with four very much more confident-sounding Beatles using the script as a basis for their lunacy. Paul starts it off by thanking people for buying their records and adds, 'We hope you've enjoyed listening to the records as much as we've enjoyed melting them.'

John, having managed to get away with bad language on the *Around The Beatles* TV special earlier in the year, gets away with it again when he comments that 'It's been a busy year Beatles Peedles.' 'Peedle' is Hamburg slang for the male organ. He then thanks everyone for buying his book *In His Own Write*.

Next is George, who thanks everyone for going to see the film *A Hard Day's Night* and mentions that the next film (*Help!*) will be in colour. Ringo then thanks the fans for just being fans and mentions the touring of 1964 and the amazing airport receptions.

Following their individual messages John starts playing the piano and begins to sing 'Can You Wash Your Father's Shirts', the first of the many songs featured on this album that are unavailable elsewhere. He is immediately joined by the remaining Beatles to perform this rather short, though still highly enjoyable song. The track finishes with all four Beatles wishing everyone a happy Christmas.

The Beatles Third Christmas Record   6:26
Recorded: 8 November 1965, EMI Studios, Abbey Road, London
John Lennon: Acoustic Guitar, Solo Vocal, Harmony Vocal and Talking
Paul McCartney: Harmony Vocal and Talking   **George Harrison:** Harmony Vocal and Talking
Ringo Starr: Tambourine, Harmony Vocal and Talking

Originally released on 17 December 1965 (Lyntone LYN 948), this, like the 1963 record, was recorded in a single afternoon session. With this recording a certain change in The Beatles' attitude begins to show. After the constant touring, Beatlemania, two films and constant media attention, they were obviously getting a bit fed up with it all.

The photograph on the front cover of the single was taken by Robert Whitaker during the filming of the Granada TV special *The Music Of Lennon And McCartney* at the beginning of November.

This track opens with all four Beatles singing 'Yesterday' that eventually goes out of tune. Following that there are various thank you messages plus the odd cynical comment such as, 'Well Ringo, what have we done this year?' asks Paul.

'We've done a lot of things this year, Paul' replies Ringo, 'Well we've been away . . . like last year.'

John then launches into a medley of lunatic songs, including an upbeat version of 'Auld Lang Syne'. Paul is next and makes a few comments before John begins to sing The Four Tops' record 'It's The Same Old Song', that is brought to an abrupt end by George shouting 'Copyright Johnny'.

Paul then says 'Ey, er, alright what are we gonna do what's out of copyright?'

'Ow about We'll Gather Lilacs In An Old Brown Shoe?' suggests John.

Ringo then says 'Let's play a request for all the boys in BEAORE' (meaning BAOR). John and Ringo then go into a send-up of Two-Way Family Favourites, a current BBC Radio requests programme, before John kicks off with a re-worded anti-war version of 'Auld Lang Syne', singing 'Should old acquaintance be forgot, and never brought to hand, down in Vietnam and old penance too, and look at all those bodies floatin', showing his thoughts on the war that was currently being fought in Vietnam. His thoughts in other directions are also made very obvious when later he says, 'It's an all-white policy in this group'.

The record continues with various comments and John performs a further lunatic song before all four Beatles return to their re-worded version of 'Yesterday'. The record finishes with the group reverting to a Liverpool scouse accent and John saying, 'This is Johnny Rhythm just sayin' good night to yez all and god bless yez.'

The Beatles Fourth Christmas Record
Pantomime: Everywhere It's Christmas   6:40

Recorded: 25 November 1966, Dick James Music, New Oxford Street, London
John Lennon: Harmony Vocal and Talking
Paul McCartney: Piano, Lead Vocal, Harmony Vocal and Talking
George Harrison: Harmony Vocal and Talking   **Ringo Starr:** Harmony Vocal and Talking
Mal Evans: Talking

The 1966 and 1967 records undoubtedly are the highlights of the seven Christmas singles sent to members of The Beatles' fan club. During this, and the 1967 record, they move away from the Merry Christmas-and-thank-you-for-buying-our-records style message of the previous three records and perform a pantomime instead. Scripted by The Beatles, under the strong influence of John Lennon and possibly various illegal substances as well, they set out to prove that indeed 'Everywhere It's Christmas (at the end of every year)'.

For this recording that was released on 16 December 1966 (Lyntone LYN 1145) and features a front-cover painting by Paul McCartney, The Beatles used a rather unusual setting away from Abbey Road – the recording studio in the offices of Dick James Music where both John and Paul had recorded a number of demos of their songs. Unlike the previous records, that were recorded at the end of other sessions, The Beatles set up a special session specifically to record this. It contains three new songs that were specially written, unlike the various throw-away songs of the earlier records. The first, 'Everywhere It's Christmas', opens the recording and features Paul on lead vocal and piano with John, George and Ringo throwing in odd comments and providing the harmony vocals. As it fades the second song, 'Orowanyna', performed by a small Corsican Choir (The Beatles), begins and so does the Goonish lunacy.

This time the lunacy includes such things as two elderly Scotsmen (John and George) high in the Swiss Alps munching on a rare cheese, and a loyal toast to the Queen on board HMS *Tremendous* (the Yellow Submarine?). The recording also includes a short sketch featuring John and George as Podgy The Bear and Jasper and a visit to Felpin Mansions where Paul who is later joined by the remaining three Beatles, performs the third specially written song, 'Please Don't Bring Your Banjo Back'. After a short message from Mal Evans the track finishes with a reprise of 'Everywhere It's Christmas'.

SIDE TWO
Christmas Time Is Here Again! (Lennon-McCartney-Harrison-Starkey)   6:10
Recorded: 28 November 1967, EMI Studios, Abbey Road, London
John Lennon: Timpani, Harmony Vocal and Talking
Paul McCartney: Bass Guitar, Piano, Lead Vocal and Talking
George Harrison: Acoustic Guitar, Harmony Vocal and Talking
Ringo Starr: Drums and Talking   **George Martin:** Organ and Talking
Mal Evans: Talking   **Victor Spinetti:** Tap Dancing and Talking

Originally released on 15 December 1967 (Lyntone LYN 1360), this recording, that features much of the studio trickery The Beatles had been experimenting with during 1966 and 1967, is based around a visit to BBC Broadcasting House and among other things, features Ringo and Victor Spinetti tap dancing! This was the last Christmas record that The Beatles recorded together as a group and is also the last of these special recordings to be produced by George Martin. The front cover, similar in style to the Sgt. Pepper sleeve, was designed by John and Ringo, and the painting on the back was by Julian Lennon. As with the *Magical Mystery Tour* album and EPs, the label of the single mentions the existence of the mysterious Apple.

Like the 1966 record, this recording features songs specially written for the occasion. The title track, 'Christmas Time Is Here Again' the only new song featured on these special records to have been copyrighted, crops up at various times throughout, while 'Get One Of These For Your Trousers' appears twice and 'Plenty Of Jam Jars' that is credited to The Ravellers, appears once.

The recording begins with the title song before developing into yet more Goonish lunacy that includes a couple of auditions, an interview with a typically evasive politician and a quiz show. Sections of these are then mixed in with one of the later appearances of 'Christmas Time Is Here Again' to create a more musical version of the idea that John was to use six months later to create 'Revolution 9'.

Mal Evans again makes a brief appearance, as does George Martin, when just near the end he says, 'They'd like to thank you for a wonderful year.'

The recording ends with George Martin playing 'Auld Lang Syne' on an organ while John, in his best Scottish accent, recites a poem, 'When Christmas Time Is Over'.

The Beatles 1968 Christmas Record   7:55
Recorded: Autumn 1968 (Locations vary)
John Lennon: Talking
Paul McCartney: Acoustic Guitar, Solo Vocal and Talking
George Harrison: Talking   **Ringo Starr:** Talking
Yoko Ono: Talking   **Mal Evans:** Talking
Tiny Tim: Ukelele, Solo Vocal and Talking

This is the first of two Christmas records compiled from recordings made by each individual Beatle. Due to a number of factors, the growing animosity between The Beatles was such that they recorded their individual sections separately: John at his home in Weybridge, Surrey; Paul at his home in St John's Wood, London; George in California, USA while he was recording side two of his second solo album *Electronic Sound* (UK: Zapple 02; US: Zapple ST 3358); and Ringo at his home in Ascot, Berkshire. The individual recordings were then given to Kenny Everett who edited the different sections together and is credited on the sleeve of the single as producer. The recording was released on 29 December 1968 (Lyntone LYN 1743/4). The painting on the front cover was by Julian Lennon.

The track starts off with an introduction from Ringo that is quickly followed by the intro of 'Ob-La-Di, Ob-La-Da'. Paul's sole contribution to the record is a new song, 'Happy Christmas, Happy New Year' that is heard twice. On the first version he accompanies himself with an acoustic guitar. This is followed by a speeded-up recording of 'Helter Skelter'. John then makes his first appearance, reading the first of two poems, *Jock and Yono*, about how he and Yoko 'battled on against overwhelming oddities, including some of their beast friends'. George, with Mal Evans, comes next and they both wish everyone a happy Christmas. Ringo makes his second appearance with a little bit of lunacy while 'Yer Blues' plays in the background. Paul then returns with a further short rendition of his earlier song and is quickly followed by John reading the second of his two poems *Once Upon A Pool Table*. Finally George introduces Tiny Tim who, with a little bit of encouragement from George, performs 'Nowhere Man' in the way that only Tiny Tim could!

The Beatles Seventh Christmas Record 7:42
Recorded: Autumn 1969 (Locations vary)
John Lennon: Acoustic Guitar, Solo Vocal and Talking
Paul McCartney: Acoustic Guitar, Electric Guitar, Solo Vocal and Talking
George Harrison: Talking
Ringo Starr: Acoustic Guitar, Solo Vocal and Talking   **Yoko Ono:** Piano, Harmony Vocal and Talking
Like the 1968 Christmas record, this was compiled by Kenny Everett who is credited on the sleeve of the single under his real name of Maurice Cole, from recordings made by each of the four Beatles. It could be described as a John and Yoko Christmas record, since the contributions by the remaining three Beatles are negligible. The longest contribution comes from Ringo who appears three times during the recording, once singing 'Good Evening To You Gentlemen', backed by an acoustic guitar, later to plug the film *Magic Christian* and finally at the end where he is heard laughing. Paul appears only once with a new song 'This Is To Wish You A Merry Merry Christmas' and George's sole contribution lasts just over four seconds.

The photograph used for the front cover of the single was taken by Ringo and the drawing on the back was by Ringo's son Zak. The single was originally released on 19 December 1969 (Lyntone LYN 1970/1).

John and Yoko, who start the track off by discussing their thoughts about Christmas, recorded their section at Tittenhurst Park, Ascot, Berks. George's contribution, recorded at Apple in Savile Row, London, is a brief happy Christmas, the only time that George appears. Next comes Ringo performing 'Good Evening To You Gentlemen' that was recorded at his home in Weybridge, Surrey. This is quickly followed by a section of The End from Abbey Road that continues playing as John and Yoko make their second appearance, this time discussing the wall around Tittenhurst Park! Paul, who recorded his section at his home in St John's Wood, London, comes next and performs two versions of his new song, 'This Is To Wish You A Merry Merry Christmas', with a brief Christmas message in between.

John and Yoko reappear and discuss the coming decade of the 1970s, during which John sings 'Good King Wenceslas'. John and Yoko then perform two versions of a rather avant-garde Christmas song with John playing an acoustic guitar. Ringo makes a brief reappearance to plug the film *Magic Christian* before a return to John and Yoko who discuss Christmas presents. The track ends with a cathedral choir singing 'Noel', and Ringo making a final laughing reappearance.

APPENDICES

THE ALTERNATIVE VERSIONS

This chapter deals with a subject that has long been popular with Beatles fans: the alternative versions of recordings issued by The Beatles. There is a considerable number of these, the earliest example being 'Love Me Do', where the original single and the version included on the *Please Please Me* album are two entirely and noticeably different recordings. It is possible to obtain seven different edits of 'I Am The Walrus', four each of 'I'm Only Sleeping' and 'Penny Lane', and at least two edits of a further 60 songs, as this chapter will reveal.

For ease of reference, the British and American releases have been used as a basic guide even though some, or most, of the recordings mentioned here are available elsewhere in the world. Collected together from these records are details of some 63 songs involving between them a staggering 139 different recordings and versions. Of these, 107 are available in both Britain and America, while 17 are available only in Britain and a further 13 are available only in America. There is also one version of 'I Am The Walrus' that is currently available only on a German single, and a different stereo mix of 'I Want To Hold Your Hand' that is, at present, available only on an Australian single

All known versions of each song have been listed together with details of timings, differences and where each recording can be found. If the same recording is available on more than one record then, most often, details of its first appearance are given. Not included as separate versions are recordings that feature a premature fade-out, as do several of the mono versions, for example, 'A Hard Day's Night', that on the mono version of the album, is a few seconds shorter than the stereo version. To include all of these would not do justice to those recordings that have differences that are considerably more noticeable. One exception to this is 'Hey Jude' that is included on the *American 20 Greatest Hits album* and is considerably shorter than the normal version. Also not included are those Alternative Versions created mainly by Capitol Records in America who, for reasons of their own, saw fit to either edit in or edit out, badly in most cases, whole sections of recordings. The worst cases of sections being edited in are on 'A Hard Day's Night', where the final vocal section has been so badly edited in on the cassette version (United Artists K-9006) that it is an embarrassment to listen to. Also on the eight-track version of Sgt. Pepper (8XT 2653) the last verse of the Sgt. Pepper reprise has been repeated with such a bad edit that it sounds as though it were carried out by a drunken amateur. As for sections being edited out, the favourite target by Capitol seems to have been the *White Album*. On the open-reel versions of this album (Capitol L-101/102) there are whole sections missing from 'Don't Pass

Me By', 'Glass Onion', 'Helter Skelter' and 'Revolution 9', plus small sections missing from many of the other tracks.

Other odd or bad edits from around the world include the version of 'Devil In Her Heart' as included on the Mexican album *The Beatles Volume 3* (Capitol SLEM 045). On this extremely bad edit a whole chunk of the coda has been so badly edited out that on first listening it sounds as though the record jumps. The same situation occurs with the Brazilian release of 'Penny Lane'. In this case it affects more than one record. For reasons known only to EMI Brazil the words 'in summer' have been edited out of almost every release of this recording in Brazil. Similarly, when 'A Day in the Life' was issued as a single worldwide in 1978, each country prepared its own master for the single. This has resulted in numerous edits, some of which have very strange beginnings.

Finally, there is also included a list of Beatles recordings that are at present available only in mono.

ACROSS THE UNIVERSE
Version 1 3:41
As included on the album *Past Masters – Volume Two* (Parlophone BPM 2)
Version 2 3:51
As included on the album *Let It Be* (Apple PCS 7096)
Although both versions of this track originate from the same recording, the first has the sound of birds at the beginning and backing vocals from Paul and Lizzie Bravo and Gayleen Pease, two girls who were invited into the recording session. It is slightly faster than version 2 that has a solo vocal from John and an orchestral backing.

ALL MY LOVING
Version 1 2:04
As included on the album *With The Beatles* (Parlophone PCS 3045)
Version 2 2:07
As included on the eight-album set *The Beatles Box* (Parlophone/World Records SM 701-708). Version 2 includes five taps of a hi-hat just prior to the beginning of the recording. These are missing from version 1.

ALL YOU NEED IS LOVE
Version 1 3:57
As available on the single (Parlophone R5620)
Version 2 3:47
As included on the album *Yellow Submarine* (Apple PCS 7070)

Although both these recordings were made on the same day and may appear to sound the same, they are entirely different. Version 1 is, at present, available only in mono. Version 2, in stereo, is not simply a stereo mix of version 1: it is an entirely different recording. There are slight but significant differences between the lead vocals and also certain sections of the backing. Version 2 is also ten seconds shorter than version 1.

AND I LOVE HER
Version 1 2:27
As included on the American version of the album *A Hard Day's Night* (United Artists UAS 6366)
Version 2 2:27
As included on the British version of the album *A Hard Day's Night* (Parlophone PCS 3058)
Version 3 2:36
As included on the eight-album set *The Beatles Box* (Parlophone/World Records SM 701-708)

The three versions of this originate from the same recording and are simply different stages of that recording. Version 1 features Paul's lead vocal, mostly on its own with only the chorus double-tracked; version 2 features Paul's lead vocal double-tracked and triple-tracked for the chorus. Version 3 has the same double-tracked lead vocals as version 2 but also has the guitar riff at the ending repeated six times, rather than four as on versions 1 and 2. There is also reputed to be a version of this song that features the ending riff repeated only twice but this has yet to be confirmed.

BABY, YOU'RE A RICH MAN
Version 1   3:03
As available on the single (Parlophone R5620)
Version 2   3:00
As included on the eight-album set *The Beatles Box* (Parlophone/World Records SM 701-708)

   Although both versions of this originate from the same four-track master tape, the mono version (version 1) has an entirely different feel to it. This is because it features tape spin, a studio trick that involves tape-delay fed back on itself, causing a gradual stuttering crescendo. Following a request for a stereo version in 1971, George Martin, assisted by Geoff Emerick, attempted to create a stereo version that also featured tape spin. After spending nearly half an hour attempting to duplicate this effect, Martin abandoned it and did a straightforward stereo mix of what was on the original one-inch master, thereby creating version 2.

BACK IN THE USSR
Version 1   2:45
As included on the mono version of the double album *The Beatles* (Apple PMC 7067-8)
Version 2   2:45
As included on the stereo version of the double album *The Beatles* (Apple PCS 7067-8)

   The sound effects as heard on both versions of this are in different places and the stereo recording includes some screams and shouts during the instrumental break that are not heard on the mono version. Right at the end of the track a final drumbeat can be heard on the mono version that is missing from the stereo recording.

BLACKBIRD
Version 1   2:20
As included on the mono version of the double album *The Beatles* (Apple PMC 7067-8)
Version 2   2:20
As included on the stereo version of the double album *The Beatles* (Apple PCS 7067-8)

   Like a number of tracks on the *White Album* there are slight, almost unnoticeable differences between the mono and stereo mixes. On this track the bird sounds included are different and also in slightly different places.

BLUE JAY WAY
Version 1   3:50
As included on the mono version of the double EP *Magical Mystery Tour* (Parlophone MMT 1)
Version 2   3:50
As included on the stereo version of the double EP *Magical Mystery Tour* (Parlophone SMMT 1)
   Both versions of this are essentially the same, but at various points the stereo recording includes backwards tapes that are not heard on the mono version. The multiple echo on the cello near the end is also missing from the mono version, as is the final organ note.

DAY TRIPPER
Version 1   2:37
As included on the stereo version of the album *Past Masters – Volume Two*, (Parlophone BPM 2)
Version 2   2:37
As included on the double album *The Beatles 1962-1966* (Apple PCSP 717)
   Although both recordings are basically the same, version 1 has the guitar intro double-tracked with each track on a separate channel, and the vocals have had echo added. Version 2 has the guitar intro single-tracked on the left-hand channel only and there is no echo on the vocals.

DON'T PASS ME BY
Version 1   3:45
As included on the mono version of the double album *The Beatles* (Apple PMC 7067-8)
Version 2   3:52
As included on the stereo version of the double album *The Beatles* (Apple PCS 7067-8)
   With the exception of the violin at the end of the track, these two recordings are the same. Version 1 is slightly faster than version 2, it has been speeded up, making it seven seconds shorter than version 2. This has the effect of transposing Ringo's voice into a higher key and giving the track a bouncier feel.

FLYING
Version 1 2:16
As included on the mono version of the double EP *Magical Mystery Tour* (Parlophone MMT 1)
Version 2 2:16
As included on the stereo version of the double EP *Magical Mystery Tour* (Parlophone SMMT 1)
   The mono version of this includes some extra bass guitar and piano at the beginning that are not heard on the stereo recording. The final section of the vocal track included on the stereo version is absent from the mono. The sound effects at the end of the track also appear earlier on the mono version.

THE FOOL ON THE HILL
Version 1 3:00
As included on the mono version of the double EP *Magical Mystery Tour* (Parlophone MMT 1)
Version 2 3:00
As included on the stereo version of the double EP *Magical Mystery Tour* (Parlophone SMMT 1)
   The stereo version includes some extra flute passages that are absent from the mono recording, as are parts of the vocal track just near the end of the track.

FROM ME TO YOU
Version 1 1:55
As included on the album *Past Masters – Volume One* (Parlophone BPM 1)
Version 2 1:55
As included on the double album *The Beatles 1962-1966* (Apple PCSP 717)
   The mono version 1 includes a harmonica during the intro that is missing from the stereo version 2.

GET BACK
Version 1   3:11
As included on the album *Past Masters – Volume Two* (Parlophone BPM 2)
Version 2   3:09
As included on the album *Let It Be* (Apple PCS 7096)

The differences between these two recordings are immediately noticeable. Version 2 has a spoken intro not included on version 1. The endings also are entirely different: Version 1 includes an extra verse and a fade, version 2 just stops and we hear John Lennon's classic statement 'I'd like to say "thank you" on behalf of the group and ourselves and I hope we passed the audition'.

GOOD DAY SUNSHINE
Version 1   2:08
As included on the mono version of the album *Revolver* (Parlophone PMC 7009)
Version 2   2:08
As included on the stereo version of the album *Revolver* (Parlophone PCS 7009)

On first listening the mono version appears to be exactly the same as the stereo mix. However, the mono version includes extra drum beats during the fade that are missing from the stereo version.

GOOD MORNING, GOOD MORNING
Version 1   2:35
As included on the mono version of the album *Sgt. Pepper's Lonely Hearts Club Band* (Parlophone PMC 7027)
Version 2   2:35
As included on the stereo version of the album *Sgt. Pepper's Lonely Hearts Club Band* (Parlophone PCS 7027)

The basic track is the same for both versions, but on the mono version the sound effects begin slightly earlier than on the stereo version.

GOT TO GET YOU INTO MY LIFE
Version 1   2:39
As included on the mono version of the album *Revolver* (Parlophone PMC 7009)
Version 2   2:31
As included on the stereo version of the album *Revolver* (Parlophone PCS 7009)
   Many people are under the mistaken impression that the vocal track differs on both versions and that the closing lines during the fade are different. In fact the mono and stereo versions are exactly the same. The reason the lyrics at the end appear to sound different is not because there are two separate lead vocals but because the mono version features an extra line of lyrics due to a longer fade-out.

HELP!
Version 1   2:16
As included on the mono version of the album *Help!* (Parlophone PMC 1255)
Version 2   2:16
As included on the stereo version of the album *Help!* (Parlophone PCS 3071)
   Although these recordings may sound the same, they have a different lead vocal. Halfway through the first verse of version 1 the lyrics are 'And now these days, . . .' whereas on version 2, the lyrics are 'But now these days. . . . ' They are two entirely different recordings.

HELTER SKELTER
Version 1   3:38
As included on the mono version of the double album *The Beatles* (Apple PMC 7067-8)
Version 2   4:30
As included on the stereo version of the double album *The Beatles* (Apple PCS 7067-8)
   Although the mono and stereo versions are the same recording, they are mixed and edited differently. The fade-out of the mono version has several notes missing and the drumming is different. When it fades it does not re-appear, as it does on the stereo version and misses Ringo's statement 'I've got blisters on my fingers' – words sometimes wrongly credited to John.

HEY JUDE
Version 1 7:11
As included on the album *Past Masters – Volume Two* (Parlophone BPM 2)
Version 2 5:05
As included on the American album *20 Greatest Hits* (Capitol SV 12245)

Although nearly two minutes shorter than version 1, version 2 is the same recording but with an early fade-out. John Lennon's profanity, that is heard five minutes 40 seconds into the recording, is missing from the shorter version.

HONEY PIE
Version 1 2:42
As included on the mono version of the double album *The Beatles* (Apple PMC 7067-8)
Version 2 2:42
As included on the stereo version of the double album *The Beatles* (Apple PCS 7067-8)

Version 1 includes an extra guitar phrase at the end of the instrumental break that is missing from version 2.

I AM THE WALRUS
There are seven versions of this song, all slightly different edits of the same recording. This should have made them all of slightly different lengths but because each one is slowed down or speeded up slightly, they all have exactly the same timing.
Version 1 4:35
As included on the mono version of the double EP *Magical Mystery Tour* (Parlophone MMT 1)

The organ intro here is repeated four times as opposed to six on some other versions. Between the lyrics 'I'm crying' and 'Sitting on a cornflake' the drum track cuts out. Later, when John repeats 'I'm crying' four times just before 'Yellow matter custard', the drum track again disappears between the first and second 'I'm crying'.

Version 2 4:35

As available on the American single (Capitol 2056)

   Again the organ intro is repeated four times, but between the lyrics 'I'm crying' and 'Sitting on a cornflake' only the hi-hat and snare drum disappear and the drum track is still present. As with version 1, during the four repeats of 'I'm crying' just before 'Yellow matter custard', the drum track again cuts out. Following the four repeats of 'I'm crying' there are some extra beats not heard on version 1.

Version 3 4:35

As included on the album *Magical Mystery Tour* (Parlophone PCTC 255)

   This version also has the organ intro repeated four times, but between the lyrics 'I'm crying' and 'Sitting on a cornflake', the main drum track cuts out leaving only the hi-hat and the snare drum. Finally, during the four repeats of 'I'm crying' the entire drum track cuts out.

Version 4 4:35

As available on the German single (Odeon 1 C 006-04 477)

   This is almost the same as version 3 except here the organ intro is repeated six times.

Version 5 4:35

As included on the stereo version of the double EP *Magical Mystery Tour* (Parlophone SMMT 1)

   The organ intro here is repeated six times and the drum track is present throughout.

Version 6 4:35

As included on the eight-album set *The Beatles Box* (Parlophone/World Records SM 701-708)

   This sixth version includes both the organ intro repeated six times and the few extra beats in the middle of the recording. It is the full version edited from versions 2 and 5.

Version 7 4:35

As included on the stereo version of the compact disc *Magical Mystery Tour* (Parlophone CDP 7480622)

   Basically this is the same as version 5 but on some of the early copies the radio noises heard just before the track changes from stereo to electronic stereo, have been repeated.

I CALL YOUR NAME
Version 1   2:05
As included on the EP *Long Tall Sally* (Parlophone GEP 8913)
Version 2   2:05
As included on the stereo version of the American album *The Beatles Second* (Capitol ST 2080)
Version 3   2:05
As included on the stereo version of the album *Past Masters – Volume* One (Parlophone BPM 1)
    Although in effect the same recording, on version 1 the backing cowbell starts at the beginning of the recording, while on version 2 it does not start until half-way through the opening line and on version 3 it does not start until after the opening line.

I DON'T WANT TO SPOIL THE PARTY
Version 1   2:33
As included on the mono version of the album *Beatles For Sale* (Parlophone PMC 1240)
Version 2   2:33
As included on the stereo version of the album *Beatles For Sale* (Parlophone PCS 3062)
    There are two whoops just before the instrumental break on the stereo version that are absent from the mono version.

I FEEL FINE
Version 1   2:20
As available on the single (Parlophone R5200)
Version 2   2:17
As included on the stereo version of the album *Past Masters – Volume One* (Parlophone BPM 1)
Version 3   2:19
As included on the double album *The Beatles 1962-1966* (Apple PCSP 717)
    Version 1 has an entirely different lead vocal from versions 2 and 3. The latter two are basically the same recording except for two seconds of mysterious whispering on version 3 just before the beginning of the track.

SHOULD HAVE KNOWN BETTER
Version 1   2:16
As included on the stereo version of the album *A Hard Day's Night* (Parlophone PCS 3058)
Version 2   2:16
As included on the American version of the album *Reel Music* (Capitol SV 12199).
   These recordings differ only in the harmonica intro. On version 1 this cuts out briefly, whereas on version 2 it is complete.

I WANT TO HOLD YOUR HAND
Version 1   2:24
As included on the stereo version of the album *Past Masters – Volume One* (Parlophone BPM 1)
Version2   2:24
As included on the Australian single (Parlophone A-8103)
   Although both versions of this are the same recording, version 2 is remixed and has the vocals that are in the centre of the stereo sound stage on version 1, mixed onto the right-hand channel. It also has the rhythm guitar that on version 1 is on the right-hand channel, mixed into the centre.

I WILL
Version 1   1:46
As included on the mono version of the double album *The Beatles* (Apple PMC 7067-8)
Version 2   1:46
As included on the stereo version of the double album *The Beatles* (Apple PCS 7067-8)
   The bass guitar that starts at the beginning of the stereo version, doesn't start until after the first verse on the mono version.

IF I FELL
Version 1   2:18
As included on the mono version of the album *A Hard Day's Night* (Parlophone PMC 1230)
Version 2   2:18
As included on the stereo version of the album *A Hard Day's Night* (Parlophone PCS 3058)
    The mono version single-tracks John's lead vocal intro, whereas the stereo version double-tracks it. Both feature a duet between John and Paul.
    When, on the stereo version, the vocal parts reach 'And I would be sad if our new love was in vain' for the second time, Paul's voice gives out on the word 'vain'. On the mono version Paul sings the complete line, although on 'vain' his voice sounds strained.

I'LL CRY INSTEAD
Version 1   1:44
As included on the British album *A Hard Day's Night* (Parlophone PCS 3058)
Version 2   2:06
As included on the American album *A Hard Day's Night* (United Artists UAS 6366)
    Both versions originate from the same recording. Version 2 includes a repeat of the first verse just before the final verse; this is missing from version 1.

I'M LOOKING THROUGH YOU
Version 1   2:20
As included on the British album *Rubber Soul* (Parlophone PCS 3075)
Version 2   2:27
As included on the American album *Rubber Soul* (Capitol ST 2442)
    Although these are from the same basic recording, version 2 has two false starts that are not included on version 1.

I'M ONLY SLEEPING
Version 1 2:58
As included on the mono version of the British album *Revolver* (Parlophone PMC 7009)
Version 2 2:58
As included on the mono version of the American album *Yesterday And Today* (Capitol T 2553)
Version 3 2:58
As included on the stereo version of the British album *Revolver* (Parlophone PCS 7009)
Version 4 2:58
As included on the stereo version of the American album *Yesterday... And Today* (Capitol ST 2553)

Versions 1 and 2 in mono, include backwards guitar during the third verse that is missing from versions 3 and 4. On version 2 there is a lot more backwards guitar during the third verse than there is on version 1. The backwards guitar at the end of version 2 starts a lot later than on any of the other versions.

Versions 3 and 4, both in stereo, appear to sound the same but have the backwards guitar in slightly different places. During the second verse the backwards guitar starts earlier on version 4 and there is also more of it than on version 3. On all versions except version 4, the backwards guitar starts immediately after John Lennon stops singing, but at the beginning of the instrumental break on version 4 it starts one beat later.

IT'S ONLY LOVE
Version 1 1:53
As included on the stereo version of the album *Help!* (Parlophone PCS 3071)
Version 2 1:53
As included on the stereo version of the compact disc *Help!* (Parlophone CDP 7 464392)

When EMI finally got round to releasing The Beatles' albums on compact disc, George Martin was called upon to prepare the digital masters for release. For the first four albums he cleaned up the mono versions and these were released worldwide on compact disc in 1987. For the *Help!* and *Rubber Soul* albums Martin returned to the original four-track master tapes and cleaned and remixed them. In doing so he also repaired a fault on the stereo version of 'It's Only Love'. On the original album version, part of the vocal track cuts out during the first chorus, this is now complete on the compact disc version.

KOMM, GIB MIR DEINE HAND
Version 1   2:24
As included on the British album *The Beatles Rarities* (Parlophone PCM 1001)
Version 2   2:24
As included on the American album *Something New* (Capitol ST 2018).

Although both recordings are almost the same, version 2 has various screams and shouts over the musical intro that are missing from version 1.

LET IT BE
Version 1   3:50
As included on the album *Past Masters – Volume Two* (Parlophone BPM 2)
Version 2   4:01
As included on the album *Let It Be* (Apple PCS 7096)

Both recordings originate from the same eight-track master tape. Version 2 is the original recording, complete with a sloppy lead guitar solo from George, while version 1 features a re-recorded and far superior, guitar solo.

LOVE ME DO
Version 1   2:22
As included on the album *Past Masters – Volume One* (Parlophone BPM 1)
Version 2   2:19
As included on the album *Please Please Me* (Parlophone PCS 3042)

Version 1 has Ringo on drums, while version 2 features session musician Andy White on drums with Ringo on tambourine. Besides not featuring a tambourine, the original version is also slightly slower and in a different key; there is also hand-clapping during the harmonica solo. For the history behind these two recordings see the *Please Please Me* album.

MAGICAL MYSTERY TOUR
Version 1 2:48
As included on the mono version of the double EP *Magical Mystery Tour* (Parlophone MMT 1)
Version 2 2:48
As included on the stereo version of the double EP *Magical Mystery Tour* (Parlophone SMMT 1)
On the mono version the sustained trumpet notes end three beats before the sustained 'now' at the end of the line 'The Magical Mystery Tour is hoping to take you away, hoping to take you away, now'. On the stereo version the sustained trumpet notes continue to the end of the sustained 'now'.

MONEY
Version 1 2:47
As included on the mono version of the album *With The Beatles* (Parlophone PMC 1206)
Version 2 2:47
As included on the stereo version of the album *With The Beatles* (Parlophone PCS 3045)
These are two different recordings. The first, in mono, is slightly slower and has Ringo tapping his drumsticks together in time with the piano intro. John's lead vocal is given more echo than on the stereo version that does not include the drumstick tapping.

NO REPLY
Version 1 2:15
As included on the mono version of the album *Beatles For Sale* (Parlophone PMC 1240)
Version 2 2:15
As included on the stereo version of the album *Beatles For Sale* (Parlophone PCS 3062)
On version 2 the first two lines of the second verse are single-tracked, on version 1 they are double-tracked. At the end of the same verse the words 'in my place' have backing vocals on all three words on version 2. On version 1 the backing vocals are on the word 'place' only.

NORWEGIAN WOOD (This Bird Has Flown)
Version 1 2:00
As included on the mono version of the album *Rubber Soul* (Parlophone PMC 1267)
Version 2 2:00
As included on the stereo version of the album *Rubber Soul* (Parlophone PCS 3075)
   On the mono version someone coughs just after the line 'She told me to sit anywhere.' This has been taken off the stereo version.

OB-LA-DI, OB-LA-DA
Version 1 3:10
As included on the mono version of the double album *The Beatles* (Apple PMC 7067-8)
Version 2 3:10
As included on the stereo version of the double album *The Beatles* (Apple PCS 7067-8)
   Version 2 includes hand-clapping during the piano intro that is missing from version 1.

PAPERBACK WRITER
Version 1 2:25
As available on the single (Parlophone R5452)
Version 2 2:25
As included on the album *Past Masters – Volume Two* (Parlophone BPM 2)
Version 3 2:25
As included on the album *Hey Jude* (Parlophone PCS 7184)
   Version 1, in mono, includes four taps during the multiple-echo sections that, together with some other minor extraneous noises, are missing from both stereo versions. Although both are in stereo, versions 2 and 3 are different mixings. Version 3 is the stereo reverse of version 2; also, the backing vocals are mixed farther forward than on version 2.

PENNY LANE
Version 1 3:00

As available on promotional copies of the American single (Capitol 5810)

This version is a much sought-after collector's item as it features seven extra notes played on a piccolo trumpet over the ending. It was distributed to radio stations in the USA and Canada in this form but when it reached the stores these seven notes had been taken off.

Version 2 3:00

As available on the single (Parlophone R5570)

This record is as version 1 but minus the extra notes played over the ending.

Version 3 3:00

As included on the double album *The Beatles* 1966-1970 (Apple PCSP 718)

This stereo version features a low trumpet after the line 'He likes to keep his fire engine clean, it's a clean machine.' This is missing from versions 1 and 2.

Version 4 3:00

As included on the eight-album set *The Beatles Box* (Parlophone/World Records SM 701-708)

This version, that is also in stereo, is version 3 with the seven extra notes from version 1 edited on to the ending.

PIGGIES
Version 1 2:04

As included on the mono version of the double album *The Beatles* (Apple PCS 7067-8)

Version 2 2:04

As included on the stereo version of the double album *The Beatles* (Apple PCS 7067-8)

The main recording is the same on both versions; the differences between the two versions are the grunts and their absence or presence at various points throughout the recording.

On the mono version, after the line 'Life is getting worse', there are three grunts; on the stereo version there are four. After the line 'Living piggy lives', there are two grunts on the stereo version but none on the mono version. After 'Clutching forks and knives', there is one grunt on the mono version that is missing from the stereo version. Finally, the grunts at the end are different: on the mono version there are about 12 and on the stereo version there are about eight.

PLEASE PLEASE ME

Version 1 2:00
As included on the mono version of the album *Please Please Me* (Parlophone PMC 1202)
Version 2 2:00
As included on the stereo version of the album *Please Please Me* (Parlophone PCS 3042)

At first listening, the mono and stereo recordings of this song appear to be the same. However, there is a slight difference in both the vocal and the lyrics between versions. On the stereo recording, half-way through the song, John fluffs the lyrics slightly. On the mono version, the lyrics are sung without fault. In addition, on the stereo version, the harmonica at the end is out of sequence with the rest of the backing, whereas on the mono version it is in sequence.

REVOLUTION

Version 1 3:22
As available on the single (Apple R5722)
Version 2 3:22
As included on the album *Past Masters – Volume Two* (Parlophone BPM 2)

The guide beat at the beginning of the stereo version 2 is missing from the mono version 1.

SEXY SADIE

Version 1 3:15
As included on the mono version of the double album *The Beatles* (Apple PMC 7067-8)
Version 2 3:15
As included on the stereo version of the double album *The Beatles* (Apple PCS 7067-8)

On the mono version, there is one tambourine tap during the piano intro and on the stereo version there are two taps. The bass guitar starts right at the beginning of the vocals on the stereo version but fades in half-way through the first line on the mono version.

SGT. PEPPER'S LONELY HEARTS CLUB BAND

Version 1 1:59

As included on the mono version of the album *Sgt. Pepper's Lonely Hearts Club Band* (Parlophone PMC 7027)

Version 2 1:59

As included on the stereo version of the album *Sgt. Pepper's Lonely Hearts Club Band* (Parlophone PCS 7027)

The main difference between the two versions is the sound effects. On the last line of the song there are two whistles between 'lonely' and 'band' on the stereo version but only one on the mono. At the end, as 'Billy Shears' is sung, the audience screams start simultaneously on the mono version but two beats earlier on the stereo version.

SGT. PEPPER'S LONELY HEARTS CLUB BAND (REPRISE)

Version 1 1:20

As included on the mono version of the album *Sgt. Pepper's Lonely Hearts Club Band* (Parlophone PMC 7027)

Version 2 1:20

As included on the stereo version of the album *Sgt. Pepper's Lonely Hearts Club Band* (Parlophone PCS 7027)

The mono version of this track features a 14-tap introduction along with an indecipherable comment from John, just before Paul says 'One, two, three, four'. The stereo version has only a ten-tap introduction and John's background comment is missing. The crowd sounds during the drumbeat sections of the opening also are different and the mono version includes laughter from the crowd that is absent from the stereo track.

SHE'S A WOMAN

Version 1 2:57

As included on the album *Past Masters – Volume One* (Parlophone BPM 1)

Version 2 3:00

As included on the EP *The Beatles* (Parlophone SGE 1)

Version 2 includes a 'One, two, three, four' count-in from Paul that is missing from version 1.

SLOW DOWN
Version 1 2:54
As included on the EP *Long Tall Sally* (Parlophone GEP 8913)
Version 2 2:54
As included on the stereo version of the album *Past Masters – Volume One* (Parlophone BPM 1)

These two versions have different vocals. The stereo version also includes John shouting 'ow' just before the last few bars of the track are played.

STRAWBERRY FIELDS FOREVER
Version 1 4:05
As available on the single (Parlophone R5570)
Version 2 4:05
As included on the album *Magical Mystery Tour* (Parlophone PCTC 255)
Version 3 4:05
As included on the double album *The Beatles 1967-1970* (Apple PCSP 718)

During the two harpsichord sections on version 1 there are eight notes, but on versions 2 and 3 there are nine. There is no fade-out or fade-in on version 1.

Versions 2 and 3, both in stereo, are different mixings. On version 2 when the orchestra joins in, it starts on the left-hand channel and immediately drifts across to the right. On version 3 it starts and remains on the right. On version 2, the slight instrumental breaks after the line 'Strawberry Fields Forever', remain in the centre, but on version 3 these instrumental breaks drift from right to left across the stereo sound stage.

At the point where version 3 fades out completely, version 2 fades only slightly; when version 3 fades back in, the horn sound drifts from right to left, unlike version 2 where it goes from right to centre and back to right. Also, version 3 has a dominant snare drum on the fade-in that is missing from version 2.

TAXMAN
Version 1 2:36
As included on the mono version of the album *Revolver* (Parlophone PMC 7009)
Version 2 2:36
As included on the stereo version of the album *Revolver* (Parlophone PCS 7009)

On the mono version the cowbell starts after the line 'Should five per cent appear too small'. On the stereo version it doesn't start until after "Cos I'm the taxman'. The entry point of the tambourine also is marginally different on both versions. On the stereo version it starts before the word 'cent', but on the mono version it starts after it.

TELL ME WHY
Version 1 2:06
As included on the mono version of the album *A Hard Day's Night* (Parlophone PMC 1230)
Version 2 2:06
As included on the stereo version of the album *A Hard Day's Night* (Parlophone PCS 3058)

However similar these two recordings may sound, they are entirely different. Aside from the fact that they are both played in different keys, John's lead vocal on the mono version is single-tracked, on the stereo version it is double-tracked.

THANK YOU GIRL
Version 1 2:01
As included on the album *Past Masters – Volume One* (Parlophone BPM 1)
Version 2 2:01
As included on the stereo version of the American album *The Beatles Second* (Capitol ST 2080)

Although both versions are from the same basic recording, version 2 includes the harmonica played twice during the track and also over the last few bars; all this is missing from version 1.

TOMORROW NEVER KNOWS
Version 1 2:59
As included on the mono version of the album *Revolver* (Parlophone PMC 7009)
Version 2 3:00
As included on the stereo version of the album *Revolver* (Parlophone PCS 7009)
    On the stereo version there is a gradual fade-in at the beginning, on the mono version the fade-in is sudden. This accounts for the one-second difference in timings. The tape loops and sound effects are different on the two versions and also are in different places.

WE CAN WORK IT OUT
Version 1 2:10
As included on the stereo version of the album *Past Masters – Volume Two* (Parlophone BPM 2)
Version 2 2:10
As included on the American album *Yesterday And Today* (Capitol ST 2553)
    These are two slightly different mixings of the same track. Version 1 has the stereo split between the two channels without anything mixed into the centre. Version 2 has sections of the organ mixed into the centre.

WHAT GOES ON
Version 1 2:44
As included on the mono version of the album *Rubber Soul* (Parlophone PMC 1267)
Version 2 2:44
As included on the stereo version of the album *Rubber Soul* (Parlophone PCS 3075)
    The lead guitar that can be heard over the ending of version 2 is absent from version 1.

WHEN I GET HOME
Version 1 2:14
As included on the British version of the album *A Hard Day's Night* (Parlophone PCS 3058)
Version 2 2:14
As included on the mono version of the American album *Something New* (Capitol T 2018)
    Version 2 features an entirely different lead vocal to that on version 1. On the line 'I'll love her more, till I walk out that door', the word 'till' comes in half a beat earlier than on version 1.

WHILE MY GUITAR GENTLY WEEPS
Version 1 4:46
As included on the mono version of the double album *The Beatles* (Apple PMC 7067-8)
Version 2 4:46
As included on the stereo version of the double album *The Beatles* (Apple PCS 7067-8)
   At the end of the mono version the 'Yeah, yeah, yeah' that can be heard on the stereo version, is missing.

WHY DON'T WE DO IT IN THE ROAD?
Version 1 1:42
As included on the mono version of the double album *The Beatles* (Apple PMC 7067-8)
Version 2 1:42
As included on the stereo version of the double album *The Beatles* (Apple PCS 7067-8)
   Included in the intro of the stereo version, along with the drumbeat, is handclapping that is absent from the mono version.

YELLOW SUBMARINE
Version 1 2:40
As included on the mono version of the album *Revolver* (Parlophone PMC 7009)
Version 2 2:40
As included on the stereo version of the album *Revolver* (Parlophone PCS 7009)
   At the beginning of version 1, together with the lyrics 'In the town. . .', is an extra guitar passage not heard on version 2. On version 1, in the middle of the song, just after Ringo sings 'As we live a life of ease', John repeats 'A life of ease' that also is missing from version 2.

YOUR MOTHER SHOULD KNOW
Version 1 2:33
As included on the mono version of the double EP *Magical Mystery Tour* (Parlophone MMT 1)
Version 2 2:33
As included on the stereo version of the double EP *Magical Mystery Tour* (Parlophone SMMT 1)
   The drum track is phased on the mono version but not on the stereo version.

THE MONO RECORDINGS

As this chapter deals with Beatles recordings that have alternative versions, it is the best place to mention the six recordings that are available only in mono. At the time of writing there are no stereo alternatives of these tracks available anywhere in the world.

'Love Me Do', 'P.S. I Love You', 'She Loves You' and 'I'll Get You' were all recorded on two-track and then reduced to mono: the original tapes were then wiped.

'Only A Northern Song' and 'You Know My Name' were reduced to mono from master tapes that still exist; these have yet to be mixed into stereo.

THE UNRELEASED TRACKS

One fascinating aspect of The Beatles' recording career is the material recorded but never released.

Unfortunately, over the years much of this material has found its way into the hands of bootleggers who have produced illegal records. It is surprising that this has been allowed to continue because The Beatles and their record and publishing companies would benefit if the material were officially issued. Many fans and collectors would prefer to buy these unreleased tracks as officially issued records rather than as inferior-quality bootlegs.

The material that remains unreleased falls into a minimum of nine different categories: auditions, demonstration recordings, radio broadcasts, television broadcasts, live recordings, interviews, recording session warm-ups, the *Let It Be* sessions and unreleased tracks plus the counterfeit records, that are described first.

BOGUS BEATLES

Before listing the unreleased tracks it is important to dispel some rumours and myths that have become associated with The Beatles over the years. A few records were thought by many to be unreleased Beatles tracks issued by other record labels than those for whom The Beatles recorded. The following five records are quite definitely *not* The Beatles.

Have You Heard The Word/Futting Around -- Fut (Beacon)

Legend has it that during the late 60s, after The Beatles had finished Abbey Road, and effectively ended their recording career, John Lennon joined the Bee Gees to record this track. Some people thought it featured all four Beatles and the Bee Gees: another theory was that it was The Beatles' last recording. It has appeared on a surprising number of bootlegs, although it is not The Beatles. It isn't exactly the Bee Gees either, but Maurice Gibb of the Bee Gees together with Steve Kipner of Tin Tin, a group discovered by the Bee Gees in the late 60s.

L.S. Bumble Bee/Bee Side -- Peter Cook and Dudley Moore (Decca)

Issued early in 1967, this recording has appeared on many Beatles bootlegs. It is a send-up of psychedelia that has a vocal that sounds a little like John Lennon. It is in fact Dudley Moore with backing by Peter Cook.

We Are The Moles Parts I And II -- The Moles (Parlophone)

Although released on the Parlophone label, this is not The Beatles under another name. Mystery surrounded the release of the record in 1968: the master tapes were deposited in a left-luggage locker in a London railway station. The locker key and a mysterious letter were sent to a leading British music paper stating that the record was to be issued on the Parlophone label. It also stated that if the record reached the top ten, the identity of the group would be revealed.

Many people assumed that the record was made by The Beatles, but even so it sold poorly. A few years later The Moles were revealed as Simon Dupree and the Big Sound (later Gentle Giant), who also recorded for the Parlophone label at the time. Again, the recording has appeared on a few Beatles bootlegs and some people still believe it to be The Beatles.

People Say/I'm Walking -- John and Paul (London)

Issued in 1965 at the height of The Beatles fame, this has appeared on a number of Beatles bootlegs and has been incorrectly identified as a duet by John Lennon and Paul McCartney. It is not but, although it doesn't even sound like Lennon and McCartney, rumours continue and so does its inclusion on Beatles bootlegs.

Ram You Hard -- John Lennon and The Bleechers (Punch)

This reggae record issued in early 1970, may well feature a John Lennon, but it is not *the* John Lennon.

The following pages describe The *real* Beatles' unreleased tracks.

AUDITIONS

During 1962, when The Beatles were trying to secure a recording contract, they had auditions with Decca and EMI. All were recorded and among the recordings are about 15 titles that The Beatles never intended for release. Although they are really quite good it was thought highly unlikely that they would ever find their way on to official records.

Fortunately, 12 of these recordings have now been issued (see *The Decca Sessions* 1.1.62 album). Among the titles recorded are Beatles versions of their own 'Hello Little Girl', 'Like Dreamers Do' and 'Love Of The Loved' that are not included on *The Decca Sessions 1. 1.62*, plus versions of other people's material such as 'Take Good Care Of My Baby', 'Besame Mucho', 'Memphis Tennessee' and 'Three Cool Cats' that are included on the *Decca Sessions 1.1.62* along with a further eight songs that they included in their early stage performances.

DEMONSTRATION RECORDINGS

These consist of songs written by Lennon and McCartney and given away to other artists, but demonstrated on record by John Lennon, Paul McCartney or The Beatles so that the artist involved could hear how the song sounded. A number of these were recorded at the offices of Dick James and are quite basic run-throughs of the songs. Others were recorded at Abbey Road and are of a higher quality, both technically and musically.

With the exception of 'I'm The Greatest', written after the split-up, the tracks included by other artists on the album *The Songs Lennon And McCartney Gave Away* were recorded originally in one form or another by The Beatles.

RADIO BROADCASTS

Between 1962 and 1965 The Beatles appeared on many BBC radio shows for which they recorded material specifically for broadcast. In addition to alternative versions of material that they did release, there were also 44 tracks recorded for broadcast but never issued. Among these are The Beatles' version of the Lennon-McCartney song 'I'll Be On My Way', together with many rock'n'roll songs.

The following is a complete list of the unreleased songs that The Beatles recorded for the BBC: 'Beautiful Dreamer'; 'Besame Mucho'; 'Carol; Clarebella'; 'A Crimble Mudley' (a medley of 'Love Me Do'; 'Please Please Me'; 'From Me To You'; 'She Loves You'; 'I Want To Hold Your Hand' and 'Rudolph, The Red Nosed Reindeer'); 'Crying', 'Waiting, Hoping'; 'Don't Ever Change'; 'Dream Baby'; 'From Us To You'; 'Glad All Over'; 'Happy Birthday Saturday Club'; 'Hippy Hippy Shake'; 'The Honeymoon Song';

'I Forgot To Remember To Forget'; 'I Got A Woman'; 'I Got To Find My Baby'; 'I Just Don't Understand'; 'I'll Be On My Way'; 'I'm Gonna Sit Right Down and Cry (Over You)'; '(I'm) Talking About You'; 'Johnny B. Goode'; 'Keep Your Hands Off My Baby'; 'Lend Me Your Comb'; 'Lonesome Tears In My Eyes'; 'Lucille'; 'Memphis, Tennessee'; 'Nothin' Shakin (But The Leaves On The Trees)'; 'Ooh! My Soul'; 'A Picture Of You'; 'Pop Go The Beatles'; 'A Shot Of Rhythm And Blues'; 'Side By Side'; 'So How Come (No One Loves Me)'; 'Soldier Of Love (Lay Down Your Arms)'; 'Some Other Guy'; 'Sure To Fall'; 'Sweet Little Sixteen'; 'That's Alright Mama'; 'Tie Me Kangaroo Down Sport (with Rolf Harris)'; 'To Know Her Is to Love Her'; 'Too Much Monkey Business' and 'Youngblood'.

Although both 'Sheila' and 'Three Cool Cats' also were recorded, they were never broadcast.

TELEVISION BROADCASTS

During the 1960s The Beatles appeared in countless television broadcasts worldwide. During some of their broadcasts on British television they performed a number of songs that have never appeared on record. The first of these was 'Some Other Guy' that was filmed and recorded at the Cavern Club, Liverpool, on 22 August 1962 and was first broadcast by Granada Television during their *People and Places* current affairs programme on 17 October 1962, 12 days after the release of 'Love Me Do'. Next came 'After You've Gone' which was performed with Terry Hall, Patsy Ann Noble, The Raindrops and The Bert Hayes Octet at the end of the BBC children's television show *Pops And Lenny* on 16 May 1963. On 4 November 1963 The Beatles appeared on *The Royal Variety Command Performance* and joined in with the rest of the cast to sing the final song of the show, 'God Save The Queen'. The show was recorded and broadcast on 10 November 1963.

During 1964, The Beatles appeared on ATV's *The Morecambe and Wise Show* and joined Eric Morecambe and Ernie Wise in a rendition of 'On Moonlight Bay'.

On 6 May 1964 ATV broadcast a Beatles special called *Around The Beatles*; during this show The Beatles mimed to recordings made on 19 April 1964. Among the songs was their version of the Isley Brothers' 'Shout!' that came complete with some very graphic expletives from John Lennon. How they got away with the language is anyone's guess! During the same show The Beatles also performed a medley of their first five Parlophone singles 'Love Me Do'; 'Please Please Me'; 'From Me To You'; 'She Loves You' and 'I Want To Hold Your Hand'.

Finally, during 1965 The Beatles were filmed on Blackpool beach singing 'I Do Like To Be Beside The Seaside' for the ATV show *Blackpool Night Out*.

LIVE RECORDINGS

Besides the recording of 'Some Other Guy' that Granada Television made at the Cavern Club in Liverpool, there are at least two other tapes of The Beatles performing live at The Cavern that are known to exist. The first was made and is still owned by Mike McCartney. Unfortunately the contents of this tape are unknown. The second tape was recorded by a Beatles' fan during July 1962 and contains among others: 'Hey! Baby'; 'Hippy Hippy Shake' and 'If You Gotta Make A Fool Of Somebody'. This second tape was bought by Paul McCartney when it was sold at Sotheby's in August 1985 for £2,100.

The Star Club Tapes also contain one further track that has yet to be issued: John's rendition of 'My Girl Is Red Hot'. The general condition of the recordings on the tape suggest that this must be of extremely poor quality for it not to have been issued.

Although numerous tapes of concerts exist, they contain only live versions of issued material and so are not relevant to this chapter.

INTERVIEWS

During various interviews one or more of The Beatles would occasionally burst into song, a situation that led to the existence of various unreleased tracks. There is, for example, a recording of John singing very badly 'Those Were The Days' that he launched into during an interview in 1968.

There is also a recording of The Beatles performing a totally off-the-cuff rendition of 'All Together On The Wireless Machine' during the first airing of the *Magical Mystery Tour* tracks on BBC Radio One on 2 December 1967.

One the most famous of the 'unreleased tracks' recorded during an interview is 'Cottonfields', sung during an interview with Kenny Everett on 18 July 1968 during a break in the *White Album* sessions at Abbey Road. The song, together with the interview, has been released as part of an interview album. In the UK it is called *Interviews II;* in the *US: The Golden Beatles*. (See the following Non-Album Tracks section for full details.)

Other unreleased tracks that are now available include 'Waltzing Matilda', a recording that was sent to an Australian DJ prior to The Beatles' Australian tour in 1964. A second version and a short rendition of 'Tie Me Kangaroo Down, Sport', has, like 'Cottonfields', been released (See the following Non-Album Tracks section for details).

RECORDING SESSION 'WARM-UPS'

There are a number of songs that The Beatles used to warm up their recording sessions. Over the years these have found their way on to innumerable Beatles bootlegs, invariably described as working versions of songs. The truth is that these short tracks were never considered by The Beatles to be serious recordings, nor did they intend to record full versions for release. They are simply recordings of The Beatles messing about in the studio, relaxing and getting ready to record by singing anything that came to mind like 'Ba Ba Black Sheep', 'Tea For Two' and 'The Third Man Theme'.

These warm-up recordings last from 30 to 90 seconds. A good example is 'Maggie Mae' on *Let It Be*.

THE *LET IT BE* SESSIONS

During the month-long fiasco of January 1969, that eventually was to become known as *Let It Be*, The Beatles, while recording the ill-fated and still unreleased *Get Back* album, also filmed the event for a television documentary. (See the *Let It Be* album.) In total 96 hours of sound film was shot, of which only 90 minutes was eventually used. The 94$\frac{1}{2}$ hours of film that remain unissued and the studio tapes contain an enormous amount of unreleased material, including Beatles versions of many songs that John, Paul and George were later to re-record for solo release. These include: 'Gimme Some Truth' and 'Jealous Guy' that was later re-recorded by John for his 1971 album *Imagine*; 'Teddy Boy', 'Hot As Sun' and 'Junk', all re-recorded by Paul and included on his *McCartney* album; and 'The Back Seat Of My Car' again re-recorded by Paul and released in 1971 on his solo album *Ram*. George's songs later re-recorded by him include 'All Things Must Pass', 'Isn't It A Pity' and 'Not Guilty'. Other songs recorded but never released include 'Shakin' In The Sixties', a Lennon-written rocker dedicated to Dick James who ran The Beatles' music publishers, Northern Songs. In addition there is a whole host of rock'n'roll, country and western and late 50s and early 60s songs.

One semi-released and copyrighted song to emerge from these sessions and featured in the film, is 'Suzy Parker', a McCartney-written song. Whether it was ever considered for release on record is open to speculation but if it were, the film soundtrack would have to be used as no known stereo master of the track exists.

UNRELEASED TRACKS

The total number of unreleased tracks recorded is open to debate, but judging by the amount of bootlegs available one would think that the rejection rate by The Beatles was 50 per cent. Bootleggers would have us believe that every single cough, splutter and twang of a guitar string ever committed to tape constitutes an unreleased track but, in all good sense, a finished recording that The Beatles once considered as a possible release should be the only material considered as unreleased tracks.

Among master tapes are numerous unreleased tracks recorded by The Beatles, but most of them were never considered for release.

There are a small number of finished tracks that were recorded, but for various reasons were not released. Among these are: 'How Do You Do It?' recorded as a possible follow-up to 'Love Me Do'; 'Leave My Kitten Alone', recorded during the sessions for the *Help!* album; 'Not Guilty' recorded during the *White Album* sessions; and the most famous unreleased Beatles track of all 'What's The New Mary Jane' also recorded during the *White Album* sessions. This was always going to be the next Beatles single, but never was.

Early in 1985 EMI planned to issue an album of unreleased tracks entitled *Sessions* that was to contain: 'Come And Get It'; 'Leave My Kitten Alone'; 'Not Guilty'; 'I'm Looking Through You'; 'What's The New Mary Jane'; 'How Do You Do It'; 'Besame Mucho'; 'One After 909'; 'If You Got Troubles'; 'That Means A Lot'; 'While My Guitar Gently Weeps'; 'Mailman Bring Me No More Blues' and 'Christmas Time Is Here Again'. This, together with a single featuring 'Leave My Kitten Alone' and an alternative unreleased version of 'Ob- La-Di, Ob-La-Da', was scrapped and returned to the vaults following objections by The Beatles.

The following list of 200 titles lists every track generally assumed to have been recorded by The Beatles in one form or another, but not released. Also included in the listing at the beginning, are eight titles that were recorded before The Beatles recorded for either Polydor or EMI Records.

Two of the eight titles, 'That'll Be The Day' and 'In Spite Of All The Danger', were recorded by The Quarrymen, John Lennon's first group, at Kensington Recording Studio, Liverpool, in 1958. The line-up for these recordings is believed to have been John Lennon, rhythm guitar and lead vocal; Paul McCartney, bass guitar and harmony vocal; George Harrison, lead guitar and harmony vocal; Colin Hanton, drums; and John Lowe, piano. There is only one known 78 rpm single of these recordings in existence, the master tapes having been destroyed.

A further three originate from a tape recorded in May 1960 in Paul McCartney's home in Liverpool, and together with John, Paul and George, also feature Stuart Sutcliffe. Although the tape contains nearly an hour and a half of various rehearsals of a number of songs, there are only three songs: 'Hallelujah, I Love Her So', 'I'll Follow The Sun' and 'One After 909', that could be described as full recordings.

The remaining three titles, 'Fever', 'September Song' and 'Summertime' were recorded by The Beatles backing Lu Walters, bass guitarist and vocalist with Rory Storme and The Hurricanes in September 1960 in Akustic Studios, Hamburg, West Germany. The recordings also featured Ringo Starr who was a member of The Hurricanes. Ringo had sat in on drums because Pete Best, then The Beatles' drummer, was nowhere to be found at the time the recording was due to take place. According to legend there were only four copies of these recordings made as one-sided 78 rpm records, but over the years they have been lost.

All songs are unpublished individual Beatle or Lennon and McCartney compositions except where stated.

The Quarrymen (Recorded in Liverpool, 1958)
That'll Be The Day (Allison-Petty-Holly)
In Spite Of All The Danger

The Beatles (Recorded in Liverpool, May 1960)
Hallelujah, I Love Her So (Charles)
I'll Follow The Sun
One After 909

The Beatles With Lu Walters (Recorded in Hamburg, September 1960)
Fever (Davenport-Cooley)
September Song (Weill-Anderson)
Summertime (Gershwin-Gershwin)

The Beatles (Recorded in London, January 1962)
Hello Little Girl
Like Dreamers Do
Love Of The Loved

The Beatles (Recorded in Liverpool, Manchester and London 1962-70)

After You've Gone (Creamer-Layton) (*with Terry Hall, Patsy Ann Noble, The Raindrops and The Bert Hayes Octet*)
Ain't That A Shame (Domino-Bartholomew)
All Along The Watchtower (Dylan)
All Shook Up (Blackwell-Presley)
All Things Must Pass
All Together On The Wireless Machine

Ba Ba Black Sheep (Trad.)
Baby, I Don't Care (Leiber-Stoller)
Back Seat Of My Car, The
Bad To Me
Beautiful Dreamer (Foster)
Be Bop A Lula (Vincent-Davis)
Be My Baby (Greenwich-Barry-Spector)
Blowin' In The Wind (Dylan)
Blue Suede Shoes (Perkins)
Bye Bye Love (Bryant-Bryant)

Carol (Berry)
Catcall
Clarebella (Pingatore)
C'mon Everybody (Cochran-Capehart)
Come And Get It
Commonwealth Song

Cottonfields (Ledbetter)
Crimble Mudley, A

Da Doo Ron Ron (Greenwich-Barry-Spector)
Digging My Potatoes (Trad.)
Don't Be Cruel (Blackwell-Presley)
Don't Ever Change (Goffin-King)
Don't Let The Sun Catch You Crying (Marsden)
Dream Baby (Walker)

Early In The Morning (Darin-Harris)
Etcetera
Every Night

Fool Like Me (Clements-Maddox)
From A Window
From Us To You

Gimme Some Truth
Glad All Over (Schroeder-Tepper-Bennett)
God Save The Queen (Trad.) (From the 1963 *Royal Variety Command Performance*)
Going Up The Country (Wilson)
Goodbye
Good Rockin' Tonight (Brown)
Great Balls Of Fire (Hammer-Blackwell)

Happy Birthday Saturday Club (Hill-Hill, Arr. Lennon)
Hare Krishna Mantra (Trad.)
Heather
Hey! Baby (Cobb-Channel)
Hi-Heel Sneakers (Higgenbotham)
Hi Ho Silver
Hippy Hippy Shake (Romero)
Hitch Hike (Gaye-Paul-Stevenson)
Home (Clarkson-Clarkson-Steeden)
Honeymoon Song, The (Theodorakis-Sansom)
Hot As Sun
House Of The Rising Sun (Trad.)
How Do You Do It? (Murray)

I Do Like To Be Beside The Seaside (Glover-Kind)
I Don't Want To See You Again
I Forgot To Remember To Forget (Kesler-Feathers)
I Got A Woman (Charles-Richards)
I Got To Find My Baby (Berry)
I Just Don't Understand (Wilkin- Westberry)
I Shall Be Released (Dylan)
I Threw It All Away (Dylan)
If You Gotta Make A Fool Of Somebody (Clark)
If You've Got Trouble
I'll Be On My Way
I'll Build A Stairway To Paradise (Gershwin-Da Silva-Francis)
I'll Keep You Satisfied
I'm Gonna Sit Right Down And Cry (Over You) (Thomas-Biggs)
I'm In Love

Isn't It A Pity
It's For You
It's So Easy (Allison-Petty-Holly)

Jealous Guy
Jessie's Dream
Johnny B. Goode (Berry)
Junk

Kansas City (Leiber-Stoller)
Keep Your Hands Off My Baby (Goffin-King)

Lawdy Miss Clawdy (Price)
Leave My Kitten Alone (McDougal-Turner)
Lend Me Your Comb (Twomey-Wise-Wiseman)
Little Queenie (Berry)
Lonesome Tears In My Eyes (Burnette-Burnette-Burlinson-Mortimer)
Look At Me (Allison-Petty-Holly)
Los Paranois
Lucille (Collins-Penniman)

Mailman Bring Me No More Blues (Roberts-Katz-Clayton)
Mama, You've Been On My Mind (Dylan)
Maybe I'm Amazed
Maybellene (Berry-Fratto-Freed)
Michael Row The Boat Ashore (Trad.)
Midnight Special (Trad.)
Miss Ann (Penniman)
Moonglow (Hudson-De Lange-Mills

Move It (Samwell)
My Girl Is Red Hot
My Kind Of Girl (Bricusse)

Nobody I Know
Not Fade Away (Allison-Petty-Holly)
Not Guilty
Nothing' Shakin' (But The Leaves On The Trees)
    (Colacrai-Fontaine-Lampert-Cleveland)

Oh Carol (Greenfield-Sedaka)
On Moonlight Bay (Madden-Wenrich) (With
    Morecambe and Wise)
One And One Is Two
Ooh! My Soul (Penniman)

Peggy Sue (Allison-Petty-Holly)
Peggy Sue Got Married (Allison-Petty-Holly)
Penina
Picture Of You, A (Beveridge-Oakman)
Piece Of My Heart (Berns-Ragavoy)
Pop Go The Beatles (Trad., Arr. Patrick)

Ramrod (Casey)
Raunchy Uustis-Manker)
Ready Teddy (Marascalco-Blackwell)
Red Sails In The Sunset (Williams-Kennedy)
Reelin' And Rockin' (Berry)
Reminiscing (Curtis)
Right String But The Wrong Yo-Yo, The (Perryman)
Rip It Up (Blackwell-Marascalco)
Rock Island Line, The (Trad.)
Rocker

Save The Last Dance For Me (Pomus-Shuman)
Send Me Some Lovin' (Price-(Marascalco)
Shake Rattle And Roll (Calhoun)
Shakin' In The Sixties
Sheila (Roe)
Shimmy Shake (South-Land)
Shirley's Wild Accordion
Short Fat Fanny (Williams)
Shot Of Rhythm And Blues, A (Thompson)
Shout! (O'Kelly-Isley-Isley)
Side By Side (Woods) (With The Karl Denver
    Trio)
Singing The Blues (Endsley)
So How Come (No One Loves Me) (Bryant-
    Bryant)
Soldier Of Love (Lay Down Your Arms) (Cason-
    Moon)
Some Other Guy (Leiber-Stoller-Barrett)
Somethin' Else (Cochran)
Spiritual Regeneration (Recorded at Rishikesh,
    India, 1967-8)
Stand By Me (King-Leiber-Stoller-Jones)
Step Inside Love
Suicide
Suzy Parker
Suzy's Parlour
Sweet Little Sixteen (Berry)

Talking About You (I'm) (Berry)
Tea For Two (Youmans-Caesar- Harbach)
Teddy Boy
Tennessee (Perkins)

Thank You Guru Dai/Happy Birthday Mike Love
  (*Recorded at Rishikesh, India, 15 March 1968*)
That Means A Lot
That's Alright Mama (Crudup)
Thingumybob
Think It Over (Allison-Petty-Holly)
Thinking of Linking
Third Man Theme, The (Karas)
Thirty Days (Berry)
Those Were The Days (Raskin)
Tie Me Kangaroo Down, Sport (Harris) (*With Rolf
  Harris*)
Tip Of My Tongue
Tom Dooley (Trad.)
Too Much Monkey Business (Berry)
Tracks Of My Tears (Robinson)
True Love (Porter)
Turn Around (Perkins)
Twelve Bar Original
Twenty Flight Rock (Fairchild-Vincent)

Walk, The (McCraklin)
Watching Rainbows
Way You Look Tonight, The
What Do You Want To Make Those Eyes At M
  For (McCarthy-Monaco-Johnson)
What'd I Say (Charles)
What's The New Mary Jane
When Irish Eyes Are Smiling (Graff-Ball-Olcott
Where Have You Been All My Life (Mann-Wei
White Power
Whole Lotta Loving (Domino-Bartholomew)
Whole Lotta Shakin' Goin' On (Lewis-David)

Yakety Yak (Leiber-Stoller)
You Are My Sunshine (Davis-Mitchell)
Youngblood (Leiber-Stoller-Pomus)
Your Feets Too Big (Benson-Fisher)
Your True Love (Perkins)

THE NON-ALBUM TRACKS

This chapter deals with generally available Beatles recordings that are not available on Beatles albums. The recordings discussed here originate from three different sources: videograms, singles and interview albums.

Four of the tracks are at present available only on the soundtracks of videograms. The first, 'That'll Be The Day', although originating from a record made by The Quarrymen in 1958, is available on the soundtrack of the videogram *The Real Buddy Holly Story*. 'Some Other Guy' was filmed/recorded in the Cavern Club in Liverpool in 1962 and a section of it is included on the videogram *The Compleat Beatles*. 'Shout!' and the 'Love Me Do Medley' originate from the 1964 TV special *Around The Beatles,* sections of that were released in 1985 on *The Beatles Live!* videogram.

During the television appearances that The Beatles made during their career they performed a number of songs including some with other artists that are not available on record. Four of those have been mentioned previously. Others, including 'I Do Like To Be Beside The Seaside', that they performed on Blackpool beach in 1965 for a film that still exists and 'On Moonlight Bay', with Eric Morecambe and Ernie Wise on *The Morecambe and Wise Show*, also in 1965, are unavailable.

Following the release by EMI of The Beatles' entire Parlophone/Apple catalogue on compact disc including two album recordings that were originally released on singles and EPs, the only Beatles Parlophone recording on a single is 'The Beatles Movie Medley' (see below).

Finally, 'Cottonfields' and 'Waltzing Matilda' both recorded during interviews were, after numerous appearances on bootlegs, finally issued during the 1980s on interview albums. These are just two of a number of songs recorded during interviews, that were described as working versions by the bootleggers. They were off-the-cuff songs that were never considered as serious recordings by The Beatles.

The following is a complete list of songs that are available only on videograms, singles and interview albums.

That'll Be The Day (Allison-Petty-Holly)
Recorded: 1958, Kensington Recording Studios, Liverpool
Availability: Videogram The Real Buddy Holly Story
John Lennon: Rhythm Guitar and Lead Vocal   **Paul McCartney:** Bass Guitar and Backing Vocal
George Harrison: Lead Guitar and Backing Vocal   **Cohn Hanton:** Drums
John Lowe: Piano

The videogram features two separate sections of the record totalling one minute 26 seconds together with an interview with Paul McCartney during which he performs an acoustic version of 'Love Me Do' plus a slower, more relaxed version of 'Words Of Love'.

The record features a young, but still very gutsy-sounding, John Lennon on lead vocals with backing vocals from Paul and George. Instrumentally, they sound extremely enthusiastic and capable. For a first recording the whole thing comes across extremely well.

Some Other Guy (Leiber-Stoller-Barrett)

Recorded: 22 August 1962, The Cavern Club, 10 Mathew St, Liverpool
Availability: Videogram The Compleat Beatles
John Lennon: Rhythm Guitar and Solo Vocal   **Paul McCartney:** Bass Guitar
George Harrison: Lead Guitar   **Ringo Starr:** Drums

Although recorded and filmed by Granada Television in August of 1962, this was not broadcast until 17 October that year, 12 days after the release of 'Love Me Do'. The sound quality of this recording can be compared to The Star Club Tapes that were recorded about four months later, but the real advantage of this film/recording is that it gives the rest of the world a chance to see what The Beatles looked and sounded like at The Cavern.

John handles this Richie Barrett song with a great deal of enthusiasm and power and is given an equally enthusiastic backing from Paul, George and Ringo.

Love Me Do Medley (Lennon-McCartney)

Recorded: 19 April 1964, IBC Studios, 35 Portland Place, London
Availability: Videogram The Beatles Live!
John Lennon: Rhythm Guitar, Harmonica and Lead Vocal
Paul McCartney: Bass Guitar and Lead Vocal
George Harrison: Lead Guitar and Harmony Vocal   **Ringo Starr:** Drums

This is the only medley of their own material that The Beatles ever purposely recorded; it predates the messy *The Beatles' Movie Medley* that was compiled without The Beatles' permission by 18 years. It is not sections of the versions previously issued edited together as is the case with *The Beatles' Movie Medley*, but a different recording entirely. However, the line-up and vocalists remain the same. The medley includes: 'Love Me Do'; 'Please Please Me'; 'From Me To You'; 'She Loves You' and 'I Want To Hold Your Hand'.

Shout! (O'Kelly-Isley-Isley)
Recorded: 19 April 1964, IBC Studios, 35 Portland Place, London
Availability: Videogram *The Beatles Live!*

John Lennon: Rhythm Guitar and Lead Vocal   **Paul McCartney:** Bass Guitar and Lead Vocal
George Harrison: Lead Guitar and Lead Vocal   **Ringo Starr:** Drums and Lead Vocal

Without doubt the highlight of *The Beatles Live!* was this rousing rendition of The Isley Brothers' 1959 classic. It was the only time The Beatles performed the song, either on stage or television, and what a dynamic performance it is! All four Beatles share lead vocals with the audience joining them on 'shout'. Paul kicks the whole thing off in his best rock'n'roll style, to be followed by George and then Ringo. To round off the foursome John begins his section and then alters the lyrics on 'Everyone f. .. in' shout now'! How they got away with that is anyone's guess.

The contents of the videogram include the unique 'Love Me Do Medley' and 'Shout!', both unavailable on record and originate from the 1964 TV special *Around The Beatles*. This was filmed on 27 and 28 April 1964 at Wembley TV studios, first broadcast on 6 May 1964 and eventually issued on 29 April 1985 by Dave Clark International through Picture Music International the video branch of EMI.

The original TV special included other artists such as Cilla Black, PJ Proby and Sounds Incorporated, but for reasons known only to Dave Clark of the Dave Clark Five, these artists were edited out, reducing the running time of the film from 50 minutes to just 18. Clark also took the curious decision to retitle the film *The Beatles Live!* and to issue it as a *Ready Steady Go!* special edition. The only connection between this and *Ready Steady Go!* is that they were both produced by Associated Rediffusion Television from whom Clark bought the rights.

The full contents of the videogram that features brand-new studio recordings made nine days prior to filming, to which The Beatles mime are: 'Twist And Shout', 'Roll Over Beethoven', 'I Wanna Be Your Man', 'Long Tall Sally', 'Love Me Do Medley' including 'Love Me Do', 'Please Please Me', 'From Me To You', 'She Loves You' and 'I Want To Hold Your Hand', 'Can't Buy Me Love' and 'Shout!', plus 'All You Need Is Love', that wasn't written or recorded until three years later and is played over the closing titles.

The Beatles' Movie Medley (Lennon-McCartney)   3:56
Recorded: Dates and locations vary
Availability: Single (UK: Parlophone R6055; US: Capitol B-5107)
John Lennon: Numerous Instruments and Lead Vocal on Six Sections
Paul McCartney: Numerous Instruments and Lead Vocal on One Section
George Harrison: Lead Guitar and Backing Vocal   **Ringo Starr:** Drums

Following the worldwide success of the 1981-2 Stars on 45 medley by Starsound, the Dutch Beatles tribute group, a medley that contained some very believable John Lennon-like vocals, Capitol Records decided to put together their own Beatles medley without The Beatles' consent using original Beatles master tapes. The medley,that contains excerpts from 'Magical Mystery Tour', 'All You Need Is Love', 'You've Got To Hide Your Love Away', 'I Should Have Known Better', 'A Hard Day's Night', 'Ticket To Ride' and 'Get Back', was then issued as a single on 30 March 1982 (Capitol B-5107).

All the excerpts were from tracks included on the newly released *Reel Music* album (UK: Parlophone PCS 7218; US: Capitol SV 12199).

In Britain, EMI Records decided that the editing together of different Beatles recordings was unacceptable and withheld release of the record but still allocated it a catalogue number. Demand for the imported copies of the US record was so high that EMI conceded and eventually issued it on 25 May 1982 (Parlophone R6055).

Despite EMI's original reluctance to issue the record in Britain it entered the charts shortly after release, eventually reaching No.7.

Cottonfields (Ledbetter)
Recorded: 18 July 1968, EMI Studios, Abbey Road, London
Availability: Single (Italy Only) (Apple DPR 108) Interview LP (UK: Interviews II; US: *The Golden Beatles*)
John Lennon: Acoustic Guitar and Solo Vocal   **Paul McCartney:** Elsewhere in the Studio
George Harrison: Elsewhere in the Studio   **Ringo Starr:** Elsewhere in the Studio

Recorded as part of an interview with Kenny Everett during the sessions for the White Album in 1968 and originally issued by Apple together with sections of the interview as part of a four-record set in Italy the same year. The entire interview, together with 'Cottonfields' and a further nine similarly spontaneous songs were issued on various interview albums worldwide during the late 1980s.

Throughout the interview John, accompanied by an acoustic guitar, launches into a number of improvised songs. Shortly after the interview opens and he has already performed three spontaneous songs, tongue-in-cheek, John launches into a perverted version of this Huddie Ledbetter classic. He is further interviewed by Kenny Everett. Between the offbeat humorous Lennon/Everett exchanges, the interview briefly touches on such subjects as John's return from India, at which point John breaks into a feigned foreign language, best described as gobbledygook.

They are joined by Paul who, with John, improvises, 'Goodbye To Kenny Everett'. John comments on Tiny Tim who was enjoying a brief spell of fame singing such songs as 'Tiptoe Through The Tulips' in a falsetto vocal. He also appears on *The Beatles Christmas Album* singing 'Nowhere Man'. John then launches into the next improvised song, 'Tiny Tim For President'. Following this, various comments are made about Kenny Everett being dismissed from the BBC because of a comment about the wife of the British Transport Minister passing her driving test.

Ringo, accompanied by drums, then proceeds to sing a further improvised song, 'Goodbye Kenny' that is followed by a further display of general lunacy. Kenny asks The Beatles to sing 'Strawberry Fields Forever' in a jazz tempo, and with Paul as lead vocalist, they perform a short a cappella version. The interview closes with Paul singing a falsetto version of Ringo's earlier 'Goodbye Kenny'.

The complete list of the songs performed during the interview is: 'Vague Idea'; 'Somebody Stole My Girl'; 'Goodbye Jingle (two versions)'; 'Cottonfields'; 'The Kenny Everett Show'; 'Goodbye to Kenny Everett'; 'Tiny Tim For President'; 'Goodbye Kenny'; 'Strawberry Fields Forever' and 'Goodbye Kenny' again.

Waltzing Matilda (Trad.)

Recorded: February-March 1964 (other details not available)
Availability: Interview LP *The Beatles Talk Downunder*

John Lennon: Lead Vocal **Paul McCartney:** Lead Vocal
George Harrison: Lead Vocal **Ringo Starr:** Lead Vocal

This short entertaining version of the traditional Australian song originates from a studio tape that was sent to Australian DJ Barry Ferber in March 1964. It is the opening uncredited track of the Australian interview album *The Beatles Talk Downunder*.

During the various interviews included on this album, one or more of The Beatles occasionally bursts into song. During the interview recorded at the President Hotel in Hong Kong on 10 June 1964, John and George perform a further version of 'Waltzing Matilda' plus a short rendition of 'Tie Me Kangaroo Down, Sport'. During a later interview recorded at the New City Hotel, Dunedin, New Zealand on 26 June 1964, Paul mentions that Ringo has written his first song, 'Don't Pass Me By'. Paul then launches into a brief a cappella rendition of the song that was to be recorded and released by The Beatles four years later.

DISCOGRAPHY

This discography is divided into four sections. First is a complete list of the international CD albums. CD singles from 'Love Me Do' to 'Let It Be' were released internationally during 1988/9. This is followed by British, American and Australian discographies of all records released in those countries up to the end of December 1988.Singles that have been re-released and also released as picture discs in Britain and have a picture disc RP prefix instead of the normal R prefix, have not been included. 12-inch singles and cassette singles, are listed only as re-releases of special editions of singles such as 12-inch singles. In all three countries, where an album has been re-released with a new catalogue number, these have been included with minimal information relating to the original release.

The International Compact Discs

POLYDOR

823 701-2 The Beatles First
Ain't She Sweet; Cry For A Shadow;
When The Saints Go Marching In;
Why; If You Love Me, Baby; (What'd I Say); Sweet
Georgia Brown; (Let's Dance);
(Ruby Baby); My Bonnie; Nobody's Child; (Ready
Teddy); (Ya Ya) (Kansas City).
*Titles in parentheses performed by Tony Sheridan
and The Beat Brothers. All other songs performed by
either The Beatles or The Beatles With Tony Sheridan.*

VARIOUS LABELS

The Decca Tapes
Three Cool Cats; Memphis, Tennessee;
Besame Mucho; The Sheik Of Araby;
Till There Was You; Searchin';
Sure To Fall (In Love With You);
Take Good Care Of My Baby; Money;
To Know Her Is To Love Her;
September In The Rain; Crying, Waiting, Hoping.

The Star Club Tapes
I'm Gonna Sit Right Down And Cry (Over You);
I Saw Her Standing There; Roll Over Beethoven;
Hippy Hippy Shake; Sweet Little Sixteen;
Lend Me Your Comb;Your Feets Too Big;
Twist And Shout; Mr. Moonlight; A Taste Of Honey
Besame Mucho; Reminiscing;
Kansas City/Hey Hey Hey Hey;
Where Have You Been All My Life;
Till There Was You;
Nothin' Shakin' (But The Leaves On The Trees);
To Know Her Is To Love Her; Little Queenie;
Falling In Love Again; Ask Me Why;
Be Bop A Lula; Hallelujah, I Love Her So; Sheila;
Red Sails In The Sunset;
Everybody's Trying To Be My Baby; Matchbox;
(I'm) Talking About You; Shimmy Shake;
Long Tall Sally; I Remember You.

PARLOPHONE

CDP 7 46435 2 Please Please Me
I Saw Her Standing There; Misery; Anna (Go To Him);
Chains; Boys; Ask Me Why; Please Please Me;
Love Me Do; P. S. I Love You; Baby It's You;
Do You Want To Know A Secret;
A Taste Of Honey; There's A Place; Twist And Shout.

CDP 7 46436 2 With The Beatles
It Won't Be Long; All I've Got To Do; All My Loving;
Don't Bother Me; Little Child; Till There Was You;
Please Mister Postman; Roll Over Beethoven;
Hold Me Tight; You Really Got A Hold On Me;
I Wanna Be Your Man; Devil In Her Heart;
Not A Second Time; Money.

CDP 46437 2 A Hard Day's Night
A Hard Day's Night; I Should Have Known Better;
If I Fell; I'm Happy Just To Dance With You;
And ILove Her; Tell Me Why; Can't Buy Me Love;
Any Time At All; I'll Cry Instead;
Things We Said Today; When I Get Home;
You Can't Do That; I'll Be Back.

CDP 7 46438 2 Beatles For Sale
No Reply; I'm A Loser; Baby's In Black;
Rock And Roll Music; I'll Follow The Sun;
Mr. Moonlight; Kansas City/Hey Hey Hey Hey;
Eight Days A Week; Words Of Love;
Honey Don't; Every Little Thing;
I Don't Want To Spoil The Party; What You're Doing;
Everybody's Trying To Be My Baby.

CDP 7 46439 2 Help!
Help!; The Night Before;
You've Got To Hide Your Love Away; I Need You;
Another Girl; You're Going To Lose That Girl;
Ticket To Ride; Act Naturally; It's Only Love;
You Like Me Too Much; Tell Me What You See;
I've Just Seen A Face; Yesterday; Dizzy Miss Lizzy.

CDP 7 46440 2 Rubber Soul
Drive My Car; Norwegian Wood (This Bird Has
Flown); You Won't See Me; Nowhere Man;
Think For Yourself; The Word; Michelle;
What Goes On; Girl; I'm Looking Through You;
In My Life; Wait; If I Needed Someone;
Run For Your Life.

CDP 7 46441 2 Revolver
Taxman; Eleanor Rigby; I'm Only Sleeping;
Love You To; Here, There And Everywhere;
Yellow Submarine; She Said, She Said;
Good Day Sunshine;
And Your Bird Can Sing; For No One; Dr. Robert;
I Want To Tell You; Got To Get You Into My Life;
Tomorrow Never Knows.

CDP 7 46442 2 Sgt. Pepper's Lonely Hearts Club Band
Sgt. Pepper's Lonely Hearts Club Band;
With A Little Help From My Friends;
Lucy In The Sky With Diamonds; Getting Better;
Fixing A Hole; She's Leaving Home;
Being For The Benefit Of Mr. Kite;
Within You, Without You; When I'm Sixty Four;
Lovely Rita; Good Morning, Good Morning;
Sgt. Pepper's Lonely Hearts Club Band
(Reprise); A Day In The Life.

CDS 7 46443 8 The Beatles (2 CDs)

Disc One
Back In The USSR; Dear Prudence; Glass Onion;
Ob-La-Di, Ob-La-Da; Wild Honey Pie;
The Continuing Story Of Bungalow Bill;
While My Guitar Gently Weeps;
Happiness Is A Warm Gun; Martha My Dear;
I'm So Tired; Blackbird; Piggies; Rocky Racoon;
Don't Pass Me By;
Why Don't We Do It In The Road?; I Will; Julia.
Disc Two
Birthday; Yer Blues; Mother Nature's Son;
Everybody's Got Something To Hide Except Me
And My Monkey; Sexy Sadie; Helter Skelter;
Long, Long, Long; Revolution 1; Honey Pie;
SavoyTruffle; Cry Baby Cry; Revolution 9;
Goodnight.

CDP 7 46445 2 Yellow Submarine

Yellow Submarine; Only A Northern Song;
All Together Now; Hey Bulldog; It's All Too Much;
All You Need Is Love; Plus incidental music by
The George Martin Orchestra.

CDP 7 48062 2 Magical Mystery Tour

Magical Mystery Tour; The Fool On The Hill;
Flying; Blue Jay Way; Your Mother Should Know;
I Am The Walrus; Hello Goodbye;
Strawberry Fields Forever; Penny Lane;
Baby, You're A Rich Man; All You Need Is Love.

CDP 7 46446 2 Abbey Road

Come Together; Something;
Maxwell's Silver Hammer; Oh! Darling;
Octopus's Garden; I Want You (She's So Heavy);
Here Comes The Sun; Because;
You Never Give Me Your Money; Sun King;
Mean Mr. Mustard; Polythene Pam;
She Came In Through The Bathroom Window;
Golden Slumbers; Carry That Weight;
The End; Her Majesty.

CDP 7 46447 2 Let It Be

Two Of Us; Dig A Pony; Across The Universe;
I Me Mine; Dig It; Let It Be; Maggie Mae;
I've Got A Feeling; One After 909;
The Long And Winding Road; For You Blue;
Get Back.

CDP 7 90043 2 Past Masters – Volume One

Love Me Do; From Me To You; Thank You Girl;
She Loves You; I'll Get You;
I Want To Hold Your Hand; This Boy;
Komm, Gib Mir Deine Hand; Sie Liebt Dich;
Long Tall Sally; I Call Your Name; Slow Down;
Matchbox; I Feel Fine; She's A Woman; Bad Boy
Yes It Is; I'm Down.

CDP 7 90044 2 Past Masters –
Volume Two

Day Tripper; We Can Work It Out;
Paperback Writer; Rain; Lady Madonna;
The Inner Light; Hey Jude; Revolution; Get Back;
Don't Let Me Down; The Ballad Of John And Yok
Old Brown Shoe; Across The Universe; Let It Be;
You Know My Name (Look Up The Number).

British Releases

PARLOPHONE-EMI/APPLE*
MUSIC FOR PLEASURE/FAME*****
UNITED ARTISTS ††

SINGLES

R4949 Love Me Do/P.S. I Love You
[5 October 1962]

R4983 Please Please Me/Ask Me Why
[11 January 1963]

R5015 From Me To You/Thank You Girl
[12 April 1963]

R5055 She Loves You/I'll Get You
[28 August 1963]

R5084 I Want To Hold Your Hand/This Boy
[29 November 1963]

R5114 Can't Buy Me Love/You Can't Do That
[16 March 1964]

R5160 A Hard Day's Night/Things We Said Today
[10 July 1964]

R5200 I Feel Fine/ She's A Woman
[23 November 1964]

R5265 Ticket To Ride/Yes It Is [9 April 1965]

R5305 Help!/I'm Down [19 July 1965]

R5389 We Can Work It Out/Day Tripper
[3 December 1965]

R5452 Paperback Writer/Rain [30 May 1966]

R5489 Yellow Submarine/Eleanor Rigby
[5 August 1966]

R5570 Penny Lane/Strawberry Fields Forever
[17 February 1967]

R5620 All You Need Is Love/Baby,
You're A Rich Man [7 July 1967]

R5655 Hello Goodbye/I Am The Walrus
[24 November 1967]

R5675 Lady Madonna/The Inner Light
[15 March 1968]

R5722* Hey Jude/Revolution [30 August 1968]

R5777* Get Back/Don't Let Me Down
[11 April 1969]

R5786* The Ballad Of John And Yoko/
Old Brown Shoe [30 May 1969]

R5814* Something/Come Together
[6 October 1969]

R5833* Let It Be/You Know My Name
(Look Up The Number) [6 March 1970]

R6013 Yesterday/
I Should Have Known Better [8 March 1976]

R6016 Back In The USSR/Twist And Shout
[25 June 1976]

R6022 Sgt. Pepper's Lonely Hearts Club Band/
With A Little Help From My Friends/
A Day In The Life [30 September 1978]

R6055 The Beatles' Movie Medley/
I'm Happy Just To Dance With You [25 May 1982]

12R4949 Love Me Do/P. S. I Love You/Love Me Do
(*12-inch Single*) [1 November 1982]

**BCS 1 The Beatles' Singles Collection
(26 Singles)**
Love Me Do to The Beatles' Movie Medley.
[4 December 1982]

12R5620 All You Need Is Love/
Baby, You're A Rich Man (*12-inch Single*)
[6 July 1987]

TC-R5620 All You Need Is Love
All You Need Is Love/Baby, You're A Rich Man
(*Cassette Single*) [6 July 1987]

12R5722 Hey Jude/Revolution (*12-inch Single*)
[30 August 1988]

Apple 58497 Free As A Bird/
Christmas Time (Is Here Again)
[4th December 1995] (US 12/12) R 6422

Apple 58544 Real Love/Baby's In Black
[4th March 1996] (US 5/3) R 6425

EXTENDED PLAY

GEP 8882 Twist And Shout
Twist And Shout; A Taste Of Honey;
Do You Want To Know A Secret;
There's A Place. [12 July 1963]

GEP 8880 The Beatles Hits
From Me To You; Thank You Girl; Please Please
Love Me Do. [6 September 1963]

GEP 8883 The Beatles No. 1
I Saw Her Standing There; Misery; Anna (Go To Hi
Chains. [1 November 1963]

GEP 8891 All My Loving
All My Loving; Ask Me Why; Money; P.S. I Love Yo
[7 February 1964]

GEP 8913 Long Tall Sally
Long Tall Sally; I Call Your Name; Slow Down;
Matchbox. [19 June 1964]

GEP 8920 Extracts From The Film
A Hard Day's Night; I Should Have Known Better;
If I Fell; Tell Me Why; And I Love Her.
[6 November 1964]

GEP 8924 Extracts From The Album
A Hard Day's Night
Any Time At All; I'll Cry Instead;
Things We Said Today; When I Get Home.
[6 November 1964]

GEP 8931 Beatles For Sale
No Reply; I'm A Loser; Rock And Roll Music;
Eight Days A Week. [6 April 1965]

GEP 8938 Beatles For Sale No. 2
I'll Follow The Sun; Baby's In Black;
Words Of Love; I Don't Want To Spoil The Party.
[4 June 1965]

GEP 8946 The Beatles Million Sellers
She Loves You; I Want To Hold Your Hand;
Can't Buy Me Love; I Feel Fine.
[6 December 1965]

GEP 8948 Yesterday
Yesterday; Act Naturally; You Like Me Too Much;
It's Only Love, [4 March 1966]

GEP 8952 Nowhere Man
Nowhere Man; Drive My Car; Michelle;
You Won't See Me. [8 July 1966]

MMT/SMMT 1 Magical Mystery Tour
Magical Mystery Tour; Your Mother Should Know;
I Am The Walrus; The Fool On The Hill; Flying;
Blue Jay Way. [8 December 1967]

BEP 14 The Beatles' EPs Collection
This 14-EP set contains all the above-listed 13
EPs plus the following free bonus EP that is not
on sale separately.

SGE 1 The Beatles
The Inner Light; Baby, You're A Rich Man;
She's A Woman; This Boy. [7 December 1981]

LONG PLAY

PMC 1202 Please Please Me
PCS 3042
Side One
I Saw Her Standing There; Misery; Anna (Go To Him);
Chains; Boys; Ask Me Why; Please Please Me.
Side Two
Love Me Do; P. S. I Love You; Baby It's You;
Do You Want To Know A Secret; A Taste Of Honey;
There's A Place; Twist And Shout. [22 March 1963]

PMC 1206 With The Beatles
PCS 3045
Side One
It Won't Be Long; All I've Got To Do; All My Loving;
Don't Bother Me; Little Child; Till There Was You;
Please Mister Postman.
Side Two
Roll Over Beethoven; Hold Me Tight;
You Really Got A Hold On Me;
I Wanna Be Your Man; Devil In Her Heart;
Not A Second Time; Money. [22 November 1963]

PMC 1230 A Hard Day's Night
PCS 3058
Side One
A Hard Day's Night; I Should Have Known Better;
If I Fell; I'm Happy Just To Dance With You;
And I Love Her; Tell Me Why; Can't Buy Me Love.
Side Two
Any Time At All; I'll Cry Instead;
Things We Said Today; When I Get Home;
You Can't Do That; I'll Be Back. [10 July 1964]

PMC 1240 Beatles For Sale
PCS 3062
Side One
No Reply; I'm A Loser; Baby's In Black;
Rock And Roll Music; I'll Follow The Sun;
Mr. Moonlight; Kansas City/Hey Hey Hey Hey.
Side Two
Eight Days A Week; Words Of Love;
Honey Don't; Every Little Thing;
I Don't Want To Spoil The Party;
What You're Doing;
Everybody's Trying To Be My Baby.
[4 December 1964]

PMC 1255 Help!
PCS 3071
Side One
Help!; The Night Before;
You've Got To Hide Your Love Away; I Need You;
Another Girl; You're Going To Lose That Girl;
Ticket To Ride.
Side Two
Act Naturally; It's Only Love; You Like Me Too Much;
Tell Me What You See; I've Just Seen A Face;
Yesterday; Dizzy Miss Lizzy. [6 August 1965]

PMC 1267 Rubber Soul
PCS 3075
Side One
Drive My Car; Norwegian Wood
(This Bird Has Flown); You Won't See Me; Nowhere
Man; Think For Yourself; The Word; Michelle.
Side Two
What Goes On; Girl; I'm Looking Through You;
In My Life; Wait; If I Needed Someone;
Run For Your Life. [3 December 1965]

PMC/PCS 7009 Revolver
Side One
Taxman; Eleanor Rigby; I'm Only Sleeping;
Love You To; Here, There And Everywhere;
Yellow Submarine; She Said, She Said.
Side Two
Good Day Sunshine; And Your Bird Can Sing;
For No One; Dr. Robert; I Want To Tell You;
Got To Get You Into My Life;
Tomorrow Never Knows. [5 August 1966]

PMC/PCS 7016 A Collection Of Beatles Oldies
Side One
She Loves You; From Me To You;
We Can Work It Out; Help!; Michelle; Yesterday;
I Feel Fine; Yellow Submarine.
Side Two
Can't Buy Me Love; Bad Boy; Day Tripper;
A Hard Day's Night; Ticket To Ride;
Paperback Writer; Eleanor Rigby;
I Want To Hold Your Hand. [10 December 1966]

PMC/PCS 7027 Sgt. Pepper's Lonely Hearts Club Band
Side One
Sgt. Pepper's Lonely Hearts Club Band;
With A Little Help From My Friends;
Lucy In The Sky With Diamonds;
Getting Better; Fixing A Hole; She's Leaving Home;
Being For The Benefit Of Mr. Kite.
Side Two
Within You, Without You; When I'm Sixty-Four;
Lovely Rita; Good Morning, Good Morning;
Sgt. Pepper's Lonely Hearts Club Band
(Reprise); A Day In The Life.[1 June 1967]

PMC/PCS 7067/8* The Beatles (2 LPs)
Side One
Back In The USSR; Dear Prudence; Glass Onion; Ob-La-Di, Ob-La-Da; Wild Honey Pie;
The Continuing Story Of Bungalow Bill;
While My Guitar Gently Weeps;
Happiness Is A Warm Gun.
Side Two
Martha My Dear; I'm So Tired; Blackbird; Piggies;
Rocky Racoon; Don't Pass Me By;
Why Don't We Do It In The Road?; I Will; Julia.
Side Three
Birthday; Yer Blues; Mother Nature's Son; Everybody's
Got Something To Hide Except Me
And My Monkey; Sexy Sadie; Helter Skelter; Long,
Long, Long.
Side Four
Revolution 1; Honey Pie; Savoy Truffle;
Cry Baby Cry; Revolution 9; Goodnight.
[22 November 1968]

PMC/PCS 7070* Yellow Submarine
Side One
Yellow Submarine;
Only A Northern Song; All Together Now;
Hey Bulldog; It's All Too Much; All You Need Is Love.
Side Two
The George Martin Orchestra. [17 January 1969]

PCS 7088* Abbey Road
Side One
Come Together; Something; Maxwell's Silver
Hammer; Oh! Darling; Octopus's Garden;
I WantYou (She's So Heavy)
Side Two
Here Comes The Sun; Because;
You Never Give Me Your Money; Sun King;
Mean Mr. Mustard; Polythene Pam;
She Came In Through The Bathroom Window;
Golden Slumbers; Carry That Weight; The End;
Her Majesty. [26 September 1969]

PXS 1/PCS 7096* Let It Be
Side One
Two Of Us; Dig A Pony; Across The Universe;
I Me Mine; Dig It; Let It Be; Maggie Mae.
Side Two
I've Got A Feeling; One After 909;
The Long And Winding Road; For You Blue;
Get Back. (PXS 1 includes *Get Back book*.)
[8 May/6 November 1970]

PCSP 717* The Beatles 1962-1966 (2 LPs)
Side One
Love Me Do; Please Please Me; From Me To You;
She Loves You; I Want To Hold Your Hand;
All My Loving; Can't Buy Me Love.
Side Two
A Hard Day's Night; And I Love Her;
Eight Days A Week; I Feel Fine; Ticket To Ride;
Yesterday.
Side Three
Help!; You've Got To Hide Your Love Away;
We Can Work It Out; Day Tripper; Drive My Car;
Norwegian Wood (This Bird Has Flown).

Side Four
Nowhere Man; Michelle; In My Life; Girl; Paperback Writer; Eleanor Rigby; Yellow Submarine. [20 April 1973]

PCSP 718* The Beatles 1967-1970 (2 LPs)
Side One
Strawberry Fields Forever; Penny Lane;
Sgt. Pepper's Lonely Hearts Club Band;
With A Little Help From My Friends;
Lucy In The Sky With Diamonds;
A Day In The Life; All You Need Is Love.
Side Two
I Am The Walrus; Hello Goodbye;
The Fool On The Hill; Magical Mystery Tour;
Lady Madonna; Hey Jude; Revolution.
Side Three
Back In The U.S.S.R.; While My Guitar Gently Weeps;
Ob-La-Di, Ob-La-Da; Get Back; Don't Let Me Down;
The Ballad Of John And Yoko; Old Brown Shoe.
Side Four
Here Comes The Sun; Come Together;
Something; Octopus's Garden; Let It Be;
Across The Universe;
The Long And Winding Road. [20 April 1973]

PCSP 719 Rock And Roll Music (2 LPs)
Side One
Twist And Shout; I Saw Her Standing There;
You Can't Do That; I Wanna Be Your Man;
I Call Your Name; Boys; Long Tall Sally.
Side Two
Rock And Roll Music; Slow Down;
Kansas City/Hey Hey Hey Hey; Money; Bad Boy;
Matchbox; Roll Over Beethoven.

Side Three
Dizzy Miss Lizzy; Any Time At All; Drive My Car;
Everybody's Trying To Be My Baby;
The Night Before; I'm Down; Revolution.
Side Four
Back In The USSR; Helter Skelter; Taxman;
Got To Get You Into My Life; Hey Bulldog; Birthday;
Get Back. [11 June 1976]

PCTC 255 Magical Mystery Tour
Side One
Magical Mystery Tour; The Fool On The Hill;
Flying; Blue Jay Way; Your Mother Should Know;
I Am The Walrus.
Side Two
Hello Goodbye; Strawberry Fields Forever;
Penny Lane; Baby, You're A Rich Man;
All You Need Is Love. [19 November 1976]

EMTV 4 The Beatles At The Hollywood Bowl
Side One
Twist And Shout; She's A Woman;
Dizzy Miss Lizzy; Ticket To Ride; Can't Buy Me Love;
Things We Said Today; Roll Over Beethoven.
Side Two
Boys; A Hard Day's Night; Help!; All My Loving;
She Loves You; Long Tall Sally. [6 May 1977]

PCSP 721 Love Songs (2 LPs)
Side One
Yesterday; I'll Follow The Sun; I Need You; Girl;
In My Life; Words Of Love; Here,
There And Everywhere.
Side Two
Something; And I Love Her; If I Fell; I'll Be Back;
Tell Me What You See; Yes It Is.

Side Three
Michelle; It's Only Love;
You're Going To Lose That Girl; Every Little Thing;
For No One; She's Leaving Home.
Side Four
The Long And Winding Road; This Boy;
Norwegian Wood (This Bird Has Flown);
You've Got To Hide
Your Love Away; I Will; P. S. I Love
You. [28 November 1977]

BC 13 The Beatles Collection (13 LPs)

Please Please Me; With The Beatles;
A Hard Day's Night; Beatles For Sale; Help!; Rubber
Soul; Revolver;
Sgt. Pepper's Lonely Hearts Club Band;
The Beatles; Yellow Submarine; Abbey Road;
Let It Be; The Beatles Rarities.[2 November 1978]

PCS 7184 Hey Jude

Side One
Can't Buy Me Love; I Should Have Known Better;
Paperback Writer; Rain; Lady Madonna; Revolution.
Side Two
Hey Jude; Old Brown Shoe; Don't Let Me Down;
The Ballad Of John And Yoko. [21 May 1979]

PCM 100 1 The Beatles Rarities

Side One
Across The Universe; Yes It is; This Boy;
The Inner Light; I'll Get You; Thank You Girl;
Komm, Gib Mir Deine Hand; You Know My Name
(Look Up The Number); Sie Liebt Dich.
Side Two
Rain; She's A Woman; Matchbox; I Call Your Name;
Bad Boy; Slow Down; I'm Down; Long Tall Sally.
[29 October 1979]

PCS 7214 The Beatles Ballads

Side One
Yesterday; Norwegian Wood (This Bird Has Flown);
Do You Want To Know A Secret; For No One;
Michelle; Nowhere Man;
You've Got To Hide Your Love Away;
Across The Universe; All My Loving; Hey Jude.
Side Two
Something; The Fool On The Hill;
Till There Was You; The Long And Winding Road;
Here Comes The Sun; Blackbird; And I Love Her;
She's Leaving Home; Here, There And Everywhere;
Let It Be. [20 October 1980]

MFP 50506** Rock And Roll Music Volume 1

Record One of PCSP 719 Rock
And Roll Music [27 October 1980]
MFP 50507** Rock And Roll Music Volume 2
Record Two of PCSP 719 Rock
And Roll Music [27 October 1980]
SM 701-708 The Beatles Box (8 LPs)

SM 701 Record 1

Side One
Love Me Do; P. S. I Love You;
I Saw Her Standing There; Please Please Me;
Misery; Do You Want To Know A Secret;
A Taste Of Honey; Twist And Shout.
Side Two
From Me To You; Thank You Girl; She Loves You;
It Won't Be Long; Please Mister Postman;
All My Loving; Roll Over Beethoven; Money.

SM 702 Record 2
Side One
I Want To Hold Your Hand; This Boy;
Can't Buy Me Love; You Can't Do That;
A Hard Day's Night; I Should Have Known Better;
If I Fell; And I Love Her.
Side Two
Things We Said Today; I'll Be Back; Long Tall Sally;
I Call Your Name; Matchbox; Slow Down;
She's A Woman; I Feel Fine.

SM 703 Record 3
Side One
Eight Days A Week; No Reply; I'm A Loser;
I'll Follow The Sun; Mr. Moonlight;
Every Little Thing; I Don't Want To Spoil The Party;
Kansas City/Hey Hey Hey Hey.
Side Two
Ticket To Ride; I'm Down; Help!; The Night Before;
You've Got To Hide Your Love Away;
I Need You; Another Girl;
You're Going To Lose That Girl.

SM 704 Record 4
Side One
Yesterday; Act Naturally; Tell Me What You See;
It's Only Love; You Like Me Too Much;
I've Just Seen A Face; Day Tripper;
We Can Work It Out.
Side Two
Michelle; Drive My Car; Norwegian Wood
(This Bird Has Flown); You Won't See Me;
Nowhere Man; Girl; I'm Looking Through You;
In My Life.

SM 705 Record 5
Side One
Paperback Writer; Rain; Here, There And Everywhere;
Taxman; I'm Only Sleeping; Good Day Sunshine;
Yellow Submarine.
Side Two
Eleanor Rigby; And Your Bird Can Sing; For No One;
Dr. Robert; Got To Get You Into My Life;
Penny Lane; Strawberry Fields Forever.

SM 706 Record 6
Side One
Sgt. Pepper's Lonely Hearts Club Band;
With A Little Help From My Friends;
Lucy In The Sky With Diamonds; Fixing A Hole;
She's Leaving Home;
Being For The Benefit Of Mr. Kite;
A Day In The Life.
Side Two
When I'm Sixty-Four; Lovely Rita;
All You Need Is Love; Baby, You're A Rich Man;
Magical Mystery Tour; Your Mother Should Know;
The Fool On The Hill; I Am The Walrus.

SM 707 Record 7
Side One
Hello Goodbye; Lady Madonna; Hey Jude; Revolution;
Back In The USSR; Ob-La-Di, Ob-La-Da;
While My Guitar Gently Weeps.
Side Two
The Continuing Story Of Bungalow Bill;
Happiness Is A Warm Gun; Martha My Dear;
I'm So Tired; Piggies; Don't Pass Me By; Julia;
All Together Now.

SM 708 Record 8
Side One
Get Back; Don't Let Me Down;
The Ballad Of John And Yoko;
Across The Universe; For You Blue; Two Of Us; The
Long And Winding Road; Let It Be.
Side Two
Come Together; Something; Maxwell's Silver Hammer;
Octopus's Garden; Here Comes The Sun; Because;
Golden Slumbers; Carry That Weight; The End;
Her Majesty. [27 October 1980]

PCS 7218 Reel Music
Side One
A Hard Day's Night; I Should Have Known Better;
Can't Buy Me Love; And I Love Her; Help!;
You've Got To Hide Your Love Away;
Ticket To Ride; Magical Mystery Tour.
Side Two
I Am The Walrus; Yellow Submarine;
All You Need Is Love; Let It Be; Get Back;
The Long And Winding Road. [12 March 1982]

PCTC 260 20 Greatest Hits
Side One
Love Me Do; From Me To You; She Loves You;
I Want To Hold Your Hand; Can't Buy Me Love;
A Hard Day's Night; I Feel Fine; Ticket To Ride; Help!;
Day Tripper; We Can Work It Out.
Side Two
Paperback Writer; Yellow Submarine; Eleanor Rigby;
All You Need Is Love; Hello Goodbye; Lady Madonna;
Hey Jude; Get Back; The Ballad Of John And
Yoko. [18 October 1982]

FA 413081*** A Collection Of Beatles Oldies
As PCS 7016 [31 October 1983]

CAV 1 Tribute To The Cavern
Side One: Various Artists.
Side Two
Love Me Do; I Saw Her Standing There;
Twist And Shout; She Loves You; Money;
I Want To Hold Your Hand; Can't Buy Me Love;
A Hard Day's Night. [26 April 1984]

MFP 41-5676-1** The Beatles At The Hollywood Bowl
As EMTV 4 [3 September 1984]

SMMC 151 Only The Beatles...
Side One
Love Me Do; Twist And Shout; She Loves You; This
Boy; Eight Days A Week; All My Loving.
Side Two
Ticket To Ride; Yes It Is; Ob-La-Di, Ob-La-Da;
Lucy In The Sky With Diamonds; And I Love Her;
Strawberry Fields Forever.
(Cassette Only) [30 June 1986]

BPM 1 Past Masters – Volumes One and Two (2 LPs)
Side One
Love Me Do; From Me To You; Thank You Girl;
She Loves You; I'll Get You;
I Want To Hold Your Hand; This Boy;
Komm, Gib Mir Deine Hand; Sie Liebt Dich.
Side Two
Long Tall Sally; I Call Your Name; Slow Down;
Matchbox; I Feel Fine; She's A Woman; Bad Boy;
Yes It Is; I'm Down.

Side Three
Day Tripper; We Can Work It Out; Paperback Writer;
Rain; Lady Madonna; The Inner Light; Hey Jude;
Revolution.
Side Four
Get Back; Don't Let Me Down;
The Ballad Of John And Yoko; Old Brown Shoe;
Across The Universe; Let It Be;
You Know My Name (Look Up The Number).
[10 November 1988]

Apple 31796 Live At The BBC (2 CDs 2 LPs)
CD Disc 1 (vinyl side A)
Beatles Greetings (speech); From Us To You;
Riding On A Bus (speech); I Got A Woman;
Too Much Monkey Business; Keep Your Hands Off My
Baby; I'll Be On My Way; Young Blood;
A Shot Of Rhythm and Blues;
Sure To Fall (In Love With You);
Some Other Guy; Thank You Girl;
She La La La La! (speech); Baby It's You;
That's All Right (Mama); Carol; Soldier Of Love.
vinyl Side B
A Little Rhyme (speech); Clarabella; I'm Gonna Sit Right
Down And Cry (Over You); Crying, Waiting, Hoping;
Dear Wack! (speech); You Really Got A Hold On Me;
To Know Her Is To Love Her; A Taste Of Honey;
Long Tall Sally; I Saw Her Standing There;
The Honeymoon Song; Johnny B. Goode; Memphis,
Tennessee; Lucille; Can't Buy Me Love; From Fluff To
You (speech); Till There Was You

CD Disc 2 (vinyl side C)
Crinsk Dee Night (speech); A Hard Day's Night;
Have A Banana! (speech); I Wanna Be Your Man;
Just A Rumour (speech); Roll Over Beethoven;
All My Loving; Things We Said Today; She's A
Woman; Sweet Little Sixteen; 1822! (speech);
Lonesome Tears In My Eyes; Nothin' Shakin';
The Hippy Hippy Shake; Glad All Over;
I Just Don't Understand; So How Come
(No One Loves Me); I Feel Fine
vinyl side D
I'm A Loser; Everybody's Trying To Be My Baby;
Rock and Roll Music; Ticket To Ride; Dizzy Miss L
Kansas City/Hey-Hey-Hey-Hey!;
Set Fire To That Lot (speech); Matchbox;
I Forgot To Remember To Forget;
Love These Goon Shows! (speech);
I Got To Find My Baby; Ooh! My Soul;
Ooh! My Arms (speech); Don't Ever Change;
Slow Down; Honey Don't; Love Me Do

Apple 34445 Anthology 1
CD Disc 1 (vinyl side A)
Free As A Bird; "We were four guys...that's all";
That'll Be The Day; In Spite Of All The Danger;
"Sometimes I'd borrow...those still exist";
Hallelujah, I Love Her So; You'll Be Mine; Cayenn
"First of all...it didn't do a thing here";
My Bonnie; Ain't She Sweet; Cry For A Shadow
(vinyl side B)
"Brian was a beautiful guy...he presented us we
"I secured them an audition...a Beatle drink even th
Searchin'; Three Cool Cats; The Sheik Of Araby;
Like Dreamers Do; Hello Little Girl;
"Well, the recording test...by my artists";
Besame Mucho; Love Me Do; How Do You Do It;
Please, Please Me

(vinyl side C)
One After 909 (sequence); One After 909 (complete);
Lend Me Your Comb; I'll Get You;
"We were performers...in Britain";
I Saw Her Standing There; From Me To You; Money (That's What I Want);
You Really Got A Hold On Me;
Roll Over Beethoven

CD Disc 2 (vinyl side D)
She Loves You; Till There Was You; Twist And Shout;
This Boy; I Want To Hold Your Hand;
"Boys, what I was thinking..."; Moonlight Bay;
Can't Buy Me Love
(vinyl side E)
All My Loving; You Can't Do That; And I Love Her;
A Hard Day's Night; I Wanna Be Your Man;
Long Tall Sally; Boys; Shout, I'll Be Back (Take 2);
I'll Be Back (Take 3)
(vinyl Side F)
You Know What To Do; No Reply (demo);
Mr. Moonlight; Leave My Kitten Alone; No Reply;
Eight Days A Week (sequence);
Eight Days A Week (complete);
Kansas City/Hey-Hey-Hey-Hey!

Apple 34448 Anthology 2
CD Disc 1 (vinyl side A)
Real Love; Yes It is; I'm Down;
You've Got To Hide Your Love
Away; If You've Got Trouble;
That Means A Lot; Yesterday;
It's Only Love
(vinyl side B)
I Feel Fine; Ticket To Ride; Yesterday;
Help!; Everybody's Trying To Be My

Baby; Norwegian Wood (This Bird
Has Flown); I'm Looking Through
You; 12-Bar Original
(vinyl side C)
Tomorrow Never Knows; Got To
Get You Into My Life; And Your
Bird Can Sing; Taxman; Eleanor
Rigby (strings only); I'm Only
Sleeping (rehearsal); I'm Only
Sleeping (Take 1); Rock And Roll
Music; She's A Woman

CD Disc 2 (vinyl side D)
Strawberry Fields Forever (demo
sequence); Strawberry Fields
Forever (Take 1); Strawberry
Fields Forever (Take 7 and edit
piece); Penny Lane; A Day In The
Life; Good Morning Good Morning;
Only A Northern Song
(vinyl side E)
Being For The Benefit Of Mr Kite!
(Takes 1 And 2); Being For The
Benefit Of Mr Kite! (Take 7); Lucy
In The Sky With Diamonds; Within
You Without You (instrumental);
Sgt Pepper's Lonely Hearts Club
Band (Reprise); You Know My Name
(Look Up The Number)
(vinyl side F)
I Am The Walrus; The Fool On the
Hill (demo); Your Mother Should
Know; The Fool On The Hill (Take
4); Hello, Goodbye; Lady Madonna;
Across The Universe

Apple 34451 Anthology 3
CD Disc 1 (vinyl side A)
A Beginning (instrumental);
Happiness Is A Warm Gun; Helter Skelter;
Mean Mr. Mustard (demo); Polythene Pam (demo);
Glass Onion (demo); Junk (demo); Piggies (demo);
Honey Pie (demo); Don't Pass Me By;
Ob-La-Di, Ob-La-Da; Good Night;
(vinyl side B)
Cry Baby Cry; Blackbird; Sexy Sadie;
While My Guitar Gently Weeps; Hey Jude; Not Guilty;
Mother Nature's Son
(vinyl side C)
Glass Onion; Rocky Raccoon;
What's The New Mary Jane;
Step Inside Love/Los Paranoias; I'm So Tired; I Will;
Why Don't We Do It In The Road; Julia
CD Disc 2 (vinyl side D)
I've Got A Feeling;
She Came In Through The Bathroom Window;
Dig A Pony; Two Of Us; For You Blue; Teddy Boy;
Medley: Rip It Up/Shake, Rattle And Roll/
Blue Suede Shoes
(vinyl side E)
The Long And Winding Road; Oh! Darling;
All Things Must Pass;
Mailman, Bring Me No More Blues;
Get Back (Live!); Old Brown Shoe; Octopus's Garden;
Maxwell's Silver Hammer
(vinyl side F)
Something; Come Together; Come And Get It;
Ain't She Sweet; Because; Let It Be; I Me Mine;
The End

Apple 521 4811 Yellow Submarine Songtrack
Vinyl Side A
Yellow Submarine; Hey Bulldog; Eleanor Rigby;
Love You To; All Together Now;
Lucy In The Sky With Diamonds; Think For Yourself;
Sgt. Pepper's Lonely Hearts Club Band;
With A Little Help From My Friends
Side B
Baby, You're A Rich Man; Only A Northern Song;
All You Need Is Love; When I'm Sixty-Four;
Nowhere Man; It's All Too Much

Apple 521 4812 Yellow Submarine Songtrack
CD
Yellow Submarine; Hey Bulldog; Eleanor Rigby;
Love You To; All Together Now;
Lucy In The Sky With Diamonds; Think For Yourself;
Sgt. Pepper's Lonely Hearts Club Band;
With A Little Help From My Friends;
Baby, You're A Rich Man; Only A Northern Song;
All You Need Is Love; When I'm Sixty-Four;
Nowhere Man; It's All Too Much

Apple UK 29325 1
Vinyl Side A
Love Me Do; From Me To You; She Loves You;
I Want To Hold Your Hand; Can't Buy Me Love;
A Hard Day's Night; I Feel Fine; Eight Days A Week
Side B
Ticket To Ride; Help!; Yesterday; Day Tripper;
We Can Work It Out; Paperback Writer;
Yellow Submarine; Eleanor Rigby
Side C
Penny Lane; All You Need Is Love; Hello, Goodbye;
Lady Madonna; Hey Jude

Side D
Get Back; The Ballad Of John And Yoko; Something;
Come Together; Let It Be; The Long And Winding Road

Apple CD 7243 5 29970 2 1
CD
Love Me Do; From Me To You; She Loves You;
I Want To Hold Your Hand; Can't Buy Me Love;
A Hard Day's Night; I Feel Fine; Eight Days A Week;
Ticket To Ride; Help!; Yesterday; Day Tripper;
We Can Work It Out; Paperback Writer;
Yellow Submarine; Eleanor Rigby; Penny Lane;
All You Need Is Love; Hello, Goodbye; Lady Madonna;
Hey Jude; Get Back; The Ballad Of John And Yoko;
Something; Come Together; Let It Be;
The Long And Winding Road

Apple CD 07243 595713 2 4 Let It Be... Naked
CD (vinyl side 1)
Get Back; Dig A Pony; For You Blue;
The Long And Winding Road; Two Of Us;
I've Got A Feeling
(vinyl side 2)
One After 909; Don't Let Me Down; I Me Mine;
Across The Universe; Let It Be
Bonus Disc
Fly On The Wall

Parlophone B000684OES The Capitol
Albums Vol 1 (Box Set)
Disc 1 (stereo)
I Want To Hold Your Hand; I Saw Her Standing There;
This Boy; It Won't Be Long; All I've Got To Do;
All My Loving; Don't Bother Me; Little Child;
Till There Was You; Hold Me Tight;
I Wanna Be Your Man; Not A Second Time

(original mono)
I Want To Hold Your Hand; I Saw Her StandingThere;
This Boy; It Won't Be Long; All I've Got To Do;
All My Loving; Don't Bother Me; Little Child;
Till There Was You; Hold Me Tight;
I Wanna Be Your Man; Not A Second Time

Disc 2 (stereo)
Roll Over Beethoven; Thank You Girl;
You Really Got A Hold On Me; Devil In Her Heart;
Money; You Can't Do That; Long Tall Sally;
I Call Your Name; Please Mr Postman;
I'll Get You; She Loves You
(original mono)
Roll Over Beethoven; Thank You Girl;
You Really Got A Hold On Me; Devil In Her Heart;
Money; You Can't Do That; Long Tall Sally;
I Call Your Name; Please Mr. Postman;
I'll Get You; She Loves You

Disc 3 (stereo)
I'll Cry Instead; Things We Said Today;
Any Time At All; When I Get Home; Slow Down;
Matchbox; Tell Me Why; And I Love Her;
I'm Happy Just To Dance With You;
If I Fell; Komm, Gib Mir Deine Hand (I Want To Hold
Your Hand)
(original mono)
I'll Cry Instead; Things We Said Today;
Any Time At All; When I Get Home; Slow Down;
Matchbox; Tell Me Why; And I Love Her;
I'm Happy Just To Dance With You; If I Fell;
Komm, Gib Mir Deine Hand
(I Want To Hold Your Hand)

Disc 4 (stereo)
No Reply; I'm A Loser; Baby's In Black;
Rock And Roll Music; I'll Follow The Sun;
Mr. Moonlight; Honey Don't; I'll Be Back;
She's A Woman; I Feel Fine;
Everybody's Trying To Be My Baby
(original mono)
No Reply; I'm A Loser; Baby's In Black;
Rock And Roll Music; I'll Follow The Sun;
Mr. Moonlight; Honey Don't; I'll Be Back;
She's A Woman; I Feel Fine;
Everybody's Trying To Be My Baby

PARLOPHONE EXPORT RECORDS

SINGLES

DP 562 If I Fell/Ask Me Why
DP 563 Dizzy Miss Lizzy/Yesterday
DP 564 Michelle/Drive My Car
DP 570 Hey Jude/Revolution
BCSP 1 The Beatles' Singles
Collection
As BCS 1 but also includes Love
Me Do picture disc.

LONG PLAY

CPCS 101 Something New
Side One
Cry Instead; Things We Said Today;
Any Time At All; When I Get Home; Slow Down;
Matchbox.
Side Two
Tell Me Why; And I Love Her;
I'm Happy Just To Dance With You; If I Fell; Komm,
Gib Mir Deine Hand.

CPCS 103 The Beatles' Second Album
Side One
Roll Over Beethoven; Thank You Girl;
You Really Got A Hold On Me;
Devil In Her Heart; Money; You Can't Do That.
Side Two
Long Tall Sally; I Call Your Name;
Please Mister Postman; I'll Get You; She Loves You

CPCS 104 The Beatles VI
Side One
Kansas City/Hey Hey Hey Hey; Eight Days A Week;
You Like Me Too Much; Bad Boy;
I Don't Want To Spoil The Party; Words Of Love.
Side Two
What You're Doing; Yes It Is; Dizzy Miss Lizzy;
Tell Me What You See; Every Little Thing.

CPCS 106 Hey Jude
As PCS 7184 but with Apple label instead of
Parlophone label.

PCS 7067-8 The Beatles (2 LPs)
As normal PCS 7067-8 release but with Parlophone
label instead of Apple label.

NON-BEATLES RECORDS
(Containing Lennon-McCartney songs)

UP 1165† † Love In The Open Air/
Theme From The Family Way
The George Martin Orchestra [23 December 1966]

4* Thingumybob/Yellow Submarine
John Fosters and Sons Ltd. Black Dyke Mills Band
[6 September 1968]

10* Goodbye/(Sparrow)
Mary Hopkin [28 March 1969]

13* Give Peace A Chance/(Remember Love)
The Plastic Ono Band [4 July 1969]

1001* Cold Turkey/(Don't Worry Kyoko)
The Plastic Ono Band [24 October 1969]

20* Come And Get It/(Rock Of All Ages)
Badfinger [5 December 1969]

NUT 18
The Songs Lennon And McCartney Gave Away
Side One
I'm The Greatest (Ringo Starr);
One And One Is Two
(The Strangers with Mike Shannon);
From A Window (Billy J. Kramer and The Dakotas);
Nobody I Know (Peter and Gordon);
Like Dreamers Do (The Applejacks);
I'll Keep You Satisfied
(Billy J. Kramer and The Dakotas);
Love Of The Loved (Cilla Black);
Woman (Peter and Gordon);
Tip Of My Tongue (Tommy Quickly);
I'm In Love (The Fourmost).
Side Two
Hello Little Girl (The Fourmost);
That Means A Lot (P.J. Proby);
It's For You (Cilla Black); Penina (Carlos Mendes);
Step Inside Love (Cilla Black);
World Without Love (Peter and Gordon);
Bad To Me (Billy J. Kramer and The Dakotas);
I Don't Want To See You Again (Peter and Gordon);
I'll Be On My Way (Billy J. Kramer and The Dakotas);
Catcall (The Chris Barber Band). [9 April 1979]

The Hamburg, Decca and Star Club Tapes

The records listed on this and the following page is a selection of the ever-growing number of releases of the Hamburg, Decca and Star Club Tapes. This is not meant to be a full discography of those recordings because to list every release would lead to confusion. Because these recordings appear to be available to anyone who may set up a record label, releases in future are likely to become as prolific and diverse as the innumerable record companies that release them.

THE HAMBURG TAPES

POLYDOR RECORDS

SINGLES

NH 66-833 My Bonnie/The Saints [5 January 1962]

NH 52-906 Sweet Georgia Brown/ Nobody's Child [31 January 1964]

NH 52-275 Why/Cry For A Shadow [28 February 1964]

NH 52-317 Ain't She Sweet/ Take Out Some Insurance On Me, Baby [29 May 1964]

EXTENDED PLAY

H 21-610 My Bonnie My Bonnie; Why; Cry For A Shadow; The Saints. [12 July 1963]

LONG PLAY

236-201 The Beatles First
Side One
Ain't She Sweet; Cry For A Shadow; (Let's Dance); My Bonnie; Take Out Some Insurance On Me, Baby; (What'd I Say).
Side Two
Sweet Georgia Brown; The Saints; (Ruby Baby); Why; Nobody's Child; (Ya Ya). [19 June 1964]

Titles in parentheses are performed by Tony Sheridan and The Beat Brothers. All other songs are performed either by The Beatles or The Beatles with Tony Sheridan.

THE DECCA TAPES

AFE RECORDS

SINGLES

AFS 1 Searchin'/Money/Till There Was You
[8 October 1982]

LONG PLAY

AFELP 1047 The Complete Silver Beatles
Side One
Three Cool Cats; Crying, Waiting,Hoping;
Besame Mucho; Searchin'; The Sheik Of Araby; Money.
Side Two
To Know Her Is To Love Her;
Take Good Care Of My Baby; Memphis,Tennessee; Sure
To Fall (In Love With You); Till There Was You;
September In The Rain. [10 September 1982]

TOPLINE RECORDS

LONG PLAY

TOP 181 The Decca Sessions 1.1.62
Side One
Three Cool Cats; Memphis, Tennessee; Besame Mucho;
The Sheik Of Araby; Till There Was You; Searchin'.
Side Two
Sure To Fall (In Love With You);
Take Good Care Of My Baby; Money;
To Know Her Is To Love Her; September In The Rain;
Crying, Waiting, Hoping. [19 October 1987]

THE STAR CLUB TAPES

LINGASONG RECORDS

SINGLES

NB 1 Falling In Love Again/ Twist And Shout
[25 May 1977]

Long Play

LNL 1 The Beatles Live! At The Star Club In Hamburg, Germany; 1962. (2 LPs)
Side One
I Saw Her Standing There; Roll Over Beethoven;
Hippy Hippy Shake; Sweet Little Sixteen;
Lend Me Your Comb; Your Feets Too Big.
Side Two
Twist And Shout; Mr. Moonlight;
A Taste Of Honey; Besame Mucho; Reminiscing;
Kansas City/Hey, Hey, Hey, Hey.
Side Three
Nothin' Shakin' (But The Leaves On The Trees);
To Know Her Is To Love Her; Little Queenie; Falling
In Love Again; Ask Me Why; Be Bop A Lula;
Hallelujah, I Love Her So.
Side Four
Red Sails In The Sunset;
Everybody's Trying To Be My Baby; Matchbox;
(I'm) Talking About You; Shimmy Shake;
Long Tall Sally; I Remember You. [25 May 1977]

AFE RECORDS

LONG PLAY

AFELD 1018 Historic Sessions (2 LPs)
Side One
I'm Gonna Sit Right Down And Cry (Over You);
I Saw Her Standing There; Roll Over Beethoven;
Hippy Hippy Shake; Sweet Little Sixteen;
Lend Me Your Comb; Your Feets Too Big.
Side Two
Twist And Shout; Mr. Moonlight; A Taste Of Honey;
Besame Mucho; Reminiscing; Kansas City/Hey Hey
Hey Hey; Where Have You Been All My Life.
Side Three
Till There Was You; Nothin' Shakin'
(But The Leaves On The Trees);
To Know Her Is To Love Her; Little Queenie;
Falling In Love Again; Ask Me Why; Be Bop A Lula;
Hallelujah, I Love Her So.
Side Four
Sheila; Red Sails In The Sunset; Everybody's
Trying To Be My Baby; Matchbox;
(I'm) Talking About You; Shimmy Shake;
Long Tall Sally; I Remember You.
[25 September 1981]

American Releases

CAPITOL/CAPITOL STARLINE†
UNITED ARTISTS††/APPLE*

SINGLES

5112 1 Want To Hold Your Hand/
I Saw Her Standing There [13 January 1964]

5150 Can't Buy Me Love/
You Can't Do That [16 March 1964]

5222 A Hard Day's Night/I Should Have Known Better
[13 July 1964]

5234 I'll Cry Instead/
I'm Happy Just To Dance With You [20 July 1964]

5235 And I Love Her/If I Fell [20 July 1964]

5255 Matchbox/Slow Down [24 August 1964]

5327 I Feel Fine/She's A Woman [23 November 1964]

5371 Eight Days A Week/I Don't Want To Spoil The Party
[15 February 1965]

5407 Ticket To Ride/Yes It Is [19 April 1964]

5476 Help/I'm Down [19 July 1965]

5498 Yesterday/Act Naturally [13 September 1965]

6061† Twist And Shout/There's A Place
[11 October 1965]

6062† Love Me Do/P. S. I Love You [11 October 1965]

6063 Please Please Me/From Me To You
[11 October 1965]

6064† Do You Want To Know A Secret/
Thank You Girl [11 October 1965]

6065† Roll Over Beethoven/Misery [11 October 1965]

6066† Boys/Kansas City/Hey Hey Hey Hey
[11 October 1965]

5555 We Can Work It Out/Day Tripper
[6 December 1965]

5587 Nowhere Man/What Goes On [21 February 1966]

5651 Paperback Writer/Rain [30 May 1966]

5715 Yellow Submarine/Eleanor Rigby [8 August 1966]

5810 Penny Lane/Strawberry Fields Forever
[13 February 1967]

5964 All You Need Is Love/Baby, You're A Rich Man
[17 July 1967]

2056 Hello Goodbye/I Am The Walrus
[27 November 1967]

2138 Lady Madonna/The Inner Light
[18 March 1968]

2276* Hey Jude/Revolution [26 August 1968]

2490* Get Back/Don't Let Me Down [5 May 1969]

2531* The Ballad Of John And Yoko/Old Brown
Shoe [4 June 1969]

2654* Something/Come Together [6 October 1969]

2764* Let It Be/You Know My Name
(Look Up The Number) [11 March 1970]

2837* The Long And Winding Road/For You Blue
[11 May 1970]

4274 Got To Get You Into My Life/Helter Skelter
[31 May 1976]

4347 Ob-La-Di, Ob-La-Da/Julia [8 November 1976]

4612 Sgt. Pepper's Lonely HeartsClub Band/
With A Little Help From My Friends/
A Day In The Life [28 August 1978]

B5107 The Beatles' Movie Medley/
I'm Happy Just To Dance With You[30 March 1982]

B5189 Love Me Do/P. S. I Love You
[12 November 1982]

EXTENDED PLAY

EAP 2121 Four By The Beatles
Roll Over Beethoven; All My
Loving; This Boy; Please Mister
Postman. [11 May 1964]

R5365 By The Beatles
Honey Don't; I'm A Loser; Mr.
Moonlight; Everybody's Trying To
Be My Baby. [1 February 1965]

LONG PLAY

ST 2047 Meet The Beatles
Side One
I Want To Hold Your Hand; I Saw Her Standing
There; This Boy; It Won't Be Long; All I've Got To
Do; All My Loving.
Side Two
Don't Bother Me; Little Child; Till There Was You;
Hold Me Tight; I Wanna Be Your Man;
Not A Second Time. [20 January 1964]

ST 2080 The Beatles' Second Album
Side One
Roll Over Beethoven; Thank You Girl;
You Really Got A Hold On Me; Devil In Her Heart;
Money; You Can't Do That.
Side Two
Long Tall Sally; I Call Your Name; Please Mister
Postman; I'll Get You; She Loves You. [10 April
1964]

UAS 6366†† A Hard Day's Night
Side One
A Hard Day's Night; Tell Me Why; I'll Cry Instead;
(I Should Have Known Better);
I'm Happy Just To Dance With You;
(And I Love Her).
Side Two
I Should Have Known Better; If I Fell;
And I Love Her; (Ringo's Theme - This Boy);
Can't Buy Me Love; (A Hard Day's Night).
Titles in parentheses performed
by The George Martin Orchestra.

ST 2018 Something New
Side One
I'll Cry Instead; Things We Said Today;
Any Time At All; When I Get Home; Slow Down;
Matchbox.
Side Two
Tell Me Why; And I Love Her; I'm Happy Just To
Dance With You; If I Fell; Komm,
Gib Mir Deine Hand. [20 July 1964]

STBO 2222 The Beatles' Story (2 LPs)
Side One
On Stage With The Beatles; How Beatlemania
Began; Beatlemania In Action; Man Behind The
Beatles – Brian Epstein; John Lennon; Who's A
Millionaire?
Side Two
Beatles Will Be Beatles; Man Behind The Music –
George Martin; George Harrison.
Side Three
A Hard Day's Night – Their First Movie;
Paul McCartney; Sneaky Haircuts And More
About Paul.

Side Four
The Beatles Look At Life: Victims Of Beatlemania;
Beatle Medley; Ringo Starr;
Liverpool And All The World! [23 November 1964]

ST 2228 Beatles 65
Side One
No Reply; I'm A Loser; Baby's In Black;
Rock And Roll Music; I'll Follow The Sun;
Mr. Moonlight.
Side Two
Honey Don't; I'll Be Back; She's A Woman;
I Feel Fine; Everybody's Trying To Be My Baby.
[15 December 1964]

ST 2309 The Early Beatles
Side One
Love Me Do; Twist And Shout; Anna (Go To Him);
Chains; Boys; Ask Me Why.
Side Two
Please Please Me; P. S. I Love You; Baby It's You;
A Taste Of Honey; Do You Want To Know A Secret.
[22 March 1965]

ST 2358 Beatles VI
Side One
Kansas City/Hey Hey Hey Hey; Eight Days A Week;
You Like Me Too Much; Bad Boy;
I Don't Want To Spoil The Party; Words Of Love.
Side Two
What You're Doing; Yes It Is; Dizzy Miss Lizzy;
Tell Me What You See; Every Little Thing.
[14 June 1965]

SMAS 2386 Help!
Side One
(The James Bond Theme); Help!; The Night Before;
(From Me To You Fantasy); You've Got To Hide Your
Love Away; I Need You; (In The Tyrol)
Side Two
Another Girl; (Another Hard Day's Night);
Ticket To Ride; (The Bitter End/You Can't Do That);
You're Going To Lose That Girl; (The Chase).
[13 August 1965]
Titles in parentheses performed by
The George Martin Orchestra.

ST 2442 Rubber Soul
Side One
I've Just Seen A Face; Norwegian Wood (This Bird
Has Flown); You Won't See Me; Think For Yourself;
The Word; Michelle.
Side Two
It's Only Love; Girl; I'm Looking Through You;
In My Life; Wait; Run For Your Life.
[6 December 1966]

ST 2553 Yesterday And Today
Side One
Drive My Car; I'm Only Sleeping; Nowhere Man;
Dr. Robert; Yesterday; Act Naturally.
Side Two
And Your Bird Can Sing; If I Needed Someone;
We Can Work It Out; What Goes On;
DayTripper. [20 June 1965]

ST 2576 Revolver
Side One
Taxman; Eleanor Rigby; Love You To;
Here, There and Everywhere; Yellow Submarine;
She Said, She Said.
Side Two
Good Day Sunshine; For No One; I Want To Tell
You; Got To Get You Into My Life;
Tomorrow Never Knows. [5 August 1966]

**SMAS 2653 Sgt. Pepper's Lonely
Hearts Club Band**
As British album [2 June 1967]

SMAL 2835 Magical Mystery Tour
As British album
[27 November 1967]

SWBO 101* The Beatles (2 LPs)
As British album [25 November 1968]

SW 153* Yellow Submarine
As British album [13 January 1969]

SO 383* Abbey Road
As British album [26 September 1969]

SW 385* Hey Jude
As British album [26 February 1970]

AR 34001* Let It Be
As British album [18 May 1970]

SKBO 3403* The Beatles 1962-1966 (2 LPs)
As British album [2 April 1973]

SKBO 3404* The Beatles 1967-1970 (2 LPs)
As British album [2 April 1973]

SKBO 11537 Rock And Roll Music (2 LPs)
As British album [7 June 1976]

SMAS 11638 The Beatles At The Hollywood Bowl
As British album [2 May 1977]

SKBL 11711 Love Songs (2 LPs)
As British album [24 November 1977]

SW 11922 Let It Be
Reissue of AR 34001 [12 March 1979]

SHAL 12060 Rarities
Side One
Love Me Do; Misery; There's A Place;
Sie Liebt Dich; And I Love Her; Help!;
I'm Only Sleeping; I Am The Walrus.
Side Two
Penny Lane; Helter Skelter; Don't Pass Me By;
The Inner Light; Across The Universe;
You Know My Name (Look Up The Number);
Sgt. Pepper Inner Groove. [24 March 1980]

SN 16020 Rock And Roll Music - Vol 1
As British album [27 October 1980]

SN 16021 Rock And Roll Music - Vol 2
As British album [27 October 1980]

SW 11921 A Hard Day's Night
Reissue of UAS 6366 [17 August 1981]

SV 12199 Reel Music
As British album [12 March 1982]

SV 12245 20 Greatest Hits
Side One
She Loves You; Love Me Do;
I Want To Hold Your Hand; Can't Buy Me Love;
A Hard Day's Night; I Feel Fine; Eight Days A
Week; Ticket To Ride; Help!; Yesterday; We Can
Work It Out; Paperback Writer.
Side Two
Penny Lane; All You Need Is Love; Hello Goodbye;
Hey Jude; Get Back; Come Together; Let It Be;
The Long And Winding Road. [18 October 1982]

CLJ 46435 Please Please Me
As British album [February 1987]

CLJ 46436 With The Beatles
As British album [February 1987]

CLJ 46437 A Hard Day's Night
As British album [February 1987]

CLJ 46438 Beatles For Sale
As British album [February 1987]

CLJ 46439 Help!
As British album [April 1987]

CLJ 46440 Rubber Soul
As British album [April 1987]

CLJ 46441 Revolver
As British album [April 1987]

SV C12P 90043 Past Masters –
Vols One and Two (2 LPs)
As British album [24 October 1988]

Polydor 549268 In The Beginning
Ain't She Sweet; Cry For A Shadow; Let's Dance;
My Bonnie; Take Out Some Insurance On Me,
Baby; What'd I Say; Sweet Georgia Brown;
When The Saints Go Marching In; Ruby Baby;
Why; Nobody's Child; Ya Ya (Parts 1 & 2).

Prior to release by Capitol Records,
some early Beatles EMI recordings
were issued by the following labels:

VEEJAY RECORDS

SINGLES

VJ 498 Please Please Me/Ask Me Why
[25 February 1963]

VJ 522 From Me To You/Thank You Girl
[27 May 1963]

VJ 581 Please Please Me/From Me To You
[30 January 1964]

VJ 587 Do You Want To Know ASecret?/
Thank You Girl [23 March 1964]

EXTENDED PLAY

VJEP I-903 The Beatles
Misery; A Taste Of Honey; Ask Me Why;
Anna (Go To Him). [23 March 1964]

LONG PLAY

VJLP 1062 Introducing The Beatles
Side One
I Saw Her Standing There; Misery;
Anna (Go To Him); Chains; Boys; Love Me Do.
Side Two
P. S. I Love You; Baby It's You;
Do You Want To Know A Secret; A Taste Of Honey;
There's A Place; Twist And Shout. [22 July 1963]

VJLP 1062 Introducing The Beatles
Side One
I Saw Her Standing There; Misery;
Anna (Go To Him); Chains; Boys; Ask Me Why.
Side Two
Please Please Me; Baby It's You;
Do You Want To Know A Secret; A Taste Of Honey;
There's A Place; Twist And Shout. [27 January 1964]

SWAN RECORDS

SINGLES

4152 She Loves You/I'll Get You
[16 September 1963]

4182 Sie Liebt Dich/I'll Get You [21 May 1964]

TOLLIE RECORDS

SINGLES

9001 Twist And Shout/There's A Place
[2 March 1964]

9008 Love Me Do/
P. S. I Love You [27 April 1964]

The Hamburg, Decca and Star Club Tapes

The records listed on this page are a selection of the growing number of releases of The Hamburg, Decca and Star Club Tapes. It is not meant to be a full discography of these recordings. To list every single release would lead to confusion.

Because these recordings appear to be available to anyone who may set up a record label, future releases will become as prolific and diverse as will the record companies that release them.

THE HAMBURG TAPES

DECCA RECORDS

SINGLES

31382 My Bonnie/The Saints [23 April 1962]

MGM RECORDS

SINGLES

K13213 My Bonnie/The Saints [27 January 1964]
K13227 Why/Cry For A Shadow [27 March 1964]

ATCO RECORDS

SINGLES

6302 Sweet Georgia Brown/
Take Out Some Insurance On Me, Baby
[1 June 1964]

6308 Ain't She Sweet/Nobody's Child [6 July 1964]

POLYDOR RECORDS

LONG PLAY

**24-4504 The Beatles – Circa 1960 –
In The Beginning**
Side One
Ain't She Sweet; Cry For A Shadow; (Let's Dance); My Bonnie; Take Out Some Insurance On Me, Baby; (What'd I Say).
Side Two
Sweet Georgia Brown; The Saints; (Ruby Baby); Why; Nobody's Child; Ya Ya. [4 May 1970]

Titles in parentheses performed by Tony Sheridan and The Beat Brothers. All other songs performed either by The Beatles or The Beatles With Tony Sheridan.

THE DECCA TAPES

AFE RECORDS

LONG PLAY

AR 2452 The Complete Silver Beatles
Side One
Three Cool Cats; Crying, Waiting, Hoping;
Besame Mucho; Searchin'; The Sheik Of Araby; Money.
Side Two
To Know Her Is To Love Her;
Take Good Care Of My Baby; Memphis, Tennessee;
Sure To Fall (In Love With You); Till There Was You;
September In The Rain. [10 September 1982]

THE STAR CLUB TAPES

LINGASONG RECORDS

LONG PLAY

LS-2-7001 The Beatles Live! At The Star, Club Hamburg, Germany; 1962 (2 LPs)
Side One
I'm Gonna Sit Right Down And Cry (Over You);
Roll Over Beethoven; Hippy Hippy Shake;
Sweet Little Sixteen; Lend Me Your Comb;
Your Feets Too Big.
Side Two
Where Have You Been All My Life; Mr. Moonlight;
A Taste Of Honey; Besame Mucho; Till There Was
You; Kansas City/Hey Hey Hey Hey.
Side Three
Hallelujah, I Love Her So;
Nothin' Shakin' (But The Leaves On The Trees);
To Know Her Is To Love Her; Little Queenie;
Falling In Love Again; Be Bop A Lula.
Side Four
Red Sails In The Sunset;
Everybody's Trying To Be My Baby; Matchbox;
(I'm) Talking About You; Shimmy Shake;
Long Tall Sally; I Remember You. [28 June 1977]

Australian Releases

PARLOPHONE/APPLE* AXIS†

SINGLES

A8080 Please Please Me/Ask Me Why
[21 February 1963]

A8083 From Me To You/Thank You Girl
[9 May 1963]

A8093 She Loves You/I'll Get You
[29 August 1963]

A8103 I Want To Hold Your Hand/This Boy
[12 December 1963]

A8105 Love Me Do/I Saw Her Standing There
[16 January 1964]

A8107 Roll Over Beethoven/Hold Me Tight
[5 March 1964]

A8113 Can't Buy Me Love/You Can't Do That
[30 April 1964]

A8117 Komm, Gib Mir Deine Hand/Sie Liebt Dich
[25 June 1964]

A8123 A Hard Day's Night/Things We Said Today
[10 July 1964]

A8125 I Should Have Known Better/If I Fell
[20 August 1964]

A8133 I Feel Fine/ She's A Woman
[27 November 1964]

A8143 Rock And Roll Music/Honey Don't
[11 March 1965]

A8153 Ticket To Ride/Yes It Is [15 April 1965]

A8163 Help!/I'm Down [23 July 1965]

A8173 Yesterday/Act Naturally
[14 October 1965]

A8183 We Can Work It Out/Day Tripper
[9 December 1965]

A8193 Nowhere Man/Norwegian Wood
(This Bird Has Flown) [24 March 1966]

A8203 Paperback Writer/Rain [16 June 1966]

A8213 Yellow Submarine/Eleanor Rigby
[25 August 1966]

A8243 Penny Lane/Strawberry Fields Forever
[16 March 1967]

A8263 All You Need Is Love/ Baby,
You're A Rich Man [13 July 1967]

A8273 Hello Goodbye/I Am The Walrus
[7 December 1967]

A8293 Lady Madonna/The Inner Light
[29 March 1968]

A8493* Hey Jude/Revolution [20 September 1968]

A8693* Ob-La-Di, Ob-La-Da/
While My Guitar Gently Weeps [20 February 1969]

A8763* Get Back/Don't Let Me Down [9 May 1969]

A8793* The Ballad Of John And Yoko/
Old Brown Shoe [19 June 1969]

A8943* Something/Come Together
[19 October 1969]

A9083* Let It Be/You Know My Name
(Look Up The Number) [13 March 1970]

A9163* The Long And Winding Road/
For You Blue [11 June 1970]

A11115 Yesterday/ I Should Have Known Better
[31 May 1976]

A11182 Got To Get You Into My Life/Helter Skelter
[July 1976]

A12000 Sgt. Pepper's Lonely Hearts Club Band/
With A Little Help From My Friends/
A Day In The Life [28 August 1978]

A689 The Beatles' Movie Medley!
I'm Happy Just To Dance With You [8 April 1982]

AB34 The Beatles Singles Collection. A boxed set
containing the above 34 singles. [October 1982]

ED48 Love Me Do/P. S. I Love You/Love Me Do
(*12-inch single*) [July 1983]

EXTENDED PLAY

GEPO 8882 Twist And Shout
Twist And Shout; A Taste Of Honey;
Do You Want To Know A Secret; There's A Place.
[28 September 1963]

GEPO 8880 The Beatles Hits
From Me To You; Thank You Girl; Please Please Me;
Love Me Do. [6 February 1964]

GEPO 8883 The Beatles No. 1
I Saw Her Standing There; Misery;
Anna (Go To Him); Chains. [19 March 1964]

GEPO 8891 All My Loving
All My Loving; Ask Me Why; Money; P. S. I Love You.
[April 1964]

GEPO 70013 Requests
Long Tall Sally; I Call Your Name;
Please Mister Postman; Boys. [18 June 1964]

GEPO 70014 More Requests
Slow Down; Matchbox; Till There Was You;
I Wanna Be Your Man. [20 August 1964]

GEPO 70015 Further Requests
She Loves You; I Want To Hold Your Hand;
Roll Over Beethoven; Can't Buy Me Love.
[19 November 1964]

GEPO 8920 Extracts From The Film
A Hard Day's Night
I Should Have Known Better; If I Fell; Tell Me Why;
And I Love Her. [10 December 1964]

GEPO 70016 With The Beatles
Devil In Her Heart; Not A Second Time;
It Won't Be Long; Don't Bother Me.
[4 February 1965]

GEPO 8924 Extracts From The Album
A Hard Day's Night Any Time At All; I'll Cry Instead;
Things We Said Today; When I Get Home.
[4 March 1965]

GEPO 70019 Beatles For Sale
No Reply; I'm A Loser; Words Of Love;
Eight Days A Week. [24 June 1965]

GEPO 70020 Beatles For Sale No. 2
I'll Follow The Sun; Baby's In Black;
Kansas City/Hey Hey Hey Hey;
I Don't Want To Spoil The Party. [2 September 1965]

GEPO 70026 Yesterday
Yesterday; It's Only Love; You Like Me Too Much;
Dizzy Miss Lizzy. [5 May 1966]

GEPO 8952 Nowhere Man
Nowhere Man; Drive My Car; Michelle;
You Won't See Me. [3 November 1966]

GEPO 70043 Help!
Help!; She's A Woman; Ticket To Ride; I Feel Fine
[16 November 1967]

GEPO 70044 Norwegian Wood
Paperback Writer; We Can Work It Out;
Day Tripper; Norwegian Wood
(This Bird Has Flown). [8 February 1968]

MMT/SMMT 1 Magical Mystery Tour
Magical Mystery Tour; Your Mother Should Know
I Am The Walrus; The Fool On The Hill; Flying;
Blue Jay Way. [14 March 1968]

GEPO 70045 Penny Lane
Penny Lane; Eleanor Rigby;
Strawberry Field Forever; Yellow Submarine.
[4 July 1968]

BEP 14 The Beatles EPs Collection
This 14-EP set contains all of the 13 EPs as
originally issued in Britain, plus a free bonus EP
that is available only as part of this collection.

That EP is:
SGE 1 The Beatles
The Inner Light; Baby, You're A Rich Man;
She's A Woman; This Boy. [April 1982]

LONG PLAY

PMCO 1202 Please Please Me
PCSO 3042
As British album [9 April 1963]

PMCO 1206 With The Beatles
PCSO 3405
As British album [13 April 1964]

PMCO 1230 A Hard Day's Night
PCSO 3058
As British album [3 September 1964]

PMCO 1240 Beatles For Sale
PCSO 3062
As British album [11 February 1965]

PMCO 1255 Help!
PCSO 3071
As British album [30 September 1965]

PMCO 1267 Rubber Soul
PCSO 3075
As British album [17 February 1966]

PMCO/PCSO 7533
The Beatles Greatest Hits – Vol 1
Side One
Please Please Me; From Me To You;
She Loves You; I'll Get You;
I Want To Hold Your Hand; Love Me Do;
I Saw Her Standing There.

Side Two
Twist And Shout; Roll Over Beethoven;
All My Loving; Hold Me Tight; Can't Buy Me Love;
You Can't Do That; Long Tall Sally.
[11 August 1966]

PMCO/PCSO 7009 Revolver
As British album [29 September 1966]

PMCO/PCSO 7534
The BeatlesGreatest Hits – Volume 2
Side One
A Hard Day's Night; Boys;
I Should Have Known Better; I Feel Fine;
She's A Woman; Till There Was You;
Rock And Roll Music.
Side Two
Anna (Go To Him); Ticket To Ride;
Eight Days A Week; Help!; Yesterday;
We Can Work It Out; Day Tripper.
[16 February 1967]

PMCO/PCSO
Sgt. Pepper's Lonely Hearts Club Band
As British album [28 July 1967]

PMCO/PCSO 7016 A Collection Of
Beatles Oldies
As British album [16 May 1968]

PMCO/PCSO 7067–8* The Beatles (2 LPs)
As British album [4 December 1968]

PMCO/PCSO 7070* Yellow Submarine
As British album [23 January 1969]

PCSO 7088 Abbey Road
As British album [17 October 1969]

PCSO 7560 Hey Jude
As British album [23 March 1970]

PXS 1 Let It Be
Includes *Get Back* book. As British album
[1 June 1970]

PCSO 7076 Let It Be
Minus *Get Back* book. As British album
[December 1970]

TVSS 8 The Essential Beatles
Side One
Love Me Do; Boys; Long Tall Sally; Honey Don't;
P.S. I Love You; Baby, You're A Rich Man;
All My Loving; Yesterday; Penny Lane.
Side Two
Magical Mystery Tour;
Norwegian Wood (This Bird Has Flown);
With A Little Help From My Friends;
All You Need Is Love; Something;
Ob-La-Di, Ob-La-Da; Let It Be.
[2 February 1972]

PCSO 7171-8 The Beatles 1962-1966 (2 LPs)
As British album [5 July 1973]

PCSO 7181-2 The Beatles 1967-1970 (2 LPs)
As British album [5 July 1973]

PCSP 719 Rock And Roll Music (2 LPs)
As British album [15 June 1976]

PCSO 7577
The Beatles At The Hollywood Bowl
As British album [5 May 1977]

PCSO 7580 Love Songs (2 LPs)
As British album [21 November 1977]

BC 13 The Beatles Collection (13 LPs)
As British album [29 November 1978]

PCSO 3077 Magical Mystery Tour
As British album [16 July 1979]

PCSO 7581 Rarities
As American album [19 May 1980]

PCMO 1001 The Beatles Rarities
As British album [December 1980]

R 91103-10 The Beatles Box (8 LPs)
As British album [March 1981]

PLAY 1005 The Beatles Ballads
As British album [3 April 1981]

PCSO 7584 A Hard Day's Night
As American album [July 1981]

AXIS 6439† Rock And Roll Music – Vol 1
As British album [10 August 1981]

AXIS 6440† Rock And Roll Music – Vol 2
As British album [10 August 1981]

PCSO 7218 Reel Music
As British album [May 1982]

PLAY 1024 The Number Ones
As British 20 Greatest Hits album but also
includes the following three-track single:
A980 Love Me Do/I Feel Fine/
Rock And Roll Music [May 1983]

BPM 1 Past Masters – Vols 1 and 2 (2 LPs)
As British album [24 October 1988]

INDEX

to *The Beatles Album File and Complete Discography*.
Bold indicates Album titles.

1 346
12-Bar Original 321
20 Greatest Hits [UK] 250, 429
20 Greatest Hits [US] 243, 443
15,000 Hz Tone, The 106
Abbey Road 136, 178, 420, 425, 442, 452
Across The Universe 158, 164, 182, 191, 204,
   242, 277, 327, 355, 375
Act Naturally 73, 200, 237
After You've Gone 407
Ain't She Sweet 15, 246, 305, 339
Ain't That A Shame 407
All Along The Watchtower 407
All I've Got To Do 50, 216, 358
All My Loving 50, 162, 171, 172, 191, 198,
   216, 257, 292, 312, 358, 376
All My Loving 422, 449
All Shook Up 407
All Things Must Pass 337, 356, 407
All Together Now 132, 204, 344
All Together On The Wireless Machine 407
All You Need Is Love 114, 135, 164, 194, 202,
   244, 252, 345, 350, 376
And I Love Her 59, 162, 174, 176, 191, 194,
   198, 220, 223, 242, 257, 312, 359, 376
And Your Bird Can Sing 86, 202, 236, 322

Anna (Go To Him) 43, 228
Another Beatles Christmas Record 362, 367
Another Girl 72, 200, 232
Another Hard Day's Night 232
Anthology 1 300, 430
Anthology 2 316, 431
Anthology 3 328, 432
Any Time At All 60, 167, 170, 223, 359
Ask Me Why 37, 44, 228

Ba Ba Black Sheep 407
Baby, I Don't Care 407
Baby It's You 46, 228, 285
Baby, You're A Rich Man 113, 202, 345, 377
Baby's In Black 64, 226, 360
Back In The USSR 119, 164, 167, 170, 204,
   356, 377
Back Seat Of My Car, The 407
Bad Boy 94, 167, 170, 187, 231, 266
Bad To Me 211, 255, 407
Ballad Of John And Yoko, The 152, 164, 204,
   252, 276, 351
Be Bop A Lula 37, 407
Be My Baby 407
Beatles, The [2 CDs] 420
Beatles, The [1960] 406

Beatles, The [1962] 407
Beatles, The [1962-70] 407
Beatles, The [1968] 116, 178, 425, 435, 442, 451
Beatles, The [EP] 423, 450
Beatles, The - Circa 1960 - In The Beginning 446
Beatles 65 226, 441
Beatles 1962-1966, The 162, 425, 442, 452
Beatles 1967-1970, The 164, 426, 443, 452
Beatles 1968 Christmas Record, The 362, 371
Beatles At The Hollywood Bowl, The 171, 426, 443, 452
Beatles Ballads, The 189, 427, 452
Beatles Box, The 195, 452
Beatles Christmas Album, The 364
Beatles Christmas Record, The 362, 366
Beatles Collection, The 177, 427, 452
Beatles' EPs Collection, The 423, 450
Beatles First, The 418
Beatles For Sale 62, 178, 419, 424, 443, 451
Beatles For Sale [EP] 423, 450
Beatles For Sale No.2 423, 450
Beatles Fourth Christmas Record, The 362, 369
Beatles Greatest Hits - Vol 2, The 451
Beatles Historic Sessions, The 31
Beatles Hits, The 422, 449
Beatles Live!, The At The Star Club, Hamburg, Germany, 1962 447
Beatles Million Sellers, The 423
Beatles' Movie Medley, The 414
Beatles No. 1 422, 449
Beatles Rarities, The 178, 180, 427, 452
Beatles' Second Album, The 218, 434, 440
Beatles Seventh Christmas Record, The 362, 372
Beatles' Story, The 224, 441

Beatles Third Christmas Record, The 362, 368
Beatles VI 230, 441
Beatles VI, The 435
Beatles With Lu Walters, The 406
Beautiful Dreamer 407
Because 142, 204, 339
Because I Know You Love Me So 356
Beginning, A 330
Being For The Benefit Of Mr. Kite 102, 202, 325
Besame Mucho 24, 35, 307
Birthday 125, 167, 170
Bitter End, The 232
Blackbird 123, 191, 332, 377
Blowin' In The Wind 407
Blue Jay Way 110, 378
Blue Suede Shoes 407
Bogus Beatles 399-400
Boys 44, 167, 170, 171, 172, 228, 313
Bye Bye Love 407

Can You Dig It? 356
Can You Take Me Back 129
Can't Buy Me Love 59, 94, 147, 162, 171, 172, 194, 198, 220, 244, 252, 255, 290, 312, 349
Capitol Albums Vol 1, The 357, 433
Carol 286, 407
Carry That Weight 145, 204
Catcall 212, 407
Cayenne 304
Chains 43, 228
Chase, The 232
Child Of Nature 356
Christmas Time Is Here Again! 362, 370
Clarabella 286, 407
C'mon Everybody 407
Cold Turkey 213

Collection Of Beatles Oldies, A 89, 424, 429, 451
Come And Get It 213, 339, 407
Come Together 139, 164, 204, 244, 339, 351
Commonwealth Song 407
Complete Silver Beatles, The 447
Continuing Story Of Bungalow Bill, The 121, 204
Cottonfields 407, 414
Crimble Mudley, A 407
Cry Baby Cry 129, 332
Cry For A Shadow 15, 246, 305
Crying, Waiting, Hoping 27, 287

Da Doo Ron Ron 407
Day In The Life, A 105, 164, 202, 324
Day Tripper 94, 162, 200, 237, 252, 271, 350, 378
Dear Prudence 119
Decca Sessions 1.1.62, The 21
Decca Tapes, The 437
Decca Tapes, The [International CDs] 418
Decca Tapes, The [US] 47
Devil In Her Heart 54, 218, 359
Dig A Pony 157, 335, 354
Dig It 159
Digging My Potatoes 407
Dizzy Miss Lizzy 74, 167, 170, 171, 172, 231, 296
Do You Want To Know A Secret 46, 191, 198, 228
Don't Be Cruel 407
Don't Bother Me 51, 216, 358
Don't Ever Change 298, 407
Don't Let Me Down 152, 164, 204, 276, 355, 356

Don't Let The Sun Catch You Crying 407
Don't Pass Me By 124, 204, 242, 331, 356, 378
Dr. Robert 87, 202, 236
Dream Baby 407
Drive My Car 76, 162, 167, 170, 200, 236

Early Beatles, The 228, 441
Early Tapes Of The Beatles, The 12
Eight Days A Week 66, 162, 200, 231, 244, 257, 315, 349
Eleanor Rigby 84, 95, 162, 202, 238, 252, 322, 344, 350
End, The 146, 204, 340
Essential Beatles, The 452
Every Little Thing 67, 174, 176, 200, 231, 356
Everybody's Got Something To Hide Except Me And My Monkey 126
Everybody's Trying To Be My Baby 38, 68, 167, 170, 226, 295, 321, 360
Extracts From The Album A Hard Day's Night 422, 450
Extracts From The Film A Hard Day's Night 422, 450

Falling In Love Again 37
Fancy My Chances With You 356
Ferry 'Cross The Mersey [Gerry and The Pacemakers] 255
Fixing A Hole 102, 202
Fly On The Wall 356
Flying 110, 379
Fool Like Me 407
Fool On The Hill, The 108, 164, 191, 202, 326, 327, 379
For No One 86, 174, 176, 191, 202, 238

For You Blue 161, 204, 336, 354
Free As A Bird 303
From A Window 209, 407
From Me To You 90, 162, 198, 232, 252, 261, 309, 348, 379
From Me To You Fantasy 232
From Then To You 362
From Us To You 282, 407
Further Requests 450

George Martin Orchestra, The 135, 162, 220, 232
Get Back 161, 164, 167, 170, 194, 204, 244, 252, 275, 337, 351, 354, 356, 380
Getting Better 101
Gimme Some Truth 407
Girl 79, 162, 174, 176, 200, 234
Give Peace A Chance 213
Glad All Over 294, 407
Glass Onion 120, 331, 333
God Save The Queen 407
Going Up The Country 407
Golden Slumbers 145, 204
Good Day Sunshine 86, 202, 238, 380
Good Morning, Good Morning 104, 324, 380
Good Night 130, 332
Good Rockin' Tonight 407
Goodbye 213, 407
Got To Get You Into My Life 87, 167, 170, 202, 238, 322, 381
Great Balls Of Fire 407

Hallelujah, I Love Her So 37, 304
Hamburg Tapes, The 436
Hamburg Tapes, The [US] 446
Happiness Is A Warm Gun 122, 204, 330
Happy Birthday 408

Hard Day's Night, A 56, 178, 220, 419, 423, 441, 443, 451, 452
Hard Day's Night, A 58, 95, 162, 171, 172, 194, 198, 220, 244, 252, 255, 291, 312, 349
Hare Krishna Mantra 408
Heather 408
Hello, Goodbye 112, 164, 204, 244, 252, 327, 350
Hello Little Girl 28, 210, 255, 306, 407
Help! 69, 178, 232, 381, 419, 424, 442, 443, 451
Help! 71, 92, 162, 171, 172, 194, 200, 232, 242, 244, 252, 320, 349
Help! [EP] 450
Helter Skelter 127, 167, 170, 242, 330, 381
Her Majesty 146, 204
Here Comes The Sun 142, 164, 191, 204
Here, There And Everywhere 85, 174, 176, 191, 202, 238
Hey! Baby 408
Hey Bulldog 134, 167, 170, 343
Hey Jude 147, 427, 435, 442, 452
Hey Jude 151, 164, 191, 204, 244, 252, 274, 333, 351, 382
Hi Ho Silver 408
Hi-Heel Sneakers 408
Hippy Hippy Shake 34, 255, 294, 408
Hitch Hike 408
Hold Me Tight 52, 216, 358
Home 408
Honey Don't 67, 226, 299, 360
Honey Pie 128, 331, 382
Honeymoon Song, The 289, 408
Hot As Sun 408
House Of The Rising Sun 408
How Do You Do It? 307, 408

I Am The Walrus 111, 164, 194, 202, 242, 326, 382
I Call Your Name 167, 170, 187, 198, 218, 265, 359, 384
I Do Like To Be Beside The Seaside 408
I Don't Want To See You Again 212, 408
I Don't Want To Spoil The Party 67, 200, 231, 384
I Feel Fine 93, 162, 198, 226, 244, 252, 266, 295, 320, 349, 360, 384
I Forgot To Remember To Forget 297, 408
I Got A Woman 283, 408
I Got To Find My Baby 298, 408
I Just Don't Understand 294, 408
I Me Mine 158, 340, 355
I Need You 72, 174, 176, 200, 232
I Remember You 39
I Saw Her Standing There 34, 42, 167, 170, 198, 216, 255, 288, 309, 358
I Shall Be Released 408
I Should Have Known Better 58, 147, 194, 198, 220, 385
I Threw It All Away 408
I Wanna Be Your Man 53, 167, 170, 216, 291, 313, 358
I Want To Hold Your Hand 95, 162, 171, 198, 216, 244, 252, 255, 262, 311, 349, 358, 385
I Want To Tell You 87, 238
I Want You 141
I Will 124, 174, 176, 334, 385
If I Fell 58, 174, 176, 198, 220, 223, 359, 386
If I Needed Someone 81, 236
If You Gotta Make A Fool Of Somebody 408
If You Love Me Baby (aka Take Out Some Insurance On Me Baby) 16, 246

If You've Got Trouble 319, 408
I'll Be Back 61, 174, 176, 198, 226, 314, 360
I'll Be On My Way 212, 283, 408
I'll Build A Stairway To Paradise 408
I'll Cry Instead 60, 220, 223, 359, 386
I'll Follow The Sun 65, 174, 176, 200, 226, 360
I'll Get You 184, 218, 262, 309, 359
I'll Keep You Satisfied 209, 408
I'm A Loser 54, 200, 226, 295, 360
I'm Down 167, 170, 188, 200, 267, 319
I'm Gonna Sit Right Down And Cry (Over You) 34, 287, 408
I'm Happy Just To Dance With You 58, 220, 223, 359
I'm In Love 210, 408
I'm Looking Through You 80, 200, 234, 321, 386
I'm Only Sleeping 84, 202, 236, 242, 322, 323, 387
I'm So Tired 122, 204, 334
(I'm) Talking About You 38
I'm The Greatest 208
In My Life 80, 162, 176, 200, 234
In Spite Of All The Danger 304, 406
In The Beginning 246, 444
In The Tyrol 232
Inner Groove, The 106
Inner Light, The 183, 242, 273
Isn't It A Pity 408
It Won't Be Long 50, 198, 216, 358
It's All Too Much 134, 345
It's For You 211, 255, 408
It's Only Love 73, 174, 176, 200, 234, 320, 387
It's So Easy 408
I've Got A Feeling 160, 335, 355
I've Just Seen A Face 74, 200, 234

James Bond Theme, The 162, 232
Jealous Guy 408
Jessie's Dream 408
Johnny B. Goode 289, 408
John's Piano Piece 356
Julia 125, 204, 335
Junk 331, 408

Kansas City 19, 408
Kansas City/Hey Hey Hey Hey 36, 66, 167, 170,
    200, 231, 296, 315
Keep Your Hands Off My Baby 283, 408
Komm, Gib Mir Deine Hand [I Want To Hold
    Your Hand] 184, 223, 263, 388

Lady Madonna 150, 164, 204, 252, 273, 327, 351
Lawdy Miss Clawdy 408
Leave My Kitten Alone 315, 408
Lend Me Your Comb 34, 308, 408
Let It Be 153, 178, 420, 425, 442, 443, 452
Let It Be 159, 164, 191, 194, 204, 244, 278,
    339, 351, 356, 388
Let It Be... Naked 352, 433
Let's Dance 17, 246
Like Dreamers Do 28, 209, 306, 407
Little Child 51, 216, 358
Little Children [Billy J Kramer and The Dakotas]
    255
Little Queenie 37, 408
Live At The BBC 280, 430
Lonesome Tears In My Eyes 293, 408
Long And Winding Road, The 160, 164, 174,
    176, 191, 194, 204, 244, 336, 351, 354
Long, Long, Long 127
Long Tall Sally 39, 167, 170, 171, 172, 188, 198,
    218, 264, 288, 313, 359

Long Tall Sally 422
Look At Me 408
Los Paranois 408
Love In The Open Air 212
Love Me Do 45, 162, 198, 228, 242, 244, 252,
    255, 257, 260, 299, 307, 348, 388
Love Me Do Medley 412
Love Of The Loved 28, 210, 407
Love Songs (2 LPs) 174, 426, 443, 452
Love You To 85, 238, 344
Lovely Rita 104, 202
Lucille 289, 408
Lucy In The Sky With Diamonds 101, 164,
    202, 257, 325, 344

Maggie Mae 159, 356
Magical Mystery Tour 107, 420, 426, 442,
    452
Magical Mystery Tour 108, 164, 194, 202,
    389
Magical Mystery Tour [EP] 423, 450
Mailman, Bring Me No More Blues 337, 408
Mama, You've Been On My Mind 408
Martha My Dear 122, 204
Matchbox 38, 167, 170, 187, 198, 223, 265,
    297, 359
Maxwell's Silver Hammer 140, 204, 338
Maybe I'm Amazed 408
Maybellene 408
Mean Mr. Mustard 144, 331
Medley: Rip It Up/Shake Rattle And Roll/Blue
    Suede Shoes 336
Meet The Beatles 216, 440
Memphis, Tennessee 24, 289
Michael Row The Boat Ashore 408
Michelle 79, 92, 162, 174, 176, 191, 200, 234

Midnight Special 408
Misery 43, 198
Miss Ann 408
Money (That's What I Want) 26, 55, 167, 170, 198, 218, 255, 309, 359, 389
Moonglow 408
Moonlight Bay 311
More Requests 449
Mother Nature's Son 126, 333
Move It 409
Mr. Moonlight 35, 65, 200, 226, 314, 360
Mr. Postman 359
My Bonnie 17, 246, 305
My Girl Is Red Hot 409
My Kind Of Girl 409

Night Before, The 71, 167, 170, 200, 232
No Reply 64, 200, 226, 314, 315, 360, 389
Nobody I Know 209, 409
Nobody's Child 18, 247
Norwegian Wood 450
Norwegian Wood (This Bird Has Flown) 76, 162, 174, 176, 191, 200, 234, 321, 390
Not A Second Time 54, 216, 358
Not Fade Away 409
Not Guilty 333, 409
Nothin' Shakin' 36, 294
Nothin' Shakin' (But The Leaves On The Trees) 409
Nowhere Man 78, 162, 191, 200, 236, 345
Nowhere Man 423, 450
Number Ones, The 453

Ob-La-Di, Ob-La-Da 120, 164, 204, 257, 332, 390
Octopus's Garden 140, 164, 204, 328

Oh Carol 409
Oh! Darling 140, 337
Old Brown Shoe 151, 164, 277, 338
On Moonlight Bay 409
One After 909 160, 308, 355, 356
One And One Is Two 209, 409
Only A Northern Song 132, 325, 345
Only The Beatles... 256, 429
Ooh! My Soul 298, 409

Paperback Writer 95, 148, 162, 202, 244, 252, 272, 350, 390
Past Masters - Volume One 258, 420
Past Masters - Volume Two 268, 420
Past Masters - Volumes One and Two 429, 444, 453
Paul's Piano Piece 356
Peggy Sue 409
Peggy Sue Got Married 409
Penina 211, 409
Penny Lane 113, 164, 202, 242, 244, 324, 350, 391
Penny Lane 450
Picture Of You, A 409
Piece Of My Heart 409
Piggies 123, 204, 331, 391
Please Mister Postman 52, 198, 218
Please Please Me 40, 178, 419, 423, 443, 451
Please Please Me 44, 162, 198, 228, 308, 392
Polythene Pam 144, 331
Pop Go The Beatles 409
P.S. I Love You 45, 174, 176, 198, 228

Quarrymen, The 406

Rain 148, 186, 202, 272
Ramrod 409
Rarities 240, 443, 452
Raunchy 409
Ready Teddy 18, 409
Real Love 318
Record 1 427
Record 2 428
Record 3 428
Record 4 428
Record 5 428
Record 6 428
Record 7 428
Record 8 429
Red Sails In The Sunset 38, 409
Reel Music 192, 429, 443, 453
Reelin' And Rockin' 409
Reminiscing 35, 409
Requests 449
Revolution 150, 164, 167, 170, 204, 274, 392
Revolution 1 128
Revolution 9 130
Revolver 82, 178, 238, 419, 424, 442, 443, 451
Right String But The Wrong Yo-Yo, The 409
Ringo's Theme (This Boy) 220
Rip It Up 409
Rock And Roll Music 65, 167, 170, 226, 296, 323, 360
Rock And Roll Music 167, 426, 443, 452
Rock Island Line, The 409
Rock and Roll Music - Vol 1 427, 443, 452
Rock and Roll Music - Vol 2 443, 452
Rocker 409
Rocky Racoon 123, 334
Roll Over Beethoven 34, 52, 167, 170, 171, 172, 198, 218, 292, 310, 359

Rubber Soul 75, 178, 234, 419, 424, 442, 443, 451
Ruby Baby 17, 247
Run For Your Life 81, 234

Save The Last Dance For Me 409
Savoy Truffle 128
Searchin' 25, 306
Send Me Some Lovin' 409
September In The Rain 27
Set Fire To That Lot! 297
Sexy Sadie 126, 332, 392
Sgt. Pepper Inner Grove 242
Sgt. Pepper's Lonely Hearts Club Band 100, 164, 202, 344, 393
Sgt. Pepper's Lonely Hearts Club Band 97, 178, 419, 424, 442, 451
Sgt. Pepper's Lonely Hearts Club Band (Reprise) 105, 326, 393
Shake Rattle And Roll 409
Shakin' In The Sixties 409
She Came In Through The Bathroom Window 144, 335, 356
She Loves You 90, 162, 171, 172, 198, 218, 244, 252, 255, 257, 262, 310, 348, 359
She Said She Said 86, 238
Sheik Of Araby, The 25, 306
Sheila 38, 409
She's A Woman 171, 172, 186, 198, 226, 266, 293, 323, 360, 393
She's Leaving Home 102, 174, 176, 191, 202
Shimmy Shake 38, 409
Shirley's Wild Accordion 409
Short Fat Fanny 409
Shot Of Rhythm And Blues, A 284, 409
Shout! 313, 409, 413

Side By Side 409
Sie Liebt Dich [She Loves You] 186, 242, 264
Singing The Blues 409
Slow Down 167, 170, 188, 198, 223, 265, 299, 359, 394
So How Come 295
So How Come (No One Loves Me) 409
Soldier Of Love 286
Soldier Of Love (Lay Down Your Arms) 409
Some Other Guy 284, 409, 412
Somethin' Else 409
Something 139, 164, 174, 176, 191, 204, 338, 351
Something New 222, 434, 441
Songs Lennon And McCartney Gave Away, The 206, 435
Spiritual Regeneration 409
Star Club Tapes, The 437
Star Club Tapes, The [International CDs] 418
Star Club Tapes, The [US] 447
Step Inside Love 211, 334, 409
Strawberry Fields Forever 112, 164, 202, 323, 324, 394
Suicide 409
Sun King 143, 356
Sure To Fall 26
Sure To Fall (In Love With You) 284
Suzy Parker 409
Suzy's Parlour 409
Swan Records 445
Sweet Georgia Brown 17, 247
Sweet Little Sixteen 34, 293, 409

Take Good Care Of My Baby 26
Taking A Trip To Carolina 356
Talking About You 409

Taste Of Honey, A 35, 46, 198, 228, 288
Taxman 84, 167, 170, 202, 238, 322, 395
Tea For Two 409
Teddy Boy 336, 409
Tell Me What You See 74, 174, 176, 200, 231
Tell Me Why 59, 220, 223, 359, 395
Tennessee 409
Thank You Girl 184, 198, 218, 261, 285, 359, 395
Thank You Guru Dai/Happy Birthday Mike Love 410
That Means A Lot 211, 319, 410
That'll Be The Day 303, 406, 411
That's All Right (Mama) 285
That's Alright Mama 410
Theme From The Family Way 212
There's A Place 47, 242
Things We Said Today 60, 171, 172, 198, 223, 292, 359
Thingumybob 213, 410
Think For Yourself 78, 234, 344
Think It Over 410
Thinking Of Linking 410
Third Man Theme, The 410
Thirty Days 410
This Boy 174, 176, 183, 198, 216, 220, 257, 263, 311, 358
Those Were The Days 410
Three Cool Cats 24, 306
Ticket To Ride 72, 95, 162, 171, 172, 194, 200, 232, 244, 252, 257, 296, 320, 349
Tie Me Kangaroo Down, Sport 410
Till There Was You 25, 36, 52, 191, 216, 290, 310, 358
Tip Of My Tongue 210, 410
To Know Her Is To Love Her 27, 36, 288
Tollie Records 445

Tom Dooley 410
Tomorrow Never Knows 88, 238, 321, 396
Too Much Monkey Business 283, 410
Tracks Of My Tears 410
Tribute To The Cavern 253, 429
True Love 410
Turn Around 410
Twelve Bar Original 410
Twenty Flight Rock 410
Twist And Shout 35, 47, 167, 170, 171, 172, 198, 228, 255, 257, 311
Twist and Shout 422, 449
Two Of Us 157, 204, 336, 355, 356

Veejay Recods 444

Wait 80, 234
Walk, The 410
Waltzing Matilda 415
Watching Rainbows 410
Way You Look Tonight, The 410
We Can Work It Out 92, 162, 200, 236, 244, 252, 271, 350, 396
What Do You Want To Make Those Eyes At Me For 410
What Goes On 79, 236, 396
What You're Doing 68, 231
What'd I Say 17, 247, 410
What's The New Mary Jane 334, 410
When I Get Home 60, 223, 359, 396
When I'm Sixty-Four 104, 202, 345
When Irish Eyes Are Smiling 410
When The Saints Go Marching In 16, 247
Where Have You Been All My Life 36, 410
While My Guitar Gently Weeps 121, 164, 204, 333, 397

White Power 410
Whole Lotta Loving 410
Whole Lotta Shakin' Goin' On 410
Why (Can't You Love Me Again) 16, 247
Why Don't We Do It In The Road 124, 335, 397
Wild Honey Pie 120
With A Little Help From My Friends 100, 164, 202, 344
With The Beatles 48, 178, 419, 423, 443, 450, 451
Within You, Without You 103, 325
Woman 210
Word, The 78, 234
Words Of Love 67, 174, 176, 231
World Without Love 211

Ya Ya (Parts 1 & 2) 18, 247
Yakety Yak 410
Yellow Submarine 85, 93, 132, 162, 194, 202, 238, 252, 343, 350, 397
Yellow Submarine 131, 178, 420, 425, 442, 452
Yellow Submarine Soundtrack [Vinyl and CD] 341, 432
Yer Blues 125
Yes It Is 174, 176, 182, 231, 257, 267, 319
Yesterday 74, 93, 162, 174, 176, 191, 200, 237, 244, 320, 349
Yesterday 423, 450
Yesterday And Today 236, 442
You Are My Sunshine 410
You Can't Do That 61, 167, 170, 171, 198, 218, 232, 312, 359
You Know My Name (Look Up The Number) 185, 242, 279, 326

You Know What To Do 314
You Like Me Too Much 73, 200, 231
You Never Give Me Your Money 143
You Really Got A Hold On Me 53, 218, 287,
    310, 359
You Won't See Me 76, 200, 234
You'll Be Mine 304
You'll Never Walk Alone [Gerry and The
    Pacemakers] 255
Young Blood 284
Youngblood 410
Your Feets Too Big 35, 410
Your Mother Should Know 110, 326, 397
Your True Love 410
You're Going To Lose That Girl 72, 174, 176,
    200, 232
You're No Good [The Swinging Blue Jeans]
    255
You've Got To Hide Your Love Away 71, 162,
    174, 176, 191, 194, 200, 232, 319